Beginning To Read:

Thinking and Learning about Print

Marilyn Jager Adams

in conjunction with the Reading
Research and Education Center at
the Center for the Study of Reading
at the University of Illinois,
Urbana-Champaign

A Bradford Book

The MIT Press
Cambridge, Massachusetts
London, England

This book could not have been written without the unending support and encouragement of my husband, Milton B. Adams. I dedicate it to him and our children, John and Jocelyn, with all my love.

Fourth printing, 1991

©1990 Massachusetts Institute of Technology

The work on which this publication was based was supported in part by the Office of Educational Research and Improvement under cooperative agreement No. G 0087-C1001. The publication does not necessarily reflect the views of the agency supporting the research.

This book was set in Palatino and printed and bound in the United States of America.

Library of Congress Cataloging in Publication Data

Adams, Marilyn Jager.
  Beginning to read: thinking and learning about print / Marilyn Jager Adams.
    p. cm.
  "A Bradford book"
  Includes bibliographical references (p.
  ISBN 0-262-01112-3
  1. Reading—United States. 2. Reading readiness. I. Title
LB1050.A258 1990   89-13716
372.4—dc20   CIP

Contents

Foreword: How I Came to Know About Beginning to Read

P. David Pearson
Center for the Study of Reading
University of Illinois at Urbana-Champaign

Everyone involved in early reading instruction and research is well aware of the strong emotional reactions incited by the mere mention of phonics. And so, in 1986, when those of us at the Center for the Study of Reading were competing for the U.S. Department of Education's Reading Research and Education Center, we could not help but notice the prominence of phonics and other issues in early reading in the Request for Proposals distributed by the Office of Educational Research and Improvement (OERI). We knew that we could not ignore these issues in our proposal. We also knew that in addressing them we would focus the phonics furor on the Center. Our solution, which became part of our proposal to OERI, was to agree to take on a major report that would thoroughly review all aspects of phonics and early reading instruction in a straightforward, evenhanded way.

In one sense, we were surprised that OERI would ask its center for reading research to undertake such a review. In two previous funding cycles, the focus of the federal government's funding for reading had a deliberate bias toward comprehension research. It was the Center for the Study of Reading, with offices at the University of Illinois at Urbana-Champaign and at Bolt Beranek and Newman in Cambridge, Massachusetts, that brought to the field *Schooling and the Acquisition of Knowledge, Theoretical Issues in Reading Comprehension,* and *Becoming a Nation of Readers,* in addition to more than 500 reports focused on issues of basic processes and instructional practices in reading comprehension. Ironically, in the end, it was *Becoming a Nation of Readers,* with its clear support of "phonics first and fast," that spawned the legislation (authored by the late Senator Zerensky of Nebraska) commissioning this report on phonics.

Finding someone to prepare such an important report became the next problem for the directors of the Center. Clearly, we wanted someone with the expertise and interest to produce a report we could support—

even be proud of. Just as clearly, that someone was Marilyn Jager Adams, a cognitive and developmental psychologist in the Center's branch at Bolt Beranek and Newman. Adams, we knew, had a long history of involvement in translating cognitive and developmental research into classroom procedures. She had designed and written a thinking skills curriculum for children. She had a strong background in basic reading processes and an equally strong interest in applied issues in word recognition. She had, for example, developed and evaluated a set of diagnostic measures for decoding skills. She also had a good working knowledge of a host of basic and applied issues and research related to language and literacy. To make a long story short, we received the award, we asked Adams to complete the phonics report, and she accepted. And now, after many months of arduous work by Adams, the report is complete.

What we had originally conceptualized as a kind of updated version of Jeanne Chall's *Learning to Read: The Great Debate* became, as Adams immersed herself in the topic, more of a "What we know about basic processes and instructional practices in word and letter identification and early reading." And that is exactly how I view the book you are reading—as the most complete review, within a single cover, of our expanding knowledge of

- the history of the English alphabet,
- the controversies surrounding phonics instruction,
- issues and research in early reading instruction,
- basic perceptual and reading processes,
- the processes involved in identifying sounds, letters, words, and meaning, and
- the processes involved in learning to read.

Several features of Adams's book distinguish it from earlier treatises on the issue of phonics and its role in reading and learning to read. First, because it was written in 1989 rather than 1967 or 1983, it has the benefit of the rapidly growing bodies of research on phonemic awareness and invented spelling (which Chall, or for that matter Bond and Dykstra, the directors of the *First Grade Studies,* did not have). Second, the book also has a tremendous theoretical advantage over the earlier works: It can place all the current and prior research on visual and auditory perception and basic reading processes within the context of Rumelhart and McClelland's work on parallel distributed processing. Such an integrated theory did not exist twenty years ago. Readers who, like me, have puzzled over how to reconcile data we considered irreconcilable (for example, data showing that every letter must be processed with data showing that there is a direct, unmediated spelling-to-meaning linkage in skilled reading) will find PDP (I like the initials) theory fascinating and illuminating.

Readers will find that the book is well written. Adams has a special talent for explaining complex theoretical concepts. She uses examples, analogies, and allusions generously. Everyone will find some comfortable ideas, some hooks to use to get a handle on what might otherwise be very abstract concepts. Furthermore, she is not afraid to use personal experience and anecdotes to drive home a point that, with only theory and data to support it, might well remain lifeless.

The book is comprehensive. Adams covers the past twenty years of basic and applied research thoroughly; her search through educational and psychological books and journals was exhaustive. She acknowledges historical predecessors (and precedents) graciously; it is clear that she has read Chall, Flesch, Bond and Dykstra, Aukerman, Balmuth, N.B. Smith, and Mathews very carefully. She even undertakes a reconciliation of some of the data coming from research on spelling and writing (invented-spelling work, for example) and sociolinguistic perspectives (Heath in the South, Teale in the Southwest) with theory and research more commonly associated with psychology.

I suspect that the book will attract some of the strong negative reactions we had originally worried about. Dyed-in-the-wool phonics advocates will be disappointed by its conciliatory tone, which they will see as too compatible with meaning-based approaches to teaching reading. They will be alarmed that Adams admits to a direct spelling-meaning connection, or that lots of students infer the entire symbol-sound system from vast exposure to print. Likewise, whole language advocates will be disappointed at Adams's insistence that the symbol-sound system be taught explicitly and early. They will be alarmed at her suggestion that phonemic awareness training ought to be one of the earliest items on the instructional agenda.

I suspect the positive reactions will be just as strong. Phonics advocates will applaud Adams's uncompromising emphasis on spelling patterns and their relation to speech patterns. At the same time, whole language advocates will appreciate her insistence that orthographic knowledge cannot simply be taught; it must be understood, and it can only be understood when it is used in meaningful engagements with print.

Especially strong reactions should come from instructional "moderates" who believe, along with the late John Downing, that the goal of all instruction—be it phonics, vocabulary, comprehension, studying, thinking, or mathematical problem solving—ought to be to promote cognitive clarity for students. That is the message I take from the book; I hope others can find it here too.

I have read the book from start to finish in a single (admittedly long) reading. But I have used it more often as a reference work, revisiting the elaborate sections on phonemic awareness because I find the concept and the research so fascinating, or poring over the sections on parallel distributed processing in yet another attempt to see how it all fits together. I think most readers will use it as a reference work, but I invite everyone to read it initially as an enlightening and enjoyable (you will like the way Adams writes) experience.

You will recall that when we at the Center undertook this (ad)venture, we had many concerns, but we hoped that Adams might be able to produce a report that we could support and even take pride in. She did! We can! We do!

Acknowledgments

I am deeply indebted to a number of people for their comments and suggestions during the preparation of this book. First among these are the members of the advisory panel: Ira Aaron, Alumni Foundation Distinguished Professor Emeritus of Reading Education, University of Georgia-Athens; Jeanne S. Chall, Professor of Education and Director of the Reading Laboratory at the Graduate School of Education, Harvard University; Bernice E. Cullinan, Professor, Department of Early Childhood and Elementary Education, New York University; Linnea C. Ehri, Professor of Education in the Division of Education, University of California-Davis; Philip Gough, Professor of Psychology and Education, University of Texas-Austin; Dorothy Strickland, Professor of Education and Deputy Director of the Institute for Urban and Minority Education, Teachers College, Columbia University; and Robert Ruddell, Professor of Education and Chair of the Division of Language and Literacy, Graduate School of Education, University of California-Berkeley. Each panel member read and commented on interim drafts of the manuscript. In addition, the entire panel convened on July 30, 1988, in Cambridge, Massachusetts, to discuss its progress and direction.

I am also indebted to the following members of the review board for their critical readings of those sections most relevant to their own expertise: Richard Allington, Department of Reading, State University of New York-Albany; Jonathan Baron, Department of Psychology, University of Pennsylvania; Roderick Barron, Department of Psychology, University of Guelph, Ontario; Isabel Beck, Learning Research and Development Center, University of Pittsburgh; Robert Calfee, School of Education, Stanford University; Doug Carnine, College of Education, University of Oregon; Anne Cunningham, Graduate School of Education, University of California-Berkeley; Mary Beth Curtis, Graduate School of Education, Harvard University; Dolores Durkin, Department of Elementary and Early Childhood Education, University of Illinois;

Usha Goswami, Merton College, Oxford, England; Connie Juel, Department of Cognition and Instruction, University of Texas-Austin; Isabelle Liberman, Department of Education, University of Connecticut; James L. McClelland, Department of Psychology, Carnegie-Mellon University; Jana Mason, Department of Educational Psychology, University of Illinois; Mark Seidenberg, Department of Psychology, McGill University; Harry Singer, School of Education, University of California-Riverside; Steven Stahl, College of Education, Western Illinois University, Macomb; Keith Stanovich, Department of Psychology, Oakland University; Rebecca Treiman, Psychology Department, Wayne State University; and Joanna Williams, Teachers College, Columbia University.

I wish also to express my appreciation for the support given by our Center liaison at the U.S. Department of Education, Anne P. Sweet, Senior Research Associate, Office of Research.

Finally, the continuing support of the following people has been invaluable: Bertram Bruce, Wayne Mesard, Yvette Tenney and especially Carl E. Feehrer at Bolt Beranek and Newman, and Richard C. Anderson, William E. Nagy, and P. David Pearson at the University of Illinois. Most of all, I thank Jean Osborn of the University of Illinois for her unfailing support in every phase of this effort.

While the guidance provided by my colleagues and each of the members of the advisory panel and the review board has factored enormously into the strengths of this manuscript, I alone am responsible for its shortcomings. With profound thanks for all the help I have received, I hope its strengths outweigh its weaknesses.

The work on which this publication was based was supported in part by the Office of Educational Research and Improvement under cooperative agreement No. G 0087-C1001. The publication does not necessarily reflect the views of the agency supporting the research.

I

Introduction

1

Putting Word Recognition in Perspective

Before you pick this book up, you should understand fully that the topic at issue is that of reading words. Before you put this book down, however, you should understand fully that the ability to read words, quickly, accurately, and effortlessly, is critical to skillful reading comprehension—in the obvious ways and in a number of more subtle ones.

Skillful reading is not a unitary skill. It is a whole complex system of skills and knowledge. Within this system, the knowledge and activities involved in visually recognizing individual printed words are useless in and of themselves. They are valuable and, in a strong sense, possible only as they are guided and received by complementary knowledge and activities of language comprehension. On the other hand, unless the processes involved in individual word recognition operate properly, nothing else in the system can either.

Operation of the Reading System

To clarify the relation of word recognition processes to the rest of the system, an analogy might be useful. Let us say that the system that supports our ability to read is like a car. Within this analogy, print is like gas. The engine and the mechanics of the car are the perceptual and conceptual machinery that make the system go.

Extending this analogy, it is obvious that print is essential to reading: no gas, no driving. But print is not enough to make the car go. Print is mute without the spark of visual perception. And just as cars are designed with more than one spark plug, so too are individual letters processed through multiple channels, all working at once, in coordination with each other. This increases the power and smoothness with which we progress. The associations among letters, like the crankshaft in a car, keep the system rolling despite occasional problems. The occasional letter that is misperceived or even wholly illegible does not stop the reading machine any more than the occasional misfire of a spark plug or drop of water in the gas stops a car.

But, of course, the engine is only indirectly responsible for making a car go. The engine turns gas to kinetic energy, and the energy turns the wheels. Similarly the perceptual system turns print to mental energy, such that it can be understood.

Obviously a car could not be driven without gas, without spark plugs, without a crankshaft, and without a differential and wheels. But it is also important to recognize that it would not be driven if drivers were obliged to attend to each of the details of its operation. Imagine if you had to push a button every time you wanted a spark plug to fire. Imagine if you had to assist the crankshaft manually in order to transform the mechanics into motion. Imagine if the mechanics were such that the car would not go more than a couple of miles per hour or that it unpredictably stalled out every few moments. You would very likely choose not to drive it at all.

These problems are analogous to the difficulties that must befall the reader who cannot quickly, effortlessly, and automatically recognize individual letters and spelling patterns and transform them to words and meanings. And, in analogy, if readers' word recognition skills are not properly operative, they very likely will choose not to read at all.

Clearly without gas, without an engine and mechanics in adequate working order, the system will not go. Suppose, however, that your reading system has plenty of print to consume and a fine mechanical system. Are you on your way?

No. First, you have to want to go somewhere, and you have to have some idea of how to get there. As you travel, you must monitor and control your path. With respect to the route, you must periodically assess how far you have gone, make sure you are on the right track, and renew estimates of how far you have to go. Simultaneously you must also pay careful attention to the local details of the road and control your car through them. These activities correspond to comprehension in its truest sense.

Depending on such variables as the familiarity of the route and its navigability—how far you can see ahead and whether the route is bumpy, windy, congested, or unpredictable—you have to invest considerable active attention in your progress. Similarly, texts that are unfamiliar in concept or difficult in wording or structure require active attention for comprehension. But to the extent that you are directing that attention to the mechanics of the system, it is not available to support your understanding. Only if your ability to recognize and capture the meanings of the words on a page is rapid, effortless, and automatic will you have available the cognitive energy and resources upon which skillful comprehension depends. Only then can you control and reflect upon your journey.

As it happens, everybody wants to go someplace. Everybody wants stimulation, new challenges, and that sense of growth and accomplishment that comes with conquering them. If reading seems unstimulating or unproductive, the individual will choose other things to do. If reading seems aversive, the individual will avoid it altogether. Apropos of this assertion, in her longitudinal study of children in one Texas school, Connie Juel found that 40 percent of the poor fourth grade readers claimed that they would rather clean their room than read. One child stated, "I'd rather clean the mold around the bathtub than read."[1]

Acquisition of the Reading System

If we want children to learn to read well, we must find a way to induce them to read lots. Moreover, the objective beneath our wish that they learn to read well is one of instilling in them the capacity and disposition to read freely. It is of ensuring that they will have ready access, beyond school, to the information and the pleasures of print. And so the circularity of the situation is extremely important: If we want to induce children to read lots, we must teach them to read well.

While accepting that everybody wants to go someplace, we must also recognize that not everybody wants to go to the same place. The materials and activities used in developing reading skill are, thus, of critical importance. To be maximally effective, they must consistently be selected with sensitivity to the needs and interests of the students with whom they will be used.

This book is principally about how to develop basic reading and reading readiness capacities among young children. Fortunately for purposes of schooling, little ones will go almost anywhere we lead them—so long as they are neither frustrated nor bored. Yet, even as that eases our task as their guides, it greatly increases our responsibility. It is up to us to lead them in the right direction.

---

1. Juel (1988).

Here the car analogy breaks down. So apt for describing the operation of the system, it is wholly inappropriate for modeling its acquisition. Building a car is a modular, hierarchical activity. From bottom up, one screws, welds, and otherwise fastens the discrete and countable parts of each subsystem together. One by one, only as each is completed, are the subsystems connected to each other.

For the reading system, in contrast, the parts are not discrete. We cannot proceed by completing each individual subsystem and then fastening it to another. Rather, the parts of the reading system must grow together. They must grow to one another and from one another.

In order for the connections and even the connected parts, themselves, to develop properly, they must be developed conjointly. They must be linked together in the very course of acquisition. And, importantly, this dependency works in both directions. One cannot properly develop the higher-order processes without due attention to the lower. Nor can one focus on the lower-order processes without constantly clarifying and exercising their connections to the higher-order ones.

The great challenge for reading educators, therefore, is one of understanding the parts of the system and their interrelations. Only such understanding enables methodical reflection on the needs and progress of each student. The value of respecting the structure and interrelations of the system lies not just in keeping the pedagogical inventory straight; much more, it greatly facilitates the task of getting through it. As the parts of the system are refined and developed in proper relation to one another, each guides and reinforces the growth of the other.

Finally, although this book is principally about developing reading skills in young children, we must remember that the attention and cooperation that any student invests in reading activities depends on the degree to which her or his interests and sense of progress are engaged. Texts and activities recommended for young children may be wholly inappropriate for older students in content, pace, and cognitive assumptions. Although instructional principles do not change for older students, instructional practice must. For developing and refining the word recognition skills of older children, computerized reading environments might hold more promise.[2] In contrast, vocationally oriented reading

---

2. See, for example, Frederiksen, Warren, and Rosebery (1985a, 1985b); Roth and Beck (1987). With special interest in improving the abilities of bilingual Hispanic youngsters, see Frederiksen (1987).

instruction may be best conducted with job materials and manuals.[3] The best idea I have encountered along these lines comes from Dorothy Strickland, who has recently proposed to help young mothers learn about print by teaching them to read to their babies.

Although issues of the personal relevance and accessibility of text are beyond the scope of this book, they must always be central to our thoughts on how to teach reading. We must also bear in mind that skillful reading encompasses much more than mastery of the basics. Indeed, none of us—neither teachers nor students—can say that we have learned (past tense) to read. Reading is and should be a continuously developing skill.

Organization of the Book

The body of this book is divided into six parts. The goal of this introductory part is to place contemporary concern over reading instruction in a broader historical and educational context. Thus chapter 2 begins with a discussion of the basic tension in any writing system between the codability of meaning and the decodability of the code. It includes a brief overview of the ways in which this tension has expressed itself in the philosophies and instructional practices of reading educators in the United States.

In part II attention is turned to the question of why phonic instruction, in particular, is so often seen as the proper cure for children's reading ills. Chapter 3 provides a review of experimental comparisons of the relative effectiveness of different approaches to beginning reading instruction. Collectively these studies suggest that, among broad classes of programs, those that include systematic phonic instruction generally give young readers an edge in spelling and word recognition skills. Yet, the class of programs that purport to teach phonics is large and varied, which leaves us wondering about the precise methods and materials from which their general advantage derives.

The focus of chapter 4 is on studies of the extent to which successful reading acquisition can be predicted by various measures of prereaders' knowledge and capacities. This body of literature indicates that familiarity of the letters of the alphabet and awareness of the speech sounds, or phonemes, to which they correspond, are strong predictors of the ease or difficulty with which a child learns to read. Research reviewed later in the book

---

3. Mikulecky (1986); Sticht (1979).

confirms that letter recognition facility and phonemic awareness are causally related to reading acquisition and that each is prerequisite for the young reader.

Even so, a catch-22 emerges. Closer analysis indicates that children who have learned their letters and acquired a solid level of phonemic awareness before entering school have also begun to learn to read before entering school. By implication, we are left with the conclusion that the likelihood that a child will succeed in the first grade depends, most of all, on how much she or he has already learned about reading before getting there.

With this finding in focus, consideration is turned to studies of the linguistic and literacy support that preschoolers normally experience. Research indicates that this support varies enormously in both nature and amount across neighborhoods. In the typical American home, parents read to their preschoolers daily—resulting in hundreds and thousands of hours of literacy exposure prior to school entry. But such practices are not normal in the homes of all preschoolers. Data from ethnographic studies indicate that some groups of children rarely even see a storybook before entering school. Unless ways are found to compensate for these differences in preschool literacy preparation, such children are unlikely to succeed with formal reading instruction.

The goal of part III, to establish more precisely the knowledge and skills that are required for proficient reading, is pursued through a review of research and theory on skillful readers. The forceful conclusion is that reading proficiency is strictly limited by the speed, accuracy, and effortlessness with which readers can respond to print as coherent orthographic, phonological, and semantic (meaning-bearing) patterns. In the course of proficient reading, the processes supporting orthographic, phonological, and semantic identification of words occur interactively and interdependently; without the complete and proper operation of all three, the reader is left with neither capacity nor support for comprehension.

The interactive and automatic manner in which skillful readers perceive and interpret words derives from a complex of associations among elementary perceptual units. As the associations bind frequently seen sequences of individual letters into coherent spelling patterns, they also connect them to pronunciations and meanings. Importantly the strength of the associative links between any two units or complexes of units depends directly on the frequency with which the reader attends and has attended to both in the course of perception. It follows from theory—and with ample empirical support—that the speed, accuracy, and effortlessness with which proficient readers move through print depend on the extent to which they have learned to process the sequences of individual letters in the words they read.

An ancillary issue that emerges in part III is that skillful readers' word recognition and comprehension processes depend on sophisticated syntactic abilities. The process through which they interpret the text is regulated by the grammatical structures and interrelationships of its phrases and clauses. Furthermore, analyses indicate that as proficient readers proceed through connected text, they identify the grammatical function of each word as it is encountered. The course through which such syntactic sensitivity develops is an area that has received too little attention from researchers.

In parts IV and V, concern is turned to the acquisition of reading and word recognition skills. Part IV lays the groundwork, discussing the general nature of learning and of what we hope to establish through beginning reading instruction. Rules may serve usefully to point out important commonalities and distinctions between experiences and thereby to help learners organize their experiences most productively. For some types of difficulties, they may also provide strategic or consciously mediated recourse for the reader. In either case, however, such guidance is useful and interpretable only as it applies to and can be absorbed by the readers' direct knowledge of the instances to which it pertains. Productive knowledge is acquired through experience and depends on thought and understanding.

Chapter 10 makes the case that in both its acquisition and fluent operation at every level, the system prospers not from unit-by-unit resolution of the information it receives. Instead and at each level of processing, recognition depends jointly on the individual units and the context in which those units occur and is critically mediated by the perceiver's prior knowledge of and familiarity with both. For example, a reader's identification of a printed word is interactively resolved through recognition of its letters both individually and in familiar sequence or relation to one another. The same holds in the identification of phonemes, words, and meanings.

More generally, to the extent that the received assemblage of information is familiar, the identities of the units and the interrelations between them will be recognized automatically and effortlessly. To the extent that it is not, its perception or understanding will require the reader's active attention.

Yet one's active attention is limited. For productive reading, it must be reserved for the process of discovering the higher-order relationships that divulge the meaning of the text. Again then, we arrive at the implication that productive reading depends on thorough familiarity with the lower-order units and relations of the text.

The goal of instruction on word recognition is to develop the reader's familiarity with frequent spelling patterns so as to enable automatic translation from spellings to meanings. To this end, as discussed in chapter 10, relationships between the spellings and sounds of words are invaluable for the young reader in a variety of ways. Nevertheless, the ability to sound words out must not be mistaken as an instructional end in itself.

In part V, concern shifts from questions of learning to those of teaching. Chapter 11 focuses on issues surrounding instruction on individual letter-sound correspondences and phonic generalizations. Research indicates that, particularly for children who enter school with weak literacy preparation, direct instruction in word analysis skills is critically important. While reading progress depends on working familiarity with spelling patterns and spelling-sound correspondences, low-readiness readers do not induce these relationships through exposure to meaningful text. What they learn in this domain depends strongly on what they are directly taught. But research also indicates that the degree to which children internalize and use their phonic instruction depends on the degree to which they have found it useful for recognizing the words in their earliest texts. It indicates, moreover, that immersion—right from the start—in meaningful, connected text is of vital importance.

One implication of these findings is that in the selection of beginning reading programs, priority consideration should be given to whether the passages in the preprimers have been designed to reinforce the word recognition lessons that precede them. Surprisingly, such coordination has been all but absent in a number of commercial packages for beginning reading instruction.

Yet there is a deeper problem here. For children with relatively little literacy preparation, basic phonic instruction can only proceed quite slowly. Instilling the most basic of individual letter-sound correspondences may require months of classroom attention. In the meantime, how can one possibly construct texts that are meaningful and engaging without extending beyond the children's established phonic knowledge?

Seemingly, the only escape from this dilemma is to find a way to increase the efficiency of spelling-sound instruction; happily, this can be done. The key to this escape lies in the recognition that spelling-sound relationships are not the basics of reading skills and knowledge. Their acquisition can be greatly eased given proper foundation and support, and it is to this objective that chapters 12, 13, and 14 are directed.

The goal of chapter 12 is to clarify, through review of experimental research, what prereaders do not automatically know and must therefore learn about spoken language in order to understand print. As in part II, phonological awareness emerges as a critical factor. Yet the emphasis of the chapter is on how such awareness might best be developed. Of special importance, when children with reading difficulties are given training in phonological awareness, they evince significant acceleration in reading achievement. Similarly, preschoolers who are given training in phonological awareness evince significant acceleration in their later acquisition of reading.

In chapter 13 the question is shifted to what prereaders must learn about print before formal reading instruction is begun. Again as in part II, broad text awareness and ready knowledge of letters are strongly implicated. With focus on how such knowledge might best be developed, the acquisition of visual letter recognition and printing skills is considered in detail. So too is the potential value of exploring the structure and functions of text through, for example, language experience and book-sharing activities.

Finally, chapter 14 examines the ways in which reading skills can grow through writing. The practice of encouraging independent writing and spelling from the beginning of first grade is firmly endorsed. The process of inventing spellings seems to sharpen both children's appreciation of the phonemic structure of words and their interest in learning about how words are conventionally spelled. For older children a strong argument is made for encouraging attention to correct spellings. And beyond spelling, the processes of composing, refining, and sharing one's own written text are of invaluable importance in helping young readers to realize that what one gets from reading depends on what one gives to it— that reading in its only productive sense is always a challenge in active thinking and understanding.

My conclusions are summarized in part VI. In brief, reading depends integrally on deep and thorough knowledge of spellings and spelling-sound relations. At the same time, both the use and acquisition of such knowledge depend on the child's fuller understanding of and interest in the reading process.

Reading Words and Meaning: From an Age-Old Problem to a Contemporary Crisis

The question of how best to teach beginning reading may be the most politicized topic in the field of education. To the uninitiated, the irrepressible question is why. One reason is that we care universally and passionately about the success of beginning reading instruction. It is the key to education, and education is the key to success for both individuals and a democracy.

But concern, even passionate concern, is not enough to politicize an issue. There must also be partisanship and, indeed, the partisanship surrounding reading instruction is fierce. One side holds that because the purpose of reading is comprehension, comprehension should be emphasized from the start. On the other side is concern that a central focus of beginning reading instruction must be that of developing the skills involved in recognizing written words; these skills, after all, are singularly lacking in the beginner and are a prerequisite to reading, however one defines it.

So where is the conflict? Don't we all want children to be able to decipher words and understand them? Yes, of course. Don't virtually all beginning reading programs endeavor to help children to learn both? Yes, of course. But the sides of the debate are deeply rooted in the nature of our writing system. To understand this, some background is in order.

The Purposes versus the Methods of Writing

Writing is a system for conveying or recording messages through constellations of visual symbols. By this definition, any number of such systems is conceivable, but an ideal system must meet three criteria:

1. The system must be capable of representing the range of expressions that its culture wishes to record or convey.

2. The symbols must be reasonably easy to produce.

3. The written message must be interpretable in the sense that it must readily symbolize for the reader what it was intended to symbolize by the writer.

Notice that while the first criterion for an ideal system of writing relates to its purposes, the second and third relate to the practicalities of its means.

Of the major writing systems that exist today, none perfectly satisfies all three of these criteria, and it is a safe bet that none ever will. Over time, every culture's uses and methods of writing must inevitably change.[1] So too do the particular concepts and ideas that they wish to record.[2] Thus even the once-perfect writing system has one of two ultimate destinies: It can remain rigidly frozen, becoming imperfect by default, or it can yield to the pressures and change. Indeed, herein lies the history of writing systems.

From Pictures to Logograms

Our earliest written records consisted of pictures.[3] In terms of the third criterion for an ideal system—that the symbols be interpretable—the advantage of pictures seems hard to beat. At least at the level of individual elements, their significance is transparent: A picture of a dog can symbolize a dog to anyone, with no need of explanation or schooling.

In view of the expressive freedom of drawing, the use of pictures for communication also seems to meet the first criterion nicely; to record a complex concept or event, one need only draw a

---

1. As examples from this century, consider the difficulties of designing, first, mechanical typeset and, now, practical keyboards for the Japanese or Chinese writing systems. In both countries, such difficulties have created pressure toward displacing their ancestral logographies with writing systems that require fewer distinct characters.

2. As examples, consider the difficulties that all countries have in representing proper nouns and topical words from other languages. In coping with such problems, the British often opt for their own labels, such as Rhodesia (after its "discoverer," John Rhodes) and Germany (Deutschland); the Americans tend to flip-flop between alternatives (Peking/Beijing, Warsaw/Warszawa, Gdansk/Danzig, Shi'a/Shiite, Tehran/Teheran); and the Chinese often just take the word as it comes, strange script and all.

3. Gleitman and Rozin (1977).

complex picture. But here lies the method's first big disadvantage: The interpretation of complex pictures is not straightforward. A complex picture may convey a thousand words, but which of those did its creator intend?

A solution to this problem—one that potentially preserves the iconic value of the symbol system but helps to constrain interpretations—can be had by insisting that each picture correspond to a single unitized idea or, better, a word. Under this so-called logographic system of writing, the notation of complex ideas is achieved not through complex scenes but through series of individual pictures. Their interpretation proceeds in reverse, by translating the pictures back into words and applying spoken language constraints.[4]

The Sumerians of ancient Mesopotamia are credited with the establishment of logographic writing.[5] This system seemed to have such merit that it spread broadly to other cultures, and logograms are the prevailing symbology[6] for a number of writing systems even today. (Chinese is the most widespread.)

In time, however, logographic systems also outgrew perfection. First and foremost, their requirement for one-to-one correspondence between pictures and words seriously restricted their expressive range; not all words are unambiguously picturable or even picturable at all. Because an acceptable system must, more than anything else, subserve the purposes of writing, this shortcoming had to be overcome. Little by little it was.

The solution was to introduce new symbols and symbolic conventions to convey unpicturable words.[7] These new additions to the writing system could not, by their very nature, have direct

---

4. Gelb (1963).

5. Balmuth (1982, p. 20).

6. In general, major writing systems cannot be perfectly categorized as logographic, syllabic, or alphabetic. Instead whatever its base symbology, each system tends to include aspects of each of the others. Thus English, though fundamentally alphabetic, freely employs logograms for signs and advertisements as well as accepting them directly in connected discourse (e.g., +, %, $, &, and 1, 2, 3, 4). Similarly, Chinese, which is at core both a logographic and a syllabic system, sometimes uses alphabetic notations, sometimes represents a new word by chaining together indigenous symbols that sound like each of the word's syllables, and more generally relies heavily on a system of "phonetic radicals" for keying the sounds of graphic characters. The Japanese writing system includes several thousand logograms in addition to a full set of syllabic symbols. For an in-depth discussion of these dimensions of variation across modern language groups, see Holender (1987).

7. See Gelb (1963).

iconic significance. They could not be consensually interpretable except by convention, that is, except through their memorization by the writer and the reader. The price of this solution, in other words, was a relaxation of criterion 3—a compromise in the ready interpretability of the symbol system.

Logograms also proved suboptimal on the second criterion, producibility: Perfectly identifiable little pictures are laborious to generate. Because of this, logograms quite naturally became simplified and stylized by writers. Over years of use, even the logograms for picturable words tended to lose their iconic transparency.[8] Again, then, a toll is taken on the interpretational accessibility of the system (criterion 3), and again the only fix lies in memorization of the conventional symbols by the writer and the reader.

How seriously do such requirements for memorization detract from the value of the system? Bear in mind that within a logography each writable word must be represented by a unique symbol. If the number of words in a spoken language is large—and the number of words in a language only grows over time—and if any sizable proportion of the logograms requires memorization, the acquisition of a fully expressive visual vocabulary must stand as a truly prodigious task.

The Chinese writing system contains as many as 80,000 basic logograms, but even Chinese adults are said to have working familiarity with only about 4,000 to 5,000.[9] In the end, as requirements for symbol memorization grow, they must in practical terms compromise all three criteria for an ideal writing system: If the full set of symbols can be neither produced nor interpreted without extensive study, criteria 2 and 3 are not met; if it can be neither produced nor interpreted even with extensive study, criterion 1 is lost too.

From Logograms to Syllabaries

In the ancestry of our own writing system, it is believed that the demise of the logographic system was set by the need to record

---

8. Holender (1987); Martin (1972).

9. Martin (1972). Note, however, that Chinese logograms are more properly said to represent morphemes, or meaning elements, than words per se. Although each character corresponds to a (monomorphemic) word, many words are combinations of more than one morpheme. In view of this, sight recognition of 4,000–5,000 logograms supports a reading vocabulary of about 15,000 words (Holender, 1987).

foreign words and proper names.[10] For this challenge, it was not satisfactory to draw a picture of the word's referent. These words were labels; it was important that their verbatim forms be retrievable from their written representations. The custom ultimately developed of representing the pronunciations of such terms with "sound-alikes" from the logographic system, that is, with strings of monosyllabic logograms.

This insight, that symbols can represent the sounds of language rather than its referents, changed our ancestral methods of writing forever. Thenceforth existing symbols were used more and more often for their syllabic (as opposed to iconic) significance, and new syllabic symbols were invented. Little by little the logographic systems of the Middle East were evolving into syllabic systems of writing.[11]

In terms of the first criterion, syllabic systems were just fine. Because all words can be analyzed into syllables, such systems allowed one to write anything that could be spoken. Yet in terms of the other two criteria, producibility and interpretability, syllabic systems have both pluses and minuses. The pluses derive from the fact that syllables are relatively salient units of spoken language. Thus the rationale behind syllabic systems was intuitively clear—so clear in fact that they were independently invented quite frequently and tended to spread rapidly.[12]

The big minus of syllabic systems derives from the fact that the sound of a word is not picturable. Because of that, syllabograms cannot be representationally transparent. Whether you want to read or write, someone must tell you what each symbol stands for, and you must memorize the answer.

Typically the number of different syllables in a language is significantly smaller than the number of different words, and to whatever extent this is true, syllabic systems hold an obvious advantage over logographies.[13] But even where this advantage is sizable, a syllabary is practical only if the absolute number of syllables in the language is relatively small. By one estimate, English contains about 5,000 syllables.[14] To be sure, this is significantly fewer than the number of different English words.

---

10. Balmuth (1982, p. 26).

11. Balmuth (1982, p. 25).

12. Diringer (1968, cited in Balmuth, 1982).

13. In Chinese a syllabary would offer little savings over a logography because the numbers of characters, monomorphemic words, and syllables are virtually identical. See Holender (1987).

14. Rozin and Gleitman (1977).

Nevertheless, a syllabic writing system would present a formidable teaching and learning task in our language.

The potential number of syllables in a language is related to the structure of the syllables in that language. In English, a syllable may consist of a single vowel sound, e.g. *a*, a vowel sound followed by one to four consonant sounds (*am, act, acts, angst*)[15]; one to three consonant sounds followed by a vowel sound (*ray, tray, stray*) or a vowel sound with one or more consonant sounds on both ends (*pit, spit, pits, spits*, . . . , *splints*). In contrast, for languages whose syllable structures are restricted to a single vowel or a single consonant plus a vowel, such as *ba, be, bi, bo, bu*, many fewer distinct syllables are possible. Such simple syllable structures are characteristic of languages in which the syllabic system thrived.[16] They were also a key factor in the eventual evolution of the alphabet.

The Alphabet

Eventually, people began representing whole syllables with nothing more than a symbol for their initial consonants.[17] This consonant-only shorthand was passed around from language to language, until it reached the Phoenicians and, by way of them, the Greeks. The Greeks adopted all nineteen of the Phoenicians' consonant symbols in sequence; however, not all nineteen of the Phoenicians' consonant sounds were present in Greek speech. Not being able to hear, much less pronounce, the extra consonants properly, the Greeks confused them for vowels.[18] The alphabetic principle was thereby set: one symbol for each elementary speech sound, or phoneme, in the language.

The invention of the alphabet is often said to be the most important invention in the social history of the world. Historian David Diringer describes it as "the creation of a 'revolutionary writing,' a script which we can perhaps term 'democratic' (or

---

15. It might be objected that in many English dialects, the letter pair *ng* often behaves not like a blend but like a digraph as in *rang* and *sang*. In this word, however, the *n* and the *g* are typically given separate, distinct pronunciation, regardless of dialect.

16. Balmuth (1982); Gleitman and Rozin (1977); Holender (1987).

17. Chao (1958, cited in Gleitman & Rozin, 1977).

18. Gleitman and Rozin (1977). Alternatively, Gelb (1963) suggests that the Greeks first represented vowels through phonetic indicators, in the manner of the *matres lectionis* of the Semitic systems, and that their status as full letters evolved from there.

rather, a 'people's script'), as against the 'theocratic' scripts that preceded it."[19]

The advantages of an alphabetic system are clear. Like the syllabaries and advanced logographies, it is capable of representing any speakable expression. Unlike either of those systems, it can do so by means of remarkably few symbols. Writing systems that were comprised of large numbers of symbols were naturally the possession of the elite. They were passed on only to those few whom it was felt should and, among those, could and would invest the amount of time and study required for their memorization. In contrast, the number of symbols in an alphabetic system tends to range between twenty and thirty-five—few enough to be memorized by almost anyone and, once memorized, adequate—at least in a perfectly alphabetic system—for purposes of reading and writing any word in the language.[20]

But the alphabetic system is not ideal. The alphabet evolved through successive compromises on the requirement that the symbology of a writing system be readily interpretable. Pictures are symbolically transparent, logograms less so, and syllabograms and letters not at all. Moreover, with passage from each of these systems to the next, the significance of the symbols became more and more abstract. Finally, the symbolic significance of the letters of the alphabet is so abstract as to not even exist in any physically robust sense. Letters map onto phonemes, and phonemes map roughly onto functionally or perceptually equivalent articulatory targets. But the sounds of individual phonemes have no constant or isolable correspondent in the speech stream, and many cannot even be produced in isolation (we can say /buh/ or /bah/ or /bih/, but not /b/).[21]

In short the merits of the alphabet are had through compromise of the criteria for producibility and consensual interpretability, but it is a special kind of compromise. The significant toll is not really one of production ease. Though it is said that the same text is significantly longer when written in an alphabetic script than in a logography,[22] this difference is compensated by the graphical simplicity of letters as compared with logograms. Nor is the toll in the number of different symbols that the reader or writer must commit to memory; there are so very few symbols in an alphabetic script. Rather, the toll is

---

19. Diringer (1968, p. 161, cited in Balmuth, 1982, p. 33).
20. Balmuth (1982, p. 31).
21. Liberman, Cooper, Shankweiler, and Studdert-Kennedy (1967).
22. Martin (1972).

cognitive; the referent of a letter is perceptually abstract and conceptually sophisticated.

For purposes of learning to read and write, the subtlety of the alphabetic principle is a significant problem all by itself. This problem is greatly compounded by the fact that written English is by no means perfectly alphabetic. In contrast to the perfectly alphabetic script, the letters of English words do not necessarily map one to one onto phonemes. Sometimes the phonemic significance of a letter is modified by the letter or even letters next door (*ran* versus *rain*, *sit* versus *sight*), sometimes by one or more nonadjacent letters (*bit* versus *bite*, *nation* versus *nationality*), and sometimes only by the identity of the word or its constituent syllables as wholes (*father*/*fathead* and *ukelele*). The situation is pithily summarized by the following poem:

Hints on Pronunciation for Foreigners

I take it you already know
Of tough and bough and cough and dough?
Others may stumble but not you,
On hiccough, thorough, laugh and through.
Well done! And now you wish, perhaps,
To learn of less familiar traps?

Beware of heard, a dreadful word
That looks like beard and sounds like bird,
And dead: it's said like bed, not bead—
For goodness' sake don't call it "deed"!
Watch out for meat and great and threat
(They rhyme with suite and straight and debt.)

A moth is not a moth in mother
Nor both in bother, broth in brother,
And here is not a match for there
Nor dear and fear for bear and pear,
And then there's dose and rose and lose —
Just look them up—and goose and choose,
And cork and work and card and ward,
And font and front and word and sword,
And do and go and thwart and cart —
Come, come, I've hardly made a start!
A dreadful language? Man alive.
I'd mastered it when I was five.[23]

---

23. From a letter published in the *London Sunday Times* (January 3, 1965), cited by Chomsky (1970). Only the initials of the author, T. S. W., are known.

Reading Instruction in the United States

In view of these complications, how should reading be taught? How should we go about inculcating such an abstract and complicated code and without losing sight of the purpose of reading: comprehension? It is from the tension between these two questions that America's controversy over how best to teach reading derives, and this tension has grown over the years. On one hand, concepts of what it means to comprehend text and of what kinds of texts the growing child should be learning to comprehend have expanded dramatically. On the other, appreciation of both the importance and the difficulty of mastering the symbol system has also matured. The trail of protests over and changes to methods of reading instruction reflect earnest concern on both sides.

From Colonial Times

The earliest methods of reading instruction followed a straightforward, two-step process: Teach the code, then have them read.[24]

Teaching about the code was based directly on the alphabetic principle. Students were first required to learn the alphabet. The phonemic significance of the letters was instilled, for example, through the presentation of key words (e.g., G is for *glass*), practice in reading simple syllables, and exercise in spelling.

Children principally read the Bible and, after the Revolutionary War, various nationalistic and patriotic essays. These selections directly subserved the prevailing notions of the sociocultural purpose of reading. Besides that, not much else was available to read (which, like the chicken and the egg, helped determine instructional goals as well as materials). Without yet having reflected on the demands of reading comprehension, the selections were neither specially written nor adapted for young minds; as a consequence, all of the complicating questions about why that might be done and how it might be done best were still moot. This approach reflected an uncomplicated translation of the nature of the writing system: Teach the means, and get on with the purpose. And thus it pretty much remained through the middle of the nineteenth century.

---

24. Balmuth (1982); Singer (1981); Smith (1974).

The Evolution of Meaning-First Curricula

The mid-1800's were marked by a resurgence of Jeffersonian ideals: The fate of a democracy was seen to depend upon the wisdom of the majority—the better educated the populace, the greater its collective wisdom. In addition, much more print had become available by that time. Indeed, literature was blossoming in America as well as in Europe. The broadening social value of reading turned inevitably to concern with how reading was taught—in particular with how best to instill in students the desire to learn, with how best to prepare them to focus on meaning, ideas, and the true rewards of education.[25]

We wondered: If children were asked to read only that for which they were intellectually ready, wouldn't the meaning-bearing value of text be self-evident? And if the mechanics of reading were properly subordinated to meaning from the beginning, wouldn't they too be easier and more pleasant to master? If we instead immersed students in the "dull drill and practice" of letter-to-sound correspondences, wouldn't we be depriving them of—even, perhaps, permanently jading them against—the higher mental activities of true reading? Indeed given the seemingly rampant irregularity of English spelling, did arduous instruction in letter-to-sound correspondences—*phonics*, as it was now called—even make sense?

Phonic and comprehension instruction had come to be seen as mutually incompatible, and highly political. In this, Horace Mann, secretary of the Massachusetts Board of Education, was a principal figure. In his annual reports for the board of education, Mann decried the "odor and fungousness of spelling-book paper" from which "a soporific effluvium seems to emanate . . . steeping [the child's] faculties in lethargy." Describing the letters as "skeleton-shaped, bloodless, ghostly apparitions," he continued, "It is no wonder that the children look and feel so death-like, when compelled to face them." In place of "this emptiness, blankness, silence and death that we compel children to fasten their eyes [on]," Mann suggested that children be taught to read whole, meaningful words first. Lessons in which words are taught first, he offered, "will be like an excursion to the fields of elysium compared with the old method of plunging children, day by day, for months together, in the cold waters of oblivion, and

---

25. The bulk of this section is distilled from Balmuth (1982) and Smith (1974).

compelling them to say falsely, that they love the chill and torpor of the immersion."[26]

At first the challenge was angrily received by schoolmasters and leading educators, but little by little its influence grew. Over the ensuing years there arose intense scrutiny of English spelling and a number of ambitious, but never quite successful, movements to reform the English alphabet and/or spelling system. In addition, the all-purpose reading books of the past were replaced with graded series—a different book for each grade—designed to match the children's age and achievement levels in linguistic complexity and content. And finally the emphasis on meaning became more and more prevalent.

The meaning-first curriculum did not gain true dominance until the second quarter of this century. At that point Americans, grappling with some serious social growing pains, were hard in search of a multiple society: Education, then as now, was seen as the key. Its purpose was to foster the productive, creative, and responsible citizenry that coalesces from knowledgeable and intellectually independent individuals. Its design and progression was to be based on the growing child's nature and needs.

From the 1930s and 1940s, major programs on beginning reading became squarely focused on comprehension. Words were introduced through meanings first—to be recognized holistically by sight. When straight recognition failed, the children were encouraged to rely on context and pictures, to narrow in on the word's identity through meaning-based inference. Phonics was relegated to the position of an ancillary tool; it was to be introduced gradually, invoked sparingly, and exercised only in coordination with the meaning-bearing dimensions of text.[27]

An Angry Protest

In the 1950s, spearheaded by an emotional book by Rudolph Flesch, we began to worry about our wisdom.[28] Had we let go of a good thing? Flesch argued that we had. Pointing out that written English is alphabetic and thus "phonetic" by definition, he continued that for English, as for any other alphabetic language, phonic instruction is the only natural system of learning how to read: Teach the children the identities of the letters, teach them the sounds that each represents, and teach them by having them

---

26. See Balmuth (1982, pp. 190–191).
27. Chall (1967).
28. Flesch (1955).

write. Once taught in this way, he asserted, the children will forever after be able to read and write—not just the words you have taught but any word in the language—all by themselves. Good readers, he explained, were good readers because they spontaneously caught on to the alphabetic nature of print. How could we deny that secret to those who would not?

Flesch's arguments were not new, but it was not from them that the book derived its impact: It was from their presentation. His appeal was as intensely political:

There is a connection between phonics and democracy—a fundamental connection. Equal opportunity for all is one of the inalienable rights, and the word method interferes with that right.[29]

I say, therefore, that the word method is gradually destroying democracy in this country; it returns to the upper middle class the privileges that public education was supposed to distribute evenly among the people. The American Dream is, essentially, equal opportunity through free education for all. This dream is beginning to vanish in a country where the public schools are falling down on the job.[30]

And it was impassioned:

It seems to me a plain fact that the word method consists essentially of treating children as if they were dogs. It is not a method of teaching at all; it is clearly a method of animal training. It's the most inhuman, mean, stupid way of foisting something on a child's mind.[31]

Addressed to the mothers and fathers of America, the book was more than thirty weeks on the best-seller list and broadly serialized by the popular press.

The Aftermath

The hue and cry of Flesch's followers eventually reached the concerned ear of the government. Polemics aside, was there something to their plea? The best scholars and researchers were enlisted to ask the question, and the answer was a resounding yes. Beginning reading programs that included early, systematic phonic instruction generally produced better results than those that did not. In response, today's introductory programs have become more eclectic, presenting systematic instruction in spelling-to-sound correspondences along with stories and exercises intended

---

29. Flesch (1955, p. 130).
30. Flesch (1955, p. 132).
31. Flesch (1955, p. 126).

to reinforce and develop comprehension skills.[32] Happily and, we hope, causally, the basic skills performance of young readers has improved.[33]

But along with the positive consequences of Flesch's little book came two definite negatives. First, Flesch did not confine his passion and politics to the issues at hand. He named names and pointed fingers. He called out the profit motive and impugned the intellect and honesty of experts, schools, and publishers. He developed conspiratorial motives, alluded to communists, and made negative insinuations about the intellectual predispositions and capacities of females and minorities. Thus, not only was the debate politicized, but it was politicized on dimensions that were wholly irrelevant to the question of how best to teach reading. Second, Flesch vastly oversimplified the issues. As he presented them, the issues were, plain and simple, phonic versus look-say pedagogy. Yet there is much more to skillful word recognition than the memorization of the alphabet and its letter-to-sound correspondences. Similarly, the issues surrounding the proper development of comprehension are complex and extend vastly beyond the ways in which one might come to identify whole words.

Thus Flesch succeeded in not only blurring the issues but in quashing rational debate of their larger substance. He succeeded, through the heated spillage of his argument, in uselessly polarizing and paralyzing a field of research that our country desperately needs.

Today one cannot promote "whole language" instruction without having half the crowd perceive it as a thinly veiled push for look-say approaches to word recognition. To some, the very term "whole language" is translated to mean an uninformed and

---

32. Popp (1975).

33. National Assessment of Educational Progress (1981b, 1985). More recent data from NAEP reflect a decline in reading achievement scores (Applebee, Langer, and Mullis, 1988). The significance of this change in test scores is difficult to interpret because of anomalies in the testing procedure. However, examining trends in the data across years and particularly the increasing proportions of very low scorers, Chall (1988) has argued that we should seriously consider the possibility that the decline is real and respond accordingly. As possible contributors to such a decline, she cites a general reduction in remedial services and library support. For the older students, she cites an increase in academic standards and curriculum requirements that has been unaccompanied with extra help for those having trouble already. For the younger students, she points to a recent decrease in attention given to systematic instruction on word recognition in the early grades.

irresponsible effort to finesse necessary instruction with "touchy-feely" classroom gratification—and worse. The term "code-emphasis" is translated by others into an unenlightened commitment to unending drill and practice at the expense of the motivation and higher-order dimensions of text that make reading worthwhile—and worse.

Toward the Future

By misinterpreting each other, we prolong a fruitless debate and, worse, we do so at the cost of precious progress and of our school children's potential reading achievement. First, we are battling over a dichotomy that should not exist: Writing has a method and a purpose; to read, one must master both. Second, more than ever before, methods of teaching reading must be the best they can possibly be.

It is not just that the teaching of reading is more important than ever before, but that it must be taught better and more broadly than ever before.[34] We are witnessing an explosion in both information and technology. Alongside, the social and economic values of reading and writing are multiplying in both number and importance as never before. It is no longer possible to guess, much less dictate, what knowledge and skills will be critical to students in their futures. Each of them must be prepared with the abilities to acquire, understand, use, and communicate information accurately, efficiently, and independently. Levels of literacy that were once held—even very recently held—to be satisfactory, will be marginal by the year 2000.[35]

But even as we come to recognize this situation, we are confronted with statistics that the ability of our students to read advanced materials is slowly but steadily declining[36]; that among industrial nations, American students' reading achievement is average or even below[37]; that compared to its industrial competitors, the United States is raising a disproportionate number of *very* poor readers[38]; that already one out of five adult

---

34. Deihl and Mikulecky (1980); Miller (1988); Resnick and Resnick (1977); Stedman and Kaestle (1987).

35. Commission on Reading, National Academy of Education (1985).

36. Applebee, Langer, and Mullis (1988); National Assessment of Educational Progress (1981b, 1985).

37. Thorndike (1973).

38. Stevenson (1984).

Americans is functionally illiterate and that these ranks are swelling by about 2.3 million each year.[39]

According to the Orton Dyslexia Society, illiterate adults account for 75 percent of the unemployed, one-third of the mothers receiving Aid to Families with Dependent Children, 85 percent of the juveniles who appear in court, 60 percent of prison inmates, and nearly 40 percent of minority youth; of people in the work force, 15 percent are functionally illiterate, including 11 percent of professional and managerial workers, and 30 percent of semiskilled and unskilled workers.[40] *Fortune* magazine reports that "of the 3.8 million 18-year old Americans in 1988, fully 700,000 had dropped out of school and another 700,000 could not read their high school diplomas"; that "in all, 84 percent of 23,000 people who took an exam for entry-level jobs at New York Telephone in 1988 failed."[41]

The future of our country depends on the extent to which it can continue to be competitively productive within the world economy. It depends, in other words, on the excellence of its populace as a whole. It is imperative that we strengthen our children's literacy skills.

In the words of *Becoming a Nation of Readers,*

Reading is important for the society as well as the individual. Economics research has established that schooling is an investment that forms human capital—that is, knowledge, skill, and problem-solving ability that have enduring value. While a country receives a good return on investment in education at all levels from nursery school and kindergarten through college, the research reveals that the returns are highest from the early years of schooling when children are first learning to read. The Commission on Excellence warned of the risk for America from shortcomings in secondary education. Yet the early years set the stage for later learning. Without the ability to read, excellence in high school and beyond is unattainable.[42]

Proficient reading comprehension depends not just on the ability to recognize words, but the ability to recognize them relatively quickly and effortlessly. Reading achievement in the early years of school depends critically on the student's facility with the printed code. If low-achieving students can be brought up to grade level within the first three years of school, their reading performance tends not to revert but to stay at grade level

---

39. Larrick (1987); Orton Dyslexia Society (1986, cited in Lerner (1988).

40. Orton Dyslexia Society (1986, cited in Lerner (1988).

41. Perry (1988).

42. Commission on Reading, National Academy of Education (1985, p. 1).

thenceforth; if we fail to bring students' reading to grade level within those first few years, the likelihood of their ever catching up is slim, even with extra funding and special programs.[43]

Classroom time is limited—a minute poorly spent on word recognition or any other activity is a minute robbed from education. In the last several decades, researchers have made enormous progress toward understanding both the psychology and pedagogy of reading. For the use of parents, teachers, and publishers and for the benefit of students, a summary of this information is in order.

Thus the Department of Education has again been asked, this time by Congress, to undertake an evaluation of phonic instruction in beginning reading programs.[44] This book is the result. The goal is not to decide whether systematic instruction on word recognition is worthwhile; it is instead to provide guidance as to how such instruction might be achieved so as to be most efficient and most effective and to provide the best support possible toward the purpose for learning to read—comprehension.

---

43. Carter (1984). Although there are no intellectual or cognitive reasons why it should be easier to teach a six year old to read than a ten year old, there are a host of attitudinal and logistical reasons why it must be more difficult to teach a ten year old than a six year old.

44. Amendment No. 2202, Human Service Reauthorization Act, 1986.

II

Why Phonics?

The charge of this book, by Congressional mandate, is to provide guidance as to how schools might maximize the quality of phonic instruction in beginning reading programs. In view of the complexity of the reading process, in view of the sheer number of skills and strategies that it involves, we are obliged to ask: Why phonics?

It is with this question that we begin, by briefly reviewing two major categories of evidence that seem to urge phonics upon us. The first category consists of comparisons of the relative effectiveness of different approaches to teaching beginning reading. The second consists of analyses of the subskills that best predict the success with which prereaders will learn to read. There is, of course, a third category of evidence that properly falls within this topic—differences between good and poor readers. However, exploration of these differences will be focal in the rest of the book.

The findings reviewed in part II are suggestive of the conclusion that something about that large and general class of programs that purport to teach phonics is of genuine and lasting value. In particular, each of these categories of evidence suggests that students must appreciate the alphabetic principle to become proficient readers: They must acquire a sense of the correspondences between letters and sounds upon which it is based.

Before beginning, a cautionary note is in order. "Necessary" is not the same as "sufficient." However critical letter-to-sound correspondences may be, they are not enough. To become skillful readers, children need much more. We return to questions of what else may be beneficial or necessary in later chapters.

3

Program Comparisons (And, by the Way, What Is Phonics?)

Perhaps the most influential arguments for teaching phonics are based on studies comparing the relative effectiveness of different approaches to teaching beginning reading. Collectively these studies suggest, with impressive consistency, that programs including systematic instruction on letter-to-sound correspondences lead to higher achievement in both word recognition and spelling, at least in the early grades and especially for slower or economically disadvantaged students.

Some of these data were collected in the realistic, but therefore complex, contexts of real classrooms. Others were collected through controlled, but therefore artifical, laboratory studies. Because both sorts of investigations have shortcomings, the data do not prove the point. Yet they do make it very difficult to dismiss.

At the end of this chapter, the issue will be pushed one step further, broaching the question of what effective phonic instruction might comprise. If in general some phonic instruction is beneficial for young readers, why in particular should that be so? Across the broad spectrum of phonic programs, what teaching activities and learning outcomes are most valuable? How much phonic instruction is beneficial and what kinds? These questions, moreover, define major themes of this book.

Jeanne Chall and The Great Debate

The Setting

More than to any single individual, current concern in the United States with the teaching of phonics is owed to Jeanne Chall. As she tells the story, it began in the fall of 1959, when the debate over the proper way to teach children to read was at its bitter peak.[1]

On one side, the most widely used reading programs still followed the whole-word, meaning-first, phonics little-and-later approach to beginning reading that had been the mode for decades.[2] On the other was not only a vociferously concerned public but an outcropping of new and rediscovered phonic approaches to beginning reading (it had been four years since the publication of Rudolph Flesch's vitriolic best-seller). In the middle were the researchers, stuck with both the responsibility and the inability to speak to the conflict.

It was then that the National Conference on Research in English invited Chall to join a small group of experts on reading instruction for a meeting at Syracuse University. The charge of this group was to identify those aspects of reading that were most in need of research. Clearly there was desperate need for research on how best to teach beginning reading. Just as clearly this issue was an extremely difficult one. The task was relegated to a subcommittee of which Chall was a member (along with Ralph Staiger and James Soffietti).

The product of this subcommittee was a plan: What was needed was a large-scale cooperative experiment, one that, through proper design and control, could evaluate the issues of whether some approaches to beginning reading were more effective than others. The study would be scientific, conducted through proper design and control; it would be efficient and open-minded, measuring program effectiveness against a variety of outcome measures; and it would be realistically complex, evaluating program effectiveness separately for different kinds of students, teachers, and schools. Eventually the plan was consummated as the now-famous U.S. Office of Education Cooperative Research Program in First-Grade Reading Instruction.[3]

The Proposal

Meanwhile Chall was hooked. Having worked so hard to identify the variables for future research, she wondered if these

---

1. See Chall (1967).

2. At the time, a survey of over 1,500 elementary school teachers indicated that basal readers were used by 98 percent of first-grade teachers and by 92 to 94 percent of second- and third-grade teachers on "all or most days of the year." (Barton and Wilder, 1964).

3. Bond and Dykstra (1967); Dykstra, (1968).

same issues might provide the necessary focus for evaluating existing methods and synthesizing previous research. She approached the Carnegie Corporation with this proposal in 1961. Her project took three years. Her product, *Learning to Read: The Great Debate*, was published in 1967. Updated and reissued in 1983, the book remains a seminal resource on the topic.[4]

The investigation to which Chall committed herself was extremely ambitious in scope. Already well-steeped in the rhetoric on alternative instructional strategies, she directed her gaze to their causes and effects.

From the Authorities

She started with the causes. What, explicitly, were the assumptions and objectives that underlay alternative programs, and what were the differences among them? To gain first-hand answers to these questions, she turned to the people responsible for creating and promoting both the reigning programs and their hottest contenders.

Each interviewed individual was asked to present his or her own convictions on the definition of reading and on the ways its nature or process might change with skill, age, or experience. They were asked to give their thoughts on reading readiness and to discuss the proper balance between emphasizing meaning and emphasizing code in terms of both pedagogical considerations and the motivations and interests of the beginning reader. They were asked to reflect on issues of vocabulary, content, illustrations, and the roles of connected reading (oral and silent) and writing in reading instruction. They were asked to comment on the classroom logistics of teaching reading and the appropriate level of parental involvement. They were asked to explain why some children fail to learn to read and whether children, in general, were learning to read less well than they had been fifty years before.

Interestingly, the general view of the respondents was not that the standards or effectiveness of reading instruction had been deteriorating. They did not believe that children were reading less well than they had in prior eras. Instead they believed that the social and cultural requirements for reading had been changing. The problem, they argued, was that it was—and increasingly would be—incumbent upon all to read more and better than ever before. The problem, in short, was born of the same

---

4. Chall (1983a).

foresighted tension that has fomented every reading and writing revolution in history.

From the Texts

Chall knew that intentions and assumptions rarely translate perfectly into products. To refine and corroborate the information gained from her authorities, she looked next to the teachers' manuals and classroom materials themselves. The twenty-two programs she examined included the two major basal series plus at least one representative of each of the most widely discussed alternative approaches of the day.[5]

Chall described each of these twenty-two programs in her book. In addition, she systematically analyzed them. Recognizing that "Too often, the emphasis has been on '*Which* [approach] works better?' and seldom on '*What aspect* of an approach (or given reading program) leads to what and why?'" she identified major instructional variables, comparing and contrasting the materials and procedures of the programs along each.[6]

Her immediate goal was to guide and organize her own work. Yet she expressed hope that in specifying major dimensions of variation among reading packages, she might also provide useful guidance to others. She hoped that explicit comparison of the similarities and differences between programs would help future researchers to design cleaner and more pointed empirical investigations. She hoped too that enumeration of the dimensions of variation would help future curriculum developers to design

---

5. These two basal series were estimated to represent about 80 percent of the total reading-series sales during that period. They were Robinson, H. M., Monroe, M., and Artley, A. S. (1956), *The new basic readers curriculum foundation series* (Chicago: Scott, Foresman) and Russell, D. H., et al. (1961), *The Ginn basic readers* (Boston: Ginn) . To get a glimpse of trends in basal series design, Chall also compared the 1956 edition of the Scott, Foresman first-grade readers to those published in 1920, 1930, 1940, and 1962.

The alternative approaches Chall examined included supplemental phonics programs, phonics-first programs, the linguistic approach (inductive phonics through regularly spelled words and word families), the Initial Teaching Alphabet or *i/t/a* (simplifying phonic correspondences through use of a reformed alphabet), the language experience approach (inducing reading abilities through writing), the responsive environment approach (Omar K. Moore's early "computer"-based approach), the individualized reading approach (self-pacing and self-selection of reading materials), and the programmed learning approach (styled on the stimulus-response programmed manuals of the era).

6. Chall (1967, p. 336).

fuller, more balanced programs and to recognize the consistencies and inconsistencies, as well as the redundancies and holes, within existing ones. The dimensions of comparison that she developed for this purpose are shown in table 3.1.

From the Classrooms

With both the authorities' views and the actual programs under her belt, Chall next headed for the schools. She visited more than 300 kindergarten, first-, second-, and third-grade classrooms located in wealthy, middle-class, and poor districts sprinkled across the United States, England, and Scotland. Her objectives were to see for herself how the programs tended to be translated into practice and to gauge their reception by and effectiveness with the children.

She had been prepared to find vast differences in the children's responsiveness to their reading lessons, and find them she did. However, whatever the prevailing mood of the classroom—excitement or boredom, enthusiasm or apathy, involvement or restlessness—it seemed independent of the philosophy or objectives of the particular program or materials in use. Interest, or lack thereof, was found regardless of the content of the stories or the emphasis on phonic rules. It even seemed surprisingly independent of class size or organization.

More than anything else, student engagement depended on the atmosphere—the momentum, support, and expectations—created by the classroom teacher. To Chall's senses the most weighty variable on this dimension was pace. It was the teacher's ability to stay tuned to that delicate interval between ease and difficulty for the students and to keep the instruction within it. She additionally observed that interest and effort tended to wane when the children were left to unmonitored seatwork, especially with workbooks and worksheets.

At the level of programs, Chall did indeed find categorical differences in classroom spirit; however, the successfulness of a program seemed due less to its nature than to its newness in the school. Innovators tended to be believers. They tended to be reflective and involved in their lessons. They tended to lift difficulty ceilings, to involve parents, and to confront rather than shrug at difficulties. And they did so regardless of the particular philosophy, format, or methods of their newly adopted program.

As Chall pointed out, the zeal and success associated with innovation must be owed in part to the self-selecting nature of

Table 3.1

Chall's analysis of reading programs.

Dimension	Measure
Completeness of Program	Total Package or Guide Only
Complete	
Partial (Letter-Sound only)	
Structure	High; Moderate; Low
Goals	Meaning, appreciation, application; or learning Code
Ultimate	
Beginning	
Motivational appeal at beginning	Primarily on Content or on Process of learning to read
Stimulus controls	
Units to control difficulty	Words; Phonic Elements; Spelling Patterns; Letters; Language Patterns
Major Criterion for Word Selection	Meaning frequency or Spelling regularity
Vocabulary Load: First Year	High; Moderate; Low
Picture Load: First Year	High; Moderate; Low; None
Content: first year	Stories-familiar experience; Stories-imaginative; Miscellaneous; Little or No Connected Reading
Learning of grapheme-phoneme correspondences (phonics)	
How?	Analytic or Synthetic
Number of verbalized rules	High; Moderate; Low; None
Teacher Guidance	High; Moderate; Low
Phonic load: first year	High; Moderate; Low
Concentrated practice on individual correspondences	High; Moderate; Low
Opportunity for transfer	High; Moderate; Low
"Set"	For Regularity or Diversity
Cues to use	Structural or Meaning
Structural Cues employed	Sounding and Blending; Visual Analysis and Substitutions; Spelling
Response Modes	
Preferred reading at beginning	Silent or Oral
Use of writing	High; Moderate; Low
Programming of meaning, appreciation, and application	High; Moderate; Low
Whole words or Letters first?	
Readiness for reading	Defined in Global or Specific terms
Need for teacher	High; Moderate; Low

those bold enough to innovate. Teachers and administrators who try something new tend to be "more ambitious and independent.... Generally, they are courageous, intelligent, industrious, and full of hope for improvement."[7]

Yet she noted another, more subtle characteristic of the delivery of new programs that may be at least as influential: Teachers presenting new programs tended to carry with them old practices. Thus, for example, while classrooms that had recently switched to phonic programs engaged in more phonic activities, they did not engage in less connected reading. Moreover, the connected reading tended to be conducted with the basals from the now upstaged and disavowed meaning-first programs. And as those basals were opened, so too were the memories of how to proceed with them. To an extent quite contrary to the philosophies of their newly adopted phonic programs, Chall watched teacher after teacher quizzing their students on the content and structure of the stories, directing their attention to the meanings of the pictures, words, phrases, and sentences before them.

To see the importance of this phenomenon, we must step back a moment. For what kinds of innovations will people stick out their necks? It is not for little changes because they can be implemented in the normal course of things. It is not for new programs that are highly similar to those already in place; even when the trouble and expense of making such swaps is deemed worthwhile, they rarely receive the acclaim or notoriety of an innovation. When people stick their necks out for an innovation, it tends to be for something really different; it tends to be for a program that strongly emphasizes some set of skills or processes that its predecessor neglected or denied.

If what Chall observed about her innovators is generally true, the power of innovation must be expected to transcend the particulars of any new program on which it might pivot. During the innovative, transitional period, while the novel aspects of the new program are being freshly addressed and the memories of the old program are still active, the students are likely to receive the best of both approaches from their teachers.

From the Research

For the fourth prong of her attack, Chall dug out the research on beginning reading. She had been amply forewarned that this

---

7. Chall (1967, p. 273).

literature was everywhere scattered and sometimes shoddy. Still she decided to pull it together to see what was really there.

Chall first looked at studies comparing the relative effectiveness of whole word ("look-say") versus phonic approaches to beginning reading instruction. As expected, the data were hard to compare across studies.[8] The various experiments had differed from one another not only in outcome measures but also in the time into the programs at which these measures were taken.

Characteristically trying to impose order on chaos, she organized the studies in a table, grouping them by grade level on one dimension and outcome measure on the other. A pattern emerged. Children who were trained through the look-say method demonstrated an early advantage in rate and comprehension of silent reading and perhaps in interest, fluency, and expression as well. In contrast, children who were taught phonics exhibited the early advantage in word recognition, particularly for untaught words, and maintained it throughout. Furthermore, there were indications that the phonics children not only caught up with but surpassed their look-say peers in silent reading rate, comprehension, and vocabulary by the end of the second grade.

Could this be? Was it even conceivable that the ever-growing advantage of the latter group was real and attributable to phonic instruction per se? Chall waded in deeper, now looking at studies comparing the effectiveness of programs employing systematic versus intrinsic phonics (essentially programs that treated phonics centrally and explicitly versus those that developed it less rigorously and as a sideline). By an overwhelming margin, the programs that included systematic phonics resulted in significantly better word recognition, better spelling, better vocabulary, and better reading comprehension at least through the third grade (where the availability of any data tapered off). Moreover, the advantage of systematic phonics—though a bit slower to kick in—was just as great and perhaps greater with children of lower entry abilities or socio-economic backgrounds as it was with readier and more privileged children.

To get one more angle on the issue, Chall examined all of the studies she could find on the correlation between letter or phonic knowledge and reading achievement. A strong, positive

---

8. Debate over the appropriate interpretation of these studies continues even today but not without firm rebuttal from Chall. See, e.g., Carbo (1988) versus Chall (1989).

correlation was reported in every one. For both young readers and prereaders, familiarity with letters and sensitivity to the phonetic structure of oral language were strong predictors of reading achievement—stronger, in fact, than IQ. Beyond the third grade, low levels of phonic knowledge continued to be a good predictor of low levels of reading achievement. However, superior phonic knowledge did not necessarily translate into superior levels of reading achievement; instead, and not surprisingly, the reading achievement of older students became increasingly associated with IQ.[9]

The Message

Chall's book is a classic because it is thorough, disciplined, and readable. It is as broad a review of the issues as exists. Even so, its staying power may derive, most of all, from the poignancy of its tone.

The observations and data she amassed seemed inescapably to suggest that—as a complement to connected and meaningful reading—systematic phonic instruction is a valuable component of beginning reading instruction. Its positive effects appeared both strong and extensive.[10] Yet the reader is left with the impression that these findings took Chall by surprise. Tucked amidst the scientific discipline of her writing, she alternately scolds, apologizes, rationalizes, and philosophizes: How could we not have known? How could we have ignored these data? She begs us never to do so again.

Other Program Comparisons

Chall's summary of the empirical data on phonics surprised a number of people besides herself. Moreover, the publishedresearch studies with which she had to work were somewhat suspect.

As mentioned earlier, Chall was a bit handicapped by the nature of the pool of studies that were available in the

---

9. It is generally the case that between early and late elementary years, the correlation between IQ and reading achievement scores rises substantially (see Singer, 1974; Stanovich, Cunningham, and Feeman, 1984). A major explanation for this pattern relates to the increasing similarity between items on the two types of tests.

10. In the introduction to the 1983 release of this book, Chall reasserts this conclusion, adding evidence that programs teaching direct synthetic phonics appear to be especially effective.

literature. Many were quite old, conducted at a time when statistical techniques were not yet in vogue.[11]   Many used homemade tests rather than standard measures of outcome. Some were flawed in design. And many failed to specify the nature or pre-experimental comparability of the students who were studied, the selection of the teachers, the time or procedures involved in the various instructional groups, or even what the contrasting methods entailed except as implied by their labels.

Naturally there followed a surge of new research on the relative effectiveness of different instructional methods for beginning readers. Some of the research took the form of massive literature syntheses, and some consisted of empirical investigations. Of the empirical investigations, some were laboratory investigations, designed for controlled examination of some small and selected set of variables, and some were classroom comparisons of whole programs. Of the classroom comparisons, some were focused on particular programs or student populations; others were not. I will refer to a number of these studies in the pages to come. Among them are some invaluable hints as to what the beginning reader needs most to be taught. In this section, however, I will limit discussion to just three.

The USOE Cooperative Research Program

The U.S. Office of Education (USOE) Cooperative Research Program in First-Grade Reading Instruction was undertaken between 1964 and 1967. As mentioned earlier, the seeds of this project were sown by the Subcommittee on Beginning Reading that was formed at the Syracuse conference in 1959. From there, it took several years and, invaluably, the persuasive persistence of Donald Durrell of Boston University for the project to take root.

This project was to fill in the empirical holes that allowed the debate over beginning reading to rage without resolution. The goal was not only to compare and contrast the effectiveness of the alternative approaches to beginning reading but to identify the nature and degree of variation owed to characteristics of the children, teachers, and schools.

The question of urgency concerned not what might be shown to work well with the particular students in a particular classroom. Much more broadly, it was what should be expected to work best for the students in any particular classroom. At the same time, the project organizers were all too aware that enormous and

---

11. See Gigerenzer and Murray (1987).

uncontrollable differences exist between the day-to-day realities of the people and dynamics involved in any given implementation.

They were thus faced with the problem that to ask any single pressing question well, they would need to involve dozens of classrooms. To investigate the range of questions on the agenda would require hundreds upon hundreds of classrooms. Moreover, the selection of each of these classrooms and the conduct and assessment of its instruction would need to be carefully supervised and controlled to rigorous scientific standards. Clearly this was more than any one project could achieve.

The solution was to initiate a host of individual projects, each involving scores of classrooms. Although each individual project was to be focused on a particular subset of the most urgent questions, they were to be collectively selected and designed so as to extend, complement, and replicate one another. The biggest questions would then be tackled by a central committee, using the combined data from the individual projects. To ensure that this could be done soundly and productively, all of the individual projects were to cooperate in the design and execution of their studies. They were to collect common information about teacher, pupil, school, and community characteristics; they were to establish common experimental controls; they were to employ common pretests and outcome measures; and they were to standardize the duration of the programs and the data collection schedule.

In response to a widely publicized invitation issued by the Office of Education, seventy-six individual projects were proposed; twenty-seven were selected. The Coordinating Center was seated at the University of Minnesota, under the direction of Guy L. Bond and Robert Dykstra.

The combined analyses of the First-Grade Cooperative Studies were published in 1967 and were directed toward three questions:

1. Which of the approaches to beginning reading instruction produces the best reading and spelling achievement at the end of first grade?

2. Does the effectiveness of the approaches vary with the reading readiness of the students? That is, are any of the approaches especially effective or ineffective with low-readiness students? Are any especially effective or ineffective with high-readiness students?

3. To what extent are various pupil, teacher, classroom, school, and community characteristics related to achievement in reading and spelling at the end of first grade?[12]

---

12. Bond and Dykstra (1967).

Let us look at the results to these questions one by one.

Which approaches were most effective? According to Bond and Dykstra's analyses, the approaches that, one way or another, included systematic phonic instruction[13] consistently exceeded the straight basal programs in word recognition achievement scores.[14] The approaches that included both systematic phonics and considerable emphasis on connected reading and meaning surpassed the basal-alone approaches on virtually all outcome measures.[15] (The exceptions were in the speed and accuracy of oral reading, for which there were no significant differences between approaches.) In addition, the data indicated that exercise in writing was a positive component of beginning reading instruction.

Did the relative effectiveness of the approaches vary with the readiness of the students? In general, reported Bond and Dykstra, the answer was no. The programs that were superior with one group of students tended to be superior with every group of students, and this was true regardless of the particular measure by which student readiness was gauged.[16] There appeared, in short, to be no basis for the widely held belief that systematic phonic instruction is useful only for brighter children.[17]

To what extent is first-grade reading achievement determined by community, school, classroom, teacher, and pupil characteristics? The projects had commonly collected a host of information on characteristics of the students' communities, schools, classrooms, and teachers. Some of these data were not sufficiently quantified to permit rigorous analysis. Of those that

---

13. The three approaches in this category are a basal plus phonics approach, a phonic/linguistic approach, and the i/t/a (initial teaching alphabet) approach which is directed toward instilling the phonic principles of English by means of a special alphabet, reformed so as to minimize letter-to-sound irregularities.

14. In grade equivalence scores, these programs resulted in an average advantage of one or two months. In gauging the size of this gain, recall that the children were only in the first grade, that is, they had only been in school for a total of a few months.

15. The two approaches in this category were basal plus phonics approach and the phonic/linguistic approach.

16 A single exception to this rule was found with the language experience approach which appeared to perform better than the basals with high-readiness students but worse than the basals with low-readiness students. Under the language experience approach, reading is taught by having the students create text. Appreciation of the functions, meanings, and structure of written text is gained through the process of creating and examining one's own and one's classmates compositions.

17. See Chall (1967, p. 126); Spache and Spache (1973, pp. 471–472).

were, virtually none was found to exert a significant, isolable influence on the students' achievement levels.

In contrast, certain pupil characteristics were strong predictors of end-of-the-year achievement. Each project had administered an extensive battery of pretests to each child at the outset of the school year. These pretests included a general intelligence test (the Pintner-Cunningham Primary Test), as well as a series of readiness tests on auditory discrimination, visual discrimination, and various indexes of language facility.

The best predictor of students' year-end reading achievement was their entering ability to recognize and name uppercase and lowercase letters. This single factor accounted for 25 to 36 percent of the variation in reading ability at the end of the year, and it did so regardless of instructional approaches. The next best predictors were the students' scores on an auditory phoneme discrimination task and a general intelligence test. Again the fundamental value of letter and sound knowledge is suggested.

Beyond these findings, Bond and Dykstra reported one more that should be recognized: Within every instructional method studied, there were pupils who learned to read with thorough success and others who experienced difficulty. Furthermore, pupils in some school systems markedly outperformed those in others for no traceable reason. This was true regardless of instructional approach. It was true even when differences in reading readiness were statistically controlled. And it could not be statistically related to any of the myriad characteristics of the teachers, schools, or community that were appraised. When students' progress was reassessed at the end of the second grade,[18] the results indicated that the particular projects in which they had participated influenced their reading ability roughly as much the particular method or materials through which they had been taught.[19]

Looking over the statistical tables for these studies, one sees a great many method effects and a great many site effects but few interactions between them. The implication is that to improve reading achievement, we must improve both programs and classroom delivery. Each seems to contribute separately and significantly to children's progress.[20]

---

18. Dykstra (1968).

19. This finding was a major impetus for recent research into the nature of the teacher/learning situation.

20. I am grateful to Steven A. Stahl for bringing this point to my attention.

Whatever the cause of such differences, their existence makes clear that—even given the most disciplined and hopeful implementation of our favorite off-the-shelf program—the success we normally achieve in teaching beginning reading falls well short of that which we could be achieving.

Follow Through

Conducted during the early 1970s, the Follow Through studies stand as another enormous federally sponsored experiment on primary education. The studies were provoked by findings that the gains made by Head Start students during preschool tended to dissipate when they left the program. The studies were intended to answer the question of what general educational approach or model succeeds best in fostering and maintaining educational progress of disadvantaged children across the primary school years.

The twenty-two instructional models examined fell into three groups: those that emphasized basic academic skills, those that emphasized cognitive or conceptual development, and those that emphasized affective development through child-centered activity. Their most extensive analysis was undertaken by Abt Associates.[21] The Abt team reported tremendous variation from school to school in educational outcomes—so much variation that even methods that on average resulted in relatively high achievement were sometimes associated with low-achieving schools. Nevertheless, of the three categories of instructional models assessed, those emphasizing basic academic skills tended to yield the best achievement scores in general. And within that category it was the University of Oregon's Direct Instruction model that generally yielded the best reading achievement scores.

The reading program used within the University of Oregon's Follow Through studies was Distar.[22] Especially developed for compensatory use, this program is highly structured, describing and even scripting classroom activities in great detail. Its emphasis is squarely and systematically on teaching the code.

The advantage of this program was strongest in the first- and second-grade evaluations, weaker in the third grade, and gone in the fourth. Notably the reading tests used for evaluation (the

---

21. Stebbins, St. Pierre, Proper, Anderson, and Cerva (1977).

22. The Distar materials are now published by Science Research Associates.

Metropolitan Achievement Tests) shift emphasis from word recognition skills to comprehension at about the fourth-grade level, and this shift may well explain the diminishing pattern of results. In any case, follow-up studies of these Follow Through students suggest that the advantages of their early instruction were lasting. In a study of fifth and sixth graders (Follow Through training stopped in third grade), Becker and Gersten found that although academic growth was slower than would be predicted from the primary grade achievement scores, they continued to outscore their non-Follow Through peers on standardized tests of reading.[23] Furthermore, return assessments of more than 1,000 of these Follow Through students in their senior year in high school indicated that they were still outperforming their cohorts,[24] not just in reading achievement but on a variety of general measures of school success.[25]

To this pattern of results Chall adds a pertinent coda.[26] Noting the unusual success of one of the Oregon Follow Through Schools, a post hoc analysis was undertaken to see if it had done anything differently.[27] It had. Specifically the students in this school had been heavily engaged in reading and interpreting stories from the first year of the program. In view of this finding, Chall takes the opportunity, once again, to surmise, "It would appear, then, that an early opportunity to do meaningful connected reading in addition to learning how to decode is needed to integrate both abilities."[28]

Not surprisingly the conclusions of the Abt report were met with protest and controversy. After all, the data on which they were based were vast and noisy; the implementations from which the data came were not designed to support direct comparisons between methods; and the instructional models beneath the various implementations embodied profound philosophical differences as to the proper nature and goals of education in the classroom.

---

23. Becker and Gersten (1982).

24. Students in schools that were in the same communities and that had comparable ethnicity and socioeconomic profiles.

25. Including, for example, lower drop-out rate, higher percentage of high school graduations, and a higher percentage of acceptances to college. For a review, see Gersten and Keating (1987).

26. Chall (1983a).

27. Meyer (1983).

28. Chall (1983a, p. 11).

All of that being so, the results of the Follow Through studies still stand in contradiction to the once broad belief that phonic instruction is a bad idea for less advantaged children. To the contrary, it seems to help at least with their mastery of the code—which is how it is supposed to help.

A Quantitative Synthesis

The last program comparison we shall examine was conducted by Susanna Pflaum, Herbert Walberg, Myra Karegianes, and Sue Rasher.[29] Unlike the Cooperative Research Program and the Follow Through studies, this comparison involved no classroom intervention. It is instead a literature synthesis. However, it is not the usual, discursive sort of literature synthesis. It is a quantitative synthesis.

In various forms but repeatedly and across a number of textbooks written for teachers of reading, Pflaum and her colleagues had encountered a disturbing assertion: that the vast research on instructional methods had yielded no useful conclusions as to the value of one approach to beginning reading versus another. Despite all of the to-do about phonics, the assertion was certainly plausible. However many studies are done on an issue, some relatively small subset tends to capture our attention and shape our opinions. Even so, the assertion did not feel right. Minimally it was worth checking.

The authors decided to examine a sample of the method comparisons directly. To avoid biases due to public acclaim and prior knowledge, they chose the to-be-examined studies through a process of random selection. They began by identifying all of the 665 method comparison studies cited in the International Reading Association's *Annual Summary of Investigations Relating to Reading* between 1965 and summer 1978, randomly pulling out 199. Screening the 199 for those involving some minimal instructional time (five sessions) and using adequate experimental design and statistical inference, they were left with 97 studies, including 341 different statistical comparisons.

To evaluate the collective findings of the studies, the authors used two different techniques. Under the first technique, they simply counted the number of comparisons for which the experimental group was statistically superior to the control (as it happened, in nearly every study conducted with elementary school students, the control group used a basal reading series).

---

29. Pflaum, Walberg, Karegianes, and Rasher (1980).

Under the second technique, they derived statistics allowing them to compare the magnitudes of the difference between the experimental and control groups across studies.

By their first technique, they counted that for 73 of the 97 studies, or roughly three-quarters, the performance of the experimental group was superior to its control. By their second technique, they determined that the average gain of the experimental groups over their controls was 23 percentile points. Under either technique, the likelihood of such a big or widespread difference due to chance alone is less than one in 1,000.

Given that the 97 selected studies included 30 different methods, this finding lends itself to a couple of interpretations, both of which may be correct. First, it lends statistical credence to Chall's observation that the introduction of new methods to a classroom, whatever their nature, tends to result in a better and more sensitive classroom dynamic. A second interpretation, suggested by Pflaum and her colleagues, is that within most researchers' best ideas about how reading ought to be taught, there lie pearls of wisdom. They suggested that the experimental techniques work better as a group because, within each, there tend to be at least some aspects that are uniquely beneficial as compared to the standard methods. The challenge left to us is that of identifying the pearls.

To complete their analysis, Pflaum and colleagues statistically examined the impact of specific study variables, including:

- Outcome measures (through what tests were gains measured).
- Control variables (how were experimental and control groups equated for IQ, income, entering achievement, and what were the methods for assigning teachers and students to groups and for ensuring objectivity).
- Subject variables (how many students were in each group and what was their classification by sex, race, family income, reading achievement, mental ability and grade level).
- Implementation characteristics (how many teachers were involved and what were the lengths of sessions in minutes, number of sessions per week, and number of weeks).
- Instructional methods used for the experimental and control groups.

Across all of these factors, they found very few significant differences,[30] but there were some interesting exceptions.[31] First, there was a tendency for longer treatments to result in bigger gains than shorter ones. The moral is that if you really believe in a method, try it for long enough to give it a chance. Second, there was a tendency toward greater gains when instruction was delivered by teachers who advocated a method as opposed to those who were less involved. In other words, if you want the greatest possible benefits from a new program, begin by converting the converters. Third, and most important within the present context, there was but one single class of instructional methods that resulted in gains significantly larger than any of the others.[32] This class of methods consisted in teaching students about letters and letter sounds, first separately and then blended together. It consisted, in short, of explicit, systematic phonics.

Summary of the Program Comparisons

In examining these program comparison studies, we have touched only the tip of the iceberg. Many, many studies fall within this category. And it is important to note that some have yielded contradictory results.

But, then, that's part of the point. Given the tremendous variations from school to school and implementation to implementation, we should be very clear that the prescription of

---

30. It is noteworthy that the great majority of sampled studies were focused on students in kindergarten, first, and second grade.

31. The productivity of this technique has been both protested and defended in the literature. See, e.g., the exchange between Slavin (1984) and Carlberg et al. (1984). Slavin is particularly critical of Pflaum et al. (1980) for "combining apples and oranges." That being so, however, it may be particularly impressive that any of the contrasts gained significance in the meta-analysis.

32. The other experimental methods included eclectic basals, analytic phonics, altered orthography, pacing of vocabulary, individualized book reading, individualized mastery system, meaning vocabulary development, comprehension skill development, advanced phonic skills, text organizers, syntax training, rate training, study skills training, reading in different content areas, tutoring, impress method, counseling, black studies, listening during reading, listening, auditory perceptual training, visual perceptual training, oral reading training, high intensity silent reading, reinforcement, grouping, teacher aide, motor training, and "other." Brief descriptions of each of these are provided by Pflaum et al. (1980).

a method can never in itself guarantee the best of all possible outcomes. However well defined the method might be, however stellar its documented research outcomes, classroom successes (and failures) depend on much more than the written agenda held out to the teacher. Indeed the remarkable power of innovation seems to derive directly from that well of possibilities between what is only on paper and what is in our hearts and minds, between what we are told to do in the classroom and how we actually do it.

The second part of the point is that the vast majority of program comparison studies indicate that approaches including systematic phonic instruction result in comprehension skills that are at least comparable to, and word recognition and spelling skills that are significantly better than, those that do not. Furthermore, approaches in which systematic code instruction is included alongside meaning emphasis, language instruction, and connected reading are found to result in superior reading achievement overall. And these conclusions seem at least as valid for children with low reading-readiness profiles as they are for their better prepared and more advantaged peers.

Before leaving this topic, it is worth adding a note and a caveat. The note is simply of interest. The major conclusions of the program comparison studies are based on masses of data gathered through formal experimental procedures and scrutinized through relatively sophisticated statistical techniques. Yet they are, point for point, virtually identical to those at which Jeanne Chall had arrived on the basis of her classroom observations and interpretive reviews of the literature.

The caveat is more subtle. There are enormous differences in the outcomes of any program depending on the particular schools, teachers, children, and implementation vagaries involved. Yet despite all of these very real and significant differences, there seems to be something about that broad class of instruction known as phonics that is of general, substantive, and lasting value.

What specifically is it within this class of instruction that is so good? The program comparisons do not begin to answer this question.

Except to argue that explicit phonics, or the provision of systematic instruction on the relation of letter-sounds to words, was more effective than implicit phonics, or the philosophy of letting students induce letter-sounds from whole words, Chall more or less finessed this issue in the 1967 edition of *The Great Debate*. In the 1983 edition, she suggests that it is direct-synthetic phonic instruction that works best—that's more specific, but not much more.

Similarly, the USOE Cooperative Research Program focused on global approaches rather than particular programs or methods within them. The Follow Through team identified a particular direct instruction and code-emphasis program, Distar, as being particularly effective with the students in their studies. However, these studies did not and were not designed either to compare Distar to other particular code-emphasis programs or to evaluate which particular aspects of the Distar program were most responsible for its success.

Finally, the quantitative analysis undertaken by Pflaum and her colleagues corroborates the influence of a central component of explicit phonic instruction: the systematic teaching of letter sounds and of blending. But there are both finer and broader issues that must be addressed in determining what, when, and how much code instruction is in order.

Exactly What Is Good about Phonic Instruction?

To ask why a given approach works, one must first answer questions of what the approach comprises. What, then, is phonics? In terms of definition, the meaning of the word is simple and straightforward. Phonics refers to a system of teaching reading that builds on the alphabetic principle, a system of which a central component is the teaching of correspondences between letters or groups of letters and their pronunciations. In terms of practice, however, phonics is harder to box in. What specifically are the instructional procedures and materials that it covers?

Virtually every reading program teaches phonics at some level. Nevertheless, some beginning reading packages term themselves phonic programs and some do not. From this perspective, the distinction between phonic and nonphonic programs is generally one of emphasis. If this is the distinction we care about, the issue before us translates from one of "what" into one of "how much."

How Much Is the Right Amount?

In grappling with this problem, it may be useful to think about it analogically. Code instruction may be likened to a nutrient, a basic building block for the growing reader. Extending the analogy, we see, first, that ingestion of the proper amount of such a nutrient is critical to students' potential development. Second, we realize that its proper metabolism will not occur in the absence of a balanced diet. And, third, we find that—however healthful it may seem—we must be careful not to dish up too much.

Although the consequences of feeding a child excessive amounts of phonics may not be as obvious as with food, the metaphor keeps on going. The extra phonic calories do not enhance growth. They are kept as unnecessary and burdensome tissue or quickly flushed as waste. Worse still, the child may become groggily sated before getting to the other necessary and complementary items on the menu.

The question of how much phonics is optimal is of genuine practical importance. Teaching phonics is a task that requires disciplined, sequenced coverage of individual elements and their interrelations, as well as continuous evaluation of students' levels of mastery. By its nature it entails lots of detail to attend to and to do. It is easy to imagine the busy teacher who short shrifts the effort, whether by teaching too little about everything or everything about too little. But it is equally easy to imagine the teacher who becomes all too immersed in the system, treating it as an end in itself, neglecting its purpose or taking that appreciation for granted.

So how much phonics is the right amount? Isn't it really a question of balance? Yes, of course. But unless that proper balance can be described, recognizing the problem as one of emphasis does little toward resolving it. What we really want to know is not just how much but how much of what kinds of instruction are warranted. We want to know when, in what order, and through what materials and procedures this instruction can be most effectively achieved. When the answer to each of these questions is established, the more global issue of "how much" will be solved.

What Do Phonic Programs Teach?

What if we restrict attention to the programs that are centered on phonics? Can we extract an operational definition of the endeavor from them? The answer is no or, at least, not easily. The problem is that there exist many, many such programs—each of Robert Aukerman's books cite over 100.[33]

---

33. R. C. Aukerman's books (1971, 1984) are very handy resources. As described in his 1971 *Preface*, each is a "compendium of approaches to beginning reading . . . organized to be encyclopedic, presenting the origins of each approach; the backgrounds of the authors and originators

To be sure, a central tenet of each of these programs is that working knowledge of the letter-to-sound correspondences underlying our system of writing is key to proficient reading. Beyond that, however, they differ greatly.

They differ in starting point as well as stopping point, with some beginning prior to what might be called phonics proper and most extending beyond. They differ in the methods, materials, procedures, and progression for everything taught in between. And they differ in fundamental strictures and assumptions about what to and what not to teach, about when to and when not to teach, and about how to and how not to teach. Moreover, while some of the differences between programs are just differences, others stand as genuine conflicts and incompatibilities. For a sense of the instructional dimensions on which different programs provide firm and opposing strictures, here are some examples:

- What fonts should be used for initial reading instruction? Should initial instruction be exclusively conducted with uppercase letters or lowercase letters? Are color and graphic aids, diacritical marks, and modified alphabets helpful, harmful, or neither?

- Is it productive or destructive to pronounce letters in isolation? Should one teach letter names or avoid using them altogether?

- In what order should the sounds of letters and spelling patterns be introduced? Should common consonants be introduced before vowels? Should vowels be introduced before consonants? Should the introduction of consonants and vowels be intermixed? Should short vowels be taught before long ones—or the other way around? For letters or spelling patterns that have more than one pronunciation, should alternative sounds be presented closely in time or considerably separated?

- Should letters that are visually easy to confuse be presented together to allow contrasts and comparisons or separated in time to minimize interference?

- Should verbalized rules (e.g., "When two vowels go walking the first does the talking"; "*g* can say /*j*/ only if it is followed by *e, i,* or *y*"; "every syllable in English must contain at least one vowel"; "a diphthong is two vowels together, both speaking, making a compound sound") be emphasized or eschewed?

- Is explicit training in blending productive or counterproductive?

---

of the various materials and methods; complete descriptions of the methods and materials, together with illustrations of the essential features of each; a capsulated summary of the significant contribution each approach to beginning reading provides; and, wherever possible, a summarization of some of the definitive research studies."

- Should initial reading vocabulary be selected on the basis of the frequency and familiarity of the words in the children's oral language or on the basis of the frequency and regularity of their spelling patterns?
- In what order should different levels of literacy skills be developed? Should the students be thoroughly versed in letter-to-sound correspondences before words are presented? Should the program begin with the presentation of some words before getting into phonics? Should meaningful, connected text be used from the start or saved until the children have achieved some level of word reading?
- Should development of writing or spelling skills be initiated before, at the same time as, or after initial reading instruction?

Where Does This Leave Us?

In short, phonic programs collectively represent not just one, but a host of theories about what instruction in English orthography ought to comprise. How, in view of this, are we to make sense of those comparative evaluation studies? Their summary conclusion is that intensive, explicit phonic instruction is a valuable component of beginning reading programs. But intensive in what respects? Explicit about what? We are left with at least three fairly obvious ways of interpreting these studies.

The first interpretation is that, any way you do it, emphasizing phonics is beneficial. But that takes us back where we started. What does "emphasizing phonics" mean? How much is enough? How much is too much? And how much of what?

The second interpretation is that the assumptions and activities found in phonic programs (or at least the sampling of programs that have been included in the comparative evaluation studies) are all good and comparably so. The up side of this interpretation is that it releases us from the problem of deciding how much of what to do: Just choose a program and do as it says. The down side of this interpretation is that it is terribly hard to believe. The programs are so complex and so diverse. How could they possibly be equally good in every way? Mustn't there at least be differences in the appropriateness of their assumptions and activities depending on the particular students to whom they are given? When one program prescribes what another proscribes, mustn't one (or both) be on the wrong track?

The remaining interpretation is that there exist a number of code-emphasis activities that are of genuine benefit to the young reader and that most phonic programs do reasonably well at some subset of these. Notice how noncommittal this interpretation is. It may be that no existing program is ideal for all students on all dimensions. It may be that most existing programs include some not-so-good activities alongside the good ones. It may be that we could build even better programs—ones that are maximally effective, minimally time-consuming, and optimally suited to the needs of our particular students—by selecting, adjusting, and combining the best of existing programs' individual assumptions and activities.

To do this, we must ask what proficient readers have learned about our system of orthography. We must ask what beginning readers need to learn, and how they might learn it most efficiently, effectively, and usefully. Looking across programs, we must assess the wisdom of major strictures, assumptions, and activities. For strictures and assumptions, we must identify their rationale and examine their justification. For activities, we must identify the instructional objectives. We must consider whether the objective is something that can and should be taught and then whether and when the proposed activity is a good means of teaching it.

One More Possibility

A seemingly gratis but unnecessary assumption about phonic programs is that, whatever their method, their success is owed to the importance of teaching children how to sound words out. If we are willing to test this assumption, a fourth interpretation of the programs' success is possible.

Specifically it is possible that the ability to sound words out—even while being an invaluable step toward reading independence—is not the primary positive outcome of phonic instruction. In the chapters to follow, it is this argument that gains most support. Laboratory research indicates that the most critical factor beneath fluent word reading is the ability to recognize letters, spelling patterns, and whole words effortlessly, automatically, and visually. The central goal of all reading instruction—comprehension—depends critically on this ability.

Acceptance of this conclusion does not diminish the general worth of phonic instruction. As we shall see, many of the activities of these programs are ideally suited toward developing these visual skills. On the other hand, as it alters our view of the goals of beginning reading, this conclusion does bear on the relative merits of individual phonic activities and the emphasis that each might best be given.

4

Research on Prereaders

The second category of evidence that seems to urge phonics on us consists of investigations of children who have not yet received formal reading instruction. What are the characteristics of such prereaders that best predict success or failure in learning to read?[1] And what implications do these findings hold with respect to what beginning readers might best be taught?

The question of best predictors was broached in discussion of the program comparisons. Based on her review of the literature, Chall reported that prereaders' knowledge of letter names was a strong predictor of success in early reading achievement—even stronger than mental age.[2] Based on analyses of the USOE first-grade studies, Bond and Dykstra reinforced and extended Chall's report: Prereaders' letter knowledge was found to be the single best predictor of first-year reading achievement, with the ability to discriminate phonemes auditorily ranking a close second. Furthermore, these two predictors were the winners regardless of the instructional approach administered.[3]

What About Mental Age?

The third best predictor in the USOE Cooperative Studies battery was mental age as measured by the Pinter-Cunningham

---

1. With the term *prereader*, I refer very simply to children who have not yet received any formal reading instruction. To those of you who prefer another label for this group of children, I apologize. None of the obvious options, including this one, seemed just right. In particular, the term *emergent literacy* was deemed problematic because it is defined differently by different authorities.

2. Chall (1967).

3. Bond and Dykstra (1967).

Intelligence Test. The visibility of this predictor is interesting in view of the once widely held view that reading instruction should not begin until a child is mentally ready. For reading instruction in general, the rule of thumb was to start at a mental age of six and a half years.[4] For phonic instruction, the rule of thumb was a mental age of seven years.

The magic age of seven for phonics is commonly attributed to a 1937 study by Dolch and Bloomster.[5] For 115 first and second graders, these investigators measured both IQ and the ability to match printed words to test words spoken by an experimenter. Not only did they find that the correlation between these two measures was significant but, further, that virtually all of children with mental ages below seven years, as derived from their IQ tests, performed poorly on the "phonic" or word-matching test. Dolch and Bloomster therefore concluded a mental age of seven years seemed necessary for a child to *use* phonics.

Yet the ability to use phonics must depend in part on whether and how a child has been taught about it. In reviewing the Dolch and Bloomster study, Chall was quick to point out that their students had been taught through intrinsic phonics.[6] The evidence indicated, she argued, that when phonics has been taught explicitly and systematically, it can be successfully used to identify new words not only by slow-learning primary students but even by normal kindergartners and preschoolers. More recent studies indicate that explicit, systematic phonics is a singularly successful mode of teaching young or slow learners to read.[7]

But the real problem associated with the Dolch and Bloomster study is that its conclusion has often been altered in transmission. Over the years some have used it to argue that phonics should not be *taught* to children with mental ages of less than seven years. The evidence forces a fundamental illogic onto this argument:

1. Letter recognition facility and phonemic awareness not only exceed mental age (as measured by IQ tests) in predicting success at reading acquisition but, further and unlike mental age (as measured by IQ tests), seem causally related to reading acquisition—which is to say that to the

---

4. This recommendation is often attributed to a report by Morphett and Washburne (1931).

5. Dolch and Bloomster (1937).

6. Chall (1967).

7. For example: Bateman (1979); Wallach and Wallach (1979); Williams (1979).

extent that children do have these skills, reading instruction can be fruitful and to the extent that they do not, it cannot.[8]

2. Individual differences in these two skills seem quite independent of mental age (as measured by IQ tests), suggesting that they may be acquired by children of high and low mental age alike.[9]

3. These two skills, unlike mental age (as measured by IQ tests), are not just positive antecedents but also central consequences of phonic instruction.[10]

In waiting on mental age, therefore, one is caught in an irreconcilable dilemma. One is left arguing that one should wait until the children are ready to teach precisely those skills that would most make them ready.

Before proceeding, I must explain my parenthetical insertion of the phrase "as measured by IQ tests" in the paragraphs above. It is a stubborn fact that what we mean by mental age or intelligence in virtually all such studies is how well an individual performs on standard IQ tests. This has remained true despite our own protestations and objections, and despite the accruing evidence that IQ tests do not measure intelligence but only a weak correlate thereof.[11]

Thus even while reading readiness is poorly predicted by IQ scores, it may be well predicted by other measures of cognitive abilities. In particular, several studies have shown that early reading achievement is quite strongly predicted by children's ability to perform such basic logical and analytical tasks as classification, seriation, and conservation of quantity.[12]

Recently Tunmer, Herriman, and Nesdale explored the force of these claims.[13] In their longitudinal study, a test of basic logical and analytical abilities was administered to children at the beginning of first grade. To evaluate the relative importance of these cognitive skills, the researchers also gave the entering students an IQ test, tests of phonemic, syntactic, and pragmatic

---

8. Stanovich (1986); Tunmer and Nesdale (1985).

9. Biemiller (1977–1978); Stanovich (1986)

10. Ehri (1980); Morais, Cary, Alegria, and Bertelson (1979); Perfetti, Beck, Bell, and Hughes (1987); Wagner and Torgesen (1987).

11. Flynn (1987). Moreover, to the extent that IQ tests do not measure intelligence, the effectiveness with which the researcher can partial out intelligence by partialing out IQ scores is also a serious concern in interpreting such studies. See Baron and Treiman (1980); Cohen and Cohen (1975); Lord (1969).

12. Arlin (1981); Lunzer, Dolan, and Wilkinson (1976).

13. Tunmer, Herriman, and Nesdale (1988).

awareness, and a Concepts about Print test. The latter test was developed by Marie Clay and is designed to assess children's knowledge of the nature and function of written text.[14] At the end of first grade, the Concepts about Print test was administered again, along with tests of decoding proficiency and reading comprehension.[15] At the end of second grade, the reading achievement tests were repeated once more.

Analyses of the combined test results indicated that the children's logical and analytical abilities were strongly and causally related to both their linguistic awareness and their concepts about print, which in turn were strongly and causally related to reading achievement. Furthermore, their logical and analytical abilities were more strongly related to their linguistic awareness than they were to their IQ scores. And, wrapping up the inquiry quite neatly, children who entered school with low levels of phonemic awareness but high levels of logical and analytical abilities had more than caught up with their classmates on phonemic measures at the end of the year. Children who had performed poorly on both the phonemic awareness test and the test of logical/analytical abilities remained significantly behind.

The seemingly inescapable conclusion of Tunmer, Herriman, and Nesdale's study is that some basic level of logical and analytical abilities makes the processes involved in learning to read much easier. Although these basic cognitive abilities proved largely unrelated to measured IQ, it is hard not to think of them as indexes of mental age. Indeed the tests of basic logical and analytical abilities that Tunmer and his colleagues used were quite Piagetian in nature.

Tunmer and his colleagues close their report with the reminder that although the cognitive abilities were strong predictors of reading achievement across two years of schooling, they seemed to influence reading achievement only indirectly—only by hastening the children's acquisition of the relevant linguistic and text-related skills. In view of this, the researchers warn against delaying reading instruction in wait of cognitive maturation. They suggest that it is both wiser and more efficient to provide all beginning readers with a variety of language games and activities designed to develop their linguistic awareness directly.

More generally, however mental age is defined, it seems to hold, at best, a remote relationship to children's reading

---

14. Clay (1979).
15. Calfee and Calfee (1981).

acquisition. Yopp and Singer[16] took issue with the mental-age-of-seven argument by pointing to researchers who had suggested that the minimum mental age for reading instruction is four years or even three.[17] Were these researchers were doing anything special? Yopp and Singer felt the answer was yes.

An examination of methods revealed that those that worked with the mentally youngest students characteristically differed from those that failed. The successful methods were far less presumptuous about what the children already knew or could do on their own; they involved the close monitoring and guidance afforded by small group or individual instruction and the explicit teaching of basic elements and processes. To cap their point, Yopp and Singer proceeded, quite successfully, to teach a classroom of kindergartners to identify new words through sounding and blending. The bottom line, they argue, is that the role of mental age is not one of limiting what a child can learn but of limiting the ways in which they can be effectively taught.

There have, in addition, been a number of empirical studies of the correlation between IQ and reading achievement. The results of these studies converge on the conclusion that IQ is only weakly and nonspecifically related to achievement in the early grades.[18]

To these findings, however, I must add a sobering afterword. Whereas IQ and general cognitive skills seem not to have much bearing on early reading achievement, early reading failures seem to result in a progressive diminution in IQ scores and general cognitive skills. In the words of Keith Stanovich, who has developed this argument with scholarship and force:

Slow reading acquisition has cognitive, behavioral, and motivational consequences that slow the development of other cognitive skills and inhibit performance on many academic tasks. In short, as reading develops, other cognitive processes linked to it track the level of reading skill. Knowledge bases that are in reciprocal relationships with reading are also inhibited from further development. The longer this developmental sequence is allowed to continue, the more generalized the deficits will become, seeping into more and more areas of cognition and behavior. Or to put it more simply—and sadly—in the words of a tearful

---

16. Yopp and Singer (1985).

17. In this vein, it is interesting to note that over the course of this century, the mental age of debate has fallen steadily. When Huey wrote on this topic in 1908, prominent authorities were arguing that the minimum age for formal reading instruction was eight (John Dewey) or ten (G. T. W. Patrick) years old (Huey, 1908/1968).

18. For a review, see Stanovich, Cunningham, and Feeman (1984).

nine-year-old, already falling frustratingly behind his peers in reading progress, "Reading affects everything you do."[19]

What about Perceptual Skills?

Among the other pretests in the USOE Cooperative studies battery were one to assess children's ability to copy simple graphic patterns and another to assess their ability to discriminate between similar and different visual patterns. Although these were not strong predictors of reading achievement, they were positively related to reading achievement. Correlations with end-of-the-year Stanford reading scores ranged from 0.27 to 0.46 for paragraph reading and 0.29 to 0.46 for word recognition.

Interest in these two measures has centered on the fact that they appear to be face-valid indexes of children's capacity for learning to read through whole-word methods. With this in mind, they have been been assiduously reexamined.

In particular, it was reasoned, not all children are alike. Some are global perceivers by nature, and some are analytic; some are auditorily attuned, and some are visual. Maybe phoneme awareness and letter-name facility are the best predictors for the auditory, analytic students. And maybe those students are even in the majority.

But what about the other students? With global, visual predispositions, wouldn't they be better off with a sight word approach to reading? Wouldn't they be fettered, even frustrated and discouraged, with a phonic approach? More generally, wouldn't it be wise to tailor instructional process and materials to children's perceptual styles or dominant modalities?

So appealing is this argument that it has been broadly advocated and adopted. In a study of special education teachers in Illinois, Arter and Jenkins found that 95 percent were familiar with the argument.[20] Of those familiar with it, 99 percent believed that modality considerations should be a primary consideration in devising instruction for children with learning difficulties.

Arter and Jenkins also found that 95 percent of their special education teachers believed that the modality argument was supported by research. Unhappily it is not. Although many

---

19. Stanovich (1986, p. 390).
20. Arter and Jenkins (1977).

empirical studies have been conducted on this issue, the hypothetical interaction between program effectiveness and preferred modalities is not supported by the data.[21]

There has also been a tremendous amount of research on whether reading acquisition can be accelerated by training various nonlinguistic perceptual and motor skills such as spatial relations, visual memory, visual discrimination, visual-motor integration, gross and fine motor coordination, tactile-kinesthetic activities, auditory discrimination, and auditory-visual integration. Despite the energy invested in such endeavors and despite the fact that many of the activities may be good for children in any number of ways, they seem not to produce any measurable payoff in learning to read.[22]

Knowing Letters

Both Chall and Bond and Dykstra reported the best predictor of beginning reading achievement to be a child's knowledge of letter names.[23] This was a highly provocative finding. For one, it did not fit with our then dominant models of cognitive development. But more, if it was true, it implied such a wonderfully direct and simple cure to problems of reading readiness. Obviously children could be taught to name and recognize the letters of the alphabet. Would teaching them to do so really give them an advantage in learning to read?

This question was addressed with a vengeance following the reports of Chall and of Bond and Dykstra. From the first wave of studies, its answer seemed to be no. Teaching children to name the letters of the alphabet did not seem to give them any appreciable advantage in learning to read.[24]

How, then, could sense be made of the predictive value of letter-name knowledge? Perhaps it was a symptom rather than a cause. Perhaps, it was suggested, children who know their letters before entering school come from homes where the right kinds of

---

21. The classic study in this area is Robinson (1972). However, the list of studies failing to demonstrate the pedagogical utility of modality-treatment interactions is long. For reviews, see Arter and Jenkins (1979); Barr (1984); Bateman (1979); Cronbach and Snow (1977); Kampwirth and Bates (1980); Stahl (1988); Tarver and Dawson (1988); Williams (1977).

22. Bateman (1979); Chall (1978); Robinson (1972); Williams (1977).

23. Bond and Dykstra (1967); Chall (1967).

24. See, e.g., Gibson and Levin (1975). For both a review and a critique of these early studies on teaching letter names, see Ehri (1983).

interests and activities are fostered. Perhaps it was only that children who know their letter names before entering school have attained the proper level of cognitive development and emotional stability, have the requisite attention span, and have enjoyed proper interaction with adults.[25] If this were so, then just teaching children letter names would be of no more use than making a fine cover for an unwritten book.

To many, this conclusion was disheartening. It was also confusing since, in study after study, letter naming facility continued to show itself as a superlative predictor of reading achievement even through the seventh grade.[26] And so research continued.

Ultimately researchers succeeded in confirming and clarifying both the negative and positive findings on letter-name knowledge. Yes, prereaders' knowledge of letters and their names is a good predictor of the success they will have in learning to read. But no, just teaching them to name the letters of the alphabet does not help much.

The accumulated research also provides an explanation for the apparent contradiction between these findings. First, it is not simply the accuracy with which children can name letters that gives them an advantage in learning to read; it is the ease or fluency with which they can do so—it is their basic familiarity with the letters. Thus, even in studies with relatively small numbers of children and limited differences in accuracy, the speed with which they can name individual letters is both a strong predictor of success for prereaders[27] and a strong correlate of reading achievement among beginners.[28]

There are at least four different explanations of what makes individual letter familiarity such a good measure. All may be correct.

---

25. Venezky (1975).

26. For example, Meuhl and DiNello (1976); Richek (1977-1978); Stevenson, Parker, Wilkinson, Hegion, and Fish (1976); Vellutino and Scanlon (1987).

27. For example, Speer and Lamb (1976); Stanovich, Cunningham, and Cramer (1984); Tunmer, Herriman, and Nesdale (1988); Walsh, Price, and Gillingham (1988).

28. Biemiller (1977–1978); Blachman (1984a). Note that for studies involving large numbers of children, letter-naming accuracy must be a fairly good proxy for letter-naming speed because children who can name most letters accurately include those who can name them most quickly while children who can name fewest letters accurately include those who name them most slowly and effortfully.

The first explanation applies to prereaders. The speed and accuracy of letter naming is an index of the thoroughness or confidence with which the letters' identities have been learned. A child who can recognize most letters with thorough confidence will have an easier time learning about letter sounds and word spellings than a child who has to work at remembering what is what.

The second explanation applies to older readers. The speed of letter naming is an index of the automaticity or effortlessness with which letter recognition occurs. Children who automatically see the letters as wholes will see the words as patterns of letters. Children who do not, will have to work on the patterns of the individual letters as well. To the extent that they invest effort in identifying uncertain letters, they have less attention and capacity left for figuring out, processing, and remembering the words. To the extent that they instead gloss over the uncertain letters, they do so at the cost of needed growth in their visual vocabularies and, possibly, the correct meaning of the text.

The third explanation relates to the fact that in general the names of letters are quite closely related to their sounds. There is evidence that a comfortable knowledge of the names of letters hastens children's learning of their sounds because it mediates their ability to remember the sounds. That is, if I, as a learner, know that this particular symbol is called *b*, then I can use that fact to help myself remember that its sound is /*b*/.

There is also abundant evidence that many children basically understand the alphabetic principle before they have fully mastered—or even been taught—our language's set of letter-to-sound correspondences. It turns out that this phenomenon is both important and related.

It is important because concern about the difficulty of conveying the alphabetic principle to children has been a major source of tension with respect to beginning reading instruction. Such concern has been the major cause of the disputes and disagreements over the best way to teach the messy letter-to-sound correspondences of English and the ambivalence as to whether such effort is productive or counterproductive in the first place. It has also been a major motive for whole word approaches to reading and for the use of reformed alphabets for initial instruction.

The alphabetic principle is subtle. Its understanding may be the single most important step toward acquiring the code. How is it that so many little prereaders figure it out on their own? The answer seems to be that while knowing the names of letters helps some children to remember their sounds, it helps others to induce them.

More specifically, these children seem to use the names of the letters to figure out their scribal significance. Thus, they spontaneously produce such words as PPL (people), KAN (can), JRIV (drive), BOT (boat), and AGRE (angry). Such invented spellings are often a little peculiar (but so are many "correct" spellings). More important, though not applied with uniform precision, the alphabetic principle is definitely there.[29]

A fourth explanation for the predictive and correlational power of letter naming speed is that the ability to name any kind of visual stimuli rapidly or "automatically" reflects a deep capacity that differs between individuals and is important for reading. This hypothesis has grown from findings that good and poor readers tend to differ in the speed with which they can name colors, numbers, and objects as well as letters.[30]

This last hypothesis is tremendously difficult to assess.[31] First, separating children on their tendency to automatize a label depends on first equating them on their degree of familiarity with the label and its referent—which is very hard to do. Second, there is an issue of common experiences, of activities that tend to go hand in hand in child rearing: If the children who come to an experiment most ready to call out the names of objects, numbers, and colors are the same as those who are (or will be) most ready to call out the names of letters, then the power of object, number, and color naming speed may stand as nothing more than a predictor-once-removed of letter naming speed.

On the other hand, the good-poor reader differences in speed of naming objects, numbers, and colors are most likely to be found when the poor readers are severely, as opposed to slightly, behind schedule in reading. It is possible that some resistance in the naming system is a constitutional and causal factor in reading disability. Whether or not it is, we are left with the same question: Can these students be brought to normal levels of fluency with letters and words through appropriate training?

---

29. For descriptions and discussions of young children's invented spellings, see C. Chomsky (1979); Read (1971).

30. Blachman (1984a); Denckla and Rudel (1976).

31. See Wagner and Torgesen (1987).

Phonemic Awareness

Bond and Dykstra's analysis of the data from the USOE Cooperative Studies indicated that the second best predictor of first-grade reading achievement was the ability to discriminate between phonemes, those smaller-than-a-syllable speech sounds that correspond roughly to individual letters or graphemic units. Follow-up investigations of this factor have clarified, extended, and underscored its importance.

It turns out that it is not working knowledge of phonemes that is so important but conscious, analytic knowledge. It is neither the ability to hear the difference between two phonemes nor the ability to distinctly produce them that is significant. What is important is the awareness that they exist as abstractable and manipulable components of the language. Developmentally, this awareness seems to depend upon the child's inclination or encouragement to lend conscious attention to the sounds (as distinct from the meanings) of words.

Why Is Phonemic Awareness a Problem?

Deep down in the machinery of our brains and long before we get to school, each of us has established a thorough familiarity with the phonemes of our language. It has been shown that at one month of age, infants make phonemic distinctions between elementary speech-like sounds.[32] They not only discriminate between such highly similar sounds as /*ba*/ and /*pa*/ but they also lump physically in-between sounds into one category or the other. Shortly after, babies begin to practice the phonemes of their language, quickly moving on to the abilities to produce and distinguish them in the rapidly flowing permutations and combinations of continuous speech.

We know that we must "know" about phonemes at some level, or we could not produce or understand speech. We know that they must have some real perceptual representation, or we could not catch people producing those articulatory errors known as Spoonerisms:

With this wing I thee red. (With this ring I thee wed.)
Heft lemisphere (Left hemisphere).[33]

---

32. Eimas, Siqueland, Jusczyk, and Vigorito (1971).

33. Attested examples from Fromkin (1973). The name *Spoonerisms* for such slips is owed to an English clergyman, William Spooner (d. 1930), who is reported to have made such errors often—and probably

Or we could not stump people with tongue twisters:

Miss Smith's fish sauce shop seldom sells shellfish;
She sells sea shells;
Rubber baby buggy bumpers.[34]

Or we could not amuse and entertain ourselves, world around, with rhymes and alliterations.

But despite our working knowledge of phonemes, we are not naturally set up to be consciously aware of them. Even adults can push a button faster when listening for a whole word than when listening for a single phoneme like /s/, and this is true even when the phoneme is the first sound of the word. It seems that adults can consciously access the presence of a phoneme only through the time-consuming and retrospective process of taking apart the syllable that they have already perceived by virtue of its presence.[35]

The deep and automatic encoding of phonemes is the product of the fact that we know them so well, that we have overlearned them even at a very tender age. It is, moreover, of critical importance to our tasks as speech producers and encoders. As Edmund B. Huey expressed in his turn-of-the-century classic on reading:

Repetition progressively frees the mind from attention to details, makes facile the total act, shortens the time, and reduces the extent to which consciousness must concern itself with the processes.[36]

In other words it is because we have so thoroughly automated, so thoroughly mechanized and sublimated, our processing of phonemes that we have attention and capacity for the higher-order meaning and nuances of spoken language.

Moreover, having learned the phonemes so well, there is almost no reason whatsoever for us to lend them conscious attention—no reason, that is, unless we need to learn to read an alphabetic script. And there is the rub. To learn an alphabetic script, we must learn to attend to that which we have learned not to attend to.

---

deliberately. Examples of his own Spoonerisms include: "You have hissed all my mystery lectures;" "I saw you fight a liar in the back quad; in fact, you have tasted the whole worm;" and "The lord is a shoving leopard to his flock." (Cited by Clark and Clark, 1977, p. 275.)

34. Examples taken from Clark and Clark (1977, pp. 289-290).
35. Savin and Bever (1970); Warren (1971).
36. Huey (1908/1968, p. 104).

After years of working with this issue, researchers now recognize that the major difference between prereaders who get high versus low scores on readiness tests of phoneme discrimination derives from their ability to understand the instructions.[37] Low-readiness prereaders can hear the difference between phonemes as well as high-readiness prereaders.[38] The difference is that the low-readiness prereaders are unprepared to analyze the sound structure of the syllables consciously in this way.

An analogy might be useful. Suppose that side by side on the table, we put two apples, one a McIntosh, and the other a New York Rome. Now suppose that we usher in a subject, point to the apples, and ask, "Same or different?" Without hesitation, any good pomologist would say "Different!"

But what about the random subject? I can easily imagine myself in such a situation. My response would be something like, "I don't know . . . . Same??? . . . Different??? . . . I don't know . . . . How do you want me to compare them anyhow?" It is not that I couldn't see any differences between these two apples or any other two apples, for that matter. The problem is that I would not know whether you wanted me to look at their similarities or their differences. And if it were their differences, I would not know which ones you cared about.[39]

Having determined that this is much the position that phonemically unaware prereaders find themselves in, we have invented better tests to assess their confusion. To provide a sense of the general nature of these tasks, as well as the similarities and differences between them, I have divided them into six categories.[40]

Phonemic Segmentation Tasks

The purpose of these tasks is to find out whether the child can decompose a syllable into its component phonemes. Preeminent in this category is the tapping task developed by Isabelle Liberman

---

37. Calfee (1977).

38. Wallach, Wallach, Dozier, and Kaplan (1977).

39. For a demonstration of the aptness of this analogy, see Experiments 2 and 3 of Treiman and Baron (1981).

40. There are in fact many more tasks than I can describe here and not all are perfectly amenable to my categorization scheme. For more comprehensive reviews of the domain, see Blachman (1984b); Lewkowicz (1980); Stanovich, Cunningham, and Cramer (1984); Yopp (1988).

and her colleagues.[41] The test consists of a series of words or syllables, each composed of one to three phonemes. The child is given a wooden dowel stick and asked to tap out the number of phonemes in each syllable.[42] For example, given the word *mat*, the child should tap three times, once for each of its phonemes: /m/, /a/, and /t/.

The test items are preceded by ample training, demonstration, and modeling and, even within the test, feedback may be given and modeling may be provided for incorrect responses. Children's failures to perform can therefore be ascribed quite confidently to their failures to understand how it is intended that each new syllable be broken into smaller segments.

In their initial experiment with the tapping task, Liberman and her colleagues looked at performance across a group of four to six year olds. The children were termed successful if they correctly tapped out the phonemes for six consecutive words. In June (at the end of the school year), none of the four year olds tested were successful, only 17 percent of the five year olds were successful, but 70 percent of the six year olds were successful.[43]

Was the performance of the six year olds related to their reading achievement? To find out, the researchers administered the Wide Range Achievement Test to these children at the beginning of second grade. Half of the children who had failed the phoneme tapping task were in the lowest third of their class in reading achievement; none of the children who failed the phoneme tapping task were in the top third.[44]

Thus the relationship between children's performance on the Liberman tapping task and their reading performance seemed real and strong. Indeed, a number of subsequent studies have confirmed the strength of this relationship.[45] Performance on the tapping

---

41. Liberman, Shankweiler, Fischer, and Carter (1974).

42. In an alternate task, developed by a Russian psychologist, Elkonin (1973), the children are asked to lay out bingo markers or counters for each phoneme. Though functionally similar to the tapping task, Elkonin's task has the advantages of avoiding its misleading rhythmicity and of requiring the child to generate a visual—and thus inspectable and discussable —record of each effort. The Elkonin version of the segmentation task has been especially useful in the training of segmentation skills.

43. Liberman, Shankweiler, Fischer, and Carter (1974).

44. Liberman, Shankweiler, Liberman, Fowler, and Fischer (1977).

45. For example, Blachman (1984a); Tunmer and Nesdale (1985); Zifcak (1981).

task at the beginning of first grade has been shown to correlate as high as 0.60 with reading achievement at the end of the year.[46]

We are nevertheless left asking which side of the relationship is the cause and which is the effect. Remember that however psychologically real a phoneme may be, it is acoustically evanescent. If we, as adults, think that we can hear the individual phonemes in a word, it is because we are used to thinking about words that way, not because the phonemes are audibly distinguishable. In actuality, the pronunciation of a word does not consist of series of discrete phonemes. It is impossible, for example, to tape-record a word and splice it into phonemes. The problem is that the attributes of each phoneme spill over into that which precedes and that which follows.

To see this, let us consider the letter *s.* For purposes of this demonstration, *s* is a good choice because it is one of the few consonants that can be pronounced in isolation: *"Ssssss."*

Now try pronouncing the words *see* and *so* to yourself. Pronounce them cleanly, as you would if you were doing it for a very young reader. And pay attention to what you do with your mouth as you pronounce the *s.* Do you feel your lips rounding as (or before) you begin the word *so?* Do you feel them stretching toward a smile as you begin the word *see?* As you change your attack on the /*s*/ in anticipation of the vowel to follow, you change the real sound of both phonemes as well, inseparably blending them together.

The purpose of this demonstration is to ground the argument that there is no way to know that, say, the word *cat* is composed of three separate phonemes except by having somehow learned that it is. The three phonemes in *cat* are audible percepts only because they are such well-learned concepts. They are not acoustically discrete. No matter how hard you pay attention, you will not hear them separately, one at a time, unless you think of them separately and one at a time.

The point of all this is to make thoroughly understandable the argument that performance on the tapping task is in part a consequence of early reading progress. This argument is consistent with the observations that performance on the tapping task increases dramatically across the first grade.[47] It has furthermore been quite pointedly supported by a number of recent studies.[48]

---

46. Zifcak (1981).

47. Liberman, Shankweiler, Fischer, and Carter (1974).

48. Perfetti, Beck, Bell, and Hughes (1987); Wagner and Torgesen (1987).

Be that as it may, the kind of phonemic awareness assessed by the tapping task appears to be a cause of early reading proficiency as well. In a study designed to probe this issue, Tunmer and Nesdale administered the tapping task along with a decoding test, a reading comprehension test, and an IQ test to first graders.[49]

Based on close statistical analysis of their data, Tunmer and Nesdale concluded that phonemic segmentation skills, as measured by the tapping task, were strongly, directly, and causally related to decoding abilities and that decoding abilities, in turn, were strongly, directly, and causally related to reading comprehension. IQ contributed directly, but weakly, to each of these abilities.

A direct peek at the children's patterns of performance tells the story just as well:

- All of the students who did well on the decoding test also passed the tapping task.
- All of those who failed the tapping task also failed the decoding test.
- An additional number of students passed the tapping task but failed the decoding test.[50]

Thus it seems that phonemic segmentation skills were a necessary precursor to being able to decode, but they were not sufficient. Those who could decode could segment. Those who could not segment, could not decode. The third group of children, who could segment but could not decode, were evidently lacking in their mastery of letter-to-sound correspondences.

One other aspect of Tunmer and Nesdale's design is relevant here. The students were divided, roughly half and half, in terms of the type of reading instruction they had received. Three of the classroom teachers followed an eclectic approach, including a heavy emphasis on the teaching of letter-to-sound correspondences. The other three teachers followed "the so-called 'psycholinguistic' approach to teaching reading, providing no incidental or formal instruction in [letter-to-sound correspondences]."[51] Depending on which instructional approach the children had received, Tunmer and Nesdale found enormous differences in reading achievement. The students who had received explicit instruction in decoding scored significantly better

---

49. Tunmer and Nesdale (1985).

50. This pattern of results has been replicated by Tunmer, Nesdale, and Herriman (1988).

51. Tunmer and Nesdale (1985, p. 421).

by every measure. However, the students did not differ significantly in their phonemic segmentation skills.

For many children, then, it seems that this sophisticated sort of phonological awareness develops around the time when they embark on formal reading instruction. But what about the others? Across studies, about one-third of middle-class children fail to gain this insight within the first grade. For less advantaged students, given the evidence that they are especially behind in phonemic awareness,[52] this number is surely much higher.

In view of the evidence that phonemic awareness is imperative for learning to read, Tunmer and his colleagues urge that all children be given instruction specifically designed to develop their linguistic awareness.[53] This is not hard to do, and it is just too risky not to.[54]

Phoneme Manipulation Tasks

In a second class of tasks that has been used quite broadly to assess phonological awareness, children are given instructions to manipulate the phonemes in each test word. For example, in a task originally developed by Bruce, the children are asked to pronounce a word after they have removed its first, middle, or last phoneme.[55] As examples, the children might be asked to say *hill* without the /h/, *monkey* without the /k/, *nest* without the /s/, or *pink* without the /k/. In other versions of such tasks, the children may be asked to reorder the phonemes of a syllable[56] or to add some extra phonemes to it.[57]

In general, performance on such phoneme manipulation tasks has yielded strong predictions of or correlations with reading achievement.[58] With a highly sophisticated and multi-leveled

---

52. Juel, Griffith, and Gough (1986); Rozin, Poritsky, and Sotsky (1971); Wallach, Wallach, Dozier, and Kaplan (1977).

53. Tunmer, Herriman, and Nesdale (1988).

54. Instruction on linguistic awareness is discussed in chapter 12.

55. Bruce (1964).

56. Alegria, Pignot, and Morais (1982); Lindamood and Lindamood (1971); Lundberg, Olofsson, and Wall (1980); Mann (1984).

57. Lindamood and Lindamood (1971).

58. Lundberg, Olofsson, and Wall (1980); Mann (1984); Rosner and Simon (1971).

battery of such tasks, strong correlations have been found all the way through grade 12.[59]

Nevertheless, tasks of this ilk have generally been found to be beyond the reach of children before the very end of first grade. This should not be surprising since, on close examination, they are seen to require all that the tapping task requires plus more. To pick out the relevant phoneme(s) from any given test word, the children must have well-developed phonemic segmentation skills. Then, whether to delete or reorder the phonemes or insert a new one and put the new word back together, must require all manner of memory skills and gymnastics. It is hard to imagine how one might succeed in such tasks without fairly well developed spelling skills.

In a valiant attempt to show otherwise, Rosner tried to train kindergartners on the phoneme deletion task. The results? Even a whole school year's worth of training resulted in precious little progress. The exception was that the children became relatively proficient at deleting the initial consonants of words.[60]

Yet the knowledge and skills required to delete the initial phoneme from a word may be very different from those involved in the ability to delete any designated phoneme from a word. So different, that we will discuss them under a separate title, syllable-splitting.

Syllable-Splitting Tasks

In these tasks, the students are asked to break off the first phoneme of a word or a syllable. In some versions, they are then asked to pronounce the phoneme in isolation (e.g., instructor says "bear," and students says "b-b-b-b"). In others, they are then asked to say what is left (e.g., the instructor says "pink," and the student says "ink").

Syllable-splitting tasks are basically easier than phoneme segmentation or manipulation tasks in that the children do not have to think about the syllable (word) as a string of phonemes to succeed. The syllable-splitting tasks require only that the children attend carefully to the sound of the syllable and that they have and apply the insight that its initial sound can be broken away.

---

59. Calfee, Lindamood, and Lindamood (1973). It is also of interest that Alegria, Pignot, and Morais (1982) found phoneme reversal performance much enhanced by phonic instruction relative to whole word instruction.
60. Rosner (1974).

Syllable-splitting tasks can thus be seen to tap an essential, if rudimentary, form of the sort of phonemic awareness presupposed by reading. Consistent with this impression, they have been shown to be strong predictors of the extent to which kindergartners will succeed with first-grade reading instruction.[61] In a massive longitudinal study involving assessment of thirty-nine different prereading characteristics—representing prereading skills, oral language ability, motor skill, social behavior, and home/background variables—Share, Jorm, Maclean, and Matthews found kindergartners' syllable-splitting performance to be the best predictor of first-grade reading achievement, accounting for 39 percent of the variance between children all by itself.[62]

The idea that the sound of a single one-syllable word can be taken apart seems truly to qualify as an insight. Perhaps we should not be surprised that this is so. The phonemes of a word are acoustically indivisible from one another. More than that, in a conversational world, the very purpose of a spoken word is to be meaningful as a whole. Forgetting about reading for a moment, we must concede that for youngsters to process the sounds of words so automatically that they can restrict active attention to their meanings represents admirable maturity in their aural language sophistication.[63]

The point is that, however easy these tasks may seem to us, they are not necessarily a piece of cake for the preschooler. Hence the youngest age at which researchers have been able to get children to do such tasks at all has depended in part on the cleverness with which the instructions are "child proofed."

For example, Zhurova working with three to six year olds in Moscow, employed toy animals and a "magic bridge." In order to cross the bridge, each animal had to say the first sound of its name to a wise old crow, perched above. To get a toy dog across the bridge, the child would have to make it say something like, "dog, d-d-d-dog, d-d-d." Otherwise the bridge would collapse.[64]

Using essentially this task, but substituting the fairyland props with intensive one-on-one tutoring by community mothers, Wallach and Wallach have shown that low-income prereaders

---

61. For example, Vellutino and Scanlon (1987).

62. Share, Jorm, Maclean, and Matthews (1984).

63. Of relevance, children seem to have less trouble analyzing the sounds of nonsense syllables than familiar, meaningful words (McNeil and Stone, 1965).

64. Zhurova (1963, cited in Routh and Fox, 1984).

can become fully proficient in splitting initial consonant sounds off words. Moreover, Wallach and Wallach report that following such training, their students had little trouble in isolating phonemes in other positions in words and, most inspiringly, in learning to read.[65]

Again, in the reverse version of the syllable-splitting task, the children are asked to break the initial phoneme off a word and to say what is left (e.g., instructor says "feel," and student says "eel"). Children's success on this version has also proved to be strongly related to early reading acquisition.[66]

In some ways, the reverse form of the task seems as if it ought to be easier. At least it avoids that foreign task of trying to pronounce a single phoneme in isolation. Musings aside, the task has proven difficult for prereaders and, again, the problem seems in part one of "child proofing" the task requirements. Feeling frustrated at his inability to get kindergartners to do much with this task, Calfee analyzed its cognitive requirements quite rigorously.[67]

Both to help children understand the instructions and to aid their memories, he tried giving them sets of four picture cards. One of the cards depicted the test word and the other three, the response choices. With this extra help, Calfee found that virtually all of the kindergartners and first graders with whom he worked could master the task very quickly. Interestingly he also found that, having introduced the task so gently, virtually all of the children went on to perform quite easily and accurately with new words and without the pictorial support—virtually all, that is, except those from nonmainstream, low-income families.

Before moving on, one more note on reverse versions of this task is in order. They are generally treated in the literature like other syllable-splitting tasks. They are generally discussed as though what the children must actually do to succeed is to recognize that initial phoneme of each word and methodically splice it away. But look at some typical stimulus-response pairs (the response is italicized): feel–*eel*, mice–*ice*; cake–*ache*; ties–*eyes*; heat–*eat*. One might as easily drop all of the phonemic analysis baggage and conceive of this task as a special kind of rhyming game. Calfee commented that many of his young students seemed to think that was what it was all about.[68]

---

65. Wallach and Wallach (1979).
66. Stanovich, Cunningham, and Feeman (1984).
67. Calfee (1977).
68. Calfee (1977).

Rhyming abilities and syllable-splitting abilities may involve different cognitive processes. On the other hand, children's rhyming abilities seem also to provide good measures of their reading readiness.

Blending Tasks

Superficially, blending tasks seem highly similar to phonemic segmentation tasks. The obvious difference is that in blending tasks, the tester provides the segments of the word (e.g., "/m/ . . . /a/ . . . /p/") and the student is asked to put them together ("map"). On closer analysis, however, blending tasks differ from segmentation tasks in at least two ways.

First, they differ in the phonemic sophistication they assess. In the segmentation task, the child must not only know that a syllable can be segmented into phonemes but, to do so, must also have a sufficient sense of what (and how big) phonemes are. In contrast the phonemic segments are given to the child in blending tasks. In terms of linguistic awareness, therefore, all that would seem to be required by the blending tasks is the knowledge that such strange little sounds can be smooshed together into a word.

Second, there are differences in the memorability of the test items presented to the child.[69] In the segmentation task, the stimulus provided by the tester is typically a single, familiar, monosyllabic word. In the blending task, the stimulus consists of between two and four subsyllabic utterances. Thus, the child is presented with more discrete sounds in the blending task than in the segmentation task—but that is only part of the point.

The other, and more important, part of the point derives from the fact that the difficulty of remembering arbitrary items depends as much on their familiarity as their number. A single, familiar, monosyllabic word should be relatively easy to remember. But what about a string of phonemes? The ease of remembering them must pivot on the child's phonemic development. In particular, if the child has previously heard phonemes produced "in isolation" and, more than that, has a comfortable familiarity with the sounds of phonemes produced "in isolation," the blending stimuli will be much easier to retain and work together.

In both their memory and performance requirements, therefore, blending tasks should stand as relatively simple and powerful

---

69. In reference are strictly the memorability of the test items. The amount of memory capacity required to *perform* segmentation must be expected to *exceed* that required to perform blending.

tests of the child's familiarity with the nature and function of phonemes. And they seem to fulfill our expectations.

With respect to the idea that blending tasks assess children's familiarity with the nature of phonemes, Fox and Routh have shown that, among four year olds, only those who could be coaxed to produce phonemes in isolation could benefit from training on phonemic blending.[70] With respect to the idea that they are relatively simple, they have been shown to be significantly easier than segmentation and deletion tasks.[71] With respect to the idea that they are powerful, blending scores obtained just prior to the beginning of formal reading instruction have been shown to be strong predictors of reading achievement not only at the end of first grade[72] but all the way through grade 4.[73]

Among the phonemic awareness tasks described so far, blending tasks have been shown to have a very special property. Through an exquisitely designed and analyzed longitudinal study of first graders' acquisition of phonemic awareness and reading skills, Perfetti, Beck, Bell, and Hughes demonstrated that blending "taps an essential but primitive knowledge of segmentation. Success at reading depends on it."[74] More specifically, their analysis showed that, whereas performance on their phoneme deletion task was more strongly a result of early reading proficiency, performance on their blending task was quite strongly the enabler—and that was true whether the children were instructed through a basal reader series or through a code-emphasis program that included direct, systematic instruction in blending.

Oddity Tasks

In oddity tasks, the child is presented with a set of three or four spoken words and asked which of the words is different or does not belong. Sometimes the children are asked to base their decision on the first sound of the words (e.g., *pig*, *hill*, *pin* or *give*, *pat*, *girl*, *go*). Sometimes they are asked to use the final sounds of the words (e.g., *doll*, *hop*, *top* or *bend*, *lend*, *mend*, *sent*). And sometimes they are asked to use the middle sound (e.g., *pin*, *gun*, *bun* or *bet*,

---

70. Fox and Routh (1975).

71. Perfetti, Beck, Bell, and Hughes (1987); Yopp (1988).

72. Lundberg, Olofsson, and Wall (1980); Perfetti, Beck, Bell, and Hughes (1987).

73. Chall, Roswell, and Blumenthal (1963).

74. Perfetti, Beck, Bell, and Hughes (1987, p. 317).

nut, get, let). Note that when middle sounds are being tested (and often final sounds as well), the task amounts to one of rhyme detection.[75]

At the conceptual level, oddity tasks are the simplest of the phonemic awareness tasks discussed so far. Oddity tasks do not require the ability to decompose a syllable into a string of individual phonemes or even the notion that it could be. They do not require the ability to fractionate a syllable or even the notion that it could be. They require only that the children be able to compare and contrast similarities and differences (that happen to correspond to phonemes) in the sounds of syllables.

In view of this, it is not surprising that oddity tasks have proved especially usable with prereaders. By thus providing a way to measure phonemic awareness before the children have begun formal instruction in reading, they allow us to separate the contribution of reading instruction to phonemic awareness from the contributions that might run in the other direction.[76]

In a classic study in this area, Bradley and Bryant gave the oddity task to hundreds of four and five year olds and then measured their reading achievement more than three years later.[77] Even after correcting for the children's chronological age, IQ, and memory for the test items, they found a highly significant relation between the children's initial oddity test scores and their later reading achievement.

But Bradley and Bryant were shrewd. At the beginning of their study, they realized that even if children's differences on the oddity task proved to be strong predictors of differences in their later reading achievement, it would not quite be enough to prove that differences in phonemic awareness caused differences in reading achievement. Maybe both types of differences were really due to some third characteristic or experience that somehow escaped measurement or control.

---

75. Among the studies in which oddity tasks have been used are Bradley and Bryant (1983); Stanovich, Cunningham, and Feeman (1984); Wallach, Wallach, Dozier, and Kaplan (1977).

76. While early assessments allow us to discount contributions of formal reading instruction, they do not allow us to negate contributions of beginning reading instruction that has occurred outside of school. Such informal instruction is largely ignored in most studies of reading predictors. Yet preschoolers' informal exercise and instruction with reading may be substantial and may be a significant factor in their development of critical prereading skills.

77. Bradley and Bryant (1983).

To hedge against this possibility, they selected sixty-five of the children who had done most poorly on the oddity test and divided them into four groups. Children in the first group received forty individual tutoring sessions on comparing the beginning, middle, and final sounds of words. Children in the second group were additionally taught how these sounds were represented by letters of the alphabet. Children in the third group spent their forty tutoring sessions learning how to categorize the words semantically (e.g., *hen* and *pig* are farm animals). Children in the fourth group received no special training at all.

What Bradley and Bryant wanted to know was whether special training in phonemic awareness per se would produce a big advantage in the children's reading comprehension scores. If it did, it would constitute strong evidence that ease of reading acquisition was directly enhanced by phonemic awareness.

Alas, the world is not that simple. When Bradley and Bryant collected the reading scores, they found that the first group of children, who had received training in phonemic awareness only, outscored their peers who had received training in semantic categories or none at all. However, the difference was not large enough or regular enough to be statistically convincing. In contrast, the reading scores of the group who had been trained both on phonemic awareness and in spelling were well ahead of the nonphonemic groups.

With this in mind, I ask you to recall the studies on training letter names. Virtually all of those studies were disappointing: Teaching children the names of letters failed to produce appreciable increases in their reading aptitude. Yet there was an exception.

Among the studies was one in which each of three different groups of first graders received instruction on letter names.[78] One group received instruction on letter names followed by instruction on sight words. Another group received instruction on sight words followed by instruction on letter names and sounds. The remaining group began with instruction on letter names and sounds and then received instruction on sight words.

After four months of instruction, each group was given a reading achievement test. The group that had received instruction on both letter names and sounds before instruction on the sight

---

78. Ohnmacht (1969).

words, was the big winner.[79] The group that had started with sight words and then received instruction on both letter names and sounds came in second. The group that had received instruction only in the names of the letters before their sight word instruction came in last.[80]

The analogy to Bradley and Bryant's efforts to train phonemic awareness with and without concurrent letter-name instruction should be obvious. Balancing the evidence, it seems that both letter knowledge and phonemic awareness are critical for the beginning reader. But it seems further that some special magic lies in the linking of these two basic skills.

Knowledge of Nursery Rhymes

As we have moved through this subsection, the tasks we have considered for assessing phonemic awareness have become simpler and simpler. The oddity tasks require little more than the detection of rhyme and alliteration. At this point we find ourselves backed into two questions. First, could there be still simpler tasks for assessing phonemic awareness? Are there tasks that could be used with still younger children? And second, where does such phonemic awareness come from anyhow?

Maclean, Bradley, and Bryant asked these questions of themselves and came up with a tantalizingly attractive hypothesis: Perhaps the rudiments of phonemic awareness are seeded in children's knowledge of nursery rhymes.[81]

To test their hypothesis, they selected sixty-six English children who were just three years and three months old. Among the children roughly half were girls and half were boys; half were from middle-class homes and half were from working-class homes; and their parents represented a broad range of educational levels.

At the outset of the study, each child was asked to recite five nursery rhymes that had been carefully selected on the basis of

---

79. Tunmer, Nesdale, and Herriman (1988) also report evidence that some degree of phonological awareness is essential before knowledge of letter names can do any good.

80. For children of average and above average IQ and reading readiness scores, this pattern of results obtained by both comprehension and word recognition measures. There were, in contrast, few significant differences between treatments for the children with low IQ and readiness scores; the single (but provocative) exception was that word recognition performance was best among those who had begun with letter names only.

81. Maclean, Bryant, and Bradley (1987).

their popularity in England; they included such favorites as "Baa Baa Black Sheep" and "Humpty Dumpty." Then every four months until the children were four and one-half years old, the experimenters returned to assess their progress on, for example, oddity tasks, rhyme and alliteration production, and, finally, recognition of letters and words.

The results of this study are extremely provocative. Across the whole study group, early knowledge of nursery rhymes varied, as might be expected, with the children's own IQs and their parents' education and social class. However, when each of these influences was cancelled out, the researchers found that early knowledge of nursery rhymes was strongly and specifically related to development of more abstract phonological skills and of emergent reading abilities. Just as one more piece of evidence for or against the argument that early nursery rhyme knowledge was specifically related to later reading skills, Maclean, Bryant, and Bradley also looked at the children's arithmetic skills; as expected, the strong predictive relationship vanished.

Summary: Phonemic Awareness

Looking across the various tasks reviewed in this section, we can identify at least five different levels of phonemic awareness.

1. The most primitive level—that measured by knowledge of nursery rhymes—involves nothing more than an ear for the sounds of words.

2. At the next level, the oddity tasks require the child methodically to compare and contrast the sounds of words for rhyme or alliteration; this requires not just sensitivity to similarities and differences in the overall sounds of words, but the ability to focus attention on the components of their sounds that make them similar or different.

3. The tasks at the third level, blending and syllable-splitting, seem to require that the child have a comfortable familiarity with the notion that words can be subdivided into those small, meaningless sounds corresponding to phonemes and, second, that she or he be comfortably familiar with the way phonemes sound when produced "in isolation" and, better yet, with the act producing them that way by oneself.

4. The phonemic segmentation tasks require not only that the child have a thorough understanding that words can be completely analyzed into a series of phonemes but further that she or he be able to so analyze them, completely and on demand.

5. The phoneme manipulation tasks require still further that the child have sufficient proficiency with the phonemic structure of words that she or he be able to add, delete, or move any designated phoneme and regenerate a word (or a nonword) from the result.

The advantage of the most difficult of these types of tasks, phoneme manipulation and phonemic segmentation, is that they yield remarkably strong predictions of and correlations with beginning reading acquisition. The disadvantage is that they are generally unattainable by children who have received no formal reading instruction, which forces us to wonder whether the skills they assess are truly causes or merely effects of beginning reading.

Direct examination of this question gives back a double-edged answer. The segmentation abilities involved in the phoneme deletion and tapping tasks seem to develop as consequences of instruction on word recognition (whether through phonic or look-say methods).[82] Those involved in the tapping task, at least, seem to be precursors to word recognition proficiency as well—again regardless of the instructional approach.[83]

The advantage of the easiest of these tasks is that they can be administered to three and four year olds and, thus, well before formal reading instruction has begun. Preschoolers' knowledge of nursery rhymes and their performance on the oddity tasks has been shown to correlate significantly with their later reading ability. The disadvantage with these easiest measures is that their predictive and correlational strength is not as strong as with the more difficult measures.

The tasks that lie in between in difficulty, blending and syllable-splitting, seem to be in between in utility. Both are more or less doable by most kindergartners and both yield strong correlations with concurrent and future reading acquisition. The results of Perfetti and his colleagues indicated that the skills involved in blending bore a truly causal relation to emerging word recognition skills.[84] On the other hand, success with either of these tasks seems to depend on possession of the idea that words are comprised of phonemes and on the ability to produce "isolated" phonemes by oneself. It is hard to imagine how a child might acquire these competencies except through the reading-directed tutelage of a sibling or adult.

---

82. Perfetti, Beck, Bell, and Hughes (1987); Tunmer, Herriman, and Nesdale (1988); Tunmer and Nesdale (1985).

83. Tunmer, Herriman, and Nesdale (1988); Tunmer and Nesdale (1985).

84. Perfetti, Beck, Bell, and Hughes (1987).

Where Do Prereading Skills Come From? Early Experience with Print

So far in this chapter we have reviewed the findings on four categories of prereader skills: mental age or IQ, perceptual skills and styles, knowledge of letters, and phonemic awareness. Under the researchers' lens, IQ proved, at best, weakly and nonspecifically related to early reading development; on the other hand, the possession of certain logical and analytical abilities was found to hasten the acquisition of reading-related skills. Moreover, we found no compelling evidence either that children's perceptual-motor development influences their general readiness for reading or that their dominant modality influences the success they will experience under one instructional approach versus another. On the other hand, knowledge of letters and phonemic awareness were found to bear a strong and direct relationship to success and ease of reading acquisition, and both seem to do so regardless of the approach through which reading per se is taught. Indeed, the harder these two variables are investigated, the stronger their predictive value appears to be.

The predictive and correlational strength of letter recognition facility and phonemic awareness bears reflection for two reasons. The first reason is that the very potency of these two skills reinforces the hypothesis that budding familiarity with letter-to-sound relations is invaluable to the beginning reader. The second is that, as predictors of reading acquisition, there is something strange about them.

Specifically, it is not clear how either letter recognition fluency or phonemic segmentation skills could be acquired except through their instruction and exercise. What, then, do they tell us about reading readiness? One irrepressible interpretation is that the likelihood that a child will succeed in the first grade depends most of all on how much she or he has already learned about reading before getting there—and this interpretation seems soberingly correct.[85]

---

85. To assess this hypothesis, Wagner and Torgesen (1987) reanalyzed Lundberg, Olofsson, and Wall (1980) data, holding constant the children's reading ability, as measured on the screening test. When this was done, the median predictive correlation of Lundberg et al.'s phonemic awareness measures dropped from 0.45 to 0.06, thus underscoring the possibility that initial differences in phonemic awareness were themselves due to differences in the children's knowledge about reading.

With this possibility in mind, the issue of whether letter familiarity and phonemic awareness skill are causes or effects of reading acquisition deserves more attention. To begin, we must recognize that the way in which this issue is typically explored by researchers consists of dividing the children, either longitudinally or cross-sectionally, into nonreaders and readers and then relating the predictor skills of each group to their ensuing reading acquisition.

Typically the way in which the children are categorized as readers or nonreaders is by whether they reach some cutoff point on some test. Most often, the "nonreaders" are those who are unable to read more than a specified number of words on a test list. But whatever the particular test, its logic typically requires that the difference between a reader and a nonreader be strictly and categorically defined: Each child is placed in one category or the other and nowhere in between.

Yet reading is not an all-or-none skill, any more than letter recognition or phonemic awareness is. The question arises, therefore: How much might a "nonreader," who has good alphabetic and phonemic skills, know about reading?

In partial answer to this question, let me describe my oldest child. John is just approaching his fifth birthday. He has been able to recite the alphabet since he was two and to recognize all of the capital letters nearly as long. He still has trouble recognizing some of the lowercase letters although he is quite interested in them.

His fine motor skills are "age appropriate for a boy," which is to say not well refined. He can print very few words on his own (his name, *MOM*, *LOVE*) and very occasionally asks us to dictate the letters of other names or words to him. I have only recently and only on a couple occasions caught him inventing spellings in the effort to teach his sister (who is almost three) how to write. When he prints he often errs on letter orientations and makes pragmatic, rather than conventional, use of space ("the *M* is very big, so I'll put it up here").

Since he was three, he has derived great pleasure from figuring out the first letter of all manner of words; it is one of his standard car seat diversions. He often asks what a printed word says, he regularly mouths along with the phonic exercises on "Sesame Street," and every now and then engages us in a binge of trying to sound words out. In addition, rhyming jokes are not only a mainstay of his four-year-old sense of humor but constitute a principal variation on the "copy cat" routine.

Has John shown extraordinary interest in learning to read? Not particularly. Clearly it is interesting. Reading is a grown-up activity and a challenge. But reading activities do not hold a candle to, for example, horsing around with his friends, watching television, or playing with his macho action figures.

Has John been extraordinarily pressured to read? I don't think so. We encourage his interest but have never sat him down for a lesson or exercise. Occasionally some of the little girls in his day care center—who seem remarkably advanced to me—do make fun of the little boys for their relative inability to read and write.

Is John unusually gifted in his prereading abilities? Apparently not. He is about average in his middle-class day care center. Moreover, at four years of age, he would have placed roughly in the middle of the middle-class preschool that Jana Mason studied in Champaign, Illinois.[86] And he would probably place roughly in the middle of countless other middle-class preschool groups around the country.

Here begins the first part of my point: If John—or almost any of his middle-class preschool peers—were given a prereader test, he would probably do quite well with the easier phonemic awareness tasks, up through blending and syllable-splitting. He would also do well on a test of letter-naming fluency—if it were on uppercase letters. On the other hand, if he were given a list of words to read by a random experimenter, I suspect that he would read none; he would be classified as a nonreader.

Thus the first part of the point is this: It is very likely that (1) if John were to participate in one of our experiments, he would be classified as a nonreader with reasonably good phonemic awareness and letter recognition skills, and (2) when John eventually receives formal reading instruction, he will do fine. Shall we then say that his success was specifically caused by his letter recognition skills and phonemic awareness at age five? Maybe. But bear in mind that John knows a tremendous amount about written English. His letter recognition skills and phonemic awareness are in some sense just tips—albeit critical and diagnostic tips—of a reading readiness iceberg. He will learn to read on schedule because he has nearly learned to read already.

The second part of the point is this: If such linguistic knowledge among preschoolers like John cannot be ascribed to rabid interest, pressure, or precocity, then where did it come from? In the literature on early readers and writers, there is some tendency to underscore the independence and spontaneity of their

---

86. Mason (1980).

achievements. Not meaning to take anything away from these children, I tend to agree with Jeanne Chall.[87] I suspect that their achievements are owed as much to many, many hours of guidance and encouragement by the older people around them.

To make this suspicion concrete, let us again consider John. Since he was six weeks old, we have spent 30 to 45 minutes reading to him each day. By the time he reaches first grade at age six and a quarter, that will amount to 1,000 to 1,700 hours of storybook reading—one on one, with his face in the books.[88] He will also have spent more than 1,000 hours watching "Sesame Street."[89] And he will have spent at least as many hours fooling around with magnetic letters on the refrigerator, writing, participating in reading/writing/ language activities in preschool, playing word and "spelling" games in the car, on the computer, with us, with his sister, with his friends, and by himself, and so on.

I believe that John's reading related experience is quite typical of that of his middle-class peers in general. In a fascinating ethnographic study of the home and community lives of three culturally different towns in the southeastern United States, Shirley Heath has shown that this kind of preschool language and literacy support is prevalent within culturally mainstream homes in general—even homes that, by economic norms, are quite poor, homes that are run by adults who are neither college educated nor professionally employed.[90]

But even while John's experience may be typical of that of culturally mainstream preschoolers in general, it is surely not identical to that of any one of them. For example, in many of the homes that Heath studied, parents read to their preschoolers before naps as well as before bedtime—a practice that might double the number of hours of a child's one-on-one interaction with written language. To account for such variation, we may therefore add or subtract a thousand hours from John's total, or we may halve it or double it.

---

87. Chall (1983b).

88. Heath's (1983) book, which examines the language, literacy, and social structures of two U.S. communities, indicates that such early and regular reading to children is characteristic of culturally mainstream homes in general.

89. He has been watching it since he was one. Because it is generally on in the morning and the evening, he probably watches it for an hour a day, on average.

90. Heath (1983).

Any way we work it, it seems a safe bet that John and the majority of his culturally mainstream peers will have experienced thousands of hours' worth of prereading activities before entering first grade. Upon this base and with the continuing help of peer pressure and parental support,[91] their first-grade teacher will attempt to teach them to read. In this endeavor, she is unlikely to spend more than 2 hours per school day. In all, she is unlikely to spend more than 360 hours over the course of the year. And, even during these hours, her attention will necessarily be divided across twenty or so students. Even so and not surprisingly, she will generally succeed. Relative to the thousands of hours of instruction that her students have received at home, that which she provides in the classroom is but a drop—albeit the quintessential drop—in the bucket.

It is easy to imagine children who have no magnetic letters on their refrigerators, no home computer with word and letter games, no reading classmates in preschool, and no ready supply of papers, pencils, and crayons lying around the house for their use. It is equally easy to imagine children whose television, if they have one, is preoccupied with programs that are less directed to scholastic readiness of preschoolers than is "Sesame Street."[92]

Yet the most important activity for building the knowledge and skills eventually required for reading is that of reading aloud to children.[93] In this, both the sheer amount of and the choice of reading materials seem to make a difference.[94] Greatest progress is had when the vocabulary and syntax of the materials are just ever so slightly above the child's own level of linguistic maturity.[95]

Rather than reading a story straight through, it seems especially important to engage the children's active attention. Recently, Whitehurst and his colleagues have reported some extremely provocative data in this area.[96] The parents of fifteen middle-class children between two and three years old were given a one-hour training session on interactive story reading. Rather

---

91. For a review of the force of these influences, see Wigfield and Asher (1984).

92. See Heath (1983).

93. C. Chomsky (1972); Commission on Reading, National Academy of Education (1985); Durkin (1966); Goldfield and Snow (1984); Johns (1984); McCormick (1977); Teale (1984).

94. Wigfield and Asher (1984).

95. C. Chomsky (1972).

96. Whitehurst et al. (1988).

than just read to their children, these parents were encouraged to pause every so often and to ask open-ended (as opposed to yes/no) questions such as "What is Eeyore doing?" They were also encouraged to expand on their children's answers, suggest alternative possibilities, and pose progressively more challenging questions. The parents were then asked to tape-record their home reading sessions with their children for one month. Meanwhile the researchers found fifteen other children matched in age and language development to the first group and asked their parents to tape-record their home reading sessions too.

Analyses of the tapes indicated that both groups read with their parents equally often—about eight times per week. They also confirmed that the parents who had participated in the training session followed its recommendations. Analyses of the children showed that at the end of the month those whose parents had been trained were eight and one-half months ahead of the others on a test of verbal expression and six months ahead on a vocabulary test—hefty differences for people who are only about thirty months old.

It is not just reading to children that makes the difference, it is enjoying the books with them and reflecting on their form and content. It is developing and supporting the children's curiosity about text and the meanings it conveys. It is encouraging the children to examine the print. It is sometimes starting and always inviting discussions of the meanings of the words and the relationships of the text's ideas to the world beyond the book.[97] And it is showing the children that we value and enjoy reading and that we hope they will too.[98]

Clearly affluence and leisure time bear on the richness of the cognitive experiences that a child might receive. After all, the more one has, the more one can give. Yet, ethnographic research makes clear that poverty is not the major determinant of the literacy preparation a child receives at home.

There are homes that do not encourage preschoolers' literacy skills in the ways described above. These homes are best identified by neither income, social class, parental education, nor race but by the values and styles of the social communities to which they belong. Children from these homes not only miss the literacy coddling of their parents but grow up in a larger environment where reading and writing are peripheral and peripherally valued activities.

---

97. Heath (1983).
98. Wigfield and Asher (1984).

Heath describes one such community in detail. In this community, adults did not make a practice of reading to their children. They did not engage their preschoolers in school-like conversations and learning situations. Their homes were empty of children's books and educational toys.

More than that, the adults generally did not buy or keep books or magazines for their own reading. When they did read, it was most often for some particular, immediate, and limited purpose such as to decipher price tags, checks, bills, telephone dials, clocks, street signs, or house numbers. More extended text tended to be read only if it was both personally relevant and unlikely to be available by any other means (such as television). More specifically, for most of the adults, such extended texts were largely limited to letters, obituaries, employment listings, and local news. And even then, reading was generally treated as social activity: Someone would read a few words; then anyone and everyone would chime in with personal interpretations, embellishments, and related stories and jibes.

Reading by oneself, in contrast,

... was frowned upon, and individuals who did so were accused of being antisocial. Aunt Berta had a son who as a child used to slip away from the cotton field and read under a tree. He is now a grown man with children, and he has obtained a college degree, but the community still tells tales about his peculiar boyhood habits of wanting to go off and read alone. In general, reading alone, unless one is very old and religious, marks an individual as someone who cannot make it socially. [99]

Children in this community are raised to be socially agile and quick with oral language. But it is not the same kind of oral language quickness that is rewarded or even accepted in school. Very quickly, reports Heath, these children fall into a pattern of school failure.[100]

Heath's story is not a fiction; it is about a real community in our own country. Moreover, similar stories have been told about the relationship between community literacy and school success in a number of different countries.[101] Perhaps Heath's case is extreme, but how extreme? Certainly it is not unique in kind.

---

99. Heath (1983, p. 191).

100. Heath (1983).

101. For example, see Clay (1976); Feitelson and Goldstein (1986). Of special interest, Feitelson and Goldstein found that about 60% of the kindergarteners in neighborhoods where children tend to do poorly in school did not own a single book. In contrast, kindergarteners in

Visiting low-income homes in San Diego, William Teale counted and timed the literacy events that occurred in the presence of each of twenty-four preschool children.[102] Using Teale's estimate that the children were awake for roughly thirteen hours per day, the frequency and durations of literacy events during observation periods can be extrapolated to an estimate of total home literacy exposure.

Categorizing the literacy events by their nature, Teale found that only one of the two most frequent classes of events in the children's homes generally involved the children themselves as participants.[103] This category was entitled "literacy for the sake of teaching/learning literacy" and included, for example, helping the child (or someone else) either with such print basics as letter and word identification or with information about the content, nature, or purpose of text.[104] Across all twenty-four children such instructional events occupied roughly 10 minutes per day for a total of 60 hours per year. Events in the category of "storybook time" occupied, on average, less than 2 minutes per day for a total of about 10 hours per year.

These events were, moreover, very unevenly distributed. Storybook reading occurred four or five times per week in three of the twenty-two homes; across the other nineteen, it averaged little more than 5 times per year. For one of the children, storybook reading averaged 26 minutes per day; across the other twenty-three, it averaged less than 20 minutes per month or less than 4 hours per year.

Extrapolating once more, we can (generously) estimate that by the time these children are six and one-half years old and entering the first grade, their home experiences will have prepared them with about 25 hours of storybook experience[105] and

---

neighborhoods where children tend to do well in school owned, on average, more than fifty-four books each.

102. Teale (1986).

103. The categories were: daily living routines; entertainment; school-related (usually of a sibling); work; religion; interpersonal communication; information networks; storybook time; and literacy for the sake of teaching/learning literacy.

104. The only more frequent category was entitled "daily living routines." As an example of what went into this category, the mother of one child was observed to have spent 22 minutes telephoning, with the assistance of the Yellow Pages, to find someone to fix her stove.

105. Assuming that this schedule of storybook reading was regularly maintained from age six months to age six and one-half years.

perhaps 200 hours[106] of general guidance about the form and nature of print.

On entering the first grade, it is patently unlikely that any such children will have learned the alphabet or mastered the skill of phonemic segmentation. Shall we say that is why they will fail? What about the thousands of hours of school-like reading experience they also lack? Is there any chance that their first-grade teacher can make up for that difference in 360 hours of one-on-twenty instruction? And on top of these questions we must ask: Why should such a child even try to catch up? What is school reading about? What is it for that is of any value or application in their own, very real worlds?

In the end, the great value of research on prereaders may lie in the clues it gives us toward determining what the less prepared prereader needs most to learn. For these children, we have not a classroom moment to waste. The evidence strongly suggests that we must help them to develop their awareness of the phonemic composition of words. And we must also teach them the letters of the alphabet and the phonemic significance of each. But what else? The "reading-ready" child enters school with a substantial base of prereading skills and a wealth of experience with and knowledge about the pleasures and functions of text and about literary language and styles.

In this context, the Goodmans' advice is forceful:

Creating A Literate Environment. The classroom and school must become an environment rich in functional use of written language. That means that there must be lots of written language [that] pupils will need and want to read. It does not mean that every chair, table, or window should be labeled. The uses of written language must be both natural and functional. Furthermore, it will be helpful if the kids are involved in creating the literate environment to give them some sense of where written language comes from. Dictating a set of "Rules for Taking Care of Our Hamster" is an example of this kind of participation.

Work, Play, and Living. Play is the child's equivalent of the work world of the adult. In language development, play forms a valuable adjunct to the real-life experiences of children. They can read real letters, but they can also create a classroom post office that delivers letters and notes between class members. . . .

---

106. Assuming that such activities occurred regularly from the age of six months, the proper estimate would be 360 hours; however, it seems more plausible that directive guidance on what print is for, what words say, and how to print letters would begin only gradually, perhaps when the child was two or three. Note, too, that the child was not necessarily personally involved in such activities; to be counted, they only needed to occur in her or his presence.

Read Something. Language, reading included, is always a means and never an end. Reading is best learned when the learners are using it to get something else: a message, a story, or other needed information. Literacy development, therefore, must be integrated with science, social studies, math, arts, and other concerns of the classroom.[107]

But even before children enter grade school, we must become universally committed to developing their appreciation of and familiarity with text. We hug them, we give them treats and good things to eat; we try to teach them to be clean and polite, good natured, thoughtful, and fair. We do these things because it is the best way we know to set them off on happy, healthy lives. We must do as much with reading. In our society, their lives depend on it.

---

107. Goodman and Goodman (1979, p. 151).

III

What Needs to Be Taught?
Hints from Skilled Readers

We have seen that, all else being equal, programs that include some explicit, systematic phonic instruction tend to produce better word reading skills than those that do not. In addition, we have seen that basic letter knowledge and phonemic awareness are the best predictors of early reading achievement. But with respect to any pedagogical implications, we have also seen that the evidence on which these summary statements are based is only vaguely and arguably suggestive. The data reviewed thus far are prescriptive in neither force nor specificity about what ought to be taught or learned in the course of reading instruction.

Our attention now turns to psychological and pedagogical explanations of these findings. More than that, it will be directed to the more fundamental question of the information and activities that may best support reading acquisition.

One promising means of determining what beginning readers ought to be taught is by basing it on models of proficient reading. To this end, the models of proficient reading to which we can turn fall into two classes.

The first class looks at reading from the outside in. What do proficient readers look and feel like they do when they read? How do they appear to behave? To what do they claim to attend? Over time, these outside-in or observational models of skilled readers have strongly influenced the teaching of reading. Yet, as will be discussed in chapter 5 of this section, the instructional guidance they have yielded has often been off base. The bottom line is that the reading process is too complex to be understood from directly observable behaviors.

The second class of models about proficient readers attempts to understand them from the inside out. What kinds of knowledge must any system possess in order to read proficiently? How must that knowledge be organized, and what are the processes involved? Anchored on psychological minutiae and built through laboratory studies and simulations, these models are complex. On the other hand, it is because they have been developed with such analytic care that their instructional implications carry special weight.

The nature of these analytic models will be explored in the remaining chapters of this part. In chapter 6 the focus is on the nature and processing of orthographic knowledge. In chapter 7 it is on the place and roles of context and meaning within the system. In chapter 8, phonological processes are added, and discussion is directed to the operation of the system as a whole.

Although orthographic, semantic, and phonological knowledge and processes are developed in separate chapters, it is imperative to understand that they do not operate separately. In the course of reading, these three types of knowledge and processes are not and cannot be invoked independently of one another. Reading reflects the coordinated, interactive knowledge and behavior of all three.

5

Outside-In Models of Reading: What Skilled Readers Look Like They Do

So highly developed are the word recognition processes of skillful readers that the rate at which they read typically exceeds five words per second.[1] They can perceive whole words as quickly and accurately as single letters,[2] and they can recognize whole phrases as quickly and easily as strings of three or four unrelated letters.[3] Moreover, the speed and accuracy of their reading seems impervious to the mutilation, substitution, or omission of letters within words.[4]

At first blush, such evidence seems to make folly of the very premise of phonic instruction, to make superfluous the alphabetic principle. Against this sort of evidence, the idea that skilled readers recognize words by translating their letters, one by one, into sounds and then blending the sounds together seems preposterous. Even the idea that skilled readers recognize words on the basis of their component letters seems indefensible. Much more plausible, it would seem, is the idea that good readers recognize words holistically, like logograms. Indeed this sort of evidence is prominently cited by advocates of whole word instruction. Earlier in this century, it provided the scientific ballast for wide scale abandonment of phonic approaches to reading.

---

1. Rayner and Pollatsek (1987).
2. Cattell (1885a/1947, 1986).
3. Cattell (1885b/1947).
4. Pillsbury (1897).

Word Shape Cues

The first salient characteristic of skillful readers is that they act as if they recognize words holistically. How might they do so? The most obvious possibility is that they have developed engrams or templates—pattern recognizers, as it were—for familiar words as wholes. The idea that children might profitably be taught to attend to the "envelope" or overall shape of words has been regularly represented in reading curricula.

Although the word-shape hypothesis has long held great appeal, it has just as long received negative empirical support. Way back in 1918, it was demonstrated that skillful readers could recognize even very long words (12–15 letters), exposed for very brief durations (one-tenth of a second), even when the words were printed entirely in capital letters—and when printed in capital letters, the shape of a word is a uniform rectangle, regardless of its identity. Summarizing such evidence in 1938, Robert Woodworth wrote:

> The most effective cue for reading a long word consists of a large share of the letters in the word, seen with fair distinctness for an instant. . . . and in reading words printed in capitals one simply must see the letters because the general shape fails as a cue.[5]

But, we may retort, can you read them as well as when shape cues are present? What about short, familiar words? And even if shape cues do not affect the perceptibility of whole words, mightn't they affect the perceptibility of frequent letter patterns?

To ask these questions experimentally, I compared skillful readers' (Brown University students) ability to report very high frequency four-letter words such as *down, make,* and *look,* both with regularly spelled nonwords (or so-called *pseudowords*) such as *fint, poat,* and *sust,* and with irregularly spelled nonwords such as *epkr, rsai,* and *tgyo.*[6] This comparison was made first with the letters printed in a single, regular lowercase font. It was then made again with each letter of each item printed in one of many different fonts; to ensure that word shape cues would be destroyed, the letters were in both upper and lower case and were selected from eighteen different fonts, ranging from 36 to 60 points in size. In short, the items to be read looked something like this:

---

5. Woodworth (1938, p. 745).
6. Adams (1979a).

*b*ac*k*   s*u*c*E*   G*T*s*i*

When presented with these items across a range of exposure durations, my adult readers were able to recognize the words much more quickly and accurately than either type of nonword and to recognize the regularly spelled nonwords better than the irregularly spelled ones—in fact, this pattern of results has been obtained by a number of researchers.[7] What I additionally found, however, was that this pattern of results was surprisingly unaffected by the distorted typography. The implication is that multiletter shape cues affect the cue value of neither whole, familiar words nor frequent spelling patterns.

Indeed to the extent that the strange typography made any difference, it was in the recognizability of the individual letters. Regardless of the typography or the type of item presented, perception seemed to be based on the recognition of its component letters. Furthermore, the encoding of the letters seemed not to occur in a strictly one-by-one manner but to overlap in time. And regardless of the typography, the difference between the words and the nonwords was that people tended to recognize the words in an all-or-none fashion. It was as though seeing any of the letters of a word brought the rest of them to clarity.

With respect to the word-shape hypothesis, my adult readers reported a particularly interesting illusion: When working with items in the strange typography, they claimed that, except at the very longest exposure durations, all appeared to be printed in a regular, homogeneous, lowercase font. They knew that none of the stimuli were typographically regular. Yet, they insisted that the items "looked" regular at shorter exposure durations. Thus it must have been that phenomenal recognition occurred *after* the actual, physical shapes of the items had somehow been discarded.[8]

From these data we can conclude that skillful readers do not depend on shape information for rapid recognition of familiar words and letter patterns. And, as it turns out, that is just as well. Such information is not very useful anyhow: Even in the legible print and constrained and frequent vocabulary of elementary school textbooks, the overall configurations of words proves a poor means for distinguishing one from another.[9]

---

7. McClelland and Johnston (1977).

8. This illusion has been reported by others including Coltheart and Freeman (1974); McClelland (1976); McConkie (1979); Pillsbury (1897).

9. Groff (1975).

Sophisticated Guessing

Although it does not seem to depend upon shape cues, skilled readers nevertheless demonstrate remarkable speed and facility in recognizing whole familiar words. How might they do so? An obvious possibility is that they are good at guessing.[10]

More specifically, for each of the words with which skilled readers are familiar, there must reside somewhere in memory either its complete spelling or information from which the word's complete spelling could be generated. If that were not true, then they could not write the words they can read.

By ready extension there follows the hypothesis that skilled readers might use such information to short-cut the visual processing involved in reading. If they knew the item they were reading was a real word, they could look at it quite cursorily. They could extract just enough information to have a fair but imperfect idea of the identity of most of its letters. Then, with this partial information in mind, they could figure out the word through process of elimination.[11]

Clearly we, as skillful readers, must be able to do this. Indeed we do do it quite often in deciphering poor handwriting or bad copy. Even so, good guessing seems not to be the principal source of our remarkable facility in recognizing familiar words. Laboratory experiments indicate that we are just plain able to perceive familiar words more quickly and accurately than unfamiliar strings of letters, and that we continue to do so regardless of the constraints, expectations, or rewards offered by experimenters.[12]

---

10. See, e.g., Broadbent (1967).

11. The usefulness of such partial information is owed to partly the fact that English orthography is highly redundant, which is to say that one letter does not follow any other with equal likelihood. As examples, having encountered a *q*, it is a near certainty that the next letter will be a *u*; if the first letter of a word is an *h*, the next must be a vowel; if the first letter of a word is a *t*, the second will probably be an *h*, an *r*, a *w*, or a vowel, and there are substantial differences among the likelihoods of these alternatives as well. By mathematical estimates, if skilled readers fully used such knowledge of likely letter sequences, they would only need to recognize 50 percent of the letters on a page. If they additionally applied their knowledge of how real whole words are spelled and their contextually driven inferences about which words could plausibly occur, they could get by with even fewer. For a discussion of the nature and role of orthographic redundancy in English orthography, see Adams (1981).

12. Adams (1979a); Johnston (1978).

Comprehension as Hypothesis-Testing

It might be argued that the processes that skilled readers use in recognizing isolated words are not necessarily the same as those they will use in reading coherent text. In particular a major difference between skillful readers and beginners is that skillful readers possess a vast, overlearned repertoire of knowledge about written text—not just about spelling but also about the syntax and semantics of language and about the normal flow of discourse. It seems an irresistible hypothesis that the reader might somehow use this information to guide and, thereby, reduce the visual work involved in reading meaningful, connected text.[13]

The process of comprehending involves not just understanding what one has read but anticipating what one will read. To see this, one has only to throw an anomalous word onto the end of an otherwise coherent and predictable ketchup.[14] Furthermore, if skilled readers are constantly and automatically generating predictions about what is to come, it is quite reasonable to expect them to use those predictions. In particular, skilled readers might use their predictions to guide their visual inspection of the text. They might skip, skim, or pore over individual letters only as necessary to confirm or correct their expectations as to its message.

This is an enormously appealing hypothesis. Not only would it seem to explain the remarkable speed and ease with which skillful readers process text, but the premise on which it does so is also compelling: Skilled readers' attention is directed to and by the meaning of the text. Not surprisingly, this hypothesis has captured a great deal of attention in both the instructional and laboratory arenas.

In the instructional arena, it has been strongly advocated by three of the field's most eloquent spokespersons, Frank Smith, Yetta Goodman, and Ken Goodman.[15] The Goodmans, moreover, have translated their theory into some excellent recommendations and activities toward developing children's appreciation of text and thoughtfulness during reading.[16]

---

13. This hypothesis is thoroughly, persuasively, and very readably advocated by Smith (1971, 1973).

14. That is, *sentence*, of course. For a review of research on this tendency, see Levy (1981).

15. For a presentation of their arguments, the reader is referred to Goodman (1972), Smith (1971, 1973), and Smith and Goodman (1971).

16. See Goodman and Watson (1977).

In the research arena, scrutiny of this hypothesis has been greatly advanced in the last decade as enabled by technological advancements that allow us to monitor and analyze readers' eye movements automatically.[17] As it happens, our eyes do not move smoothly across the letters, words, and phrases of a text while reading. Instead the eyes leapfrog through the text, alternately pausing on a word and jumping quickly to another.

The movements themselves take very little time—slightly more or less than one-seventieth of a second, depending on how far the eye must travel. In contrast, the pauses, or fixations, average about one-quarter of a second in duration, but vary greatly depending upon such factors as the difficulty of the text for the reader. The fixations account for roughly 95 percent of our reading time, and this is as it should be: While our eyes are moving between words, visual processing is suppressed; it is while our eyes are still that we acquire visual information from the page and process its meaning. More specifically, given normal text, the eyes can resolve up to three or so letters to the left of their fixation point and about twice that number to the right.

By studying the locations and durations of readers' fixations, psychologists have been able to learn a great deal about the dynamics of connected reading. Of particular relevance in the present context, they have been able to investigate the reality of the hypothesis that skilled readers use contextual constraints to reduce the amount of information they sample from the page. To review these findings more clearly, let us break the issue down into several smaller questions.

1. Do skilled readers skip over any significant number of words in meaningful text?

Not really. Normal adult readers fixate most of the words of a text, regardless of its difficulty. When they do skip, they almost never skip more than one single word, and skipped words tend to be very short. There is thus some tendency to skip over function words (such as *of, in, to, and,* and *the*). Nevertheless many function words and the vast majority of content words receive the reader's direct gaze.[18]

---

17. The recent boom in eye movement studies is owed to computer-mediated tracking, recording, and analytic techniques that have greatly reduced the labor and expense involved. However, the nature of eye movements has been appreciated by psychologists for over one hundred years. Our appreciation—and much of our understanding—of their significance as an indices of cognitive processes may be owed most to the work of Guy Thomas Buswell, undertaken between 1920 and 1945. (See Kolers, 1976).

18. For the most part, readers' decisions about the location to which they will shift their eyes is governed by noncognitive perceptual and motor

2. Do skilled readers spend more time on the "important" words of a text?

Sort of, but apparently not because they are investing more effort in graphemic processing. The strongest determinant of the amount of time for which a reader fixates on a word is its length in letters, and this seems directly due to the visual labor required to recognize it. A second determinant of fixation durations is the word's familiarity, but this effect seems due to the time required to access its meaning. When consideration is shifted from individual words to larger units of text, such as phrases and clauses, people do tend to spend more time gazing at thematically important material than details, but again this effect seems owed, not to closer visual attention, but to nonvisual processes involved in thinking about its meaning.[19]

3. Readers can discriminate letter-level information as much as seven or eight letter positions to the right of where they are fixated.[20] Do they use this information to preprocess the words to come?

Yes, but not in a way that allows them to skip over such words. Readers apparently gain information about the location of the next word in a text and use that information to tell their eyes how far to move.[21] If coupled with contextual cues, the visual information they gain about an upcoming word enables them to recognize the word more quickly when they do fixate it.[22] Still, they seem not to process its identity until it is fixated.[23]

4. Even if skilled readers look at every word, they might not process every word in equal detail. Do skilled readers sample the visual features of predictable text less thoroughly?

No. Regardless of semantic, syntactic, or orthographic predictability, the eye seems to process individual letters. Whether or not graphemic details are consciously noticed, they seem quite reliably to be processed by the eye. Disruptions in adult readers' eye movements indicate that the visual system tends to catch the slightest misspelling, involving a visually similar letter and buried in the very middle (and thus least informative) part of long words that are highly predictable by the preceding context.[24]

---

heuristics (McConkie, Kerr, Reddix, and Zola, 1987). However, some degree of cognitive control must be involved because normal readers are more likely to skip short function words than short content words (Just and Carpenter, 1987).

19. Carpenter and Just (1981). For a broader discussion, see Just and Carpenter (1987).

20. Underwood and McConkie (1985).

21. McConkie, Kerr, Reddix, and Zola (1987).

22. McClelland and O'Regan (1981).

23. McConkie, Zola, Blanchard, and Wolverton (1982); Rayner (1975).

24. McConkie and Zola (1981).

5. Can readers choose or be taught to use context to guide their fixation patterns?

Apparently not. Studies of skimmers and speed readers indicate that they in fact fixate fewer words, but the words they do fixate are not necessarily the most important ones. To the extent that speed readers use any special strategy for choosing the words on which they will fixate, it seems to depend on the words' length in letters. And importantly, while speed readers may be quite good at extracting the gist of a text,[25] their knowledge of details diminishes with the sparseness of their fixations.[26]

In summary, the eye movement research lends little support to the notion that skilled readers use contextual constraints to reduce the visual processing involved in reading. To the contrary, when reading for comprehension, skilled readers tend to look at each individual word and to process its component letters quite thoroughly. The other aspect of skilled readers' performance that is underscored by this research is the remarkable ease and speed with which they achieve such letter-based word recognition, requiring only a few one-hundredths of a second to recognize each additional letter.[27]

Semantic Preprocessing

If skilled readers do not use their active comprehension processes to anticipate the print they are about to see, do they at least use them to anticipate its meaning? That in itself would speed their reading. And if one additionally assumes that semantic and syntactic expectations hasten perceptual processing, it should also speed letter-level processing. Again this is an issue that has received an enormous amount of attention from research psychologists. And again, the answer that is emerging is rather surprising.

Relevant context generally does speed readers' ability to decide whether an item is a word and what it means. For skilled readers, however, it seems to do so only after they have quite thoroughly identified the word—both visually and semantically.[28]

Consider the following two clauses:

---

25. In developing the inferential confidence and abilities to do so is almost surely where the effectiveness of speed reading courses lies.

26. Carver (1985); Just and Carpenter (1987).

27. Just and Carpenter (1987).

28. See Stanovich (1981).

They all *rose*.[29]
John saw several spiders, roaches and *bugs*.[30]

Although the meaning of the last (italicized) word of each of these clauses is thoroughly ambiguous, the context seems automatically to select the correct interpretation. Thus, *rose* means "stood," not "flower"; and *bugs* means "insects or other arthropods," not "surreptitious listening devices." Intuitions aside, when adults are asked to read sentences such as these, they immediately access both meanings of the ambiguous words. Only after both (all) meanings have been activated does context select the appropriate one. Very quickly (tenths of a second) thereafter the activation of the inappropriate one(s) fade away; in contrast, the appropriate meaning hangs around at least until it is integrated into the evolving interpretation of the clause as a whole.[31]

If these findings seem introspectively unlikely, be consoled: It is rare that readers become consciously aware that they have computed multiple meanings when only one fits. Unless the inappropriate meaning is significantly more frequent or otherwise on the mind of the reader, it is highly unlikely that it will gain attention.

Sounding Words Out

If mature readers do not recognize words holistically, even though that's what they look like they do; and if mature readers do not use context to help them recognize words, even though that's what they feel like they do; then we must at least consider the possibility that they recognize words by sounding them out, even if that's not what they look *or* feel like they do.

This hypothesis merits consideration not just through the process of elimination. It is also begged by the developmental literature—by the predictive power of prereaders' phonemic segmentation skills, by the diagnostic power of poor readers' difficulties in decoding pseudowords, and by the relative success of instructional programs that emphasize sounding and blending.

---

29. Tanenhaus, Leiman, and Seidenberg (1979).

30. Swinney (1979).

31. For a review and further evidence on this phenomenon, see Seidenberg, Tanenhaus, Leiman, and Bienkowski (1982).

As it turns out, skilled readers typically do recode printed words into their spoken images.[32] Moreover, they do so with such effortlessness and automaticity that they even do so against their own best interests and intentions not to.[33]

On the other hand, skilled readers' ability to recognize a word does not depend on its phonological translation. Through a variety of clever experimental techniques, psychologists have made clear that skilled readers can recognize a word without generating its phonological image. For skilled readers, the path from print to meaning does not depend on sounding words out.[34]

The fact that skilled readers generally do but do not have to turn print to sound while reading has most often been taken as evidence for a "dual-route" theory of skilled word recognition. Quite simply, this theory holds that skilled readers can recognize printed words through either of two distinct and independent processes: (1) by direct, visual recognition or (2) by applying some set of spelling-to-sound rules to translate the print into an image of its spoken equivalent. For instructional purposes, the invited inference is that it matters little which of these routes we develop first.

Support for the dual-route theory goes beyond laboratory experiments on the ways in which skilled readers recognize real words. In addition—and perhaps most persuasively—the dual-route theory is philosophically compatible with the alphabetic basis of our orthography. Beyond that, it provides a way to explain the remarkable speed and facility with which skilled readers read unfamiliar words and pseudowords. And it gives us a way to understand two clinical syndromes known as "deep" and "surface" dyslexia.[35]

Both of these syndromes are types of acquired dyslexia; they generally pertain to adult patients who have lost the ability to read due to brain damage. Briefly (and with oversimplification), deep dyslexics lose the ability to read aloud unfamiliar words and pseudowords correctly, but they can still recognize and understand the meanings of familiar words. In contrast, surface dyslexics can pronounce regularly spelled nonwords correctly but have great difficulty in recognizing irregularly spelled words and

---

32. For reviews, see Barron (1981a, 1981b, 1986); Patterson and Coltheart (1987).

33. Tannenhaus, Flanigan, and Seidenberg (1980).

34. For a review, see Spoehr (1981).

35. See Coltheart, Patterson, and Marshall (1980); Patterson, Marshall and Coltheart (1985).

suffer confusions between homophones (such as *bury* and *berry*). The dual-route theory handles these syndromes quite neatly: Deep dyslexics have lost the phonological route but kept the direct route; surface dyslexics have lost the direct route but kept the phonological route.

After years of careful and thorough scrutiny, however, dual-route theories are increasingly faulted on both logical and empirical grounds.[36] In the end, cleaner explanations are being offered even for the deep and surface dyslexics.[37] The emerging view is that skillful word recognition involves both direct visual processing and phonological translation. However, these two routes stand, not as independent alternatives to one another, but as synergistic parts of the same process.

Summary

Each of the hypotheses reviewed in this chapter was provoked by the same apparent paradox: Skillful readers' processing of text seems far too fast and efficient to be based on letterwise processing of its print. Similarly each of these hypotheses has been transported to the educational domain with the same well-intentioned motivation: If we could release children from letterwise processing of text, we could expedite their graduation into efficient, skillful readers. Yet the single immutable and nonoptional fact about skillful reading is that it involves relatively complete processing of the individual letters of print.

On reflection, we realize that none of these hypotheses is entirely wrong. The problem is that none of them is sufficiently right. Skillful readers do have and do use knowledge about word patterns, orthographic redundancy, and complete spellings; they can and normally do produce spelling-sound translations; and though they seem not to use it to avoid visual processing, they are highly attuned to the semantic and syntactic constraints of text.

Each of these sorts of knowledge and skills is a real asset for the skilled reader—all the more, if they work in concert with rather than displacement of one another. As we shall see, that is in fact how they do work: The force of the theory and research

---

36. For an all-points attack on these theories, see the article by Humphreys and Evett (1985) and its accompanying "Open Peer Commentary." For a discussion of the shortcomings of dual-route theories in explaining the behaviors and capabilities of beginning readers, see Barron (1986).

37. Patterson, Seidenberg and McClelland (in press).

reviewed in the next chapters is that they operate in parallel. Depending on the situation, they operate in dominance, complement, or deference to each other. Such coordination is possible because they are commonly anchored in the knowledge and processes involved in individual letter recognition.

6

Analyzing the Reading Process: Orthographic Processing

So how do skilled readers recognize words? The answer to this question has been evolving, bit by bit. It is the product of many people, the collective outcome of myriad research studies and theoretical papers. Even so, a grand share of our theoretical progress is owed to James L. McClelland, David E. Rumelhart, and the colleagues with whom they have worked over the last fifteen years. Repeatedly the theoretical frameworks these psychologists have produced have glued together the pieces and thrust the field forward.

The framework I present is primarily derived from a recent paper by Seidenberg and McClelland,[1] which in turn was based largely on earlier theoretical work by Seidenberg, McClelland, and Rumelhart.[2] Within this framework, skillful word reading is held to depend, not just on the appearance or orthography of words, but also on their meanings and pronunciations. The ways in which these three types of information are believed to be represented and processed by the reader will be developed in three separate chapters. Importantly, this discussion is split into three parts for rhetorical purposes only: Perhaps the single most important tenet within this modeling framework is that these three types of information are not processed independently of one another. Skillful reading is the product of the coordinated and highly interactive processing of all three.

Instructional inferences that can be drawn from this framework are summarized at the end of each chapter. In the bodies of the chapters, I concentrate on individual aspects of the theory,

---

1. Seidenberg and McClelland (1989).

2. For presentation of McClelland and Rumelhart's recent work, see their two books (McClelland and Rumelhart, 1986; Rumelhart and McClelland, 1986). An overview of Seidenberg's work is presented in Seidenberg (1985).

discussing their relevance to the larger reading process as well as their logic and justification.

Skilled Readers Look at the Letters and See Letter Patterns

Skillful readers of English thoroughly process the individual letters of words in their texts. The impressive ease and speed with which they do so is owed to the fact that they have learned, at an automatic level, a great deal about the sequences of letters they are likely to see. In essence, because of their vast experience in looking at English words, skillful readers do not recognize the letters of a word independently of one another. Instead, within their memories, the units responsible for recognizing individual letters have become linked to one another by an intermediating set of association units.[3] The strengths of the associations between these units reflect the frequency with which the corresponding letters have been seen together in particular order and combination.[4]

Although the growth of the associations between letters can be emulated on a computer with relatively simple statistical learning rules, their ultimate nature seems quite complex. To be sure, the associations capture the relationships between ordered pairs and triples of letters (called bigrams and trigrams in the research literature), and skillful readers' sensitivity to frequent bigrams and trigrams has been well documented in the

---

3. The importance of these intermediating units is that they expand the processing capabilities of the network. In particular, if the letter units were only linked directly to one another, its capacity to learn about complex patterns would be much more limited (Rumelhart and McClelland, 1986). Nevertheless, to simplify the verbiage, I will generally ignore their existence in descriptions of the letter recognition process.

4. Seidenberg and McClelland have shown that for monosyllabic words, the associative network need not attend to the ordered position of every letter in a word at once. It is instead sufficient that it respond to overlapping sets of ordered triples. As an example, the word MAKE is treated by their model as the set of letter triples [_MA, MAK, AKE, and KE_], where _ symbolizes the empty space at the beginning or end of a word. Seidenberg and McClelland point out that this scheme of ordered "triples" could easily be extended to cover the more complex patterns found in longer, polysyllabic words. In addition, it offers an intuitively pleasing heuristic by which the associative network can learn about the normal order of letters; it implicitly requires only that each individual letter (the center of a triple) be directly sensitive to the frequency with which various letters occur right next to it in sequence, either immediately before or immediately after.

laboratory.[5] However, through experience, the network of associations additionally comes to capture the ordered sequences of letters that represent whole familiar words. And eventually, through their overlapping representation of many individual words, it becomes responsive to frequent spelling patterns independent of the particular word presented.

The basic workings of the letter recognition network are quite simple. When the reader fixates on a word, the visual percepts of the letters directly stimulate its corresponding letter recognition units. The associative links leading from each of visually stimulated letter recognition units then pass along a fraction of their excitation to other letter recognition units.

The nature of the stimulation passed along from a donating to a receiving letter depends on the frequency with which the two letters have occurred together in the reader's lifetime of reading experience. Letters that have often been seen with the donating letter will receive positive excitation; the more often they have been seen together, the stronger this positive excitation will be. Conversely letters that have rarely been seen with the donating letter will receive negative excitation, or inhibition, that is proportionate to the rareness of their co-occurrence.

The perceptual facilitation that may result from this architecture is substantial. It is, moreover, a classic case of the whole working better than the sum of its parts. To see how this system of interletter associations helps the reader, let us consider the perceptual course of a single familiar word: *the*.

As the eye fixates on the word *the*, the letter recognition unit for the letter *t* receives direct, visual stimulation. In English, when the letter *t* occurs in the initial position of a three letter word, the next letter is extremely likely to be an *h*.[6] The strength of the associative link from the *t* to the *h* should therefore be very strong and positive, resulting in considerable excitation of the *h* unit. Thus as a consequence of the reader's having seen the initial *t*, the *h* unit reaches its own seeable level of excitation more quickly than had it been waiting on direct visual excitation alone.

But this description captures only a fraction of the full visual effect. In particular when the reader fixates on the word *the*, all three of its letters lie in full foveal view. Because of this, the

---

5. For example, Juel and Solso (1981); Massaro, Venezky, and Taylor (1979).

6. In fact, *h* is more than fifty times more likely than the next highest contender, which is *o* (Mayzner and Tresselt, 1965).

units corresponding to each of its letters receive direct visual stimulation at once. In turn, all of these units simultaneously receive and pass excitation to each other at once.[7] Thus, not only does the *t* help the *h*, but the *h* helps the *t*, and similarly for the *e*. In this way, the whole word is truly more perceptible than the sum of its parts. Even so, to appreciate this system fully, a couple more points are in order.

First and most important, the entire workings of the system depend squarely on the individual letters that fall within the reader's field of view. Even in the worst case, when the reader is faced with a highly unlikely string of letters, the most disruptive thing that the interletter associations can do against the direct visual information is to cause activation to be dispersed unhelpfully around the letter units.

As an example, suppose that instead of *the*, our reader were presented with the letter string *tqe*. The reader's *h* recognition unit would still receive excitation from the sight of the letters *t* and *e*. However, without any direct, visual stimulation, the *h* is unlikely to be seen; furthermore it will have little energy to pass back to the *t* and the *e*. Meanwhile, the *q* will pass excitation to the *u* unit, which itself will sit in a state of unrequited titillation. Worse still, the presence of a *q* between the *t* and the *e* is highly unlikely—so unlikely, in fact, that the *q* unit is expected both to receive and to pass strong inhibitory signals to the *t* and the *e*.

And what will be the result of all this? It is not that the reader will be unable to see the string. Nor is it that she or he will mistakenly see *the* instead. Even as the individual letters of an unlikely string, such as *tqe*, work against each other, each is simultaneously accruing direct stimulation from the image on the page. Because the direct visual information will eventually win out, the result of the associative interference is only that the perception of the string will take a bit longer; it will need to await full stimulation from the direct visual processing of its letters.[8] As soon as the visual processing is complete, the string of letters will be distinctly and unambiguously seen as it appears on the page.[9]

---

7. In a three letter word, *h* follows *t* roughly ten times more often than it follows any other initial letter; *h* precedes *e* roughly twenty times more often than it precedes any other letter; and *e* follows *h* roughly five times more often than any other letter (Mayzner and Tresselt, 1965).

8. Skilled readers reliably take longer to "see" the letters of irregularly spelled nonwords than those of pseudowords or real words.

9. Interestingly, the theory suggests that if the direct visual processing of a word could somehow be prematurely terminated, then the association

The point is—and this is very important—that the help that skilled readers gain from their knowledge of words and spelling patterns can neither supplant nor overcome the direct visual information available from the actual letters of the fixated string. For both familiar whole words and regularly spelled but novel strings, the skilled reader's recognition is speeded as a result of the interletter associations. However, even the extent to which this can happen depends on the reader's processing each component letter of the string. Only by virtue of being viewed, can any letter of a word productively send or receive excitation to others. Readers can get the system to work for them only by visually processing the individual letters of the words they read.

A second point that should be emphasized is that the inner workings of the skillful reader's letter recognition apparatus are, in actuality, quite baroque. In the examples developed, I considered only associations between adjacent letters. Although I did so to simplify the example, it seems patently incorrect. Both computer simulations and validation studies with skilled readers indicate that the nature of the interletter associations is vastly more complex. The associations bind together multiple letter units in such a way that even words with unusual spelling patterns like *guide, aisle,* and *fugue* are recognized with ease and automaticity—provided that the reader has attended to these words some reasonable number of times in the past. It is by binding together the total, ordered letter sequences corresponding to whole familiar words that the interletter associations give us the sense and appearance of recognizing these strings instantly and holistically.

---

network might indeed override "truth." This prediction is supported by laboratory studies. The key to these studies lies in finding a method to terminate the visual processing of the word prematurely. This cannot be done by simply removing the word or flashing it at the viewer very briefly. The human visual system maintains a virtual image of what it has seen for several tenths of a second after the physical image has been removed from view, more than long enough for a skilled reader to complete the visual processing of a legibly printed word. However, if the brief exposure of the word is immediately followed by a different, letterlike pattern, the new pattern overwrites the image of the word such that no basis for its further visual processing remains. When psychologists have used this procedure with nonword strings, the influence of the letter association network often becomes strikingly apparent. Under these conditions, for example, skilled readers may insist that they saw *youth* when the presented string was *yoth;* they may insist that they saw *tiny,* when the presented string was *iytn;* even more extreme, one subject was absolutely positive that he had clearly and distinctly seen *snow* when the presented string was *uwos* (Adams, 1979a).

The Importance of Automatic Letter Recognition

If the recognition of a word depends on the recognition of its letters, one might reasonably ask how the reader manages to recognize the letters. The answer, it seems, is that letter recognition is the product of a bank of associated feature recognizers. Working with the minutiae of curves, oblique lines, and horizontal bars, the feature recognizers excite and inhibit each other to facilitate letter recognition in much the same way as the letter recognizers do to facilitate word recognition.[10] In this way the skilled reader is able to recognize the component letters of a fixated word automatically, with near instantaneity, and almost regardless of typestyle.

There exists a wealth of evidence that the speed and accuracy with which young readers can recognize individual letters is a critical determinant of their reading proficiency and future growth.[11] Here we have found the reason why this is so. To see this, let us imagine two different young readers. Both have trouble recognizing letters, but they cope with their difficulties in different ways.

First let us imagine a child who basically finesses the difficulty. Maybe the child relies on context; maybe he relies on the few letters of the word that he does know; maybe he uses a combination of context and, say, the first letter of the word. But, one way or another, he avoids worrying about or working on the letters that are not recognized easily. As often as not, this child may succeed in identifying such partially recognized words correctly. Yet even if he does, the experience of having "read" the words will contribute minimally to the growth of his orthographic facility. To the extent that he has ignored their letters, it cannot.

Next let us imagine a second child who has difficulty identifying letters but copes by poring over their every detail. In the long run, this may be a better strategy because it helps to establish the configurations of the individual letters in her memory. Until that happens, however, this child will not only have word recognition difficulties, she will also fail to improve her knowledge of how the words she has studied are spelled. If it takes more than a moment to resolve the visual identities of successive letters in a word, then the stimulation of the visual

---

10. McClelland and Rumelhart (1981).
11. See chapter 4.

recognition unit for the first will have dissipated by the time that the second has been turned on. Unless the units are active at the same time, there is no way for the system to learn about the conjoint occurrence of their letters.

To be sure, the letter recognition effort ascribed to imaginary child number two is extreme. But the logic is extendable: The more time a child takes to identify each successive letter of a word, the less is the concurrent activity of the word as a whole; the more time it takes a child to identify each successive letter of a word, the less she or he can learn from that reading about the spelling of the word as a whole.

What Else Do the Letter Associations Do for Us?

We have seen that the associative links between individual letter recognition units are responsible for the automatic and holistic manner in which we perceive whole, familiar words; for the speed and accuracy with which we can see pseudowords and other well spelled, visually novel strings; and for the relative difficulty and sluggishness with which we perceive irregularly spelled nonwords. Still there are at least two other important services that this network of interletter associations performs for us.

Processing Letter Order

An extremely important role of the interletter associations is that they help us to encode the proper order of the letters we see. Although the visual system is quite fast and accurate at processing item information (such as the identities of the individual letters of a word), it is both slow and sloppy about processing their spatial locations. Indeed, the system's capacity for processing spatial information is too limited to support the speed and accuracy with which skilled readers can recognize words.

According to William Estes, the visual system's primary means of encoding the location of information in the visual field is in terms of the physical, neural channels through which the information is passed from the eye to the brain.[12] However, the density of these input channels is limited. Thus when letters are small and arrayed closely together—as they are in most adult

---

12. Estes (1977).

text, they necessarily share input channels with each other. As a consequence, the reader has no sensory basis for distinguishing their respective locations.

Yet it is not enough to know just the identities of the letters; the identity of a word depends critically on their order as well. There are important differences, for example, between *sprite, stripe, ripest,* and *priest.*

It follows that to read well, skillful readers must somehow reconstruct the order of the letters they see. Furthermore, they must do so quickly, accurately, and effortlessly. Skillful readers almost never make mistakes in reporting the order of the letters in words and pseudowords, nor are they aware of mucking with them. The key to their proficiency lies in the network of interletter associations: As the associations automatically impose the readers' knowledge of whole words and frequent spelling patterns, they automatically rectify the reader's noisy information about letter order.[13]

If this is true, then less skilled readers might be expected to demonstrate difficulties with letter orders. A study of skillful and less skillful high school readers suggests that this is so.[14] Like their skillful peers, the less skilled high school readers in this study almost always reported (wrote down) the order of the letters in real high-frequency words with perfect accuracy. Unlike their skillful peers, however, they frequently misreported the order of the letters of pseudowords (such as *fint, poat,* and *sust*).

It appeared, then, that while these less skilled readers had learned the whole spellings of real, familiar words, their knowledge of spelling patterns that are smaller than words—for example, of letters that are and are not likely to occur next to each other—was weak. This inference was corroborated by asking the students to view and report ordered pairs of letters. Whereas the skilled readers' performance on this task was strongly sensitive to the overall frequency with which the letter pairs appear in printed English, the performance of the less skilled

---

13. Notably the order of the letters in irregularly spelled nonwords is frequently misreported by skilled readers. This may be attributed to two different forces: First, the ordering of the letters is jumbled as it arrives; second, it gets jumbled further through the pressures of the interletter associations to facilitate an orthographically acceptable pattern. As evidence of the latter force, the skilled reader is found to mess up the letter order of irregularly spelled nonwords even more when the nonwords are intermixed with real words than when they are the only type of letter string that is expected (Adams, 1979b; 1981).

14. Adams (1979b).

readers was not. Indeed, the less skilled readers benefited very little from the frequency of a letter pair unless it was a pair that occurs very frequently as the first two letters of English words.[15]

Clearly a weakness in poor readers' knowledge about smaller-than-word spelling patterns could go a long way toward explaining their special difficulty in reading pseudowords. But it also connects with several more mundane dimensions of literacy lore and practice.

First, because of the crudeness with which the visual system processes spatial information, readers with poorly developed knowledge of the spelling patterns of English are likely to have difficulty with the order of the letters they read. They are, that is, unless the print is sufficiently large and spaced out that no two letters will share the same visual input channel. We note the time-honored practice of setting primers in large type.

Second, given smaller print and weak knowledge of English spelling patterns, the only means by which a reader could avoid ordering errors would be to fixate on each word either repeatedly or for relatively prolonged periods of time.[16] We note that for young, poor, and dyslexic readers, the number and duration of fixations tend to be far greater than for skillful readers.[17]

Third, letter reversals and transpositions are frequently cited as characteristic of very poor readers, but they have traditionally been interpreted as evidence of neurological dysfunction or "primary dyslexia." An alternate view is that such behaviors may reflect nothing more than inadequate knowledge of the orthographic structure of English. In keeping with this, the study reported above suggests that letter ordering difficulties are common among below-average high school readers, if less extreme than among dyslexics.

Breaking Words into Syllables

Most of the variation in the frequency of the subword spelling patterns in English is due to the ways in which we spell single syllables. In turn, the ways we spell single syllables are primarily due to the fact that our orthography is fundamentally

---

15. Frederiksen (1978).

16. The assumption that longer fixations are helpful derives from the assumption that visual nystagmus, or the jitter of the fixated eye, causes slight variations in the input channels through which the letter information is shipped to the brain and that such variation could be used for sorting out the letter's relative positions.

17. Just and Carpenter (1987).

alphabetic. Only certain sequences of phonemes are permissible within the spoken syllables of our language, and even among those some occur far more frequently than others.

To the extent that graphemes symbolize phonemes, their sequencing must be expected to mimic this pattern. Reflecting the structure of the languages' spoken syllables, certain strings of graphemes must be expected to occur frequently, infrequently, or not at all, depending on the phonemes they represent. As the important consequence of this, our overlearned knowledge of the spelling patterns of English must automatically break our perceptions of long, written words up into syllables.

Syllabic Cues from Consonants

To see how this is so, let us first consider the consonants. With the exception of a few institutionalized peculiarities of our spelling system (such as *kn___*, *___ght*, *wr___*, and *ch____*), the differences in the likelihoods with which one consonant follows another can be directly traced to the phonological structure of our spoken syllables.

For example, *dr__* is a syllabic form that we can and do use in speech and *dn__* is not. In keeping with this, letter counts of printed English show that a *d* is forty times more likely to be followed by an *r* than by an *n*.[18] By implication, when the reader sees *dr* on a printed page, the *d* and *r* recognition units must pass considerable excitation to each other such that they hang together as a spelling pattern. In contrast, when the two letters are *dn*, they are more likely to pass inhibitory signals to each other and not to evoke any learned spelling pattern.

It is important to note that the letters *d* and *n* do appear in sequence in printed English. However, when they do, they straddle syllable boundaries: e.g.,

> *midnight*
>
> *baldness*
>
> *redness*
>
> *Sidney*

If we look at each of these *dn* words carefully, we notice something else characteristic about their structure: The letter that precedes the *d* in each case also precedes *d* in a number of relatively common English words and syllables; for example:

---

18. Mayzner and Tresselt (1965).

> __id: *did, side*
> __ld: *child, would*
> __ed: *red, wanted.*

And the same is true of the letters that follow the *n*:

> *ni__:* *nice, unit, genius*
> *ne__:* *new, near.*

Thus while the *d* and *n* are expected to inhibit each other, each is also expected to excite and be excited by its neighbor on the other side. Because of the pattern of excitation and inhibition thereby produced, the interletter associations must effectively pull the syllables apart. From each of our example *dn* words, the interletter associations are expected to create two strongly integrated spelling patterns, one for each syllable, with a weaker connection between them: *mid-night, bald-ness, red-ness, Sid-ney.*

This situation is not unique to *dn*. It is generally the case that letter sequences that occur frequently in printed English occur within rather than across syllable boundaries. Sampling English words three to seven letters in length, Mayzner and Tresselt found that across all character positions, *d* was followed by one of only eight letters in more than 90 percent of its occurrences.[19] Each of these eight letters is a common companion of *d* within single syllables. As examples:

> *da: day, damage, sandal*
> *de: dear, delete, under*
> *di: did, divine, predict*
> *do: dog, donor, adore*
> *dr: drop, drastic, address*
> *ds: heads, intends*
> *du: dull, industry*
> *dy: dye, candy*

In the other 8 or 9 percent of *d*'s occurrences, it is followed by one of the other eighteen letters of the alphabet. And, again, almost any of these eighteen unlikely letters can follow *d*, but when it does, it is likely to lie on the opposite side of a syllable boundary: *handball, hardcover, riddle, gadfly*, and so on.

---

19. Mayzner and Tresselt (1965).

Syllabic Cues from Vowels

The vowels also play a vital role in helping the reader to perceive the syllabic structure of long words but in a slightly different way. As we saw, the predictability with which one consonant follows another is largely a reflection of the alphabetic principle. Each consonant symbolizes one or, at worst, a few speech sounds, and the spelling sequences in which the consonant most often occurs in print reflect the articulatory sequences with which those sounds occur in speech. In terms of spelling-to-sound entropy, the worst consonant may be *c*, with at least five distinct behaviors: *city, cat, chair, chrome, suspicious.* Even so, the speech sound that the *c* represents is strongly predictable from the letter next door.

In contrast to the consonants, the alphabetic conduct of the vowels is just plain disorderly. In print, each vowel can represent any of many different sounds or none at all. As an example, compare the sound of the *a* across the words *say, cat, abut, ma, flaw, bean.* There are six different sounds, all fairly common. Furthermore, the particular sound that a vowel is to represent is at best ambiguously marked by its neighbors; compare the sounds of the *a* in *cake–have, bear–hear, lead–lead, nation–nationality, Arab–Arabian, gauge–gauze, naive–waive, guard–guano–dual.*

The vowels are not only the most unruly symbols in our alphabetic script, they are also the most frequent. The six primary vowels account for roughly 39 percent of the character spaces in written English text.[20] The facts that vowels are both so frequent and so phonologically uninformative has provoked two diametrically opposing sets of suggestions about how to improve our orthography.

The first set of suggestions is that we add more vowels to the alphabet. If there were enough vowels that each one could represent a specific and different speech sound, then the majority of the "irregularities" of our spelling system would be gone. This suggestion is embodied in reformed alphabets, such as UNIFON and the i/t/a. In each of these, the number of different vowels is more than tripled.[21]

The second set of suggestions is that the vowels be eliminated from English orthography altogether. This suggestion is embodied in the kinds of instant shorthand courses that are advertised in magazines. It is, moreover, a good enough idea to have warranted

---

20. Mayzner and Tresselt (1965).
21. See Aukerman (1971).

explicit testing. In a laboratory study, Miller and Friedman[22] found that when all of the vowels were removed from printed English texts, adults could reconstruct the texts almost perfectly:

Ths dmnstrts tht txt s stll mr r lss lgble whn th vwls hv bn rmvd.[23]

In contrast, when a similar proportion of randomly selected letters was removed, median reconstruction accuracy was less than 20 percent:[24]

Tis dosts that ex bome elatey ilgi when a pabl ropoon f rndoml lec etters a ben eov. [25]

It may be that vowels contribute minimally to word identification in spoken language as well. It is, after all, the vowel sounds that vary most noticeably across dialects. As another boost for this point of view, try reading the first sentence of this paragraph aloud while uniformly substituting each of the vowels with a schwa sound ("uh"). Although it is surprisingly hard to do, the sentence remains more or less comprehensible.

If we did eliminate vowels in our orthography, our written texts would become 39 percent shorter in character spaces. More important, perhaps, we would do away with the majority of English spelling-to-sound irregularities and have much less to worry and argue about with respect to how to teach letter-to-sound translations. We might also make phonic instruction easier. After all, the task of splitting vowels away from consonants is among the most difficult of phonemic segmentation skills.[26] Furthermore, studies of children's invented spellings indicate that the vowels are the last of the phonemic entities to be perceived.[27]

Is it really reasonable to contemplate so doing? I think not:

Th prps f th dmstrtn s t shw tht th trnsprnc f th nttn dcrss prcptsl whn th txt s comprsd f rltvl lng r nfrqnt wds nd bcms vrtll mpntrbl f wds r nt smntcll r sntctcll prmd, vz.

prcpn,

---

22. Miller and Friedman (1957).

23. Translation: This demonstrates that text is still more or less legible when the vowels have been removed.

24. Miller and Friedman (1957).

25. Translation: This demonstrates that text becomes relatively illegible when a comparable proportion of randomly selected letters has been removed.

26. Gleitman and Rozin (1977); Liberman, I., Shankweller, Liberman, A., Fowler, and Fischer (1977); Treiman (1988b, in press).

27. Ehri (1986).

swd,

dmtr,

trnp,

tmlg,

nnsns. [28]

And so we are left asking what vowels are good for. As it happens, a certain variety of vowel sounds is essential in spoken language, though for a nonintuitive reason: It allows listeners to estimate the size of a speaker's vocal tract, which is necessary for converting acoustical signals into phonemic information.[29] In addition, whether speaking or writing, vowels provide the critical distinction between such words as *bit* and *bat* or *bare* and *bore*.

For reading, however, the most important function of vowels may be orthogonal to their phonemic significance.[30] Their primary function may instead be that of promoting the syllable as a perceptual unit:

Th* p*rp*s* *f th*s d*m*nstr*t**n *s t* sh*w th*t th* *mp*rt*nc* *f v*w*ls c*nn*t b* f*ll* *xpl**n*d *n t*rms *f th**r ph*n*m*c s*gn*f*c*nc*, f*r th* l*g*b*l*t* *f th* t*xt *s *lm*st c*mpl*t*l* r*c*v*r*d *f th* v*w*ls *r* n*t *m*tt*d b*t r*pl*c*d w*th s*m* ph*n*m*c*ll* n*ns*gn*f*c*nt s*mb*l — *nd th*s *s tr** *v*n f*r l*ng, *nfr*q**nt, *nd c*nt*xt**ll* *npr*d*ct*bl* w*rds, v*z.,

d*ff*d*l

h*rps*ch*rd

*g*c*ntr*c

r*ct*ngl*

*ll*str*t**n

c*mpr*h*ns**n [31]

---

28. Translation: The purpose of this demonstration is to show that the transparency of the notation decreases precipitously when the text is comprised of relatively long or infrequent words and becomes virtually inpenetrable if words are not semantically or syntactically primed, viz. porcupine, seaweed, odometer, turnip, etymology, nonsense.

29. Gerstman (1967).

30. Adams (1981).

31. Translation: The purpose of this demonstration is to show that the importance of vowels cannot be fully explained in terms of their phonemic significance, for the legibility of the text is almost completely recovered if the vowels are not omitted but replaced with some phonemically nonsignificant symbol—and this is true even for long, infrequent, and contextually unpredictable words, viz., daffodil, harpsichord, egocentric, rectangle, illustration, comprehension.

More specifically, there is one way in which the vowels in our written language are completely obedient to the structure of our spoken language: Just as every spoken syllable must be vocalized, there must be at least one vowel in every written syllable. Because of this, the likelihood that any given consonant in English text will be followed by a vowel is very high. Furthermore, because there are so few vowels in the English alphabet, the likelihood that any given consonant will be followed by any particular vowel is also very high.[32]

The implication is that vowels must pull their adjacent consonants into tightly associated activation patterns. Furthermore, for polysyllabic words, each vowel must pull its surrounding consonants toward itself at the same time as the unlikely letter pairs that straddle the syllable boundaries are pushing them away.

All Together: Consonants, Vowels, and Spelling Patterns

The implication of this analysis is that because of their overlearned knowledge of frequent spelling patterns, skilled readers break long words down into syllabic units. They do so automatically and in the very course of perceiving them.

At the nucleus of each syllabic unit will be its vowel(s), strongly attracting the consonant that precedes it and ready to accept the one that follows.[33] When two vowels sit on either side of a single consonant, the consonant is most likely to attach itself to the vowel that follows, and this is by direct extension of the foregoing analysis. Whereas the letter that follows any consonant is highly likely to be a vowel, vowels are relatively indifferent as to what letters they may precede. In general, then, the associative link between a consonant-vowel pair is expected to be quite strong, while the link between a vowel-consonant pair is expected to be of intermediate value. Operationally this means that such words as *preface* and *cumulate* are likely to be processed

---

32. Mayzner and Tresselt (1965).

33. Whereas the next letter after any consonant is very likely to be a vowel, vowels are relatively indifferent as to what letters they may precede. In general, then, the associative link between a consonant-vowel pair is expected to be quite strong, while the link between a vowel-consonant is expected to be of intermediate value. Operationally, what this means is that such words as *preface* and *cumulate* are likely to be processed as *pre-face* and *cu-mu-late* rather than, say, *pref-ace* and *cum-ul-ate*.

as *pre-face* and *cu-mu-late* rather than, say, *pref-ace* and *cum-ul-ate*.[34]

In view of this, the following instructions from a sixteenth-century English speller are quite interesting:

> Teache the childe in spelling his syllabes, to leaue the consonant, that commeth before a vowell to the syllabe following, exãple: in the word, *manifold,* Let him spell for the first syllabe *m* and *a* onely, for he may not take *n* vnto them, because, *i* the vowel followeth: to the second syllabe he must take but *n* and *i,* for *f* hath *o* the vowell next after him. To the third syllabe he must take the foure letters that remaine, *f, o, l,* and *d.* In this order than let him spell it, saying: *m, a, ma: n, i, ni: f, o, l, d, fold, manifold.* [35]

When the vowels surround two or more consonants, which way the consonants go depends most of all on the bonds between themselves. Consonants that belong to frequent consonant blends and digraphs tend to move together, while less likely pairs tend to split apart. Thus *napkin, thoughtful, ketchup,* and *double* are expected to be parsed as *nap-kin, thought-ful, ket-chup,* and *dou-ble.*

Finally, on top of and potentially overpowering the attractions between individual letters are the bonds corresponding to the reader's familiarity with the spellings of whole words and syllables. It is due to their contribution that the skilled reader reads such words as *preamble, fathead, disheartening,* and *retroactive* correctly instead of as *pream-ble, fa-thead, di-shear-te-ning,* and *re-troac-tive.*

Still, to make this whole system work properly, one more note must be added: We can specify no fixed and final set of letter-based rules about how the mind will divide a syllable. We cannot take any given letter string, say, *par* and proclaim it to be a pattern that the mind will categorically treat as a syllabic unit. Sometimes it will—*par-tial, par-take*—and sometimes it will not—*part-ly, pa-rade.* Whether it does depends on the larger orthographic context in which it occurs.

More generally, the consonants that any vowel nucleus attracts must be a matter of competition. The letters will be pulled together or apart depending on the *relative* strengths of the interletter, spelling pattern, or word-level associations between them. As is illustrated by the *partial / partake / partly / parade* example, the strongest patterns of mutual attractiveness and

---

34. Consistent with this, listen to the way in which speakers tend to split the word *another,* as in "a whole nother. . . ."

35. Clements (1587, cited in Balmuth, 1982, pp. 162–163).

interfacilitation will win out, even over competitors that would have won in some other situation.[36]

Seeing Syllables

Having asserted that skilled readers automatically break long words down into syllables in the course of perceiving them, it is appropriate to ask about the proof that this is so. Here the best evidence comes from D. J. K. Mewhort, who in his laboratory and with a number of colleagues has been systematically investigating this issue over the last twenty years.[37] Mewhort's cumulative results inarguably indicate that skilled readers parse long words into syllabic units during visual scanning, not afterward. Furthermore, they do so in the course of identifying the individual letters of a word, not afterward. They do so automatically; the process is not under conscious control. They do so for pseudowords as well as real words. And their ability to perceive longer letter strings depends on such instantaneous syllable parsing. We will examine just a sample of this work to illustrate its compellingness.

If each of the letters of a polysyllabic word is presented one by one, left to right, and in its correct position but very, very briefly (one two-hundredth of a second), skilled readers' ability to recognize the word depends strongly on the duration of the dark interval between letters. When one letter comes on immediately as the preceding one goes off, the word is recognized. However, when the time between the offset of one letter and the onset of the next is lengthened to just a few hundredths of a second, recognition drops precipitously. This delay is too long to allow the percepts of the letters to peak simultaneously; because of that, the associative linkages between them cannot do their job.[38]

---

36. Consistent with this, Seidenberg and McClelland (1989) argue persuasively that there are no such things as "whole word units" in our heads. Instead even our recognition of whole words is the product of activity distributed across the letter recognition machinery. For very familiar words, the whole pattern of activity has occurred so many times that it reinforces itself as a whole, allowing us to recognize the words holistically. For less and less familiar words, this is less and less true, such that the difference between our responses to words and well-spelled pseudowords is a matter of degree rather than kind. Put another way, words are visually nothing more than "superfamiliar pseudowords" (Mewhort and Campbell, 1981).

37. A review of this work is presented in Mewhort and Campbell (1981).

38. This is analogous to the word recognition difficulties that result from slow letter recognition skills.

At the same time, a few hundredths of a second is also too short to allow the reader to process the letters one at a time. If the delay is lengthened to a quarter of a second—so that the reader has a chance of processing the letters one at a time—performance begins to recover.[39]

In contrast, when polysyllabic words are arrayed syllable by syllable rather than letter by letter, the words are accurately recognized regardless of the length of the dead interval between the pieces. However, when the words are instead presented in nonsyllabic groups of letters (e.g., *ind-ust-ry* and *sp-eci-fic*), performance is relatively poor except when there is no delay between presentation of letter groups.[40]

Skilled readers' ability to recognize a long word depends on whether they can chunk it into syllables in the course of perceiving it. Moreover, their ability to chunk a word into syllables in the course of perceiving it, depends on the nearly simultaneous activation of the component letters of each syllable.[41] The manner in which this capacity depends on the temporal characteristics of the display is thus wholly consistent with the supposed dynamics of the interletter association network: Syllables cohere because their letters mutually reinforce each other when simultaneously perceived.

Learning about Likely and Unlikely Letter Sequences

There is relatively little literature comparing skilled and less skilled readers' sensitivity to likely and unlikely spelling patterns. Even so, that which does exist is consistent with the idea that it is an important and methodically acquired capacity among normal readers and a key deficit among slower readers.

First, developmental investigations of this capacity show that it accrues in a gradual but systematic fashion.[42] Kindergarten and first-grade readers are generally insensitive to whether the spellings of the strings they see are regular. Whether reading words, pseudowords, or nonwords, they tend to process them in a

---

39. Mewhort (1974).

40. Mewhort and Beal (1977).

41. For additional evidence that adult readers process written words in syllabic units, see Seidenberg (1987).

42. For a review, see Barron (1981).

simple letter-by-letter manner[43] and are unable to distinguish between which of the strings are "wordlike" and which are not.[44]

For normal readers, such sensitivity begins to develop toward the end of first grade. At this point, given three-letter strings (but not four-letter strings),[45] they begin to show a distinct advantage for pronounceable consonant-vowel-consonant sequences such as *rop* over irregular and unpronounceable nonwords such as *rjp*.[46] Over the course of second grade, normal readers (but not poor readers) additionally become sensitive to the consonant pairs that frequently occur at the beginnings of words, such as *bl-* and *pr-*.[47]

Furthermore, even given relatively long (seven-letter) strings, the speed with which normal second graders can decide whether or not it is a real word proves sensitive to the frequency of the spelling patterns. Nonword decisions are slowed by both the likelihood of the individual consonant pairs in the strings (e.g., *shrnld* is slower to be rejected than *hgjcpl*) and the presence or absence of vowels (e.g., *turild* is slower to be rejected than *shrnld*). Moreover—and perhaps most interestingly—the mere presence of one or more vowels is enough to slow their rejection of even an otherwise unlikely string (e.g., *kugafp*, *vbejic*, and *gsecfp* are slower to be rejected than *dtscfk*, etc.).[48]

By the time normal readers are in the fourth grade, the presence of a vowel slows their ability to decide that a string is not a word only if it appears in likely surroundings in the string (e.g., *clasty* and *grilts* but not *kigafp* and *vbejic*).[49] By that time, the children generally exhibit the adult pattern of pseudo-word/nonword differences, even for long strings.[50] In addition, it is during the fourth grade that the adult ability to perceive syllables as units emerges; at this point, normal readers begin to perceive syllables more quickly and accurately than single letters.[51]

---

43. Juola, Schadler, Chabot, and McCaughey (1978); Lefton and Spragins (1974); McCaughey, Juola, Schadler, and Ward (1980).

44. Lefton, Spragins, and Byrnes (1973); Rosinski and Wheeler (1972).

45. This is compatible with Seidenberg and McClelland's (1989) assumption that the orthographic processor works first with sets of ordered letter triples.

46. Doehring (1976); Gibson, Osser, and Pick (1963); Thomas (1968).

47. Santa (1976–77).

48. Henderson and Chard (1980).

49. Henderson and Chard (1980).

50. Gibson, Osser, and Pick (1963); Lefton and Spragins (1974).

51. Friedrich, Schadler, and Juola (1979).

The literature on differences between good and poor readers' sensitivity to regular spelling patterns is even more limited than that on its normal development, but the studies that exist suggest that the differences are real and significant. A number of investigators have shown that, when processing nonwords, poor readers gain significantly less help from regular spelling patterns or likely letter pairs than do good readers.[52] Although these results are consistent with the idea that low sensitivity to spelling patterns causes reading difficulty, they are a bit too abstract to confirm it.

More direct evidence is available from a study conducted by a team at Bolt, Beranek, & Newman Inc.[53] We administered a battery of decoding tasks to above- and below-average readers in the second through fifth grades.[54] Our goal was to discover particular subskills that might explain the poor readers' difficulties, and sensitivity to spelling patterns was among the primary hypotheses considered.

For the first task in their battery, the children were timed as they read aloud each of ten lists of words and pseudowords. Among these lists was one that consisted of long, single-syllable pseudowords (e.g., *splange, trolves, brength*) and another that consisted of two-syllable pseudowords of the same length (e.g., *cribble, frastic, ruction*). We had hypothesized that, until children had acquired the skills enabling automatic recognition of syllable boundaries, these two lists would be of comparable difficulty. After that point, however, we expected the two-syllable items to be significantly easier than the single-syllable items; after all, the two-syllable items would thenceforth resolve into pairs of simple, familiar syllables.

In keeping with our expectations, we found that these two lists were of comparable difficulty for all of the younger readers. For the above-average readers, the two-syllable pseudowords became significantly easier than the long, single-syllable pseudowords in the fourth grade—which is consistent with the developmental studies reported. For the below-average readers, however, this did not happen until the fifth grade.

---

52. Frederiksen (1978); Mason (1975); Massaro and Taylor (1980).

53. Adams et al. (1980).

54. "Above-average" readers were those who scored in the fifth stanine or above on both the Gates-McGinnitie and Stanford reading comprehension test; "below-average" readers were those who scored within or below the fourth stanine on both tests. Essentially the same pattern of results was obtained in both an urban and a suburban school system.

More interestingly, regardless of when this shift appeared, it coincided with a number of other substantial changes in the children's list reading ability. Suddenly the children exhibited a leap in the speed and accuracy with which they could read both two syllable real words (e.g., *pocket, monkey*) and longer polysyllabic real words (e.g., *refrigerator, comfortable, helicopter*). In addition, it was only after this shift that they showed any appreciable ability to read polysyllabic pseudowords at all (e.g., *unberritate, prolativity, indection*).

To assess the differences in these children's sensitivity to orthographic patterns further, we gave them two additional tasks. Each was designed to simulate the orthographic conditions that we believed to prompt syllabification but in a way that better controlled for children's familiarity with the strings to be parsed.

In the first, the children were timed as they read aloud very frequent four-letter words that were embedded in a string of unrelated consonants:

wgfbackvcb

qsroadhnpm

lhcpmakezr

As with the lists, performance improved dramatically at the fourth-grade level for the above-average readers and the fifth-grade level for the below-average readers. But more, differences between the above- and below-average readers were enormous. It was not until the fifth grade that the performance of the below-average readers exceeded that of the above-average second graders.

In the second task, the children were asked to read aloud a series of spaceless sentences. Some of these sentences were meaningful:

thatboywentlast

and some of them were not:

whatbuywantland

Again there were big differences in the performance of the above- and below-average readers and, again, on the meaningless strings, it was not until fifth grade that the performance of the below-average readers met that of the above-average second graders.

Beyond all of these studies is the familiar classroom observation that poor readers of all ages have special difficulty with long words.[55] When I first observed this phenomenon, it struck me as truly paradoxical. How could a reader have no trouble with a single-syllable word like *thought* or even a pseudoword like *crought* but be entirely unwilling or able to read a long word like *information?* Most of the syllables of long, polysyllabic words, I observed, are orthographically regular bigrams and trigrams; the only significant exceptions to this rule are extremely frequent suffixes as in *in-for-ma-tion*. It seemed to me that if a child could conquer the long, orthographically odd syllables of items like *crought*, then the short, regular ones in words like *information* ought to be easy.

At the time I felt the tendency of poor readers to block on long words was a matter of confidence. Others have attributed it to problems of vocabulary, but poor readers even have trouble with very high frequency long words.[56] I now believe, in keeping with the theme of this section, that poor readers' difficulties with long words may be due most of all to poorly developed knowledge of spelling patterns.

Lest any reader is still unconvinced of the importance of being able to parse long words into syllables, consider figure 6.1.[57] The figure gives a blow-by-blow account of a fifth grade reader's attempt to read the word *reverence*. After fifty-one seconds of trying, this child finally reaches the end of the word but still doesn't succeed in identifying it. How could she? Anyone who tried to identify a long word by sounding out its individual letters would run out of memory space long before she or he was done.

For the skilled reader, the perception of words and syllables is effortlessly and automatically driven by the associative connections among letters in their memories. Unless unskilled readers are wholly familiar with the identities of individual letters and encouraged to attend to the spellings of words, they may not develop the orthographic knowledge on which this system depends.

---

55. For laboratory corroboration of such observations, see Just and Carpenter (1987) and Samuels, LaBerge, and Bremer (1978).

56. Adams et al. (1980).

57. From Farnham-Diggory (1985, p. 145; 1984, p. 67).

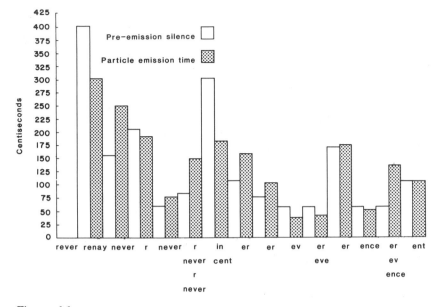

Figure 6.1
Laura reading the word *reverence.*

Summary and Instructional Implications

When the skilled reader fixates on a word, each individual letter activates its own recognition unit in the reader's memory. These directly activated units, in turn, send activation to each other, with the result that the associations between them are strengthened as the automatic consequence of having looked at the word. Over time, as the reader encounters more and more words, the associations between the letter units will ultimately come to reflect the more general orthographic structure of the printed language.

Strong associations develop between the units representing sequences and patterns of letters that have been seen frequently. As a result, any word composed of these sequences and patterns is perceived more or less holistically: Because of the learned associative linkages, every one of its component letters effectively primes and reinforces the perception of every other. In contrast, weak or inhibitory associations develop between letters that have rarely occurred together. As a result, long words are automatically broken into syllables: Because the letter sequences within syllables are quite predictable, the perception of the syllable as a whole coheres; because the sequences of letters that occur between syllables are unpredictable, the percept of the word becomes somewhat dissociated at the syllable boundaries.

In short, then, although the skillful reader's Orthographic processor requires sequences of individual letters as input, it effectively perceives whole words and syllables. In reverse, however, the ability to perceive words and syllables as wholes evolves only through complete and repeated attention to sequences of individual letters. With concern toward how best to develop word recognition skills, the theory thus carries several strong implications.

First, it is extremely important that young readers be able to recognize individual letters accurately before word recognition instruction begins. Individual letters are the input to the network. If a child cannot recognize a letter, it will not activate its appropriate unit within the network. Unless the letter activates its appropriate unit within the network, it cannot share excitation with the other letters of the word under study. Unless the letter shares excitation with the other letters of the word under study, the associations between them cannot be strengthened. Only through the strengthening of these associations can word study enhance word recognition capacity.

Second, for the development of word recognition proficiency to proceed at its optimal rate, young readers must be able to recognize individual letters relatively quickly. The association between one letter and another is strengthened or created only when both recognition units are active at the same time. If the child spends any measurable amount of time recognizing the second letter in a word, then, by the time it is resolved, the activation of the first will have uselessly dwindled away. Difficulties in individual letter recognition thus subtract directly from any potential profit to be gained from studying whole words.

Third, for immature readers—readers who have not yet acquired a set of associations to match the print before them, it is important not just that they look at the word before them but that they attend carefully to its complete ordered sequence of letters.

Toward hastening the development and refinement of the letter recognition network, students should be engaged in activities that encourage attention to the ordered, letter-by-letter structure of the syllables and words they are to read. (Remember that the order of the letters in a sequence is poorly perceived until the sequence becomes familiar.) Many of the most common practices of reading programs—including synthetic phonics, writing, exercise with frequent blends and digraphs, and practice with word families—seem ideally suited to this end.

In this context, the allure of phonics, or the exercise of discovering a word by sounding out its spelling, is that it inherently forces the child to attend to each and every letter of the word, in left-to-right order. The motivation for its recommendation has little to do with the value or importance of actually sounding the word out.[58] It is, from this perspective, merely a gimmick to focus the child's attention on its spelling. Note too that phonic activities that direct the child's attention to individual letters rather than sequences of letters do not seem useful to this end.

The value of having the children write and spell is also strongly reinforced. It has been shown that the act of writing newly learned words results in a significant strengthening of their perceptual integrity in recognition.[59] This is surely a factor underlying the documented advantages of programs that emphasize writing and spelling activities.[60] In this vein, it is interesting to note that except for their general emphasis on writing and spelling, these programs differ markedly from each other in method and philosophy. They include, for example, such diverse approaches as i/t/a, language experience, the phonic/linguistic method,[61] and the Spalding method.[62]

---

58. However, as will become clear in the chapters that follow, both of the attendant activities of translating its letters to sounds and searching for its semantic identity should significantly enhance the orthographic learning that would come from the left-to-right study of its letters alone.

59. Whittlesea (1987).

60. Bond and Dykstra (1967).

61. The relation between the success of the i/t/a, language experience, and phonic/linguistic approaches and their emphasis on writing and spelling is discussed in Bond and Dykstra (1967). By way of reminder, the primary goal of the i/t/a curriculum is to enhance the children's awareness and acquisition of phonics by developing reading and writing through a reformed, phonemically regularized alphabet. The phonic/linguistic approach generally eschews exercise in blending and in individual letter-to-sound correspondents, seeking to instill the alphabetic principle through induction, by use of regularly spelled words and word families. Under the language experience approach, the emphasis is on the communicative and expressive functions of written language; reading skills are developed as a consequence thereof by encouraging children to dictate and, later, to write their own stories and experiences.

62. Spalding and Spalding (1986). For a review of the classroom effectiveness of this program, see Aukerman (1984).

By writing and spelling, I mean writing and spelling of whole words, as when a child composes her or his own story, writes to dictation, or even copies words over.[63] Workbook exercises that have the child fill the appropriate letter in a blank do not serve the same purpose because they do not force the child's attention to the spelling patterns of the words as wholes.

Exercise on frequent blends and digraphs such as *bl, st, pr, th, sh,* and *ch* also seem worthwhile. As attention to such letter groups serves to strengthen the associations among their letters in memory, it should hasten the children's ability to perceive such strings quickly and holistically.[64] In the same spirit, instruction on frequent prefixes and suffixes may similarly be helpful for the reader who is sufficiently advanced to be working on polysyllabic words.

Word families, or phonograms, are lists of words that by design share some significant fragment of their spelling and sound pattern, such as *bill, fill, pill, will, hill.* Within the present context, exercise with word families fulfills the desirable goal of reinforcing the integrity of frequent spelling patterns even as they participate in different words. For both skillful readers and computer simulations of skillful readers, the orthographic representations of words with such overlapping spelling patterns are tightly interrelated in memory.[65]

The theory suggests further that children be discouraged from skipping or glossing over words that are difficult for them. When they encounter a word that is hard to read, they should take the time to study it. They should look carefully at its spelling and sound out its pronunciation; then they should repeat this process

---

63. It is worth taking the time to watch individual students copying words. Some persist in looking at the word to be copied, writing down one single letter and then looking back for the next single letter. With respect to orthographic learning, however, the benefits of copying are expected to come from looking at the text to be copied, remembering a whole word or syllable, and writing that down before looking back to check one's spelling or to get the next word or syllable to be copied. Sometimes letter-by-letter copying seems to be nothing more than a habit, as though it simply has not occurred to the child to go for whole words or syllables. In these cases, the problem may be fully remedied by providing a little guidance on the method and increased efficiency of treating the to-be-copied materials in a word-by-word or syllable-by-syllable manner.

64. In addition, the ability to break such blended letters apart from one another is among the more difficult hurdles in phonemic segmentation. Direct instruction in blending may help to develop essential dimensions of phonemic awareness as well as appropriate orthographic sensitivities.

65. See Seidenberg and McClelland (1989).

until they can read off the word with something close to normal ease and speed. Happily, for children who are normal readers, this level is reached with only a couple encounters of the word, even if the encounters are separated by several days.[66]

Importantly, such focused word study during corrected reading should be relatively infrequent in practice. Intuitions and research concur that students' reading abilities are best advanced by giving them texts in which the vast majority of words are manageable.[67] When students are stumbling on too many words, the best solution is no longer to ask them to reread; it is to give them an easier text. Note further that the objective here is not to force children to study and reread difficult words while you are watching; it is to help them develop the inclination to study and reread words when they are reading by themselves.

These qualifications notwithstanding, repeated readings of difficult words and passages result in marked improvements in children's speed, accuracy, and expression during oral reading and, most important, in their comprehension.[68] In view of this, we should choose texts that are worth rereading and, whenever it seems worthwhile, we should have the children reread them.

In view of the importance of syllabification skills, one might infer that they too ought to be taught. Is this inference supportable? Opponents of syllabification training have argued that it is circularly unproductive. In order to break a word down into syllables, they argue, the reader must first sound the word out. But being able to sound the word out was the goal of breaking it into syllables in the first place. Consistent with this argument, various efforts to teach children how to divide words into syllables have generally produced little measurable improvement either in children's ability to divide new, untrained words into syllables or in their overall vocabulary and reading comprehension scores.[69]

As exceptions, several recent studies have obtained improvements in children's ability to pronounce two-syllable words by training them to compare each syllable to known one-syllable words (e.g., *problem—rob, them*).[70] Although these children did not become better at syllabifying words to dictionary specifications, a caution is in order as to the value of this

---

66. Reitsma (1983).

67. See Rosenshine and Stevens (1984).

68. Dahl and Samuels (1979); Herman (1985); Samuels (1985).

69. See Johnson and Bauman (1984).

70. Cunningham (1979).

measure. The word divisions that appear in American dictionaries are largely due to the pronouncements of one man, Noah Webster. Although his decisions were based on his own best judgments, they may or may not correspond to the ways in which an able reader breaks words up. There is, moreover, no obvious instructional purpose in worrying about whether or not they do.[71]

Another obvious approach to teaching children how to syllabify is to teach them rules about the letter pairs that cannot straddle syllable boundaries. Given our analysis of why and how skillful readers perceive syllables, however, this approach does not seem promising.

First, the forces that attract a letter into one syllabic unit or another are relative. The members of any given letter pair may join the same syllable as each other or split into different ones depending on the larger orthographic context in which they occur. The definitive property of a syllable boundary is not how unlikely its bounding letter pair is; it is how unlikely it is compared to the other pairs in the vicinity. To make the point another way, what nature of letter-level rules could one possibly teach children that would allow them, automatically and accurately, to syllabify both members of each of these pairs:

cowlneck, cowlick

cornice, corncob

handsome, handsbreadth

costly, costive.

Not only does the idea of drilling children on unlikely letter pairs have limited positive appeal, it may also be a counterproductive endeavor from the start. To drill such pairs one must ask the children to attend to them and work with them repeatedly. Yet, the syllabification skills of proficient readers seem to derive from the fact that syllable boundaries fall across letter pairs that have *not* been seen or attended to very often.

Overall, the best instructional strategy for orthographic development is to induce children to focus on the likely sequences that comprise syllables, words, and frequent blends and digraphs. As the children become familiar with these spelling patterns, their ability to syllabify will naturally emerge along with the

---

71. For discussions of Noah Webster's influence on the spelling and syllabification of American English, see Balmuth (1982) and Venezky (1980).

automaticity with which they will recognize the ordered spellings of single syllables. Beyond that, the strongest implication of the theory toward developing solid word recognition skills is that children should read lots and often.

7

Analyzing the Reading Process: Use and Uses of Meaning

Obviously the recognition of a printed pattern is not an end in itself for the reader. Where does meaning enter in? For skilled readers it seems that meaning, too, is largely the product of effortless and automated activities. Moreover, the nature of the relationships between orthographic and semantic processing also holds a number of implications with respect to the skills that young readers must develop.

The Relationship between Meaning and Orthography

Figure 7.1 shows the relation between the readers' knowledge and processing of orthography, word meaning, and the broader context in which a word occurs.[1] The ellipse labeled "Orthographic processor" contains all of the individual letter recognition units and the associative linkages between them. Note that the Orthographic processor is the only one that receives input directly from the printed page: The first important point of the figure is that, when reading, it is visual, orthographic processing that comes first and that causes the system to kick in.

The second important aspect of this figure is that between the Orthographic and Meaning processors, there are arrows leading in both directions. As the visual image of a string begins to take form, it sends excitatory signals to units representing word meanings. And as the visual information begins to resolve itself and settle in on fewer and fewer meaning candidates, they reciprocally send excitation back to the letter patterns they require.

---

1. Seidenberg and McClelland (1989).

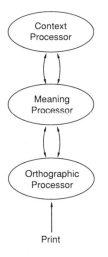

Figure 7.1
The relation of the Orthographic processor to the meaning and context processor.

The third important aspect of this figure is that the Meaning processor is connected in both directions to the Context processor. These connections serve to facilitate the perception of contextually appropriate words and to select a contextually appropriate interpretation of words whose meanings are ambiguous or diffuse. Let us consider each of these phenomena in turn: first, contextual facilitation and then meaning selection.

The Context Processor

The Context processor is in charge of constructing a coherent, ongoing interpretation of the text. As it does so, it sends excitation to units in the Meaning processor according to their compatibility with its expectations; this process is symbolized by the arrow leading from the Context processor to the Meaning processor in Figure 7.1. Within the Meaning processor, such contextual priming produces a boost in the excitation levels of all units that are compatible with the reader's ongoing interpretation of the text.

Contextual Facilitation and Word Recognition
The exact amount of excitation that the Context processor will contribute to any given meaning unit depends on exactly how predictable it is. If the context is only weakly predictive of the

word to follow, then its energy will be dispersed across as many units in the Meaning processor. If the context is strongly predictive of the word to follow, that word's meaning should receive a strong and focused boost in excitation.

In effect, such boosts in the excitation of a meaning give it a head start toward reaching consciousness. To the extent that a meaning is already turned on, it needs less input from the letter recognition network to become fully active. In keeping with this, predictive context speeds people's ability to decide whether any given string of letters is or is not a word. The more highly predictive the context is, the more it does so.[2]

The Context processor is also responsible for selecting among alternate meanings of a word. This is important not just for blatantly ambiguous words (such as soccer *ball* versus inaugural *ball*) but to a lesser extent for almost any word. For example, the word *Wyoming* brings different images to mind, depending on whether the surrounding topic is national parks or national elections. The Context processor's job is to pick out and emphasize those aspects of a word's meaning that are most important to its evolving interpretation of the text.[3]

Yet even while the Context processor facilitates the reader's awareness of appropriate words and meanings, it does not prevent excitation of inappropriate ones. Given a sentence such as

John saw several spiders, roaches, and *bugs*.

people very briefly show signs (albeit not conscious awareness) of having interpreted the last word to mean both insects and spying devices.[4]

The brevity of this phenomenon shows that the Context processor is quick to settle the issue. On the other hand, its very existence demonstrates that, among skilled readers, the contributions, even of relatively strong context, are not preemptive—even at the level of meaning selection. In particular, this example demonstrates that contextual selection cannot overcome orthographic information; it is not even strong enough to prevent the incoming orthographic information from turning on each of its own appropriate meanings.

---

2. For a review, see Fischler and Bloom (1979).

3. Sanford and Garrod (1981) is an excellent book on the ways in which readers' understanding of larger context influences their interpretation of individual words.

4. Seidenberg, Tanenhaus, Leiman, and Bienkowski (1982).

For skillful readers, then, the implication is that context can respond to orthographic information; it can speed and assist its interpretation; but it cannot overcome it. Consistent with this, study after study has shown that context significantly affects the speed or accuracy with which skilled readers can perceive familiar words only when the experimenter has done something to slow or disrupt the orthographic processing of the word. This can be accomplished in either of two ways: (1) by reducing the contrast or by adding or subtracting bits of visual information so as to make the letters harder to see or (2) by choosing words whose orthography is unusually difficult.[5]

The fact that contextual cues prove especially helpful for orthographically difficult words is not only consistent with our analysis of how the system ought to work but is quite comforting. The implication is that by its very design, the Context processor gives us decoding assistance when we need it most. And in keeping with this, a number of investigators have shown that context exerts a much stronger effect on word identification performance of younger and less skilled readers.[6]

The capacity of the Context processor to help readers across orthographic difficulties must be of tremendous everyday significance to the young reader.[7] As it helps to reduce the time and effort that they must invest in orthographically difficult words, it must significantly increase their capacity for comprehending the text.

Contextual Facilitation and Comprehension

In essence, text comprehension is a hierarchically layered process. At the bottom level, the reader must retrieve the meaning of each individual word encountered. When the spelling of the word is only marginally familiar, contextual excitation can sometimes significantly assist this process. First, where a spelling pattern is only partially processed, contextual excitation can augment orthographic excitation so as to select the intended word from any competitors. Second, where orthographic processing is laborious or uncertain, indirect excitation, originating in the Context processor, can help to speed its progress.

---

5. For a review, see Stanovich (1980).

6. For reviews, see Perfetti (1985); Stanovich (1980).

7. On the other hand, overreliance on contextual clues should be a source of concern rather than pride for the educator for it is a strong sign that the reader's orthographic knowledge and skills have not been properly developed.

At the next level of text interpretation, readers must collapse the meanings of the individual words they have read into a composite interpretation. They must, in other words, periodically interrupt their word-by-word progress through the text to interpret the collective significance of the chain of words they have been reading. Skillful performance at this level depends on two factors: (1) the ability to recognize the opportunities at which recoding is most appropriate and (2) the ease and speed with which the individual words are recognized.

In general, for skillful readers, these interpretive pauses regularly occur at major syntactic boundaries.[8] As this effectively ensures the internal coherence of the string of words to be recoded, it is extremely important.

More specifically, the skillful reader's selection of recoding opportunities reflects a trade-off between the importance of the syntactic boundary and the length or difficulty of the phrase or clause that it bounds. Where there is a choice, major boundaries are preferable because they allow the reader to put together a more significant fraction of the sentence at once. However, when the number or difficulty of the words (or concepts) between major boundaries is high, skillful readers recode at earlier and more subtle junctures. Otherwise, their capacity for the remembering the uncollapsed string of words might be exceeded. As a consequence, some of the information to be put together would be lost, and comprehension would suffer.

Note that if readers try to recode at a syntactically inappropriate point in the sentence, they find themselves in the position of trying to interpret a syntactically anomalous set of words. In this case, too, comprehension must suffer.

Research confirms that the syntactic sensitivities of younger and less skilled readers are quite undeveloped and provides evidence that this may significantly contribute to their comprehension difficulties.[9] However, the second factor—the time and effort which readers must invest in recognizing the individual words of the syntactic unit—looks to be at least as important.[10]

The greater the time and effort that a reader must invest in each individual word, the slimmer the likelihood that preceding words of the phrase will be remembered when it is time to put them all together. Yet word recognition difficulties are ubiquitous

---

8. Kleiman (1975).

9. Adams (1980); Huggins and Adams (1980).

10. Perfetti (1985); Perfetti and Lesgold (1977).

for younger and less skilled readers. There must be some relief from this bind, or comprehension would be a rare event.

One way of circumventing decoding problems is to skip over difficult words. Although this is a common strategy even among better readers,[11] its drawbacks with respect to preserving the meaning of a text are obvious, especially in the extreme. The other source of relief is to be gained from the Context processor. For the reader with marginal word recognition skills, the speed and facilitation that the Context processor lends to the decoding process could well make the difference between comprehension and word calling.

At the third level of the comprehension process, readers must combine their understanding of the just-interpreted phrase or clause with their overall interpretation of the text so as to revise and update their understanding of what the text means and where it is going. At this step, the reader's working materials are no longer locally defined. Full understanding may require retrieval of particular facts or events presented many pages earlier in the text. It may also require consideration of knowledge and construction of argument that are entirely extraneous to the text. And it certainly requires the critical and inferential activities necessary for putting such information together.

It is, in short, this third level of interpretation that we think of as true understanding. Interpretation at this level requires active attention and thought; it is not automatic. It will be only as fruitful as the discipline and effort that the reader invests in it, and the training of this discipline and effort is an area in which contemporary education in the United States clearly falls short.[12]

In view of the attentional requirements of comprehension, the immediate point is that the automatic facilitation that context imparts to word recognition may be critical. At least for marginal decoders, contextual facilitation may make the difference between whether or not they have sufficient resources to allow such comprehension to happen at all. Within the larger context of this book, the more important point is that the comprehension of a text, in its deepest and most productive sense, must be impeded unless and until the reader has mastered the knowledge and skills required for the automatic recognition of its words.

---

11. Freebody and Anderson (1983).

12. Chall (1983b); National Assessment of Educational Progress (1981a); National Commission on Excellence in Education (1983).

The Meaning Processor

The inner workings of the Meaning processor are similar in nature to those of the Orthographic processor. In particular, its units do not correspond to whole, familiar words. Instead, just as the spellings of familiar words are represented in the Orthographic processor as interassociated sets of letters, the meanings of familiar words are represented in the Meaning processor as interassociated sets of more primitive meaning elements.

For example, a person's understanding of the word *dog* would be represented neither by some self-contained "dog node" nor by any list of definitive properties but instead as the interassociated distribution of properties that collectively represent the person's total history, direct and vicarious, of experiences with dogs. Because the nature of these interconnected sets of meaning units holds implications for comprehension and vocabulary growth, it is worth examining in a little more detail.

Acquiring Concepts

Let us suppose that a child is encountering some particular thing, say a cat, for the first time.[13] As the cat is observed, the sets of meaning units representing its characteristics—its color, its fur, its voice, its tail, its shape and size, its behavior, its environment, and so on—become activated and interconnected in the child's Meaning processor. At that point, the child's concept of a cat will correspond precisely to that particular, interconnected constellation of meaning units. If the child is told that this creature is called a cat, the word *cat* will also correspond precisely to that particular, interconnected constellation of meaning units.

Now suppose that our child encounters another cat—and another, and another, and another. Whether these encounters involve the same cat in different situations or different cats in their own situations, none will be identical to that very first encounter.

To the extent that they are the same, they will activate overlapping sets of meaning units. Eventually, through their repeated and simultaneous activation, these overlapping sets of meaning units will become strongly interlinked, collectively representing the child's core concept of a cat. A creature that

---

13. This framework for concept acquisition is based most closely upon Hintzman (1986).

evokes their majority in proper configuration will be conceived as a cat; one that does not, will not.

To the extent that the cat encounters are different, they will activate different meaning units. Such dispersion of meaning serves to make the child's concept of a cat more flexible, to keep it from being tied to that first, unique image of a cat. It effectively broadens the child's understanding of what a cat can be like and can do.

Over time, as the child encounters more and more cats, there will also emerge subclusters of characteristics corresponding, for example, to barn cats and house cats, Siamese cats and Persian cats, stalking cats and curled-up cats. When the child sees a cat that matches one of these subclusters, it will evoke not only the general concept of a cat but also the entire subset of meaning units with which it is tightly connected, providing such responses as "better not pet a barn cat."

Acquiring the Meanings of New Words

Because of the direct connections between the Meaning processor and the Context and Orthographic processors, vocabulary acquisition can be seen to proceed in much the same way. Suppose that while reading a story, a child encounters a word that she or he has neither seen nor heard before. Because the meaning of the word is totally unknown, it has no established connections to the units in the Meaning processor. The associative pathways from the Orthographic processor to the Meaning processor ensure that it gets shipped up. Yet without a destination, its energy will diffuse, without constraint, around the meaning units.[14]

If the word had been presented in isolation, that might be the end of it. However, our imaginary child encountered this word while reading a meaningful text. As a consequence, the meaning units will not be homogeneously unprepared for its arrival. Those that are compatible with the ongoing interpretation of the text will have been excited already by the Context processor. Rather like radar, looking for a blip, the orthographic pattern will find these activated meaning units, and as their excitation intermingles, a bond will begin to form between them.[15]

The impact of such an incidental learning experience is expected to be small. Context is rarely pointed enough to predict the precise meaning of a word. The pattern of activation that it

14. See McClelland and Rumelhart (1986a).
15. McClelland and Rumelhart (1986a).

creates across the meaning units is likely to be quite diffuse. It is likely to miss some of the aspects of the word's meaning, and it is likely to include a number that belong only to the context and not to the word at all. Further, the more diffusely it is spread across meaning units, the weaker can be its contribution to any one. Thus, although our imaginary child will have learned something about this word through its accidental encounter, that something may well be too weak and too imprecise to be useful by itself.

But think about what will happen when the child sees this word again. It will evoke the configuration of meaning units that it encountered before. In addition, it will meet the pattern of excitation set off by the new and different context in which it currently occurs. Where the meaning units of the earlier and current context overlap, their excitation will be mutually reinforced. They will therefore become more strongly bonded to each other and to the orthographic pattern of the word. As a consequence, they will also be the units that are most strongly evoked on the next encounter of the word.

Given a number of encounters with this word over a variety of different contexts, the units that context evokes most often will be those that belong to the meaning of the word itself. Beneath them will be subclusters of units that correspond to its frequent usages and connotations. Units that have been excited in only one or two contexts will become lost in the noise. In this way, the meaning of the word itself will eventually be learned well enough to contribute independently and appropriately to the meaning of a text, even if not to allow the child to generate a well-articulated definition.

Strategic Use of Context Should Be Taught

A caveat is in order. The kind of vocabulary acquisition I have described above is a bit slipshod. It is capable only of providing the word with the meaning anticipated by the immediately preceding context, and it requires only that the reader has looked carefully at the unknown word and has understood the context preceding it. Other than that, it is passive; it happens effortlessly and automatically.

If, in contrast, the reader takes the time and effort to analyze the contextual clues available, a far more precise and useful concept of the word may be established on its first encounter.[16]

---

16. More generally, productive learning depends on thinking as much as recognizing. The interplay between memory and thought will be discussed in chapter 9.

Such analysis may extend beyond the immediate context of the word. At best, readers will thoughtfully search for and interpret cues that precede the word more remotely. At best, they will additionally look for clues or definitions that might follow it. Although such methodical exploitation of context is not automatic, it can be taught, to the considerable benefit of the reader.[17]

Vocabulary Instruction

Intuitively, such incidental and incremental meaning acquisition should not be as efficient, word for word, as methodical vocabulary instruction. And, indeed, it is not.[18]

To gain an overview of the effectiveness of vocabulary instruction, Steven Stahl and Marilyn Fairbanks conducted a meta-analysis of relevant research published through April 1985.[19] Their study was addressed to three questions:

1. Does provision of vocabulary instruction generally result in an increase in students' word knowledge?

The answer to this question was a definite yes. Across studies, whether outcome tests measured children's knowledge of word definitions (e.g., through multiple-choice or short-answer items) or usages (e.g., through sentence anomaly or cloze tests), children who had received instruction on the tested words significantly outperformed those who had not. In addition, children who had received vocabulary instruction significantly (though, of course, less dramatically) outperformed the others on global vocabulary measures, such as standardized tests, indicating that vocabulary instruction effectively enhanced learning of words that were not explicitly taught as well.

2. Does vocabulary instruction result in any increase in students' reading comprehension?

Again the answer was yes. Instructed children demonstrated significantly better comprehension of passages containing taught words than uninstructed children. More concretely, the fiftieth-percentile-student in the instructed group was effectively advanced to the level of the eighty-third-percentile student in the uninstructed group. The instructed children also demonstrated slight but significant gains over their uninstructed peers on standardized measures of reading comprehension, corresponding to an advance from the fiftieth to the sixty-second percentile.

---

17. For a review of research on strategies for exploiting context, see Calfee and Drum (1986).

18. Nagy, Herman, and Anderson (1985); Stahl and Fairbanks (1986).

19. Stahl and Fairbanks (1986).

3. What kinds of vocabulary instruction are most effective?

Across studies, methods in which children were given both information about the words' definitions and examples of the words' usages in contexts resulted in the largest gains in both vocabulary and comprehension measures. Although methods providing repeated drill and practice on word definitions resulted in significant improvement on measures designed to assess children's specific knowledge of the words taught, it produced no reliable effect on the comprehension scores.

The limited effectiveness of having children learn the definitions of words deserves further consideration. After all, how many times did your parents say, "Look it up!" when you came to them with a vocabulary question?

In fact, a common vocabulary exercise in the classroom is to give children a list of words, ask them to look each up in the dictionary, and use it in a sentence. To get a closer look at the productivity of such instructions, George Miller and Patricia Gildea examined several thousand sentences written in response by fifth and sixth graders.[20] Examples of the sentences produced by the children follow in the column on the left. The dictionary definitions from which the children worked are given in the column on the right:

Student's Sentence	Dictionary Definition
Me and my parents <u>correlate</u>, because without them I wouldn't be here.	**correlate**. 1. be related one to the other: *The diameter and circumference of a circle <u>correlate</u>.* 2. put into relation . . . .
I was <u>meticulous</u> about falling off the cliff.	**meticulous**. very careful or too particular about small details.
The <u>redress</u> for getting well when you're sick is to stay in bed.	**redress**. 1. set right; repair; remedy: *King Arthur tried to <u>redress</u> wrongs in his kingdom.*

All things considered, one might conclude that the children used the definitions quite well; nevertheless, the sentences are peculiar. The productive understanding of a word requires much more than knowledge of its definition.

A study by McKeown, Beck, Omanson, and Pople is among those that have demonstrated that the number of times that children encounter a word is a strong predictor of how well they will learn it; this is consistent with the basic principle of associative learning.[21] But McKeown and company also found that the next

---

20. Miller and Gildea (1987).

21. McKeown, Beck, Omanson, and Pople (1985).

best predictor of learning was the richness and variety of meaningful contexts in which the words had been encountered and used. Of particular interest, rich and diverse experience with a word yielded a special advantage in the children's abilities to understand its connotations or submeanings in specific contexts and to exploit its extended meaning in the course of story comprehension. This is exactly as our portrayal of the Meaning processor would predict.

While affirming the value of classroom instruction in vocabulary, we must also recognize its limitations. By our best estimates, the growth in recognition vocabulary of the school age child typically exceeds 3,000 words per year, or more than 8 per day.[22] This order of growth cannot be ascribed to their classroom instruction, nor could it be attained through any feasible program of classroom instruction.

First, the amount of direct instruction prescribed in teachers' guides and curriculum materials is relatively small compared to this number. Examinations of basal reading series show that the number of word meanings to receive explicit instruction generally ranges between 200 and 500 per year.[23] Second, counting the number of vocabulary items listed in the basals greatly overestimates the number of new words that children are likely to learn through classroom instruction. It seems that the majority of the words listed for instruction by the basals are already familiar to most children.[24] Further it seems that teachers tend to spend very little time on direct vocabulary instruction in any case. Dolores Durkin observed that, of 4,469 minutes of reading instruction, only 19 were directed to vocabulary instruction.[25] Similarly, Roser and Juel found that the third-, fourth-, and fifth-grade teachers they observed spent an average of 1.67 minutes on vocabulary per reading lesson; most often they spent none at all.[26]

Not only does it seem that classroom vocabulary instruction is not the principal source of children's vocabulary growth, it also seems that even under the most supportive circumstances, it could

---

22. Miller and Gildea (1987); Nagy, and Anderson (1984); Nagy and Herman (1987).

23. Calfee and Drum (1986); Nagy and Herman (1986).

24. For example, in a study of third, fourth and fifth graders, Roser and Juel (1982) found that 72 percent of the "new" words that the basal listed for instruction were already known by students. Even among students in the lowest reading groups, 48 percent of the words were already known.

25. Durkin (1979).

26. Roser and Juel (1982).

not be. To gain more direct insight into this problem, Isabel Beck and her colleagues designed an intensive regimen of vocabulary instruction for fourth-grade children. The program was designed to teach the meanings of 104 words and took five months—seventy-five half-hour lessons—to complete.[27]

Children have been shown to learn well under this program, mastering about 80 percent of the trained words. But 80 percent of 104 words is only 81 words—a lot fewer than 3,000. Besides that, consider the amount of time it took. If this training were extended to a full year, one might expect the children to learn as many as 200 new words through it. Even if it were the only subject taught, all day long, every day, the total number of words that could be covered would barely exceed 3,000, and—especially under these circumstances—the total number of covered words that would be learned would surely be many fewer.

Importance of Learning New Words from Context

So how do children learn so many new words each year? Is it possible that they do so mostly on their own, from encountering the words in context? Thanks to work of William Nagy, Richard C. Anderson, and their colleagues, we can give this question a confident yes. Piece by piece, they have put this puzzle together, and here are the pieces[28] :

1. How many words of print do children read each year?

A study of fifth graders indicated that the amount out-of-school reading ranged from practically none to nearly 6 million words per year, with half the children reading at least 650,000.[29] Adding in-school reading to this total, they conclude that the average fifth-grade student encounters more than 1 million running words of text a year.[30]

2. How many unknown words does a child encounter in a year?

---

27. Beck, Perfetti, and McKeown (1982); McKeown, Beck, Omanson, and Perfetti (1983).

28. Nagy, Herman, and Anderson's (1985) original study was smaller and its estimates less conservative than those provided in a more recent paper: Nagy, Anderson, and Herman (1987).

29. Based on data collected by Fielding, Wilson, and Anderson (1987).

30. Nagy, Herman, and Anderson (1985). To this, Nagy, Anderson, and Herman (1987) add the observation that the ninetieth percentile student reads about 200 times more text per year than the tenth percentile student.

The average (fiftieth percentile) fifth grader is likely to encounter between 16,000 and 24,000 unknown words per year in the course of reading.[31]

3. What is the likelihood that the child will learn the meaning of an unknown word through a single encounter while reading meaningful text?

On immediate testing, there is a 20 percent chance that through a single encounter of a word in meaningful, grade-level text, the child will have acquired enough of its meaning to express a very vague aspect of its sense; there is a 10 percent chance that the child will have learned enough about it to express a fairly clear understanding of its meaning; and there is a 15 to 20 percent chance that the child will be able to pick out its meaning on a multiple-choice test.[32] When testing is delayed for about a week, multiple-choice performance falls to about 5 percent.[33]

4. What is the total number of new words that a child is expected to learn through independent reading?

If we use the most conservative estimates above, the answer is at least 5 percent (the likelihood of learning) of 16,000 to 24,000 (the number of unknown words encountered in a year), which equals 800 to 1,200 new words per year.

It is thus clear that learning from context is a very, very important component of vocabulary acquisition. But this means of learning is available only to the extent that children engage in meaningful reading and, even then, only insofar as they bother to process the spelling—the orthographic structure—of the unknown words they encounter. Where they skip over an unknown word without attending to it, and often readers do,[34] no learning can occur. Acquisition of the meaning of a word from context depends on the linkage of the contextually evoked meaning with the structural image of the word.

Meaningfulness and Orthographic Knowledge

While the acquisition of new vocabulary items depends on attending to orthography, it also happens that acquisition of new orthographic patterns is enhanced by attending to meaning. This is because the Meaning processor is directly linked to the Orthographic processor (figure 7.1).

In particular, when the Orthographic processor ships a meaningful spelling pattern to the Meaning processor, the Meaning processor returns excitatory feedback. The effect should be one of

---

31. Anderson and Freebody (1983).
32. Nagy, Herman, and Anderson (1985).
33. Nagy, Anderson, and Herman (1987).
34. Anderson and Freebody (1983).

adding reinforcement to the activated spelling pattern which should contribute to its consolidation. Whittlesea and Cantwell have shown that this is exactly what happens. When a pseudoword is given a meaningful definition, the perceptibility of its letters is significantly enhanced. Moreover, it remains so at least twenty-four hours later and whether or not its meaning can be remembered.[35]

Knowledge about Prefixes, Suffixes, and Word Stems

The direct linkage between the Orthographic and Meaning processors may also be responsible for skilled readers' perceptual sensitivity to the roots or meaning-bearing fragments of polysyllabic words and nonwords.[36] It moreover raises the prospect that it might be a good idea to teach students about the derivational morphologies of polysyllabic words—to teach them, for example, that such words as *adduce, educe, induce, produce, reduce*, and *seduce* are similarly spelled because they share a common meaning element: *duce*, "to lead."

By sharpening the connections leading from the Meaning to the Orthographic processor, such instruction might be expected to improve both spelling and visual word perception. Conversely, by refining the connections from the Orthographic to the Meaning processor, such instruction should strengthen students' vocabularies and refine their comprehension abilities.

In keeping with this, after giving seventh graders thirty ten-minute lessons on the derivational morphologies of words, Otterman found that they were more proficient with both the meanings and spellings of the studied items.[37] The students did not, on the other hand, demonstrate any significant improvement in their general vocabulary and comprehension scores or in their ability to interpret new derivationally complex words. Nor, by our analysis, could such improvement be expected unless, along with the word parts they had been taught, they were also trained in the strategies and discipline for inducing meaning from morphological components. Although the linking of particular orthographic patterns with particular meanings can be accomplished entirely through the mechanisms of the

---

35. Whittlesea and Cantwell (1987).

36. Although this sensitivity seems real, it is not very strong. Some of the papers that have addressed this issue are Fowler, Napps, and Feldman (1985); Manelis and Tharp (1977); Taft (1985); Tyler and Nagy (1987).

37. Otterman (1955, cited in Johnson and Bauman, 1984).

Orthographic and Meaning processors, making an independent habit of so doing requires additional and sophisticated cognitive control.

In addition, a cautionary note is in order about teaching the derivational morphologies of words: The morphemic and syllabic structures of polysyllabic words rarely coincide. As an example, the syllabic segmentation of *information* is *in-for-ma-tion;* morphologically it is *in-form-ation*. Given that word recognition is driven by the Orthographic processor, one might expect readers to be more responsive to the syllabic structure of a word than to its morphology. Studies of skilled readers indicate that this is often the case.[38]

One wonders, moreover, whether our visual compulsion to syllabify is not partly responsible for the fact that we are not more sensitive to morphology.[39] Syllabic parsing, after all, disintegrates the *busy* in *business* and the *current* in *concurrent*. Though it might help us to see the *port* in *deport* or even *comportment*, it breaks it up in *importance* and *transportation;* though it might help us to see the *form* in *deform*, it hides it in *information*, *performance*, and *conformative;* and similarly for the *pos(e)* in *impose* and *repose* versus *position, positive,* and *imposter*.

Although teaching older readers about the roots and suffixes of morphologically complex words may be a worthwhile challenge, teaching beginning or less skilled readers about them may be a mistake. Juel and Roper/Schneider have demonstrated that the spelling patterns to which young children are asked to attend significantly influence the spelling patterns to which they respond during word perception.[40] More than that, children's word recognition facility is particularly influenced by their familiarity with "versatile" spelling patterns—ones that appear in a variety of words.[41] Where there is a difference, the syllabic segments of a polysyllabic word are, by their nature, orthographically more common or versatile than its morphological segments. To avoid conflicts with the goal of establishing solid sensitivity to frequent spelling patterns, instruction on morphology may best be postponed. The perceptibility of syllables is too important.

---

38. Goldblum and Frost (1988).
39. Kaye and Sternberg (1982).
40. Juel and Roper/Schneider (1985).
41. Juel (1983).

Instructional Implications

Several instructional themes follow from this discussion of meaning and orthography. The first is that reliance on context to the exclusion of orthography is a good strategy neither for reading nor for learning to read. For the skilled reader, meaning is effortlessly and automatically driven by orthographic processing. Unless young readers are encouraged to attend to the spelling patterns of words, they may not develop the orthographic knowledge on which this system depends.

To this end, it again seems that children should be encouraged not to skip over words that are difficult for them.[42] When they encounter a word that is hard to read, they should, of their own volition, take the time to study it. In addition to reflecting on its spelling, they should methodically consider its meaning, using not just the immediate drift of the context but also looking for definitions, paraphrases, and contrasts that follow or more remotely precede the word.

After they have worked over a new word, they should return to the beginning of the phrase and then the sentence to which it belongs, rereading the whole thing. This is not only valuable for purposes of reinforcing the orthographic structure and meaning of the new word: It is necessary for comprehension of the sentence. More generally, repeated reading of text is found to produce marked improvement in word recognition, fluency, and comprehension.[43]

An additional benefit of repeat readings may be toward the reader's appreciation of the syntax of the passage.[44] Because readers must interpretively collapse text at and only at syntactic boundaries, such sensitivity stands as a strong, if indirect, determinant of comprehension. Thus, when readers are asked to undertake repeat readings in unison with an expressive model (such as a professional reader on tape), marked improvements in their own phrasing are also found.[45] Before (or while) asking students to reread an important or difficult passage, we should not hesitate to read it aloud ourselves to them (or as they read silently) and with expression. Syntactic sensitivities can also be

---

42. Again, any child who has difficulty with more than a few words per paragraph should be given something easier to read.

43. Herman (1985); Samuels (1985); Taylor, Wade, and Yekovich (1985).

44. Carbo, M. (1978); Schreiber, R. (1980).

45. Carbo (1978).

strengthened by asking students to construct tables or flowcharts of the text—that is, by engaging them in tasks that inherently require thoughtfulness about the text at the level of propositional units and the relations between them.[46]

In this context, it is worth reflecting on the fact that readability or text difficulty is not a unary dimension: A text can be more or less difficult at the level of words, syntax, or concepts.[47] The aspects of a text that are best pushed beyond or kept within the students' level of mastery depend on the purpose for which the text is intended. If its purpose is to expand word recognition skills, then a larger proportion of new words can occur but its syntactic and conceptual structure should be entirely manageable. Similarly, if its purpose is to expand syntactic sensitivity, then the topic should be familiar and the vocabulary should be controlled. In contrast, if the purpose is to impart new concepts, grade-level control of syntax and vocabulary makes sense.

Within readability formulas, syntactic complexity is generally estimated by the number of words in a sentence.[48] Given text that has been written as clearly as possible, the average number of words per sentence provides a reasonable statistical index of its overall syntactic complexity. Among other things, it provides an estimate of the number of meaningful ideas that the reader must interrelate in interpreting the sentences.[49] Thus, proposition by proposition,

The dog chased the cat. The cat killed the rat. The rat ate the malt.

describes the situation in more digestible units than does

This is the dog that chased the cat that killed the rat that ate the malt.

But while the number of words between periods is a correlate of syntactic complexity, it is not its cause. To illustrate, we can significantly shorten our complex sentence as follows:

This is the malt the rat the cat the dog chased killed ate.

And, conversely, we can increase the comprehensibility of our simplest sentences by adding more words:

---

46. Sticht (1979).
47. See Klare (1984).
48. Klare, G. R. (1974–1975).
49. Kintsch and Keenan (1973).

First, a rat ate the malt. Then, a cat killed the rat. Then, this dog chased the cat.

The key to syntactic ease or complexity is not just the number of words or ideas in a sentence. It is also the transparency; it is the obviousness of the syntactic boundaries between clauses and phrases and the clarity of the meaningful relations between them.[50]

Turning from readability back to word meaning, it would seem that vocabulary instruction is generally a worthwhile endeavor. Although such instruction may produce relatively little direct increase in the children's vocabularies, it provides a general forum for experimenting with the uses of words and the ways in which their meanings differ. It supports the attitude that learning new words and being thoughtful about their meanings is worthwhile, and it sets up a context for discussing the larger meaning of the text.

In addition, explicit training on the strategic use of context for defining word meanings seems wholly warranted. Sometimes the meaning of a new word is inferable from or even explicitly provided by the text. However, theory indicates that neither the ability nor the tendency to exploit contextual clues that follow or more remotely precede a word can be automatic. By implication, the processes and benefits of using such information should be taught.

The idea of teaching students about the spellings and meanings of the roots and affixes of derivationally complex words seems promising but unproved. My own belief is that such knowledge is valuable on both orthographic and semantic dimensions. For example, once one sees that *concurrent* consists of "with" (*con-*) plus *current*, the word is no longer a spelling problem. I further sense that my appreciation of the meaning of such words changes qualitatively and profitably from appreciation of their derivations. Somehow, the insight that *fid* means "trust" or "faith" significantly alters and connects my understanding of words like *confidence, fidelity, fiduciary*, and *bona fide*; the discovery that *path* means "suffering" alters and connects my understanding of words like *sympathy, psychopath*, and *pathologist*; and so on. In reverse, I also find it quite helpful to look at morphology clues in inferring the meanings of new words. Yet it is also my impression that such insights are never automatic. The only way I seem to discover such relations is by consciously looking for them.

---

50. Huggins and Adams (1980).

Perhaps the objective of such lessons should be one of developing children's inclination to look for such relations as much as teaching them about any particular sets of words. In any case, when and if the worth or effectiveness of lessons on derivational morphology is firmly demonstrated (or otherwise accepted), there is reason to suspect that such training would be best postponed until later grades of schooling when the student's knowledge of frequent spelling patterns has been thoroughly established and automated. In an nutshell, it is less important for the orthographically inexperienced to be facile with the *form* in *information* than with either the *for* in *information, for, forty, forget,* and *misfortune* or the *ma* in *information, major, automation,* and *flammable*.

Finally, the most important point of this section is that meaningful experiences with words are important to the acquisition of their spelling, as well as their usage and interpretation. The best way to build children's visual vocabulary is to have them read meaningful words in meaningful contexts. The more meaningful reading that children do, the larger will be their repertoires of meanings, the greater their sensitivity to orthographic structure, and the stronger, better refined, and more productive will be their associations between words and meanings.

8

Adding the Phonological Processor: How the Whole System Works Together

Although skillful readers do not depend on phonological translation for recognizing familiar words, they seem quite automatically to produce such translations anyway. In this chapter, we examine why and how they do so. Far from being superfluous, such phonological translation adds a critical degree of redundancy to the system. Without it, even skillful readers would find themselves faltering for fluency and comprehension with all but the very easiest of texts.

The Nature of the Phonological Processor

Figure 8.1 illustrates the way in which readers' phonological knowledge and processes are theoretically related to the rest of the system as it is involved in reading.[1] As with the Orthographic and Meaning processors, the Phonological processor contains a complexly associated array of primitive units. The auditory image of any particular word, syllable, or phoneme corresponds to the activation of a particular, interconnected set of those units.

In figure 8.1 the arrows between the Phonological and Orthographic processors run in both directions. The arrow that runs from the Orthographic processor to the Phonological processor indicates that as the visual image of a string of letters is being processed, excitatory stimulation is shipped to corresponding units in the Phonological processor. If the letter string is pronounceable, the Phonological processor will then send excitatory stimulation back to the Orthographic processor; such feedback is represented by the arrow that runs in the other direction.

---

1. See Seidenberg and McClelland (1989).

The Phonological processor is also connected in both directions to the Meaning processor. In this way, the activation of a word's meaning results in the excitation of the phonological units underlying its pronunciation. Conversely, the activation of its pronunciation automatically arouses its meaning.

It is especially important that the Orthographic, Phonological, and Meaning processors are all connected in both directions to each other. This circular connectivity ensures coordination between the processors. It ensures that all three will be working on the same thing at the same time. More than than, it ensures that each processor will effectively guide and facilitate the efforts of the others. As we shall see, this is critical both to reading and to learning to read.

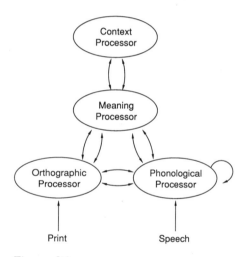

Figure 8.1
Adding the Phonological processor.

The Phonological processor has two other features that set it apart from the others. First, like the Orthographic processor, it accepts information from the outside. However, the information that it accepts is speech. Note that the Orthographic processor is still the only one to receive information directly from the printed page, reflecting the fact that reading depends first and foremost on visual processing. Second—and this is an important asset in the reading situation—the knowledge represented within the Phonological processor can be activated or reactivated at our own volition. Not only can we speak, we can also subvocalize or generate speech images at will.

The Importance of Phonological Processing in Reading

The direct connections from the Orthographic to the Phonological processor suggest that phonological activation is an automatic and immediate consequence of visual word processing, and indeed it is.[2] But the Orthographic processor is also directly connected to the Meaning processor, implying that for skilled readers at least, the meaning of a word may be activated just as quickly as its sound.

Meaning activation is, of course, the whole point of reading a word. If it does not depend on phonological translation and, further, may happen just as quickly as phonological translation, one is left wondering why phonological translation should be set up as an automatic aspect of the system. What is the function of the Phonological processor? Why is it there?

One capability it supports is that of reading aloud with fluency. Yet this hardly seems an adequate design criterion for making it so integral a part of the system. If our heads were designed by a computer engineer, there might instead be a little toggle switch that turned the Phonological processor on when it was time to read aloud and off otherwise. After all, when phonological translations are superfluous, why invest any energy in carrying them out?

The answer is that for optimal reading performance, phonological translations are rarely superfluous; perhaps they are never predictably so. The activities of the Phonological processor provide two invaluable services to the system. First, they provide an alphabetic backup system—a redundant processing route—that is critical for maintaining the speed as well as the accuracy of word recognition necessary for productive reading. Second, they provide a means of expanding the on-line memory for individual words as is essential for text comprehension. Let us examine the nature and value of each of these services in turn.

Interactions among All Three Processors: The Alphabetic Backup System

Both the immediate and long-term impact of reading depend critically on the speed as well as the accuracy with which readers can identify the individual letters and words of the text.

2. Perfetti, Bell, and Delaney (1988); Tannenhaus, Flanigan, and Seidenberg (1980); Van Orden, Johnston, and Hale (1988).

This is because the utility of the associative linkages, both within and between processors, depends on the speed and completeness of the input they receive. When the words of a text are processed too slowly or scantily, readers forfeit any automatic facilitation and guidance that the associative connections would otherwise provide. Commensurately, they also forfeit the opportunity to recognize, learn about, and understand what they have read.

The accuracy and speed of written word recognition depend first and foremost on the reader's familiarity with the word in print. The more frequently a spelling pattern has been processed, the more strongly its individual letters will facilitate each other's recognition within the Orthographic processor. The more frequently a written word has been interpreted, the stronger, more focused, and thus faster will be its connections to and from the Meaning processor. The more frequently a spelling pattern has been mapped onto a particular pronunciation, the stronger, more focused, and thus faster will be its connections to and from the Phonological processor.

In short, when readers encounter a meaningful word that they have read many times before, the Orthographic processor will very quickly resonate to the pattern as a whole. Further, the word's meaning and phonological image will also be evoked with near instantaneity. For texts consisting entirely of such highly familiar words, it follows that phonological translation might indeed be somewhat superfluous (except when reading aloud). However, such texts are highly unlikely.

To estimate the frequencies with which students do encounter different words, Carroll, Davies, and Richman sampled 5,088,721 words from school books, grades 3 through 8, and counted the number of times each different word occurred.[3] Fully 50 percent of their sampled words consisted of just 109 very commonly used words. Moreover, roughly 75 percent of the sample was made up of only 1,000 different words and 90 percent of only about 5,000 different words.

In contrast, the *total* number of different words that these researchers encountered was 86,741.[4] Individually the 80,000 or so words that make up the remaining 10 percent of the sample must be encountered relatively infrequently by readers. Collectively,

---

3. Carroll, Davies, and Richman (1971).

4. Carroll et al. (1971) treated each distinct string as a different word such that, for example, *word, Word, word's, worded, wordiness, wording, words, Words,* and *wordy* appear as separate entries in their count.

however, they represent more than 94 percent of the different words the young reader is expected to encounter. Moreover, each of these 80,000 less common words is expected to be understood by the schoolchild, or it would not appear at all.[5]

But the point is not simply that there are frequent and infrequent words. It is that there is a tremendous range in the frequencies of the different words that students encounter in print.[6] The most frequent word in the Carroll, Davies, and Richman count (which is *the*) is expected to occur more than 73,000 times in every million words of reading. The hundredth most frequent word (*know*) should occur about 1,000 times in every million words of reading;[7] the thousandth most frequent word (*pass*) should occur about 86 times per million words; the five thousandth most common word (*vibrate*) should occur about 10 times per million; and occurring less often than that, are thousands upon thousands of other good words (e.g., *crayon, warn, fiction, kiss, sweater, bump, remark, yell, lizard, disappointment, astronomer, suggestion, pebble, iceberg, magician, horrible, wink*). There must be an analogous range in the students' familiarity with the words they read.

It is in the reading of less familiar words that the presence of the Phonological processor or, more significantly, the presence and circular connectivity of all three processors becomes so advantageous. One reason for this advantage is that the processors are distinct from one another in terms of both the kinds of input they receive and the internal knowledge with which they work. Because of this, each is vulnerable to its own types of error- and speed-related failures and difficulties. The other reason for this advantage is that none of the processors "knows" whether

---

5. Carroll et al.'s (1971) findings for the third-grade sample were similar to those for the sample as a whole. The third-grade sample was comprised of 840,857 words of running text, representatively selected from a set of textbooks, tradebooks, workbooks, reference books, and magazines. Of these, 50 percent were accounted for by roughly 100 words, 75 percent by roughly 800 words, and 90 percent by roughly 2500 words. In contrast, the total number of distinct words encountered was 23,477.

6. The same holds true for adults. Sampling 1,000,000 words of adult reading matter, Kucera and Francis (1967) found 50 percent accounted for by just 133 words.

7. Bear in mind that there are many chance factors underlying which word occurs at which particular rank in a word count — the more so as the rank of the word decreases. The word *know* is therefore better taken as illustrative of the class of words that are about the hundredth most frequent in printed school English rather than as the particular word that will actually hold that position in any particular sample of text. And the same goes for the less likely examples presented above.

a string is actually a word. Instead each processor is capable only of producing its own rather mechanical and frequency-driven responses to its own type of input. Because of this, each processor by itself would be blindly vulnerable to its own distinct set of confusions.

The coordinated and interactive attack on word identification that the processors pull off together generally serves to overcome the confusions and to compensate for the difficulties in speed or resolving power that any one of them alone might suffer. To understand this more fully, let us detail the specific kinds of difficulties and confusions that may arise within each of the processors, along with the compensation provided by the rest of the system. Be warned: Because this discussion pivots on the timing and logic of the interactions among all of the processors, it is necessarily complicated.

Orthographic Processing

Vulnerabilities of the Orthographic Processor

The Orthographic processor takes individual letters as input and responds to the familiarity of the ordered string by linking the letters together into multiletter patterns. The strength and speed of the Orthographic processor's response to a word depend upon two factors: the speed and adequacy with which the individual letters are perceived; and the familiarity of the spelling patterns comprising the word.

The Orthographic Processor's Dependence on the Speed and Adequacy with which the Individual Letters Are Perceived. To the extent that the individual letters of a word are poorly perceived or mistaken, the Orthographic processor lacks the full and proper complement of information with which to work. In these cases, its response may consist of a number of relatively slow-to-develop and weak candidate patterns instead of any single rapid and correct image of the word presented.

The best operation of the Orthographic processor requires that the letters be resolved not just accurately but quickly as well. Specifically, letter identification must proceed quickly enough that the units representing all of the letters within a spelling pattern are near peak excitation at once. Without simultaneous excitation of the letters of a spelling pattern, the associative network is debilitated; it has no way of knowing that the letters have co-occurred. It can bestow no benefit on the reader in terms of processing speed and guidance and can produce no holistic image of the pattern. In the extreme, where the excitation of each letter dwindles away before the excitation of the next is turned on, the system can do nothing more than work out each letter of the word, one by one and independently of the others.

Difficulties in the speed or quality of individual letter resolution may be caused by physical factors, such as illegible print or the sorts of laboratory manipulations described earlier. But they may equally be caused by insufficient familiarity with letter identities.

The Orthographic Processor's Dependence on the Familiarity of the Spelling Patterns Constituting the Word. Given adequate perception of the individual letters of a word, the speed and strength of the Orthographic processor's response depends on the familiarity of the spelling pattern. The more familiar the spelling pattern is, the stronger the associations are between its letters. The strength of such associations directly affects the speed of perception because of the way in which they serve to share and redouble the excitation of the individual letters. The strength of such associations also determines whether the response to a word will consist of a single cohesive pattern or some collection of more loosely linked fragments.

Compensating for Orthographic Difficulties

Although even skillful readers may occasionally encounter illegible letters or less familiar spelling patterns, they typically overcome such problems almost without notice. The mechanisms lie in their associative knowledge about spellings, sounds, and meanings.

Compensating for the Orthographic Processor's Difficulties with Letter Recognition. If the identity of the letter and the spelling of the word are well known to the reader, compensation for poor letter resolution may be achieved within the Orthographic processor itself. Selfridge's well-known example provides a case in point:[8]

TAE CAT

---

8. Selfridge (1955).

Note that although the two middle characters of each of these words are, in fact, identical, one actually seems to "look like" an *H* and the other like an *A*. At the level of individual letter identification, the ambiguous character must be mapped onto both the *H* and the *A* units in the Orthographic processor. Within each of the three-letter strings, however, one of the candidates is highly familiar while the other is unacceptable. The illusion arises as the surrounding letters in each string associatively reinforce the familiar candidate and inhibit its competitor.

If the hard-to-identify print occurs in context, even greater illegibilities may be overcome.[9]

Pole vaulting was the third event of the meet.

After dinner, John went home.

This happens because excitation from the Context processor reinforces the relevant response in the Meaning processor, allowing it to dominate despite the vagueness of the orthographic information.

Such words may even "look" more legible in context; if so, it is because of excitation that the Meaning processor relays to the relevant units in the Orthographic processor both directly, and indirectly through the Phonological processor. Indeed, because phonological responses are relatively tightly associated with spellings, excitation that arrives from the Phonological processor may even increase the apparent legibility of spelling patterns that are not highly familiar to the Orthographic processor.

Compensating for the Orthographic Processor's Lack of Familiarity with the Spelling of a Word. The Phonological processor can lend a great deal of assistance toward recognizing visually unfamiliar words. Specifically, we can sound the word out.

For skilled readers, because the associations between the Orthographic processor and the Phonological processor are built on complex spelling and phonological patterns, such "sounding-out" may occur quite effortlessly and efficiently—so much so that skilled readers may read an aurally familiar word with little outward sign that they have never seen it before.

To illustrate, you will probably have little trouble reading aloud any of the following even if you have never seen them

---

9.   Figure from Nash-Webber (1975, p. 352).

before: *diatessaron, gerentomorphosis, epilimnion, trypsinogen, anfractuosity,* and *thigmotaxis.* If these words were in your listening vocabulary, identification would be easy and complete. More to the point, reflection should verify that the manner in which you sounded out these words was something closer to syllable by syllable or morpheme by morpheme than it was to letter by letter. You naturally exploited the sophisticated patterns that your Orthographic and Phonological processors have acquired.

For comparison, try next to sound out these words: *Karivaradharajan,*[10] *Wloclawek, Verkhneudinsk, Shihkiachwang, Bydgoszcz, Quetzalcòatl.* When confronted with words whose spellings are strange by English standards, skilled readers are reduced to less efficient, less confident, and more effortful processing. For younger and poorer readers, the sounding-out process tends to proceed in an effortful letter-by-letter fashion even when the words are relatively short, frequent, and regular.[11]

If a familiar response to the word is aroused in either the Meaning or Phonological processors, its orthographic image will be reinforced through the feedback they provide. Further, almost any orthographic string that finds a familiar response in one of these other processors will find a familiar response in both, thus doubling the feedback it will receive.[12] And if the other processors have anticipated the word—as when the word occurs in a meaningful context or a rhyming situation—their responses will be still stronger and more rapid[13] —sufficiently so, perhaps, to compensate wholly for such orthographic difficulties.

---

10. The major obstacle with proper Indian names such as this one, is not so much that the spelling within syllables is so difficult but that there are so many syllables. It is therefore interesting to note that Indian readers treat such names as compounds of smaller, more familiar patterns, e.g., *Kari-varadha-rajan,* much as we do when reading very long English words, e.g., *anti-dis-establishment-arian-ism.*

11. Frederiksen (1982).

12. If we know the meaning of an orthographically unfamiliar word, we generally know its pronunciation (if it is orthographically unfamiliar, how else might we have learned its meaning?). Similarly if we have learned a pronunciation for an orthographically unfamiliar word, we have surely associated it with some sort of conceptual information, if only the context in which it occurred. In general then, if either the Phonological or the Meaning processor responds to the word, both will, with the result that both will relay a fraction of their excitement back to the Orthographic processor. The notable exceptions to this generality are pseudowords invented for testing and experimentation.

13. For a review, see Carr and Pollatsek (1985).

Finally, this sort of feedback from the other processors not only speeds and clarifies the perception of visually less familiar words. In addition, as it returns extra activity, extra reinforcement, to the associative links between the letters of the word, it provides the reader with extra support toward learning the orthography of the word as well. But, of course, this works only if the reader takes the time to resolve the orthography rather than just making do with its interpretation.

Compensating for the Orthographic Processor's Inability to Distinguish Real Words from "Well-Spelled" Frauds. For each of the difficulties discussed so far, the Orthographic processor found no solid response where it should have had one. But the reverse can also occur: The Orthographic processor can be satisfied with a response where it should have had none. This vulnerability stems from the fact that it has within itself no basis for assessing anything about a word save the familiarity or regularity of its spelling.

For skillful readers, the Orthographic processor is quick at resolving the spellings of whole, frequent words. But its responses to piecewise familiar nonwords, such as *sust* and *bome*, are very nearly as quick and cohesive. The speed and coherence of the Orthographic processor's responses to such well-spelled nonwords may even exceed its responses to less frequent and less regularly spelled real words, and this is true for simulations of the model as well as for people.[14]

When skillful readers are asked to judge as rapidly as possible whether or not each of a series of orthographic strings is a word, they are willing and able to do so on the basis of its spelling pattern alone—provided that the words are regularly spelled and that the nonwords are not. However, if either regularly spelled nonwords, like *sust*, or irregularly spelled words, like *aisle*, are included among the items to be judged, this strategy becomes unreliable. In these situations, their decisions must await confirmation from the other processors, and, that being so, their responses are a few hundredths of a second slower and show sensitivity to the phonology and the meaningfulness of the words.[15]

But do not mistake the point here. The point is not that word recognition is slower when it involves phonological or meaning

---

14. Seidenberg and McClelland (1989).
15. Waters and Seidenberg (1985).

processing. Except in certain artificial and purposefully truncated tasks (such as the rapid word/nonword decision tasks of the laboratory), word recognition always involves phonological and meaning processing. The point is that under appropriate laboratory conditions, we can demonstrate the separate—and sometimes crucial—backup assistance that each of these processors adds to the total word recognition process.

Phonological Processing

Vulnerabilities of the Phonological Processor

The Phonological processor takes letters or multiletter patterns as input from the Orthographic processor. It responds with any and all pronunciations that it has associated to that letter or spelling pattern. The speed and strength of its response(s) depend on three factors: the instantaneity and quality of the orthographic information it receives; the number of different responses that the orthographic input elicits; and the familiarity of the appropriate response.

The Dependence of the Phonological Processor on the Speed and Quality of the Orthographic Input. The Orthographic processor does not wait until it is done with a word to ship information to the Phonological processor. Rather the associative connections between the two processors (and all of the connections within the system, for that matter) are like little short circuits. As soon as any individual letter receives excitation (and in exact proportion to the strength with which it does so), it will relay the same to the Phonological processor.

For skilled readers given legible print, the letters of a whole, familiar spelling pattern are orthographically resolved and bonded together almost at once. In these cases, the Phonological processor instantaneously receives excitation corresponding to the whole, integrated pattern and responds nearly as quickly with a holistic phonological translation.

However, if Orthographic processing is disrupted, fractionated, or slowed down, the picture is different. Rather than receiving the spelling pattern at once and as a whole, the Phonological processor must get it more slowly and in pieces. Moreover, because early processing of an unfamiliar string may include the indirect excitation of inappropriate letters, the Phonological processor may also have to put up with certain false leads.[16]

Bear in mind that the Phonological processor is comprised of an associative network very similar to that within the Orthographic processor. Like the Orthographic processor, its job is to bind together its input into the largest coherent response pattern that it can.

When the incoming string is a whole familiar word or a regularly spelled syllable, its task is easy. All pertinent phonemic units will be excited at once and at once will excite each other. Through this collective excitation, the appropriate phonological translation of the whole string will quickly be consolidated, overcoming any alternative phonological translations that its individual letters or subsets of letters might also have triggered.

In contrast, suppose that the letters arrive one by one from the Orthographic processor. The first letter perceived (which is typically but not necessarily the first one in the printed string)[17] will evoke all of its various phonemic translations, and each of these phonemic units will relay excitation to all others with which it has become associated. But the direct guidance thus provided must be very slim. First, any single letter may map onto a number of phonemic translations; for example, *c* may signal /*s*/ as in *city* and *dice*, /*k*/ as in *cat, income,* and *ache,* /*ch*/ as in *chin* and *bocci,* or /*sh*/ as in *suspicion* and *chute.* Second, there are only about forty phonemes in our language; so few that each must be associated with a relatively unhelpfully large number of others. The Phonological processor's efforts to build a word from the phonemic translations of a single letter must be very much like playing "Name that Tune" with just one note.

The response of the Phonological processor may be further diffused by any failures of the Orthographic processor to resolve the identities of individual letters. In general, visual letter recognition failures do not result in no response; they instead result in some number of relatively weak responses—as many as the perceived aspects of the letter evokes. In these cases, the Phonological processor not only misses the preemptive activation of the correct letter but must also cope with the misguided activation from all of the alternative candidates.

---

16. Remember the *tqe* example in chapter 6.
17. Adams (1979a).

The Phonological Processor's Difficulties with Multiple Spelling-Sound Translations. The greater the number of phonological responses associated with any given orthographic input, the more ways its excitation must be divided, and the more weakly and slowly each candidate translation will mature.

Thus the Phonological processor should respond uniquely and quickly to phonologically unambiguous spelling patterns, such as _ust and _ame: Whatever the first letter(s), its responses should rhyme with *just* and *name*. On the other hand, the processor's response to _ear will be slower: Should the winning response rhyme with *bear* and *wear* or with *dear* and *fear?* Similarly, responses to graphophonemically irregular words, such as *aisle* and *corps*, will be slowed as their component letters trigger a number of partial but more regular, more frequent, and thus more volatile competing responses. The naming times of both people and simulations of the model are found to be consistent with these predictions.[18]

The Phonological Processor's Dependence on its Familiarity with a Spelling Pattern. Again, the speed and strength of any given response is a direct product of the frequency with which it has been coupled with the spelling pattern in the past. And, again, because of the associations among units, the most evocative aspects of a spelling pattern are its largest familiar parts.

Thus although the Phonological processor should be ambivalent, and thus slow, with pseudowords such as *mave* (should it rhyme with *have* or *gave?*), it should respond quickly, appropriately, and uniquely to very frequent but graphophonemically exceptional real words, such as *have*, because it should respond to them as familiar wholes. Again the response patterns of both people and simulations of the model are consistent with this prediction.[19]

Similarly, for words that are sufficiently familiar to be processed holistically, the normal slowness of processor's responses to words with "strange" spelling-to-sound correspondences is also expected to be overcome. In keeping with this, skilled readers' naming times are relatively long for less frequent "strange" words, such as *heir* and *tsar*, but as quick as any for frequent ones such as

---

18. For reviews, see Carr and Pollatsek (1985); Seidenberg and McClelland (1989).

19. Seidenberg (1985).

once and *climb*.[20] This pattern of behavior is also obtained in simulations of the model.[21]

Finally we recall that it is not the general frequency with which a word occurs in print but the frequency with which it has occurred in the experience of the person reading it. It is, after all, one's personal experience with a word or spelling pattern that determines the strengths of the associations it evokes. Thus, words that behave like high frequency items among more experienced, skillful readers, behave like low frequency items among younger[22] and less skilled readers.[23] Words that are pronounced quickly and easily by experienced, skillful readers are pronounced slowly and effortfully by younger and less skilled readers. Words whose pronunciations are generated holistically by more experienced, skillful readers, are pronounced in accordance with piecewise rules by younger and less skilled readers (e.g., *island, busy*, and *whom* tend to be read, respectively, as "izland," "bussy," and "wom").[24]

Compensating for Phonological Difficulties

Print is not uniformly legible; the familiarity of words and spelling patterns range widely for all readers; and ambiguous spelling-sound correspondences are a fact of English orthography. Although such problems never go away, readers learn to overcome each of them. The key again lies in the interactive capabilities of system as a whole.

Compensating for the Phonological Processor's Problems with Slow Orthographic Processing. In contrast to the Orthographic processor, the workings of the Phonological processor are not necessarily defeated by slow letter recognition. This is because of the Phonological processor's autonomous capacity to renew its own stimulation. Specifically, readers can vocally, subvocally, or

---

20. Waters and Seidenberg (1985). Interestingly skilled readers may even respond slightly more quickly to frequent "strange" words than to frequent regular words. This is presumably a combined effect of the words' holistic familiarity and the failure of their "strange" spellings to evoke any serious response competition.

21. Seidenberg and McClelland (1989).

22. Backman, Bruck, Hèbert, and Seidenberg (1984); Waters, Seidenberg, and Bruck (1984).

23. Backman, Bruck, Hèbert, and Seidenberg (1984); Seidenberg, Bruck, Fornarolo, and Backman (1986).

24. Adams and Huggins (1985); Backman, Bruck, Hèbert, and Seidenberg (1984).

mentally repeat the candidate phonological fragments (e.g., "t - t - t - rrr - t - rrr - t - rrr - ap -t - rrr - ap - trr - ap - trr - ap - trap!"). In so doing, they renew the excitation of the relevant phonological units which in turn pass renewed excitation both to each other and to the orthographic units to which they are currently linked. In this way, poor orthographic resolution may be overcome within the Phonological processor itself.

If the word in attention is aurally familiar, then the phonological translation will also activate a response in the Meaning processor. The meaning response will then reciprocally strengthen the phonological response as well as sending activation directly to the orthographic response.

Compensating for the Phonological Processor's Difficulties with Multiple Spelling-to-Sound Correspondences. The Phonological processor's problems with ambiguous spelling-to-sound patterns in real words, such as *bear* and *dear*, are rarely a problem in actual reading. First, the ambivalence of the Phonological processor's response to such spelling patterns as _ear derives largely from the fact that both translations occur in more than one word that it knows and thus with considerable frequency across words. Second, individual words that have regular spellings and irregular spelling-to-sound correspondences tend to be quite frequent.[25]

Taken together, the implication is that letter sequences that have such ambiguous spelling-to-sound correspondences are likely to be highly familiar visually. As a consequence, they should be quickly processed and integrated within the Orthographic processor and, from there, quickly passed on as wholes to the other processors. If the Phonological processor does not immediately respond holistically and thus, uniquely, to an irregularly spelled word on its own, activation of the correct pronunciation from the Meaning processor should quickly ensure that it will.

In keeping with this, skillful readers' responses to words with regular spellings and irregular pronunciations (such as *bear*, *have*, *done*, and *great*) tend to be just as fast and accurate as their responses to wholly regular words.[26] Their response to an

---

25. Hooper (1977); Wang (1979).

26. Seidenberg (1985). Note further that this speed and accuracy does not indicate that the Phonological processor is circumvented but only that the words' pronunciations are resolved despite any doubts that it might have. As evidence, prior reading of, e.g., *come*, significantly slows the reading of

irregularly pronounced word tends to be slower only if the word is relatively infrequent—but, even then, only by a few hundredths of a second.[27]

In contrast, the speed with which skilled readers name nonwords with ambiguous spelling-to-sound translations (such as *mave* and *gough*) is reliably slowed.[28] Further, preceding such a nonword with a similarly spelled word strongly influences its pronunciation.[29] If *mave* is preceded by *gave*, it tends to get a long *a*; if preceded by *have*, it tends to get a short one. The explanation, following the model, is that the residual phonological excitation of the just-presented word is often sufficient to raise the consistent pronunciation of the ambiguous spelling pattern to dominance.

Again, because it is really the frequency of a word within the reader's own experience that matters, what is effectively a high-frequency word for a highly experienced, skillful reader may be an infrequent word for a young or poor reader. As a consequence, the speed with which younger and poorer readers can pronounce or recognize words is slowed much more by irregular spelling-to-sound correspondences, and this is true even for moderately frequent words.[30] Such less skilled readers also display a tendency to regularize the words—for example, to pronounce *deaf* as "deef" or *touch* as "towch."[31] Whether due to the absence of convergent support from the orthography-to-phonology connection or the presence of interference from it, it is clear that word identification in these cases is not effectively established through the direct orthography-to-meaning route.

Compensating for the Phonological Processor's Difficulties with Weak Spelling-to-Sound Familiarity. When reading meaningful, connected text, the Meaning processor receives activation from the Context processor as well as from the Orthographic and Phonological processors. To the degree that this contextual activation overlaps with orthographic or phonological activation

---

home: This can only indicate that the Phonological processor was involved in the reading of each (Taraban and McClelland, 1987).

27. Brown (1987); Taraban and McClelland (1987).

28. Glushko (1979); Taraban and McClelland (1987).

29. Taraban and McClelland (1987).

30. Seidenberg (1985).

31. Adams and Huggins (1985); Backman, Bruck, Hèbert, and Seidenberg (1984).

from the word, it will speed and strengthen the Meaning processor's response. This, in turn, will boost the strength of the feedback that the Meaning processor returns to the Orthographic and Phonological processors, such that spelling and sound difficulties may be overcome. Indeed, children with deficient word recognition skills are found to rely especially heavily on such contextual compensation.[32]

Compensating for the Phonological Processor's Indifference to Homographs and Homophones. Homographs are words that are spelled identically but mean something different. Homophones are words that are pronounced identically but mean something different.[33] Neither of these types of words can be disambiguated by the Phonological processor alone.

Homographs that have different pronunciations, such as *lead* the horse and *lead* pipe, present a special problem to the Phonological processor: Should *lead* rhyme with *bead* or *bed?* In general, both pronunciations are activated and sent to the Meaning processor, though the Phonological processor's response to most frequent candidate is faster and stronger.[34]

If the word has appeared in isolation, the speed and strength of the Meaning processor's responses depend on the relative frequencies of the candidates' meanings. Because the most frequent meaning necessarily corresponds to the most frequent pronunciation, the Meaning and Phonological processor will thus reinforce each other's choice. In contrast, if the word appears in connected text, contributions from the Context processor should ensure the correct choice.

The problem with homophones, such as *rose* and *rows*, is that the Phonological processor's responses are strictly phonological in nature. Thus, the responses it sends to the Meaning processor for *rose* and *rows* are indistinguishable. Fortunately for the Meaning processor, *rose* and *rows* are orthographically distinct. For skilled readers, at least, that is enough to keep them from being confused: The orthographic differences will compensate for the phonological similarities.

Even given relatively strong contextual expectations, such as the prior display of "*a type of flower*", skilled readers are liable to

---

32. For a review, see Stanovich (1980).

33. Of course, some homographs are homophones and vice-versa, but not all.

34. For a review, see Seidenberg and McClelland (1989).

confuse such words as *ROSE* and *ROWS* only when orthographic processing is aborted prematurely—as through special laboratory techniques[35] and, by conjecture, through the sorts of cursory visual processing that accompany skimming, the reading of highly predictable material, and hasty treatment of visually unfamiliar words. It is worth emphasizing that the errors in these cases do appear to be phonologically inspired: Under these circumstances, people are significantly more inclined to mistake *ROWS* for *ROSE* than to mistake *ROBS* for *ROSE* despite the fact that *ROWS* and *ROBS* are of comparable visually similarity to *ROSE*.

Laboratory evidence suggests that to verify its interpretation of such homophonic words, the Meaning processor literally undertakes a spelling check. Starting with each of the ambiguous word's meanings, it retraces the links to the Orthographic processor seeking evidence of whether its particular spelling was presented.[36]

Processing Meaning

The Meaning processor is in a unique position within the system. In arriving at its own response to an incoming word, it receives input from every one of the other processors. The responses of the Meaning processor are therefore influenced by the speed and accuracy or precision of all of the other processors but at the same time are less dependent on the timeliness and completeness of any one.

Although the information from any one of the other processors—Orthographic, Phonological, or Context—would often be sufficient for the Meaning processor to select a single dominant response from its repertoire, the convergent activation from all three serves two purposes that are critical to the system. First, it boosts the speed and strength of appropriate responses in the Meaning processor and, through them, of appropriate responses in each of the others. Second, the separate, multiple inputs imbue the system with a critical degree of reliability: Where any one of the inputs is ambiguous or misleading, the others should provide for the correction or detection of its incompatibility.

The optimal operation of the Meaning processor depends both on its receiving definitive, correct, and timely input from each of the other processors and on its possessing a well-integrated response to their input. It will clearly be at a general loss if it

---

35. Van Orden (1987).
36. Dennis, Besner, and Davelaar (1985); Van Orden (1987).

receives inadequate input from all three of the other processors. Moreover, to the extent that the input from any one is too poor or too slow, it cannot conduct the parity checks between them that ensure interpretive reliability. If, for whatever reason, the Meaning processor can produce no coherent response, all is for naught: The meaning of the word cannot be established and, without the word's meaning as the focus of activity, neither new information nor reciprocal feedback can be issued to any of the other processors.

As the Meaning processor receives and reciprocally sends activity to each of the other processors, it is in the unique position to regulate the responses of the system as a whole. Further, the proper evocation of meaning is the ultimate goal of individual word recognition in reading.

The responses of the Meaning processor are, thus, uniquely important to the reading process. Yet it, too, may fail or go astray. When it does, no quick fixes are available; its response is already the product of the system's total resources. The only sound remediation for problems in the Meaning processor is more learning.

Vulnerabilities of the Meaning Processor

Given that the Meaning processor does in fact possess a solid representation of a word's meaning, the speed and strength of its response depend on three factors: the contribution of context; the quality and completeness of the orthographic and/or phonological input it receives; and the strength of the associations between the word's meaning and its orthographic and/or phonological representation.

The Meaning Processor's Dependence on Context. As discussed in the previous chapter, the reader's understanding of the context in which a word occurs can help to emphasize or boost the activation of contextually relevant components of the word's meaning, to select among alternative interpretations of ambiguous words, and even to create a meaning for the word where there otherwise might be none. More generally, context serves to reinforce and thus to increases the strength, speed, and appropriateness of the system's understanding of a word's meaning. As it does so, it automatically increases the strength, speed, and appropriateness of its orthographic and phonological response to the word as well.

There are at least two major determinants of the speed and strength of the assistance that the Context processor can lend to the Meaning processor. The first derives from the definitiveness and appropriateness of the Context processor's expectations. If the Context processor's expectations of the word are vague, it cannot provide much help. Compare, for example, the ease of completing the following two sentences:

The entire group examined the ???
At the farmstand, we got tomatoes and corn on the ???

By the same token, the expectations of the Context processor may be inappropriate. As an example, consider this sentence:

At the farmstand, we got tomatoes and corn on the *car*.

From the previous example, you know that your Context processor expected *cob*, not *car*. Fortunately you had orthographic information to straighten things out. Without orthographic guidance, such misleading expectations can be quite unsettling:

Though smelly and ugly to look at, the *sewer* makes beautiful clothes.

Research verifies that while strong, appropriate contextual cues can speed word processing, strong, inappropriate ones typically slow it down, and everything in between typically has an in-between effect.[37]

The second factor influencing the help that the Context processor can provide, is the conscious attention that the reader devotes to it. Some limited degree of contextual facilitation occurs automatically. For example, the presentation of the word *doctor* will automatically facilitate the perception of the word *nurse*. However, the inhibition of inappropriate responses as well as the facilitation of more complexly determined appropriate responses—which, importantly, includes that critical question of what word is likely to be next in a sentence—require considerable time and the reader's conscious attention to accrue.[38]

In actual reading, the extra time involved in establishing useful contextual guidance is not expected to be a problem. Since such guidance begins to mature before the to-be-resolved word is encountered, it will generally be ready when it is time to digest the phrase or clause as a whole.[39]

---

37. Fischler and Bloom (1979); Stanovich (1984).

38. Neely (1977).

39. Indeed, looking to our model, an alternative explanation for these findings might be that automatic context effects arise within the Meaning

On the other hand, the Context processor's dependence on conscious effort and attention may often be a problem. First, the reader's available pool of conscious attention is inherently limited. To the extent that such attention is being directed to other activities in the system, less is available for these crucial interpretive activities. In particular, the reader may have no conscious capacity left for integrating the meaning of the word with its prior context and assessing its sense if she or he is investing conscious effort in resolving the word's orthographic structure, in sounding it out, or in retaining the prior wording of an incomplete phrase.

Further, processes that require conscious attention are, as a group, optional rather than automatic. For any of a variety of reasons, therefore, the reader may simply neglect their execution. It is of interest in this vein that when asked to read aloud such sentences as

John said, "Does are in the park, aren't they?"

second graders often, and without the slightest signs of perturbance or confusion, read *does* as "duz."[40]

The Meaning Processor's Dependence on the Quality and Completeness of the Orthographic and/or Phonological Input. Neither the Orthographic nor the Phonological processor waits until it is done with a word to ship excitation to the Meaning processor. Rather, just as soon as a spelling or phonological unit receives excitation, it relays that excitation to all associated constellations of units in the Meaning processor.

For skilled readers given legible print, the letters of a whole, familiar word are orthographically resolved and bonded together almost at once. In these cases, the Meaning processor instantaneously receives excitation from the Orthographic processor corresponding to the whole, integrated spelling pattern and quickly responds with its meaning. Nearly as quickly, it also receives excitation from the Phonological processor of the whole, integrated phonological translation of the word.

---

processor itself, whereas attentional context effects arise only when the phrase is compiled by the Context processor.

40. Daneman and Carpenter (1983). The tendency to rely more heavily on orthographic than contextual clues typically begins to appear sometime in the second grade (Biemiller, 1970).

However, if orthographic processing is disrupted, fractionated, or slowed down, the Meaning processor must receive the spelling and phonological patterns more slowly and in pieces. In these cases, the speed and definitiveness of the Meaning processor's response depend on such factors as the base familiarity of the word and its meaning and the extent to which it is predictable from the preceding context.

With poor orthographic and phonological resolution and little or no contextual facilitation, the reader may fail to recognize the word altogether. On the other hand, if the word is highly predictable from context, relatively little orthographic or phonological information may be needed for some one response to dominate all others comfortably.

As valuable as such contextual compensation may be, it also has a negative side. If the Meaning processor relies too heavily on context, it is liable to miss orthographic distinctions that the reader should care about. This happens, for example, when one reads one word for another while skimming, when one misses typographical errors while proofreading (this is a special problem when one is proofing highly predictable material, such as material that one has written),[41] and, most relevant in the present context, when one lacks both the capacity to resolve the spelling of the word automatically and the time or discipline to resolve it with effort.

The latter is a particularly vexing problem in the instructional arena. Younger and poorer readers tend to rely significantly more heavily on context than do more experienced and skillful readers.[42] On the one hand, such compensatory use of context is a positive behavior—it is ultimately a critical component of productive reading. On the other, to the extent that children use context to avoid fully processing and, thereby, learning about the spellings of words, it may in the long run slow their reading growth. We will return to this trade-off in chapter 10.

The Meaning Processor's Difficulties when the Connections between a Word and its Meaning are Weak. The strengths of the associations between a constellation of meaning units and the word whose meaning they represent influence not only the speed but the very likelihood that a meaning will be elicited. Given a well-developed representation of meaning, the strength with which it

---

41. See also Healy and Drewnowski (1983).
42. For a review, see Stanovich (1980).

is evoked by a particular orthographic or phonological pattern depends on the frequency with which it has been coupled to that pattern in the reader or listener's experience.

Among other things, these couplings influence the relative ease of accessing different meanings of a word. Presented in isolation, the strength with which alternative interpretations of a word are aroused depends on the frequency (or recency) with which the word has been coupled with each of those interpretations. In isolation, therefore, the word *does* is more likely to be interpreted as "acts" than as "female deer." Because more frequent meanings are also more likely meanings, this tendency is surely helpful on balance. When it is not—as when the competing meanings are of comparable frequency or the least frequent one is the most appropriate—activation from the Context processor will usually sort them out.[43]

Again, what is at issue here is not knowledge of the word's meaning per se but the connection between such meaning and the orthographic or phonological representation of the word. Thus one might have a wholly adequate understanding of the word *groin* and still be at a loss for understanding the word *groyne*—unless one were aware that these two words were alternate spellings for the same thing.

Indeed, this example seems to illustrate a basic principle of the Meaning processor's operation: When it does receive complete input from the Orthographic processor, it is inclined to respect it. Thus, encountered in isolation, a good reader would not assume that *groyne* meant *groin* even while pronouncing it the same way; encountered in context, a good reader would at least pause to wonder. Such deference to orthography is functional: It is the means by which we so reliably distinguish between such words as *rose* and *rows;* moreover, given the architecture of the system, the inadequacy of sophisticated-guessing or hypothesis-testing theories of word recognition can only be owed to skilled readers' tendency to process orthography completely.

For unfamiliar words that are irregularly spelled, however, the system's deference to orthography-based interpretations can result in certain confusions. For example, it was in graduate school that I discovered that the word /in-dikt/, which I had read so often, was the same as the word /in-dite/, which I had heard so often; and, even then, I discovered this only when I happened to say the word aloud. This same deference undoubtably underlies

43. Carpenter and Daneman (1981); Simpson (1981); Swinney (1979).

younger and poorer readers' tendency to mispronounce irregularly spelled words even in context, as in

The girls rowed the boat to the *island* (read /*izland*/).[44]

It must also be skilled readers' deference to orthographic information that allows them to decide so quickly and accurately that strings such as *brane* are not words[45] and that sentences such as *"Tie the not"*[46] do not make sense. On the other hand, even for skilled readers, such judgments are typically slower (by a few hundredths of a second) and/or slightly less accurate than when shown pseudowords or sentences that do not "sound" meaningful. This interference reflects the competing contribution of the Phonological processor.

Although the interference produced by sound-alikes is slight among skilled readers, one might expect it to be relatively strong among readers with less consolidated orthographic knowledge. Specifically, suppose that a young reader is confronted with a sentence such as

We swim in the see.

As the child reads each word, the Orthographic processor will send its results both to the Phonological processor and to the Meaning processor. The response of the Phonological processor is indifferent to the word's spelling—it neither knows nor cares whether the word was "see" or "sea." Moreover, because both words are aurally quite familiar to the child, the phonological translation will easily find both meanings in the Meaning processor, and the Context processor will easily agree that one of them makes sense and reinforce it.

Meanwhile, since this is a young and inexperienced reader, the strength of the link between the Orthographic processor and the Meaning processor is expected to be relatively weak and possibly incomplete. It would not be surprising if it could not overcome the self-reinforcing, self-sustaining activity that the Phonological, Meaning, and Context processors were mutually supporting. It would not be surprising, in other words, if the orthographic inappropriateness of the word went entirely unnoticed and, indeed, this is what happens.

---

44. Adams and Huggins (1985); Backman, Bruck, Hèbert, and Seidenberg (1984).

45. For a review, see Dennis, Besner, and Davelaar (1985).

46. Baron (1973).

Working with children aged six to ten years, Doctor and Coltheart found that the youngest judged the majority (70 percent) of twenty-four sentences such as "We swim in the see" and "The sky is blew" to be meaningful. Even the oldest children accepted 20 percent of such sentences. In contrast, children of all ages accepted correctly spelled, meaningful sentences while rejecting sentences that did not sound meaningful most of the time.[47]

The hypothesis that these children's confusions were owed largely to the interactive and parallel contributions of the Phonological, Meaning, and Context processors is also supported by Doctor and Coltheart's study. Specifically, the children's sentence judgment errors greatly exceeded both their tendency to misspell the words when dictated in context and their tendency to define the homophone rather than the printed word itself when presented in isolation.

Remediating the Meaning Processor's Weaknesses

The responses of the Meaning processor are the combined product of all of the knowledge and processing the reader has applied to the text. If the Meaning processor commits an error or oversight, it is because the reader's knowledge and processing have not been adequate to the challenge presented by the text. The only way to minimize such problems is by maximizing the knowledge, skill, and interpretive control that the reader will readily bring to bear.

Supporting Appropriate Use of Context. The key to reconciling text with context lies in the competent operation of the other processors. For skillful readers, a word's orthographic and phonological resolution is normally so fast, so complete, and so strongly bound to its meaning that contextual guidance can produce little gain in interpretive speed while contextual misguidance is generally overcome. Moreover, the activities involved in resolving the word's orthography, phonology, and meaning are so automatic and effortless that skilled readers can devote nearly all of their conscious attention to the combined sense of a word and its context. Not only do they readily select a unique meaning for a word when that is appropriate, but they can also entertain the alternatives—as is evident from their ability to understand the double entendres of puns, poetry, and jokes.

---

47. Doctor and Coltheart (1980).

For readers with less orthographic facility, one might expect word recognition to depend much more strongly on contextual cues. Research confirms this hypothesis. Younger and poorer readers tend to rely significantly more heavily on context than do more experienced and skillful readers.[48] Not only do they rely more heavily on context for initial word identification, they seem also to rely on it with a differential inflexibility for word interpretation. Younger children seem remarkably resistant to considering multiple meanings of a word even when all are perfectly well known.[49]

It is reasonable to wonder whether this inflexibility might be more apparent than real. Perhaps in the social context of interpreting a sentence for an adult, children feel that a single, definite response is most appropriate. Perhaps they actually recognize the ambiguity, but suppress one of the responses so as not to look confused or uncooperative.

Perhaps. But that does not explain young children's universal bumbling of jokes and puns. Gleitman and Brill have shown that, although "any self-respecting five year old" will laugh at a well-delivered pun, only one side of the ambiguity is typically understood.[50] This can hardly be a matter of politeness.

As an example, here is one of the riddles that circulated through my son's preschool class:

Where do sheep get a haircut? At the baa-baa shop.

I laughed when I first heard this joke as, no doubt, did most of the (Yankee) parents. And so it was followed for weeks thereafter with a host of variations that were clearly perceived as equally hilarious by the children:

Where do cows get a haircut? At the moo-moo shop.
Where do dogs get a haircut? At the bow-wow shop.
Where do lions get a haircut? At the (ROAR) shop.

. . . And so on.

It seems that children are not predisposed to considering more than one interpretation of what they read or hear. While this tendency makes folly of jokes, it must limit their capacity to monitor and adjust their interpretations of reading materials in more deleterious ways. By conjecture, it might be a very good idea to bring jokes, puns, and other sorts of double entendres

---

48. For reviews, see Stanovich (1980, 1984).
49. Asche and Nerlove (1960).
50. Brill (1974, cited in Rozin and Gleitman, 1977, p. 192).

deliberately and systematically into the classroom. Exercise with such materials is a regular component of some reading and language curricula and may be far more valuable and important to the students' comprehension development than would appear at first blush.[51]

Developing Appropriate Deference to Orthographic Information. Whatever else may be required for the development of reflective reading, able and effortless lower-level processing is essential. The contribution of context takes on its proper weight in the system only when orthographic processing becomes comparably sure and quick. Moreover, the thoughtful exploitation of context—that which is required for establishing the full and proper meaning of text—becomes possible only when sufficient attention is available for its reflective processing.

Exercise in comprehending connected text must be complemented by activities to encourage and enhance the children's knowledge and facility with the visual identities of individual words. Such activities include not only spelling-sound instruction in the beginning, but repeated readings and writing/spelling activities throughout. And again, the reading of connected, meaningful text provides the very best opportunity for learning the orthography and meaning of less familiar words.

Reinforcing the Links between Words and their Meanings. Clearly the Context processor provides invaluable help toward the fuller interpretation of poorly learned or partly forgotten word meanings. Yet a less obvious source of assistance is also suggested by the model. Specifically, in normal, skillful reading, the units in the Meaning processor will receive excitation from both the Orthographic and the Phonological processor. The two processors thus provide a redundant look-up process. Even where the activation of one of them might not be enough to bring any fragment of the word's meaning to consciousness, the conjoint activation of both just might—and once any critical subset of the meaning units is activated, it will automatically excite others to which it is bound.

But neither of these sources of assistance is robust. The cohesiveness of a word's meaning representation depends most of all on the frequency with which it has been activated and reinforced. If we want children to learn the meanings of new

---

51. Bereiter, Hughes, and Anderson (1986).

words, we should take care to give them the opportunity to read and use those words repeatedly. More generally, it is repeated experiences with a word in different contexts that strengthens both its meaning and its ties to orthography. The more a child reads, the stronger both will be. To this end, regular encouragement of silent reading is strongly recommended. But oral reading, though logistically more cumbersome and less efficient, is also worthwhile: Given the graphophonemic unruliness of English, reading aloud provides valuable opportunities to reconcile irregularly spelled words with their phonological translations.

Summary: Interactions between Processors

The goal of this section has been to clarify how the parallel and interconnected operation of the Orthographic, Phonological, and Meaning processors complement and compensate for each other's vulnerabilities and weaknesses in the course of reading. In explaining these interrelations, I dwelled mainly on catastrophic failures of each of the individual processors—situations in which the proper response was just plain not forthcoming of its own accord. Although such catastrophic failures must be fairly rare in the normal, daily reading of competent readers, lesser difficulties—or at least inconsistencies—in the ease and speed of resolving the orthography, phonology, and meaning of words must occur within nearly every paragraph we face.

Line by line in running text, most words are common words— words that are seen frequently and that we must generally recognize instantly and easily with no need of phonological support. Carroll, Davies, and Richman reported that 90 percent of school children's running text consists of just 5,000 common words, and a similar distribution is found in adult texts.[52]

Nestled among these common words, however, are myriad less common ones. Specifically, the remaining 10 percent of school children's running text consists of more than 94 percent of the different words they must read. On average these words occur only four times in every million words of text; none occurs as many as ten times in every million words of text. For the average child, in other words, none is encountered as many as ten times in each year's worth of reading. The sheer arithmetic of the situation argues that relatively few of these words can be visually overlearned.

---

52. Carroll, Davies, and Richman (1971); Kucera and Francis (1967).

The importance of such less frequent words is underscored by the fact they impart a disproportionate amount of meaning to text. The information conveyed by words varies inversely with their frequency.[53] The less frequent a word is, the greater is the amount of meaning that it is expected to contribute to a passage; the less frequent a word is, the more strongly the meaning of a passage is expected to depend on its full and proper interpretation.

While competent reading depends on resolving these words, it also depends on resolving them quickly and completely. The nature of the system is such that identification of individual words depends on simultaneous activation of the units corresponding to their orthographic or phonological components. Similarly, the comprehension of phrases and sentences depends on simultaneous activation of the units corresponding to their component words. The problem is that while simultaneous activation of successive units depends on rapid activation of each, the response of any one of the processors to less familiar words is expected to be relatively slow and possibly fuzzy.

It is in overcoming this problem that the connectivity among the processors is so critical to the skilled reader. By mutually facilitating, reinforcing, and reminding each other of their relevant knowledge, they collectively ensure that we will recognize printed words, ranging in frequency and familiarity from *the* to *syzygy*, with the greatest speed and accuracy possible.

For this role alone, the Phonological processor is an indispensable part of the system. Yet its second role, as memory enhancer, is at least as important.

Supporting the Reader's Running Memory for Text

At the bottom-most level, the connections between the Orthographic and Phonological processors capture the ways in which the graphemes of our language symbolize its phonemes. Thus, a seemingly reasonable hypothesis about the Phonological processor is that its existence is a consequence of the alphabetic foundation of our script and its use, a fortuitous vestige of having learned to read by sounding out words.

To be sure, phonic instruction must contribute invaluably to the definition, strengthening, and refinement of these connections between print and speech. Yet phonic training cannot be the whole

---

53. Finn (1977–1978).

explanation for their existence, and support of the alphabetic principle cannot be the whole explanation for their use.

Automatic phonological translation has been found among normal, skilled readers of every language studied.[54] This includes readers of Chinese, whose script is principally logographic.[55] And despite the fact of automatic phonological translation among readers of Chinese, the translations they produce seem unrelated to—even disjoined from—the processes of visually recognizing and accessing the meanings of individual words.[56] The suggestion is that phonological translations subserve some additional purpose, distinct from word identification, in the reading process. Theory and research confirm that this is so.

Text comprehension is a two-stage process. In the first stage, the reader identifies each successive word and its appropriate meaning as defined by its immediate context. In the second, the reader interprets the entire string of words just read, considering the relationships among the just-read words to each other as well as to any relevant background knowledge and larger understanding of the text that can be brought to bear. In order for this second stage to result in a complete and sensible interpretation, there are two conditions on its execution.

First, it is best undertaken at major syntactic boundaries. Otherwise, the string of words to be compiled will be syntactically incomplete and make no.[57] The performance of skilled readers indicates that they generally prefer to recode at the boundaries between sentences or whole clauses. In keeping with this, when skilled readers are in the course of reading a clause, their ability to recall its precise wording is extremely rapid and accurate; in contrast, this fine, verbatim memory for the clause is all but lost just as soon as they start reading the next.[58] As another outward sign of this recoding, skilled readers characteristically pause at the end of major syntactic units.[59] Appropriately, the duration of this "wrap-up" time is significantly increased if the interpretation of the just-read clause requires inference or subtle resolution of pronouns.[60]

---

54. Tzeng and Wang (1983).

55. Tzeng, Hung, and Wang (1977).

56. Trieman, Baron, and Luk (1981); Tzeng and Wang (1983).

57. That is, ". . . make no sense."

58. Chang (1980); Kleiman (1975).

59. Aaronson and Scarborough (1976); Just and Carpenter (1987).

60. For the term "wrap-up" as well as a discussion of such findings see Just and Carpenter (1987).

The second condition on the success of the wrap-up process, is that it get the proper input. Specifically, its success depends upon the reader's having a complete and correctly ordered memory of the just-read words. Again, if the reader's memory for the just-read words is incomplete or misordered, then a sensible interpretation may be precluded.

Baddeley, Vallar, and Wilson have illustrated the importance of these two conditions through work with individuals whose immediate verbal memory capacity has been reduced through brain damage.[61] In their first patient, phonological memory capacity had been impaired by a stroke to the point that she was capable of retaining the wording of sentences no more than six words in length. Her ability to understand short simple sentences, and even series of such sentences, was unimpaired. However, within lengthy clauses, she showed difficulty in connecting pronouns and other indirect references to their antecedents. In addition, she was entirely unable to judge the sense or nonsense of longer written or spoken sentences that required precise retention of wording and order. Examples of these sentences include:

The earth divides the equator into two hemispheres the northern and the southern.

One could reasonably claim that sailors are often lived on by ships of various kinds.[62]

Due to a prolonged seizure, the sentence memory of a second patient had been reduced to just three words. This is too few for most of the sentences we see and hear. In keeping with this, the patient "complained of comprehension difficulties, saying that he could always understand the beginning of a conversation, but that after the first few phrases, his mind became cluttered 'like a noisy television screen.' "[63]

When reading, if given enough time, this patient could correctly interpret such sentences as

The girl is pushing the horse.

Baddeley, Vallar, and Wilson show how, with three-word units and by dint of work, this is possible:[64]

---

61. Baddeley, Vallar, and Wilson (1987).
62. Baddeley, Vallar, and Wilson (1987, p. 514).
63. Baddeley, Vallar, and Wilson (1987, p. 515).
64. Baddeley, Vallar, and Wilson (1987, p. 527).

> The girl is . . .
> . . . girl is pushing . . .
> . . . is pushing the . . .
> . . pushing the horse.

The correct interpretation can be had by focusing on the second and fourth triplets.

But other sentences eluded this patient, regardless of the time invested:

The book the pencil is on is red.

For sentences such as this, no combination of two or three triplets will unlock its sense:

> The book the . . .
> . . . book the pencil . . .
> . . . the pencil is . . .
> . . . pencil is on . . .
> . . . is on is . . .
> . . . on is red.

Given clauses that are extremely long and complex, similar difficulties must threaten healthy, skillful readers. It is not the capacity of one's verbal memory but the capacity relative to the requirements of the task that makes the difference.

How do normal, skillful readers cope with such difficulties? They exploit their phonological translations: Skilled readers can neither remember nor comprehend a complex sentence when they are prevented from subvocalizing its wording.[65]

It is important to note that suppression of subvocalization does not disrupt the interpretation of single words or simple sentences. The effect here has nothing to do with word identification. Rather the mechanism at work is our so-called "articulatory loop"—our ability to extend phonological memory through verbal rehearsal.[66] By speaking or thinking the spoken images of the words to ourselves, we effectively renew their phonological activation, thus extending the longevity and holding capacity of our verbatim memory.

In contrast with skillful readers, younger and poorer readers are expected to exploit this capacity relatively ineffectively. First, the capacity of immediate memory varies directly with the

---

65. Baddeley (1979); Levy (1977); Levy (1978); Waters, Caplan, and Hildebrandt (1987).
66. Baddeley (1986).

speed with which the items to be remembered are encoded[67]—but the decoding speed of younger and poorer readers is relatively slow. Second, the capacity of immediate memory varies directly with the amount of effort that is simultaneously being invested in processing activities[68]—but younger and poorer readers must invest considerable effort in all aspects of reading. Third, evidence suggests that, as a group, younger and poorer readers are relatively disinclined to engage in verbal rehearsal in the first place.[69] Moreover, where young readers are actively engaged in sounding out individual letters and syllables, the Phonological processor is clearly unavailable for retaining the wording of clauses.

Not surprisingly, then, memory for the prior wording of an in-process clause has been shown to be significantly poorer among younger than among older students and among low-ability readers than among high-ability readers.[70] Such deficits might well be the explanation of why poor readers are inclined to supply such words as *pizza* in a fill-in-the-blank test like the following:

When I got home from work, I wanted to eat a fruit. I went to the refrigerator and got a _____.[71]

Although normal reading does not consist of fill-in-the-blanks, this kind of behavior points up the impoverished comprehension and consequent dysfluency that poorer readers may face.

Perfetti and his colleagues found, more specifically, that their poorer third-grade readers could not remember as many as three words back in a clause.[72] The interpretive situation in which such youngsters find themselves must be very much like those described earlier for memory-impaired adults, with one important difference: While the impaired adults exercised the control and determination to overcome such deficits whenever possible, children may not.

Finally, although skilled readers prefer to undertake this second, integrative level of interpretation at sentence boundaries, they are relatively flexible about overriding that preference. If

67. Baddeley, Thomson, and Buchanan (1975); Case, Kurland, and Goldberg (1982); Dempster (1981).

68. For a discussion of trade-offs between processing and storage demands in the reading situation, see Daneman and Tardif (1987).

69. For a review, see Jorm and Share (1983).

70. Perfetti (1985).

71. Perfetti and Roth (1977).

72. Goldman, Hogaboam, Bell, and Perfetti (1980).

the nature of the task or sentence so dictates, they will instead pause for wrap-up at clausal or phrasal boundaries. Clearly their ability to do so depends on their ability to recognize amenable syntactic boundaries, but this, too, is a process that has become highly automatic.

Skilled readers interpret the syntactic structure of what they are reading on the fly. As a consequence, they quite reliably stumble on such garden-path sentences as:

The conductor stood before the audience left the concert hall.
The old train the young.[73]

But importantly, they stumble as soon as they fixate the word *left* in the first sentence and the second *the* in the second. This indicates that they do not wait until the end of a clause or sentence to interpret its syntax: Instead they interpret (and, when necessary, reinterpret) it on a word-by-word basis.

The syntactic sensitivities of younger and poorer readers are not well developed.[74] For this reason alone, they are unlikely to break a sentence down into appropriate and tractable subunits even if they know they cannot manage its wording in its entirety.[75] And so, beyond having less immediate memory capacity and less inclination to expand it through verbal rehearsal, younger and poorer readers also have less flexibility in controlling its requirements.

Both the causes and consequences of inadequate memory for wording restress the value and importance of repeated readings of more difficult texts. In addition, they supply the rationale for the common use of short, simple sentences in primers—though, of course, the mastery of more complex ones can come about only through experience with them.[76]

Summary: The Importance of Phonological Processing

For the skillful reader, automatic phonological encoding subserves two distinct and critical processes. First, as an alphabetic backup system, it increases the speed and completeness with which the

---

73. Just and Carpenter (1987).

74. Huggins and Adams (1980).

75. See Adams (1980).

76. Adams (1980) argues that both the requirement and the opportunity for developing sensitivities to more complex syntactic structures arise through *reading* language, not listening to it.

meanings and orthography of less familiar words can be processed. Second, through the "articulatory loop," it expands the reader's verbatim memory capacity in support of proper comprehension.

For skilled readers, in short, phonological processing adds a critical degree of insurance and efficiency to the reading system. Paradoxically this added insurance and efficiency is generally denied to younger and poorer readers precisely because of the reasons that they need it all the more; it is precluded precisely because of the otherwise inefficiency of their processing capabilities.

The situation is succinctly summarized by Charles Perfetti and Alan Lesgold:

The poor reader is slower at getting to the point in the comprehension process beyond which exact wording is not needed, but he is also poorer at retaining exact wording. Thus, he is confronted with a double whammy—slower processing and lower tolerance (in terms of working memory), both of which combine to create more processing needs [resulting in still more slowing and still less tolerance] than might otherwise exist.[77]

In his recent book, Perfetti has explored the relationship between processing efficiency and comprehension potential in depth.[78] He has examined data on the realities and consequences of all manner of processing inefficiencies, from single letter recognition to subtleties of discourse processing. Perfetti makes very clear that reading comprehension is an extremely complex behavior and that its efficiency is influenced by many, many factors. Nevertheless, his ultimate conclusion is that the most frequent, pervasive, and profound reading problems derive from difficulties in recognizing the orthography and identifying the meanings of individual words.

---

77. Perfetti and Lesgold (1977, p. 178).
78. Perfetti (1985).

IV

Thinking, Learning, and Reading

In part III, we saw how, for the accomplished reader, the Orthographic, Phonological, Meaning and Context processors work together, autonomously and in synergy, to allow progress through the text with comprehension and fluency. This coordination depends on an enormous complex of highly overlearned knowledge and skills. How are such knowledge and skills acquired?

Toward answering this question, part IV is devoted to background information. Chapter 9 examines the structure of knowledge and the ways in which its acquisition is influenced by experience, thinking, and rules. Chapter 10 focuses on the special relationships among the Orthographic, Phonological, Meaning, and Context processors that inhere in beginning reading.

The Nature of Learning
(Words or Otherwise)

What does it mean to have learned something? When we recognize a scene, for example, what is it that makes it familiar? Most obviously, it is that we recognize the things it contains: the house and the tree that shades it, the flower-spattered field and the rough-hewn fence that encloses it. But this is not any house, any tree, any blooming field, or any old fence. We recognize the scene because this is the same house, tree, field, and fence that we have seen there before.

How do we know that they are the same? Because we look at the house and recognize the soft, regular striping of its whitewashed clapboards, the shapes and locations of its windows and doors, the gingerbreading around its eaves, and the warm blue-greyness of its worn asphalt shingles.

But what makes these parts familiar? It is that we recognize the rhythmic contrast of whites and greys that reveal the clapboard; we recognize the rectangle of the house's frame and the pattern of rectangles within it that are made by its doors and windows; we recognize the horizontal and vertical crisscrossing of its shingles and the disturbances of that pattern where the roofing has curled and warped.

Gradually, as we scrutinize each of these parts to see what makes them special, a paradox arises. It is the parts of the parts, and the parts of the parts of the parts, that makes the scene unique. Yet, the parts are less distinctive than the whole, and the parts of the parts are less distinctive than the parts. Other scenes have houses, trees, or fenced-in fields. Other houses have clapboards, and many other objects have stripes. Other houses have rectangular frames, windows, and doors, and many things besides houses, windows, and doors are rectangular.

Indeed, if we were to continue this componential analysis of our scene, we would eventually find ourselves focusing on colors, arcs, line segments, and contrasts in brightness. These are the basic elements of visual perception, the elements whose presence defines every visual event in our mental universe. Considered piece by piece at this level of analysis, everything we ever will see must be familiar already. And, of course, that is the point. We do not "see" the scene as an array of colors, arcs, line segments, and brightness contrasts. We perceive and remember it as a particular house, tree, and fenced-in field of wildflowers, all in specific relation to each other.[1]

The Structure of Knowledge

The central assumption of connectionist theories of learning is that knowledge is built upon the elements, pieces, or components of our experiences but that it consists of learned relations among them.[2] Because these theories of learning are built from the bottom or most elementary levels of representation up, the easiest way to understand their logic may also be from the bottom up. For a moment, imagine that you are a baby.

Perhaps even in your first encounter with a rectangle, you see it as a whole. But inside, the wholeness of this new pattern is represented as an appropriately interrelated set of four line segments. The rectangle is created from your prior knowledge of its simpler parts by linking them in a new and particular interrelation with one another.

---

1. Eye movement studies show that, when viewing a complex scene such as this, we do not evenly sweep it with our eyes. We do not look directly at most of it at all. Instead we jump our fixations between its complexly meaningful parts — the house, the tree, the fence, and any center of interest in the field (Antes, 1974; Buswell, 1935; Mackworth and Bruner, 1970; Mackworth and Morandi, 1967; Yarbus, 1967). Scene recognition studies show that our memories, even for distinctive, namable, and well-studied elements of a scene, are tightly bound up in their spatial relations to other parts of the scene (Biederman, 1972; Biederman, Rabinowitz, Glass, and Stacy, 1974). In addition, studies of scene reconstruction indicate that memory for scenes tends to be hierarchical such that two parts are remembered in direct association with one another only if they are part of same, immediately higher-order unit (Stevens, 1978). Thus the parts of a window might be directly associated only with other parts of that window; in turn, the entire complex of associations representing that window is directly associated en masse to other global aspects of the house; and the whole memory of the house is in turn directly associated to the whole memories of the tree, the field, and the fence.

2. For a more formal and complete but relatively readable theoretical overview, see McClelland, Rumelhart, and Hinton (1986).

Having once been studied, the rectangle's perceptual support will now be different, for the interrelated assemblage of parts it aroused must now reside in your memory. On next encounter, it will be received by the entire, connected representation of its prior occurrence, and you will respond to it as a familiar whole. The more you encounter or study it, the stronger those interrelations will grow, the more familiar (better remembered) it will become as a whole, and the more quickly you will respond to it as such.

Still, no matter how many times you see this rectangle and no matter how well-integrated and holistically familiar it becomes, it will at core be comprised of the same set of interrelations among the same elementary line segments. When you encounter some different rectangle, it too must be perceived as an interrelated set of four line segments. And as you encounter another, and another, and another, you will eventually accrue a whole lot of rectangle memories that as a group substantially overlap. Each will share some aspects of its underlying representation with others, and each of those, in turn, may overlap with your first rectangle, with each other, or with still others. In this way, what will accrue is a family or distribution of rectangles, perceptually bound together by their common representational base. In perceiving rectangle, after rectangle, after rectangle, you will eventually come to perceive each as a member of a class.

In this oneness of the core representations of knowledge, lies only half the key to learning. The other half derives from the fact that on separate encounters, you may never have identical experiences with any object or event. Your first rectangle was not an abstraction but a real thing: It had a color, a texture, and a size; perhaps it also had a weight, a taste, and a feel. Moreover, you did not see it in a vacuum: It was located in a particular situation, distinguished not just in time and space but also by its particular visual, auditory, verbal, social, conceptual, and motor context.

All attended aspects of your experience with the rectangle will be remembered, and they will be remembered in association with one another. Those parts of the experience with which you were already familiar—perhaps the room in which it occurred, or the person with whom you were playing—will be experienced, reinforced, and remembered as coherent patterns or associated bundles of elements in themselves. But these bundles too—by virtue of their co-occurrence in this experience—will be associated with each other and with your memory of the rectangle.

The next time you encounter this same rectangle, the situation cannot be identical. The parts of it that are different will be written in as new associations to each other and to the rectangle. The parts that are similar or the same will arouse and reinforce your earlier memory of the rectangle. The perception of the rectangle itself (its color, size, texture, and so on) must, of course, be similar since it is the same rectangle. But your second experience with it may also be similar in still other ways. Maybe you are in the same room; maybe your mother is there again; maybe she is playing the same game. These repeated features of the experience will also be recalled with the result that their associations to the rectangle will also be reinforced.

None of these ancillary features may be identical in detail with their occurrence in the first scenario. However, they do not need to be. They need only to be sufficiently similar to evoke the same complex responses. Thus, your mother may say and do some different things the second time you play the game with the rectangle, and these new things will be newly entered into your memory of the rectangle and its context. On the other hand, all the ways in which the game is the same as in the last encounter will be evoked and reinforced, as will all of the things that make this person your mother, this place your room, and so on. And the more recently it was that you and your mother played this game with this rectangle, the more forcefully each familiar part will recall the entire situation since each will have been associated with fewer other things in the interim.

Moreover, every time you encounter this rectangle, each of these repeated elements of the experience will be evoked and thereby linked ever more strongly together. Meanwhile those aspects of your various experiences with the rectangle that were unique to each situation will be lost in the noise. After a while, whether actually present or not, each of the most frequent past experiences with the rectangle will be evoked and reminded whenever you see it. You will have learned not just about the physical characteristics of this particular rectangle but also about the contexts and uses with which it is normally associated and, by default, the contexts and uses with which it normally is not.[3]

In this way—in effect by the classical principles of association (contiguity, recency, frequency, and similarity)—we acquire concepts. We acquire categorical knowledge about the objects and events in our environment and about their forms, their uses, and

---

3. For a more formal and disciplined discussion of these issues, see McClelland and Rumelhart (1986).

their contexts: This is the rectangle we drop in our shape-sorter, and this is how we do it.

Eventually we experience many rectangles, each similar and different from one another in particular ways. And, quite automatically, as their similarities overwrite each other, their differences become distinct. Eventually we learn, for example, that this rectangle is the shape of our crib, that these are the shapes of other beds in our house, and that these are the shapes of beds in general. We learn that this one is the overall shape of the picture on our wall, that these are other pictures on other walls, and that these are pictures on walls in general. We learn that this one is the cover of our favorite book, that these are the covers of our other books, and that these are the covers of books in general.

And eventually, to help us where our direct experiences do not appropriately cluster or separate one set of concepts from another, we also acquire labels.[4] Labels in effect serve as glue with which we build concepts from experiences. For example, as we learn that no matter the functions or contexts of objects, they may commonly be called rectangles, we also learn that all of those objects that can be called rectangles are similar in overall shape: Every one can be seen as a closed figure of four orthogonal line segments.

Our awareness of the common and definitive properties of such commonly labeled objects may be quickly established if someone explicitly directs our attention to them. Alternatively we may become aware of them only gradually, through induction. As the same label is applied to one after the other of some family of patterns, it must eventually be, not the individual patterns, but the commonalities among them with which the label has been most frequently associated. It must thereby be the commonalities among them to which the label becomes most strongly associated. This way in which labels can serve to bundle together and, thereby, make salient the commonalities of otherwise dissimilar or disperse experiences, has been termed *acquired equivalence* in the literature.

Through the same mechanisms, labels can also work in the reverse direction to support *acquired distinctiveness* of experiences that are otherwise highly similar.[5] Thus where all meat might once have been "chicken," children eventually learn that some is instead beef, pork chops, or turkey. Where all dogs might once have been "doggies," they eventually learn that some are

---

4. Miller and Dollard (1941).

5. Miller and Dollard (1941).

dachshunds, some are poodles, and some are dalmatians. Little by little, they refine and solidify their knowledge of the features that set each of these labels apart.

As conceptual organizers, labels must be extremely important. In view of the all-absorbing nature of our memories and the haphazardness of our experiences, this must be true. At least at the first order of analysis, the organization of our personal knowledge must be communally appropriate. We must learn to attend to the similarities and differences among objects and events that are deemed significant and functional by the people around us. What else, besides labels, could so broadly ensure that we do?

Perhaps it should not be surprising that, beyond passively enjoying the service of such labels, we tend eventually to exploit their utility in more active ways. For example, when told that lions, tigers, and panthers are cats, we are likely to respond by looking for similarities between these animals and our household feline; the same label means communally respected commonalities. When told that this is a leopard but that is a cheetah, we are likely to look for other ways to distinguish them; different labels mean communally respected differences.[6]

It is, in short, through all of these processes that we eventually come to think of windows, doors, and buildings as rectangles when we have to, but more fully and just as easily as windows, doors, and buildings. We do so because our minds, through experience, have acquired the associations that bond together all of their other sensed characteristics—their overall shapes, plus their construction, ornamentation, sizes, locations, functions, and states—as well our own responses to them—how we have opened, closed, locked, walked through, waited before

---

6. In the world of educated adults, this tendency is ubiquitous. "The problem is not with so much with underarm deodorant sprays as with halogens in general," says the ecologist. "What are halogens and why?" you reply. "This is an analgesic rather than an anti-inflammatory," says the doctor. "What's the difference?" you ask. This is clearly a highly effective and efficient habit for the lifelong learner, but it is also somewhat mysterious. Specifically, it is quite unusual for people to exhibit awareness of subconscious control mechanisms. (Witness, as a case in point, our long debates about how we "see" words.) One wonders therefore whether this tendency is owed less to any autonomously derived appreciation of the passive benefits of labels that all of us have enjoyed than to a more superficial response learned directly from the specific teaching styles that some of us have enjoyed. That is, toward developing this tendency, it may be as important to tell (or elicit from) children *why* two things have the same or different names as to tell them what those names are.

them, and, importantly, how we have labeled them and used their labels, both literally and metaphorically.

It is by virtue of their tenet that an object's sensed features as well as our responses to it become tied together in the same associated bundle, that connectionist theories are potentially able to capture the compelling aspects of many of their rivaling theoretical predecessors.

Comparisons of Connectionist Theories with Others

Among theories and models, the connectionist framework meets and explains the data on human word recognition performance exceptionally well. It is for this reason alone that I have adopted it in this book.

Still it must be recognized that interest in connectionist theory extends well beyond issues of human word recognition. As a general theory of knowledge representation and an architecture for machine learning, its potential applications and extensions are many. Until its details are resolved and its performance is proven, a certain degree of skepticism about the theory is scientifically warranted.

Meanwhile, as with any new theory, connectionism is met with pockets of stubborn resistance. Some react that its underlying structure is too reminiscent of behaviorist theory. Others charge that its overriding flavor is too much that of artificial intelligence. While resonating to both of these suggestions, I nevertheless believe the theory is worthy of serious reflection regardless of one's philosophical persuasions. Although its actual power and longevity cannot yet be judged, it offers an interesting amalgamation of viewpoints about psychology and epistemology.

In particular, connectionist theory offers a bridge between empiricist and nativist views of knowledge. The canon of the empiricist is that what is known is owed strictly to experience while what can be experienced is owed strictly to the senses. The nativists, in contrast, point out that what is known transcends what can be sensed: They agree that knowledge is built from experience, but only as the elements of that experience are selected, structured, and interconnected or disjoined by the mind in accordance with its own fundamental interpretive predispositions.[7]

---

7. See, e.g., Watson (1971).

The debate between the empiricists and the nativists has been raging for at least 2,500 years and is as highly charged with emotion as any in science. Despite its sometimes academically alkalinized treatment, it gives us ulcerous identity crises: Are we, ourselves, the products of nature or of nurture? Are we truly creative or but finite state automata? Do we have free will and choice, or is our every action inescapably preprogrammed, the product of determinism?[8]

According to connectionist theory, yes, learning accrues through experience. And, yes, our perceptions are received by those simple sensory transducers and detectors that we are all innately given. However, we also remember, and we remember not just the central sensory event but also its total context and all of our responses to it—verbal, motor, affective, or reflective. In this way, though driven by empiricist principles (contiguity, recency, frequency, and similarity), what we learn automatically becomes organized not just in terms of the similarities and differences of its sensory format, but also by those of its contexts, name, uses, affect, social valence, and so on.

Moreover, experiences are remembered not in a separate compartment of our heads, but as associated patterns within the very structure of our recognition apparatus. As a result, the way in which we perceive the world becomes organized this way as well. We learn to perceive the world not as flecks of light and bits of sound, but as parts of patterns that, on their partial activation, recall their balance so as to create expectations, to fill in sensorial blanks, and to guide our responses. In bridging the nativist-empiricist impasse, connectionist theory is also potentially capable of reconciling many of the lesser (but still fierce) debates that psychology has aired in this century.

All learning is mediated by our nervous system and thereby modulated by any differences in the speed, entropy, disposition, or what-have-you with which we might be innately, nutritionally, or environmentally endowed. Moreover, everyone's experiences are unique, and so too are the vagaries of their attention and interest; probabilistically speaking, each of us can only be unique.

---

8. That this debate is about something other than science and logic (perhaps our personal convictions about the knowability or changeability of personal destiny?) is evident from the curious tendency of those who believe most strongly in the nativist notions of free will and creativity to reject nature (genetics) in favor of nurture as the major determinant of our personal strengths and weaknesses and, vice-versa, the tendency of those who subscribe to empiricist theories of learning and cognition to subordinate nurture to nature in explaining individual differences.

Learning is the product of neither discrimination nor generalization but both. It depends as much on detecting invariants as on attending to distinctive or differentiating features.[9] The mediating responses are neither need reduction,[10] localizing movements,[11] nor cognitive categories,[12] but all or any of the above and more, each learned, in part, by virtue of the others' presence. In what we perceive, the whole will be greater than the sum of its parts[13] in that the activation of part of a pattern will evoke the rest—but this happens only because, in what we have learned, the whole consists precisely of the sum of its parts. We behave like probabilistic cue-learners in that the complete familiar image is not necessary to provoke recognition; a fragment of its cues can activate its entire interassociated complex of patterns in memory. To this end, some subsets of cues may be adequate and some may not. Their adequacy depends on their match to our memory as modulated by our attention, such that superficial similarity may do the trick in one instance[14] while purposes, attitudes, or contexts[15] may do it in another. The theory is entirely compatible with the schema theory[16] that has been so broadly advocated of late, but adds to it the representational microstructure and learning mechanisms that it so badly needed.[17]

Finally, within the connectionist framework, learning—that is, the creation or strengthening of associations—comes with their activation. Such activation may be directly evoked by an outside stimulus (as when you reencounter an object or event); it may be indirectly evoked by the similarity, along one dimension or another, of an experience (as when one experience seems to resemble or reminds you of another); or it may be internally directed. When we reflect on our knowledge, we do so by activating it. Reflection or study thus strengthens learning. When

---

9. Appreciation and exploration of this contrast is strongly owed to Eleanor and J. J. Gibson. See, e.g., E. Gibson (1969).

10. For example, Hull (1943).

11. For example, Carr (1935).

12. For example, Bruner (1957).

13. For example, Koffka (1935).

14. For example, Brunswik (1955).

15. For example, Ittelson (1962).

16. In this, I refer to the psychologists' versions of schema theory, which differs significantly from the version developed and promoted by computer scientists. (See Adams, 1989.)

17. See Hintzman (1986); Rumelhart, Smolensky, McClelland, and Hinton (1986).

we turn our attention from one memory to another, comparing and contrasting their parts, we activate each and create associations between them. Thinking thus results in new learning. When we attend to some aspect of one set of memories and look for it in another, we raise awareness to (and thereby strengthen) commonalities that may have inobtrusively nestled into the otherwise distinct and separately integrated patterns of each. Directed attention to aspects of our memories thus results in "perceptual reorganization"—in insight and creativity.[18]

But note: Associative networks do not think. As they associatively register our experiences, they provide the input or medium for thought, and they record its output. But they do not think.

The Relation of Knowledge to Thought and Understanding

In support of thought, the network's capacity for making complex patterns holistically familiar is extremely important.[19] It is precisely this sort of well-integrated perceptual, conceptual, and procedural knowledge that is seen to distinguish the mature reader from the beginner in responding to a flash card. Differing in scope and level but not kind, this sort of knowledge is also seen to distinguish speed and sensitivity of the "expert" from the promising novice in playing chess,[20] solving algebra problems,[21] understanding physics,[22] sight reading music,[23] and interpreting fables.[24] To the extent that we have learned to respond to a complex challenge more or less holistically, we can turn our active attention to its higher-order relations. To the extent that we have not, we can, at best, struggle to put its parts together.

Thought and understanding thus depend critically on our associated memories, but the converse is also true: The cogent growth of the associational network depends critically on understanding and active thought. The network will, quite of its own design, establish associations between knowledge components corresponding to their superficial similarities and their physical

---

18.   Koffka (1931); Köhler (1925).
19.   See Glaser (1984).
20.   Chase, and Simon (1973). Chi (1978).
21.   Hinsley, Hayes, and Simon (1977).
22.   Larkin, McDermott, Simon, and Simon (1980).
23.   Allport, Antonis, and Reynolds (1972).
24.   Adams and Bruce (1982).

and temporal contiguities. To a large degree, however, conceptual learning depends on associations between temporally disjoint and perceptually disparate components of memory. It is because we establish these remote and abstract connections that we possess minds rather than something more like intricately programmed video discs. It was the seeming undeniability of this "transcendental synthetic Unity of Apperception"—this characteristically human tendency to construct concepts and cause-effect relations, to impose order on the "manifoldness" of sensory knowledge—that led Kant[25] and so many after him away from the pure empiricist doctrine.[26] To Kant, these higher-order organizational tendencies seemed necessarily to reflect innate or a priori properties of thought.

Clearly we are independently capable of insight and creativity. We rummage through our minds provoked by our own questions of how, why, what if, and what else. We conduct our own, self-driven searches for more global and abstract conceptions of what, when, and where. Nevertheless, a significant portion of our conceptual knowledge must be socially instigated.

In particular, much of what we learn is learned through language. Certainly most of our formal education is acquired through language. These observations seem almost too common to set in print. Yet, they turn from banal to deeply paradoxical with the realization that we can only learn through language that which we in some sense already know. That is, through language, novel concepts can only be communicated in the form of novel combinations of familiar concepts.

As an example, we can directly access the meanings of only the words we already know. The referents of new words can be verbally explained only in terms of old words. This can be done either explicitly, by presenting their definitions, or implicitly, by setting them in a context of old words that effectively constrains their meanings. The analogous situation holds for objects, events, and ideas. If familiar, they may be brought to mind by the slightest and most oblique reference. If unfamiliar they can be communicated through language only by comparing and contrasting them with familiar concepts, by decomposing them into familiar concepts and then piecing together the whole, or by setting them in or against a familiar context.

It is, in short, misleading to speak of language as a means of expressing one's thoughts to others. Language is instead a means of

---

25. Kant (1781/1929).
26. Watson (1971).

directing others to construct similar thoughts from their own prior knowledge.

In view of this, the effectiveness of a linguistic message is seen to rest on three requirements. The speaker (or writer) must: (1) correctly presuppose what sorts of related knowledge their intended listener (or reader) already has, (2) produce expressions that will evoke appropriate subsets of that knowledge, and (3) present or structure those expressions in a way that will induce the listener to interrelate the evoked knowledge in a way that most nearly captures the meaning intended.

The burden of comprehensibility can alternatively be shifted to the listener (or reader). As such, the first of these criteria stipulates that she or he possess the knowledge presumed by the message while the second stipulates adequate vocabulary and linguistic facility. As we shall see, a major problem with each of these criteria is that its attainment is easily misjudged in the task of reading instruction. But the third requirement is a bit different. How can a speaker "induce" listeners to interrelate their evoked knowledge as intended?

Innate or not, our capacity for communication—and cognitive growth in general—would seem to require the ability and even predisposition to direct one's attention to activated overlap among established memories. It would seem to require the proclivity to search such overlap for coherent patterns of interrelation and, perhaps, to be uncomfortable when none can be found. Moreover, to be successful, it would seem to require that the interpretor have some sense of the kinds of relationships for which she or he was to search amid the meshwork of conjoint activity; it would seem to require, in other words, that she or he have some expectations, some prior understanding with respect to the nature of the relationship at issue.

The Relevance to Word Recognition

First, the learning of a pattern—visual, auditory, motor, or conceptual—consists of building associations among its familiar parts. It is by building new links between old knowledge that we learn new patterns and elaborate and modify old ones. A major goal in learning to read is to interlink the printed appearance of words with one's knowledge of their sounds, contexts, functions, and meanings such that all will be evoked together. Once established, this whole complex of associations will be automatically strengthened and refined each time the word is encountered again.

Second, if for no other reason than frequency of co-occurrence, memory tends to organize itself hierarchically. Thus while skilled readers' visual memory for individual printed letters are built from interrelations between line segments and arcs, their visual memories for spelling patterns are built from interrelations among letters, and their visual memories for words are built from spelling patterns.

Taking both of these points together, we get a very important third: In order for any memory to be economical and robust and to do what it is supposed to do, one must first have learned to respond to each of its nodal parts as wholes. Thus, in order to remember a word or spelling pattern as a sequence of letters rather than an array of smaller visual features, one must have first learned to respond to the component letters as wholes. This example is perhaps obvious. However, the underlying theme of the chapters to come is that a major aspect of the task of learning to read consists of precisely this—establishing the appropriate kinds of parts and their relevant interrelations at each level of analysis.

Encoding the Parts versus the Associations between Them

There is another way to get to this same point. Learning to decode is essentially a challenge in what is known as paired-associate learning: When shown *p*, you must learn to respond with the phoneme /*p*/; when shown *pen*, you must learn to respond with the name and thought of a pen. At core, such paired-associate learning challenges consist of three distinct tasks: You must learn to recognize the visual stimulus, *p*; you must learn the phonemic response, /*p*/; and you must associate or interconnect the visual stimulus and the phonemic response, *p* - /*p*/.

There exists considerable evidence that poor readers have no particular problem with paired-associate learning provided that the task does not require verbal encoding.[27] The implication is that there is nothing basically wrong with the speed or effectiveness with which their minds establish associations. What then could be their problem in learning to read? Clearly it has something to do with verbal encoding, but we need a more specific answer. We need an answer that is sufficiently specific to

---

27. For a review, see Vellutino (1979).

allow us to prevent or repair reading difficulties wherever possible and with the greatest efficiency possible.

Analysis of the reading process suggests that that answer must lie in one or both of the following alternatives.

1. Either the children are failing to recognize the printed stimulus.

This could be due to unreliable letter recognition skills, poorly developed knowledge of spelling patterns, or both.

2. Or they are not properly encoding the verbal response.

For learning the sounds of individual graphemic units, the proper units of response are phonemes. For learning longer subword spelling patterns, the proper units of response are bigger phonological patterns, which, to allow efficient and robust learning, must be composites of individual phonemes. For learning the sounds of words, the proper units of response are spoken words, and these too must be coherently represented not only in themselves but as the top-level composites of their phonemes and multiphoneme phonological patterns.

To make the picture complete, we must push down one more level of analysis. The productive learning of letter-sound correspondences involves more than just recognizing the letters and coupling them to appropriate sounds. Most children, including many of those who will be reading disabled, can accurately identify printed letters by the end of first grade.[28] Many children who are certifiably reading disabled have also learned basic letter-sound correspondences. Given the word *bat*, for example, they can often respond /b/ - /æ/ - /t/, all by themselves. Yet, even having done so, they may steadfastly fail to realize that the printed string before them says *bat*. Urging them to "say it faster" or "blend it together," is to no avail. It is as though these children can find no connection between the sequence of sounds they have produced and the highly familiar word which they have "read."[29]

It is not enough to memorize the sounds that go with each letter. To make use of those sounds, the child must realize that they are the subsounds of language. The trick in letter-sound learning is not in linking the letters to a sequence of new sounds; that should be easy enough for any child, but it is unproductive.

---

28. Kolers (1972); Liberman, Shankweiler, Orlando, Harris, and Berti (1971); Vernon (1971).

29. Johnson, and Myklebust (1967). The citation and the point are owed to Liberman (1973).

The trick in productive letter-sound learning lies in linking the letters to a particular set of familiar sounds. Specifically it lies in linking the letters to the phonemic sounds that one has already learned so well, to the phonemic sounds that are already so deeply and integrally a part of one's knowledge of spoken words. To create such links, however, the child must first become attuned to the existence and relevance of those phonemic components—but, again, phonemic awareness is not easily established.

Still worse than having difficulty with just the stimulus or just the response, the poor reader may have difficulty with both. The system is set up such that mastery of one side of the spelling-sound equation should hasten resolution of the other. But by the same mechanisms, it is also set up such that difficulties with either side will impede progress with the other. Again, an underlying theme of the chapters to come is that a major aspect of the task of learning to read consists of establishing the appropriate kinds of "parts"—the appropriate "terms" for the print-to-meaning equation—at each level of analysis.

What Are the "Parts" (and the "Parts" of the "Parts")?

More specifically, in order to learn to read words, there are certain classes of parts, certain categorical concepts, about both speech and print of which a child must be aware. Within the domain of speech, children must become consciously aware of those categories or classes of spoken units called *words* and *phonemes*. And, to get from the words to the phonemes, they must also be able to focus their attention on spoken *syllables*, which lie in between. Within the domain of print, children must become consciously aware of *words* and their *spellings*. And to get from the words to the spellings, they must also become aware of *letters*, which lie in between.

Although the knowledge that the child must acquire about speech and print are distinct from one another, they relate to each other in form and function. Building the links between modalities requires certain expectations about the relations between print and speech. Effective use of this complex of knowledge in reading and writing depends further on a host of expectations about the higher-order physical and linguistic structure of text. Whether in acquisition or operation, such knowledge can function in proper interrelation only if it is taught in proper interrelation.

What About Rules?

Learning consists in the strengthening and refinement of associative links among the features of a pattern, and accrues through repeated experiences with the pattern. As a direct consequence, memory tends to organize itself hierarchically: The most complex patterns are represented by an associated bundle of patterns that are slightly less complex; these patterns are represented by an associated bundle of patterns that are still less complex; until, at the bottom-most level of a memory, there are patterns composed of associated bundles of elementary perceptual units. As it happens, this sort of hierarchical, frequency-based learning will automatically and implicitly but quite unintentionally result in "ruleful" behavior.[30]

Recall that the elementary letter, phonemic, and meaning units upon which our knowledge of words is built are relatively small in number and are not duplicated. Essentially the lowercase *a* in all the words you have seen that contained a lowercase *a* is represented by a single bundle of associated features. More generally, perceptually similar patterns are perceptually similar because they are comprised of many of the same parts.

Earlier we saw how such representational overlap may guide and speed perception. For example, when a test word is immediately preceded by another that is semantically, phonologically, or orthographically similar, it is recognized more quickly. To the extent that the repeated or overlapping parts of the test word's representation are still partially excited, its full resolution is accelerated.

Such overlap between similar patterns also provides the means for passive acquisition of abstract, categorical, or "ruleful" knowledge.[31] To illustrate, when a regularly spelled but novel string, say a pseudoword, is encountered, there will be no unique, preestablished set of associated units to meet it in memory. On the other hand, there will be a host of similar but not quite matching patterns. By virtue of its representational overlap with each of these patterns, the pseudoword will evoke them all. Thus brought to mind in unison, their commonalities, by sheer strength of number, will dominate their particulars, and the pseudoword will be read in accordance with the "rule" that they collectively instantiate. A pseudoword like *kail* will be read to rhyme with *ail*,

---

30. I am indebted to Phil Gough for reminding me not to overlook this issue.

31. See Rumelhart and McClelland (1986).

bail, fail, Gail, hail: "When two vowels go walking, the first does the talking." A pseudoword like *shate* will be read to rhyme with *ate, bate, date, fate, gate:* the "final *e* rule."

More generally, an important distinction develops from this perspective between abstracted and abstract knowledge. A pattern becomes *abstracted* when it is coupled with a consistent response across a number of nonidentical contexts. For spelling patterns, this response may be either sound-based, as in *ail, bail,* and *fail,* or meaning-based, as in *nation, national, nationality.* In time, as the commonalities among such patterns overwrite each other, their overlap emerges with a strength that is greater than that which can be owed to any one of the individual patterns from which it has grown.

In contrast to rules that are abstracted through experience, those that are learned in the *abstract*—including, perhaps, "When two vowels go walking, the first does the talking"—are by definition divorced from the specific, concrete contexts of their application. As such, they must lack the representational underpinnings to be directly absorbed into the associative network.

It is automatic, frequency-based pattern recognition that is responsible for the speed and reliability with which skillful readers process the spellings, sounds, and meanings of words and the spellings and sounds of pseudowords. This facility is the product of the clusters and subclusters of associated units that they have acquired through their experience with print; it is the product of their *abstracted* rules. In contrast, rules that are acquired only as abstract principles must live in another part of the head—the part in charge of conscious interpretation, not the part in charge of automatic, frequency-based responding.

Does that mean that the articulation of spelling-sound rules in reading and writing instruction is a waste of time? No. For purposes of instruction and learning, rules and definitions may be viewed as well-specified labels. As such, they may subserve the same, valuable function as labels, only more directively.

The articulation of a rule is a reasonable means of pointing a reader's attention to an aspect of a spelling under study. Such direct attention to or prolonged consideration of the particular relations among letters (and their sounds or meanings) can serve only to strengthen the associations that bind them together. Moreover, once the students have been exposed to some sampling of pertinent instances, provision of the rule should help them to notice the commonalities between them. The point is only that rules, definitions, and labels cannot substitute for the perceptual, conceptual, and procedural experiences to which they allude.

They can, on the other hand, be very useful in helping the learner to organize such experiences, to notice or reinforce important relationships among their components.

Does that mean that requiring students to memorize such rules is a waste of time? For purposes of directly affecting those associations to which the rules pertain, the answer would seem to be yes. When the interletter associations are in place and doing their job, the rule is unlikely to be consciously accessed and is in any case superfluous.

On the other hand, there are circumstances in which abstract rules stand as a useful backup system. In particular, when the recognition system fails to resolve a word, we may pause to give it direct, conscious attention. In this mode, we are in the position to recall the abstract rule and to conduct the conscious analysis on which its application depends. Even skilled readers may occasionally find themselves in this mode—especially, for example, in reading foreign words or in trying to decide how to pronounce some proper noun.

Moreover, for purposes of writing (as opposed to reading), where retrieval of spelling patterns is generally under conscious reflection, such rules may be quite helpful. In writing, I often find myself reciting the poem:

> *i* before *e*,
> Except after *c*,
> Or when sounded as *a*,
> As in *neighbor* and *weigh*.
> *Either, neither, leisure*, and *seize*
> Are four exceptions
> If you please.

In summary, an analogy might be helpful.[32] You cannot teach a person to be an expert tennis player by teaching her the rules of skillful return. The tennis player needs first to acquire the kind of understanding of the game that comes through direct experience. The tennis player needs to have watched enough balls leave her opponent's racquet to be able to estimate their trajectory. She needs to have watched the opponent's swing enough times to know if the ball will be spinning and how that will alter its path. She needs to have played the wind enough to know how to read the game across its distortions. She needs to have returned enough balls of every different kind that her preparation, swing, and

---

32. With concern toward classroom instruction, a more useful analogy is had in analyses of the utility of rules in the teaching of thinking. See Adams (1989).

follow-through are part of a single well-integrated response. Although an instructor's articulation of signals and principles may hasten and sharpen the player's tendency to attend to the critical cues of the situation, her expertise is embedded in her rapid, automatic responses to familiar game situations. Her ability to make use of such rules depends upon her having internalized some collection of experiences to which they can apply, as well as the kinds of expectations and deep understanding of the game that support their timely and appropriate application. The same is true for the reader.

On the Goals of Print Instruction: What Do We Want Students to Learn?

Implicit in many discussions of reading instruction is the assumption that the goal of early instruction on word recognition is one of teaching students how to sound words out. In fact, the connections between orthography and phonology are extremely important for the young reader; as for the skillful reader, however, the importance of phonological processing is as a means or support system. Development of spelling-sound relations is not an end in itself. The only reason for learning to read words is to understand text.

The Importance of Phonological Processing in Learning to Read

In part III we saw that phonological processing is an invaluable asset to experienced readers. On the other hand, each of the benefits it was seen to provide depends on some minimal competence with visual word recognition. Indeed we have seen again and again that skillful reading depends critically on the speed and completeness with which words can be identified from their visual forms.

For the beginning reader, visual word recognition skills are uniquely absent. How does the system deal with this? How does it support their acquisition? The answer is that the development of the Orthographic processor is owed primarily to the guidance and input of the Phonological processor. The reasons that this is so are simple and obvious on reflection.

• *Independence and "self-teaching."* Well before orthographic competence begins to settle in, the Phonological processor is already richly linked to the Meaning processor. Even when children are told the identity of a written string, the Phonological processor mediates their understanding of it. Beyond that, the ability to sound words out gives them the capacity to identify and thereby learn new words on their own.

- *Remembering the order and identities of letters.* To the extent that English is alphabetic, its spelling mimics its pronunciation. Thus, if the units in the Orthographic and Phonological processors are properly interconnected, children's appreciation of the spoken structure of a word will automatically guide and reinforce the knowledge they acquire of its spelling.

- *Building orthographic associations through oral communication.* Through speech, the Phonological processor provides the channel for communicating with students about letters, words, and meaning. The principal means by which we help children learn to read is by talking with them.

Each of these formative relations between spelling and sound is important, and in this chapter each will be examined in turn. On the other hand, neither singly nor together are these spelling-sound relations the be all or end all of word reading competency. With this in mind, we will back off a bit at the end of the chapter so as to reexamine their importance from the larger perspective of what the young reader must learn about written words.

Independence and "Self-Teaching"

Perhaps the most well-respected value of letter-sound instruction is that it provides children with a means of deciphering written words that are not familiar as wholes. Applying their knowledge of letter-to-sound correspondences, they can sound the word out, discovering or confirming its identity by themselves.

Jorm and Share emphasize a further advantage of the ability to sound words out: It serves as a self-teaching mechanism. They argue quite persuasively that sounding words out "may be the principal mechanism by which beginning readers learn to use the more efficient visual route and eventually achieve skilled performance."[1]

Jorm and Share point out that children should be able to learn the complete spellings of individual words visually, that is, without phonological recoding. The problem is that they cannot learn enough words that way. Even in first- and second-grade texts, more than a third of the words occur only once; the majority

---

1. Jorm and Share (1983, p. 114).

occur five times or fewer.[2] Because most words are afforded so few learning opportunities, adequate growth in a child's visual vocabulary is not likely to result from the learning of one whole word at a time.

Children who can neither recognize a word as a whole nor sound it out have only two options toward its identification: They can rely on contextual cues or ask someone else. The drawbacks of depending on someone else are obvious, but let us review the drawbacks of relying on context.

The major problem with using contextual cues for word identification is that they are unreliable.[3] And this is all the more true since it is the less frequent words that contribute the most meaning to a passage.[4] Here is the dilemma: The child depends on the meaning of the passage to infer the meaning of its less familiar words, yet the meaning of the passage depends disproportionately on the meanings of its less frequent words.

The strategy of relying on context is also less than ideal for purposes of word learning. Where context is strong enough to allow quick and confident identification of the unfamiliar word, there is little incentive to pore over its spelling. And without studying the word's spelling, there is no opportunity for increasing its visual familiarity. Thus even if the child guesses right on one occasion, she or he may be no better prepared to identify the word on the next. On the other hand, where contextual cues are not strong enough to reveal the word's identity, there is little point to studying its spelling; without a meaning or pronunciation to hold it together, it is not likely to be remembered anyhow.

In contrast, with working knowledge of letter-sound correspondences, the child should, in theory, be able to sound out and from there identify any written word that is in his speaking or listening vocabulary. Furthermore, the very process of sounding the word out entails careful visual study of its spelling. To paraphrase Jorm and Share, every success in sounding out an unfamiliar word is a productive learning trial in visual identification.[5]

---

2. Firth (1972, cited in Jorm and Share, 1983); Rodenborn and Washburn (1974, cited in Jorm and Share, 1983). See also Beck (1981).

3. For recent evidence on this point, see Schatz and Baldwin (1986).

4. Finn (1977–1978).

5. The literal quotation is "Every failure to identify an unfamiliar word is essentially a learning trial missed as far as visual identification is concerned." (Jorm and Share, 1983, p. 132.)

Remembering the Order and Identities of Letters

A second valuable return on learning letter-sound correspondences is that they provide a means of remembering the identities and orderings of the letters within words. Let me relate this argument in the way I came to appreciate it.

In working with schools for the deaf, I learned that many teach reading through phonics. On discovering this, I was dismayed: How counterproductive and egocentric of us to make written English, which the children need so badly, parasitic on spoken English, which the children barely have. It seemed to me that for deaf children, any useful dependence between modalities should run in the opposite direction; rather, spoken English, if it need be taught at all, should be built on a preestablished knowledge of written English. Then it came to me.

Imagine that I set before you the task of learning a notational system for the English language. Within this system, words are represented by ordered sets of just a few elementary symbols. More specifically, let us suppose that my system contains twenty-six such symbols but, just to make it interesting, let us say that some 90 percent of the time I will use only fifteen of them.[6]

Imagine further that the composition of my symbol set has been essentially arbitrary. The individual elements are completely meaningless in themselves. They have no obvious iconic significance. They are visually confusable with one another; indeed, they look more like each other than anything else you have learned to date. And they are unrelated to the sounds of the words in whose representations they occur.

In short, the only basis you have for memorizing the words within this system is in terms of the specific, ordered sets of visually nondescript and indistinct symbols by which I designate them. Half of the words that I present will be quite short, consisting of seven symbols or fewer. The remainder may be indefinitely long, although few will exceed fifteen symbols in length.[7]

What criterion shall I set for passing this task? For sportspersonship, I will make it easy. Let's say that you, like the average American high school student, must learn the combinations and permutations of symbols corresponding to at least 50,000 words.

What an awful task. And yet the system I have just described corresponds precisely to our own system of writing—with one

---

6. As in English (Mayzner and Tresselt, 1965).
7. As in English (Miller, Newman, and Friedman, 1958).

important exception: My system lacks any symbol-to-sound correspondences. And that, of course, is the point.[8]

English is fundamentally alphabetic. With obvious exceptions, the letter sequences of its written words mimic the phonemic sequences of its spoken words. True, there are irregularities, but the majority of these irregularities are owed to the vowels.

With relatively few exceptions, the consonants are quite well behaved. There are a few consonant polygraphs that must be translated as wholes rather than letter by letter, such as *ch-*, *sh-*, *th-*, *ph-*, *kn-*, *-ght*, and *wr-*. There are also a few consonants and consonant digraphs that map onto more than one phoneme (but rarely more than two): *c(at)–c(ity)*, *g(asp)–g(ist)*, *h(ope)–h(our)*, and *(tou)gh–(bou)gh*. In addition, consonants are occasionally "silent" or phonemically misleading for reasons peculiar to their word's printed history—as examples, *island*, *debt*, and *psalm*.[9] By and large, however, the occurrence of each consonant can be traced to its simple phonemic significance with a high degree of predictability.

As for the vowels, we have seen already that it may be their presence rather than their identities that is most important for purposes of word identification. It may matter more that you know that there is one than that you know what it is with certainty. Thus, with the exception of the "silent" ones, vowels, too, are recalled by phonology. In chapters to come, we shall see that even the behavior of the vowels is more rule bound than might be apparent from a letter-by-letter analysis of spelling-sound correspondences.

The bottom line is that however fuzzy one's knowledge of spelling-sound correspondences might be, it must be of invaluable assistance toward memorizing the order and identities of the letters that distinguish written words.[10]

---

8. Note that, in effect, it is the reader's ability to learn about and exploit the orthographic redundancy of English that is under discussion here. Sensitivity to orthographic redundancy is a powerful correlate of reading proficiency. The argument above might thus be recast in terms of the Phonological processor's role in promoting its acquisition. For a discussion, see Adams (1981).

9. See Balmuth (1982).

10. Though inspired by my work with deaf children, the force of this argument, by its very logic, may apply only to hearing children. The issues surrounding the question of how best to teach deaf children to read are extremely complicated and will not be addressed in this book.

Linnea Ehri has proposed that the process of learning about the identities and orderings proceeds very gradually.[11] At the first level, children must acquire a working familiarity with the shapes and sounds of letters. In addition, they must acquire basic phonemic awareness and, in particular, the ability to detect systematic relationships between the sound segments of spoken words and the letters in their spellings.

Working from these abilities, the children begin to build orthographic images of the words they read by matching the letters of each to its phonemic segments. At first children may proceed by matching just a few—probably the first and maybe the last—of the individual graphemes of each word to its phonemic segments. As they become more and more familiar with the words and with the grapheme-phoneme relationships, their orthographic images become more and more complete and cohesive—such that, eventually, the full image of a word may be evoked at a glance. As the children's repertoires of printed words grow in number and completeness, they begin to learn about more complex spelling-sound patterns too. As these complex patterns support more efficient mapping of spellings to sounds, it thus becomes easier and easier for them to read and remember newly encountered words. Meanwhile, through their reading experience, semantic and syntactic information also becomes "amalgamated" with the orthographic images of the words.

Ehri's "word identity amalgamation theory" is strongly reminiscent of the psychological theory and research described in part III. Yet, its force derives from the fact that it was conceived quite independently of that literature. Ehri's theory was based directly on research and observation of the behaviors and developmental patterns of children in the course of learning to master print.

Building Orthographic Associations through Oral Communication

The primary duty of the Phonological processor is that of processing speech, not print. It is precisely for this reason that the Phonological processor figures so heavily in instruction about print. In the classroom or the home, reading instruction revolves around print but is propelled through speech.

We tell our students and children what to do, when to do it, and how. We tell them to sit down, to open their books, and to complete their assignments, and we ask them questions: "Why do

---

11. Ehri (1980).

you think Jack's mother threw the beans out the window?" Although this sort of speech is essential to reading development, it is not directly instrumental in orthographic development, and it is not the sort that I have in mind right now.

Instead I am thinking of certain speech acts and speech knowledge that serve directly to seat and refine the capabilities of the Orthographic processor. I am thinking of particular ways in which both we and the children use spoken language in the course of reading instruction that can only contribute formatively to the development of those crucial associations both within the Orthographic processor and between it and the rest of the system.

Examples are myriad. When we say a letter's sound or call it by name while asking the children to look at it, we create linkages between its visual form and its spoken translation or label. When we say, "No, that's *hat*, not *hot*. Look at the *a*. It says *haaat*," we refine the linkages between its spelling and its sound. When we sound out a word, emphasizing but blending its separate phonemes, we create linkages among its left-to-right sequence of letters and between them and its temporal sequence of sounds. When we or the children spell a word, we reinforce the left-to-right linkages of its letters still further. When we present the children with rhymes or phonograms (e.g., *bent*, *dent*, *sent*, *tent*, *went*), we reinforce their similar spelling patterns and connect them to their similar sounds. When we speak a written word, its spoken syllables automatically resonate as well-integrated phonological patterns, there to meet and reinforce the spelling patterns that the children are beginning to build. When we speak a written word, we activate its meaning, providing for it, too, to be linked to its orthographic image. And when we read text aloud, we arouse and thus impose the children's knowledge of spoken language on their interpretation of the text.

Children, in short, understand spoken language, and we depend on that. It is from speech and through speech that they must come to understand written language as well. The very architecture of the system ensures that when print is both viewed and spoken at once, it will automatically result in the growth and refinement of the associations to, from, and within the child's Orthographic processor—provided that the child has sufficient familiarity with the units that are to be associated. In the chapters to follow, we will turn to the issues of what those units are and how their familiarity is acquired.

Spelling-Sound versus Spelling-Meaning Relationships

Thus far in this chapter, I have focused on the value of the phonological link in both the learning and teaching of reading. Yet, if you look back at each of the supporting arguments presented, you will notice that in each case the importance of phonological processing was as a means, not an end.

For skilled readers, printed word identification is first and foremost a visual process. It is visual information that sets the system in action, drives the Phonological and Meaning processors, governs the readers' patterns of eye fixations, and allows skilled readers to perceive familiar words and spelling patterns so efficiently. Although the Phonological, Meaning, and Context processors are always engaged in printed word identification, they are subordinate to the Orthographic processor in both order and power. They serve not only to receive but, reciprocally, to speed and corroborate the Orthographic processor's perceptions. When conflicts between the processors arise—as may occur with homophones, garden path sentences, and misleading context—it is visual information that normally presides.

It is important not to overstate this case. The challenge for beginning readers is not just to acquire the visual patterns corresponding to letters and words; such visual knowledge will do no good at all unless it is properly linked to it corresponding representations in the Phonological and Meaning processors. On the other hand, the primary goal of beginning instruction on printed word identification should not be seen as one of teaching students how to sound words out. The primary goal is, instead, to teach children about orthography and how orthography maps onto the sounds and meanings of words, and that is quite different.

Skillful reading cannot proceed solely through the process of sounding words out. If you still need convincing, try reading the following rendition of "Little Red Riding Hood" to yourself:[12]

---

12. This text was brought to my attention by A. W. F. Huggins. It was slightly adapted from the *Co-Evolution Quarterly* (17, 1978, p. 7), where it is accompanied by the following footnote:

Does anyone know the true origin of this strangeness? It was sent to us by Wylie Wilson, Long Beach, California, xeroxed from *Language in America* (1970, World Publishing Company), whose author, Charlton Laird, footnotes: "This tale exists in many forms because many people have had fun contributing to it, so that it has become a bit of folklore, a communal folk production of the literate mind, if that is not a contradiction in terms. I quote it from *Word Study*, XXVIII, no. 5 (May, 1953), p. 4. The editor pronounced it anonymous; it has been associated especially with the name of Professor H. C. Chase." All we know is it's a bitch to proofread. In

LADLE RAT ROTTEN HUT

Wants pawn term, dare worsted ladle gull hoe lift wetter murder inner ladle cordage honor itch offer lodge dock florist. Disc ladle gull orphan worry ladle cluck wetter putty ladle rat hut, end fur disc raisin pimple colder ladle rat rotten hut. Wan moaning rat rotten hut's murder colder inset: "Ladle rat rotten hut, heresy ladle basking winsome burden barter and shirker cockles. Tick disc ladle basking tudor cordage offer groin murder hoe lifts honor udder site offer florist. Shaker lake, dun stopper laundry wrote, end yonder nor sorghum stenches dun stopper torque wet strainers."

"Hoe-cake, murder," resplendent ladle rat rotten hut, end tickle ladle basking an stuttered oft. Honor wrote tudor cordage offer groin murder, ladle rat rotten hut mitten anomalous woof.

"Wail, wail, wail," set disc wicket woof, "evanescent ladle rat rotten hut! Wares or putty ladle gull goring wizard ladle basking?"

"Armor goring tumor groin murder's," reprisal ladle gull. "Grammars seeking bet. Armor ticking arson burden barter end shirker cockles."

"O hoe! Heifer blessing woke," setter wicket woof, butter taught tomb shelf, "Oil tickle shirt court tudor cordage offer groin murder. Oil ketchup wetter letter, an den—O bore!"

Soda wicket woof tucker shirt court, end whinny retched a cordage offer groin murder, pick dinner window an sore debtor pore oil worming worse lion inner bet. Inner flesh disc abdominal woof lipped honor betting adder rope. Any pool dawn a groin murder's nut cup and gnat gun, any curdle dope inner bet.

Inner ladle wile ladle rat rotten hut a raft attar cordage an ranker dough bell. "Comb ink, sweat hard," setter wicket woof, disgracing is verse. Ladle rat rotten hut entity bet rum end stud buyer groin murder's bet. "Oh grammar," crater ladle gull, "Wart bag icer gut! A nervous sausage bag ice!" "Buttered lucky chew whiff, doling," whiskered disc ratchet woof, wetter wicket small. "Oh grammar, water bag noise! A nervous sore suture anomalous prognosis!" "Buttered small your whiff," inserter woof, ants mouse worse waddling. "Oh grammar, water bag mousey gut! A nervous sore suture bag mouse!"

Daze worry on forger nut gull's lest warts. Oil offer sodden throne offer carvers and sprinkling otter bet, disc curl and bloat Thursday woof ceased pore ladle rat rotten hut an garbled erupt.

Mural: Yonder nor sorghum stenches shut ladle gulls stopper torque wet strainers.

I am embarrassed to admit how much time I spent deciphering this passage. The difficulty lies not with the slightly inappropriate spelling-to-sound correspondences: If I could read it aloud for you, you would surely understand it perfectly. Nor does

---

fact, we found an error in the book ("grammer" instead of grammar once). Mural: Loss of redundancy is loss of correctability. —SB.

I found a couple more misspellings — thanks only to the speller on my word processor.

the difficulty lie in the accessibility of the spelling-to-sound correspondences. Presented in isolation, I bet you would pronounce every one of the words in this passage appropriately without hesitation. Further, once you have figured out what this passage "says," you will find that the stress patterns (strong and weak syllables) of its individual words never violate the prosodics of its encrypted sentences.

What, then, causes this passage to be so hard to understand? It derives from the accessibility of the spelling-to-meaning correspondences. If you look back at the passage—or, easier still, read it backwards—you will find that every word in it is familiar; in any normal context, you could read off, recognize, and understand each one in an instant.

In part III, it was asserted that the Orthographic processor passes its output directly to the Meaning processor. In this example, you see an effect of this relationship. The Meaning and Context processors cannot understand what the Phonological processor is "saying" because there is no way that they can reconcile it with what the Orthographic processor is "seeing."

There is no way to just shut-down the spelling-to-meaning link; in reading, it is dominant. When (and if) you do decipher this passage, it will be through either or both of two means. You can repeat each phrase to yourself without looking at the print (though even without looking, it is hard to keep from imagining it) and rely heavily on your Context processor (that is, your prior familiarity with the story of "Little Red Riding Hood" and with sentences). Or you can ask a friend to read it aloud to you. In either case, the trick is to escape the orthographic stimulation.

The Importance of Automatic Word Recognition

The fact that we can understand the "Ladle Rat Rotten Hut" passage when someone else reads it aloud is significant in itself— for, after all, even when the text is read aloud, the individual words will not be quite right. Thus, while we know that the meaning of a text depends on the meanings of its individual words, we see clearly from this demonstration that the converse is also true: The meanings of the individual words become available through the meaningfulness of the text. Paradoxical as this may seem, it is consistent with our understanding of the perceptual and conceptual performance of the system.

First let us consider the problem perceptually. As the sounds of continuous speech are heard, they automatically activate familiar patterns in the Phonological processor. If the speech stream consisted of a series of distinct and discrete individual words, the effect would be one of activating our phonological memories for each of those words, one after the other, in rapid sequence. (And we would find oral renditions of "Ladle Rat Rotten Hut" just as befuddling as the written one.)

In reality, however, the enunciation of individual words and speech sounds is neither discrete nor distinct but highly variable in running speech. The acoustical cues for any given phoneme are highly dependent on those which precede and follow it. They are also altered by such factors as the rate of speech,[13] the stress contour of the utterance, the speaker's particular diction and dialect, the size and shape of her or his vocal tract, and the basic pitch of her or his voice.[14] On top of all that, we rarely hear speech in acoustically ideal environments; as often, our messages are heard despite the presence of competing background talk, extraneous noise, distortions, and so on.

The most obvious consequence of this "signal variability" is that spoken words will often be imperfectly received. Indeed, confusion between similar phonemes, such as $/g/-/k/$, $/b/-/p/$, and $/r/-/l/$, is relatively common among listeners.[15]

A second consequence is that, over time, the phonological image that we will have acquired for any given word must be relatively diffuse. It will consist not of any one "correct" pattern that has been evoked and reinforced over and over but of a host of patterns corresponding to the range of pronunciations of that word that we have experienced. En masse this distribution of patterns should center on the "correct" or typical pronunciation of the word. However, any phonological event that overlaps any fragment of a word's distribution should cause it to become activated to a greater or lesser extent.

McClelland and Elman have more specifically hypothesized that the excitation of any given phoneme recognition unit results in excitation of all of the words with which that phoneme has been linked.[16] By implication, the reception of any given word should result in some activation of all of the words to which any of its perceived phonemes have been linked. When we consider this broad responsiveness of the memory system together with the impreciseness of the acoustical signal, we see that phonological

---

13. Miller (1981).
14. See Klatt (1980); Repp and Liberman (1984).
15. Bond and Garnes (1980).
16. McClelland and Elman (1986).

reception must, in general, be a rather messy affair. Any given word in the spoken stream will never activate exactly and only its intended phonological image. Instead, it will, to a greater or lesser degree, evoke many different words—as many as overlap with the (appropriately and inappropriately) evoked components of its phonological structure.

How, in view of this chaos, can we possibly understand the spoken message? Though they differ on the mechanisms and processes by which it happens, theorists agree that a major means by which we do so is through knowledge of words.[17] Within the connectionist framework, the word that best matches the received sequence of phonemes wins the competition. As it does so, it inhibits all competing word candidates while reinforcing its own proper phonemic composition through feedback.[18]

When "Ladle Rat Rotten Hut" is read aloud, the phonological structures of its actual words are slightly but perceptibly different from those we must "hear" to understand the story. Thus, as critical as such whole word recognition capabilities seem to be, they cannot explain this illusion. Nor can they provide sufficient basis for us to cope as well as we do with normal connected speech. In particular, the boundaries between the individual words of running speech are not consistently or reliably marked by pauses or any other physical cue.[19]

Even if our phonologically driven word recognizers were perfect, we would still have difficulties distinguishing, for example, "assorted collection" from "a sordid collection" or "electricians too" from "elect Trish and Stu." The situation is aptly summarized by Cole and Jakimik: "Ream ember, us poke can cent tense off in contains men knee words that were knot in ten did tube bee herd."[20] The problem, again, is with the entropy of the input. There are just too many phonologically supported word candidates with which to work.

In the same way that resolution of the intended phonemic structure of an utterance cannot be had by focusing on the individual phoneme units that are received, resolution of intended

---

17. See, e.g., Klatt (1980); Marcus (1981); Marslen-Wilson (1987); Tyler and Frauenfelder (1987).

18. McClelland and Elman (1986). Here again is our paradox, one level removed: While the perception of a word depends on the perception of its phonemes, the perception of the phonemes depends on the perception of the word to which they belong.

19. Cole and Jakimik (1980).

20. Cole and Jakimik (1980, p. 139).

wording cannot be had by focusing on the individual word units that are activated. To select among candidate phonemic units, the Phonological processor backs off to examine words or, equivalently, the coherence of the relations among the candidate phonemes. Similarly, to select among candidate words, the Meaning and Context processors must direct their attention, not to the individual words, but to the relations among them.

Toward explaining conceptual processing, one might alternatively offer that the system chooses among candidate words on the basis of semantic or syntactic factors. Reflecting on this hypothesis, however, we find that it amounts to the same thing. The issue is not which of the phonologically activated word candidates has syntactic import or meaning: All of them will—else they would not have had the status of whole, familiar words on which their activation depended. Yet, many words can subserve more than one syntactic function. Further, although every word is associated with a broad distribution of meaning, only a fraction of that distribution will be relevant in any given context.

Homonyms provide the most obvious demonstration of this phenomenon. Recognition that the word *ball* in the expression *inaugural ball* refers to a gala celebration rather than a bouncy, round projectile is available not from inspection of the semantic field associated with *ball*; it requires inspection of the semantic field that is conjointly associated with *ball* and *inaugural*. In the same way, though less blatantly, it is inspection of such semantic overlap that must be responsible for the cogent interpretation of any word in context.

To see this, let us consider the interpretation of proper nouns. In the sense that the denotation of a proper noun is not just unambiguous but unique, proper nouns may be seen to lie at the opposite end of the referential continuum from homonyms. In view of this, one might imagine that the meaning evoked by a proper noun should be stable across contexts. Yet, conceptual selectivity still operates. In a discussion of national parks, mention of *Wyoming* is more likely to evoke thoughts of Yellowstone or the Tetons than of electoral college representation; in a discussion of strategic itineraries for presidential election campaigns, the reverse is true.

More generally, in interpreting meaningful speech, we readily conceive contextually appropriate examplars of a named class: In hearing, for example, that "Jim Rice smacked the *ball* over the fence," we do not envision a basketball; in hearing that "Larry Bird shot the *ball* from midcourt," we do not envision a baseball. Similarly, we readily recognize contextually relevant properties of a named class (e.g., "The child fell on the [slippery] *ice*" versus "The lemonade needed more [cold] *ice*"). This ability depends on analysis, not of the total semantic field of the individual words, but of the activated overlap between them.[21] (Note that our ability to interpret and produce metaphorical language can also be explained in this way.)[22]

Although the tasks of selecting intended from received phonemes and of selecting intended from activated words (and their meanings) are similar to one another, they also differ importantly. Specifically, we select the most plausible sequence of phonemes from the possibilities evoked by the speech stream on the basis of familiar words or, equivalently, on the basis of learned or previously established associations among the phonemes. We need not attend to this selection process; it will be executed automatically by our memory system, through preemptively overlearned excitatory and inhibitory links. In contrast, the ability to convey new information depends on creating sentences that include novel combinations of words and that thereby evoke novel combinations of meanings. Yet, unless the relevant relationships are preemptively familiar, the system cannot extract them for us; we must find them. We must examine the overlaps among the candidate words and their meanings, we must search the relationships embedded in them, and we must assess their coherence.

We have seen this requirement before. In chapter 9 we arrived at the conclusion that

our capacity for communication—and cognitive growth in general—would seem to require the ability and even predisposition to direct one's attention to activated overlap among established memories.

And thus we find our thoughts returned to the issue of printed word recognition. Human attention is limited. To understand connected text, our attention cannot be directed to the identities of individual words and letters. In reading as in listening, the process of individual word perception must proceed with relative

---

21. Note that this argument is consistent both with the laboratory demonstrations that multiple meanings of a polysemous word are activated even in semantically constraining context and with the fact that people become consciously aware of only one such meaning. Thus, Seidenberg et al.'s (1982) finding that, for example, the word *bugs* in the sentence "*John saw several spiders, roaches, and bugs*" briefly but measurably activates the concept of surreptitious listening devices, is reconciled with our conscious or attentive conviction that it does not.

22. See Adams (1989).

automaticity, and such automaticity is afforded only through learning. The system must have learned about the relations among visual features that signal individual letters; it must have learned about the relations among individual letters that correspond to frequent words and spelling patterns; it must have acquired the associations that link spelling to speech and, most important, to meanings. Only having perceived the individual words can we direct our attention to the relationships between them. Only as their perception has become relatively automatic can we devote our active attention to the process of understanding them.[23]

A similar argument has developed around Posner and Snyder's "two-process theory of expectancy."[24] Briefly, this theory posits that the guidance afforded by context during language comprehension arises from two distinct processes. The first operates automatically and derives from the semantic overlap between the context and a to-be-perceived word; to the extent that the meaning of a word has already been partially activated, that word will more quickly gain perceptual dominance over any competing orthographically (or phonologically) evoked alternatives.

The second process, in contrast, is under the control of the reader's conscious, limited-capacity attentional focus, and the contextual effect it produces is bivalent. Not only is the perception of contextually appropriate words speeded, but the perception of contextually incongruous words is slowed. Interestingly, although such bivalent effects of context are commonly observed among younger and poorer readers, they are found among skilled readers only when the to-be-perceived word is temporally delayed or physically degraded.[25] In either case, the explanation is the same: When perceptual resolution of the word is slow, readers anticipate the word's identity by focusing their active attention on the contextually activated sectors of memory. The long response times for semantically incongruous words thus reflect the extra processing load involved in shifting that active attention from the predicted to some unexpected region of memory.

In the reading literature, Posner and Snyder's two-process theory of expectancy is sometimes coupled with what might be

---

23. It may be that cognitive processes never become entirely capacity free (Cheng, 1985).

24. Posner and Snyder (1975).

25. Stanovich (1980).

described as a two-stage model of word recognition. The idea is essentially that the process of recognizing a word consists of directing our attention to its specific location in memory: Context delimits the neighborhood; orthography specifies the address; the word's identity is affirmed by directing our active attention to that address. Within the kinds of laboratory tasks from which Posner and Snyder's two-process theory derives its support, this would seem a nearly optimal strategy. (In these tasks, the viewer is asked to decide as quickly as possible whether the last "word" of each of a series of sentences is a real word or a nonword.) It may, more generally, be a productive tactic whenever a word of interest is, for example, unfamiliar, artificially delayed, physically degraded, or semantically incongruous.

In fluent reading or listening situations, however, where the orthographic or phonological activation of words is automatic, this sort of word-wise verification procedure would seem unnecessary. Through the combined activation of semantic priming and perceptual input, the intended word should dominate all other candidates without active selective processing, much as the intended phonemes are expected to dominate through the conjoint constraints of acoustical input and lexical knowledge. Furthermore, if comprehension depends on our ability to attend not to the individual words but to the semantic overlap between them, then a compulsion to focus attention directly on each individual word would also seem suboptimal.

The notion that in normal listening situations we tend not to focus attention directly on the individual words might explain the otherwise puzzling fact that many prereaders are unaware of words at the level of isolable and independently meaningful components of speech. Further, the notion that we are inclined to accept the dominant word candidate without directly or thoroughly scrutinizing its phonology is consistent not only with our ability to understand "Ladle Rat Rotten Hut" when read aloud but also with the sorts of contextually and lexically appropriate misperceptions people are found to commit when listening to meaningful speech.[26] Moreover, if this is indeed the

---

26. When listeners are required to "shadow" or concurrently repeat someone else's continuous speech, they tend to correct errors in the original speaker's articulation. This tendency is heightened when the contextual predictability of the word is increased, which is consistent with the argument that a word's activation derives in part from semantic priming. It is also heightened when the articulation error occurs later as opposed to earlier in the word, which is consistent with the argument that a word may be "perceived" as soon as its level of activation dominates any competing candidates. Because such phonological restorations occur

way in which language comprehension normally proceeds, it may explain the developmental patterns witnessed in young readers' use of context.

Learning to Attend to Spellings and Meanings

From observations of first graders' reading errors, recorded from October to May, Andrew Biemiller identified three successive stages in the trade-offs between orthographic and contextual processing.[27] In the first stage, although the children's errors tended to be contextually acceptable (74 percent), most (81 percent) seemed graphically unrelated to the print on the page. This is consistent with the idea that the children were accustomed to comprehending language without focusing their attention directly on the perceptual identities of its individual component words.

In the second stage, the proportion of graphically compatible misreadings increased, but so too did the tendency to look at a difficult word without responding at all. This is consistent with the idea that the process of attending to the graphically defined identities of the individual words was both effortful for the children and disruptive of their comprehension process.

In the third stage, the children's misreadings tended to be both contextually appropriate (83 percent) and graphically similar (44 percent) to the misperceived word. In this last stage, we see the beginnings of orthographic automaticity. At least some of the graphic information was being registered with the ease and speed

---

with near instantaneity and are not accompanied by increases in shadowing latency, they appear to be the result of automatic perceptual processes rather than conscious inference and correction.

In contrast, when such articulation errors are not corrected but faithfully reproduced, an increase does result in the shadowing latencies for subsequent words. Perhaps this is because the anomalous word creates a contextual hiatus; perhaps it is because it causes the listener to divert attention from the process of comprehension to the word itself. Both explanations are consistent with the present framework.

Of further interest, when listeners are asked not to shadow but to listen carefully for phonemic errors, the influence of contextual constraint all but vanishes. However, the tendency to overlook errors late in a word is just as strong. Again we see that the perception of phonemes is the combined product of what has been heard and what the system knows to be lexically permissible. See Marslen-Wilson and Welsh (1978).

27. Biemiller (1970).

required to complement rather than disrupt the comprehension process.

In an independent study of first graders' oral reading errors, Rose-Marie Weber obtained a similar pattern of results.[28] Although the children were occasionally observed to omit a word, insert a word, or scramble the order of words in the text, the vast majority (80 percent to 94 percent) of their errors consisted of substituting the printed word with another. To be sure, the better readers made fewer errors per line of running text than did the poorer readers. Nevertheless, whether the children were in the high, middle, or low reading group, the majority (87 percent to 92 percent) of their substitution errors were grammatically compatible with the preceding context. Overall, reported Weber, the distribution of errors "indicate a heavy dependence on contextual cues and disregard of the graphic display and its relationship to the sound system of English."[29]

Although most of the children's substitutions shared at least one letter (83 percent to 90 percent) with the word on the page, the better readers tended to capture more of the graphemic detail than did the poorer readers. Even so—and regardless of the children's reading ability—errors that were grammatically incompatible with the preceding context tended to exhibit *more* correct graphemic detail than those that were compatible. Weber observed that "in the relatively rare cases when the readers disregarded the grammatical constraints of preceding context, their attention was directed to analyzing the details of the graphic display, or even to working out the relationships between the letters of the stimulus and its pronunciation."[30] Again we find the suggestion that when children focus their attention on the perceptual resolution of a word, they do so at the potential cost of losing the meaning of the sentence.

In view of all of this, one might be tempted to discourage beginning readers from poring over the graphemic details of their texts. Toward developing the child's comprehension skills, one might sense that such preoccupation with the spellings and sounds of individual words is counterproductive. But such conclusions are hasty.

The young reader's tendency to take time out for decoding is, to the contrary, functional: The only way to learn the spelling patterns of the words is to study them. Moreover, its disruptive

---

28. Weber (1970).
29. Weber (1970, p. 154).
30. Weber (1970, p. 154).

potential is temporary: As the spellings of more and more words are learned by the system, it will happen less and less often. And finally, as John Downing explains, this tendency represents the first of three necessary phases in the acquisition of a complex skill:

The first phase is the *cognitive phase* in which the learner attends closely to the functions and techniques of the various tasks he must undertake to become a skilled performer. He tries to find out what behaviour is relevant and what is irrelevant for performing the skill. In more complex skills there may be a considerable effort involved in understanding the tasks set for the learner. The second phase is the *mastering phase* in which the skill is practised until mastery is gradually achieved. The third phase is the *automaticity phase* when the learner practises beyond mastery until he can perform the skill without any conscious concern for it.[31]

Like skilled readers, beginners are attuned to the linguistic and semantic flow of their texts as they read.[32] However, to the extent that necessary lower-order skills are lacking, the role of such higher-order constraint changes. Instead of complementing orthographic processing, it may substitute for it. In particular, until the processes involved in visual word recognition are fairly well developed, many readers apparently find that they can often guess the identity of a word as accurately as and more easily than they can actually decode it. Thus even among older students with poor decoding skills, contextually appropriate substitution errors are frequent[33] and word recognition performance is especially sensitive to the presence and compatibility of meaningful context.[34]

Although such sensitivity to context can only be a good sign, its dominance is not. The syntactic and semantic cogency of such errors is evidence of productive comprehension processes; however, their frequency is symptomatic that orthographic processing is proceeding neither quickly nor completely enough to do its job. The seriousness of this concern is underscored by the evidence that

---

31. Downing (1979, p. 34).

32. Provided that the text is not too difficult: see Stanovich (1984).

33. Allington and Strange (1977); Juel (1980).

34. Allington and Fleming (1978); Biemiller (1977-1978); Samuels, Begy, and Chen (1975-1976); West and Stanovich (1978). For excellent review and discussion of this interaction between decoding proficiency and contextual reliance, see Stanovich (1980, 1986).

weaknesses in basic decoding skills may be the most common and can be the most debilitating source of reading difficulties.[35]

Although the tendency among young readers to pause and study an unfamiliar word should be encouraged, the teacher should be aware that such efforts, even when successful, are likely to disrupt the flow of comprehension. Children who pause on many words should be given an easier text.[36] Children who pause occasionally should be helped, if necessary, to figure out the troublesome word. After identifying such words, they should be encouraged to begin their sentences anew so as to recover comprehension.

With proper practice, support, and motivation, orthographic automaticity will come. Meanwhile, our challenge is not to quash the cognitive phase. It is to find ways to help the children through it as efficiently and effectively as possible. Only as orthographic processing has become relatively automatic—only as it can be achieved relatively quickly, completely and effortlessly—can it properly work in concert rather than in competition with contextual processing.

For skillful reading, the connections between print and language must be thoroughly developed. To this end, certain lessons that fall properly within the domain of phonic instruction are invaluable. But here too our perspective may be confused. In discussing the value of phonic instruction for beginning readers, it is generally spelling-to-sound translations that we speak of. In keeping with this, it is generally the importance of spelling-to-sound translations that we think of.

But reading depends on connections between spellings, speech sounds, *and* meanings. Further, although the central goal of instruction on visual word recognition is to establish self-supportive paths *from* print *to* the rest of the system, it is essential for both expert and novice that the connections between each pair of processors run in both directions. Moreover, in setting the system up, the use and development of the mappings *from* speech and meaning *to* spelling are critical. When reading instruction is viewed from this perspective, the wisdom of our instructional practices often becomes much clearer.

---

35. Perfetti (1985); Stanovich (1986); Vernon (1971).
36. Clay (1979); Rosenshine and Stevens (1984).

V

Learning How to Read

Finally, in this part, we turn consideration to the acquisition of reading. What must children learn on their way to becoming good readers, and what can we do to give them the most help?

Throughout this book the importance of learning about spelling patterns and spelling-sound relationships has been stressed. We therefore begin part V with a chapter on the merits and demerits of teaching phonics first. The conclusion of this chapter is that, as valuable as phonic knowledge may be, its very learnability depends on prior possession of a variety of other sorts of knowledge about language and print.

In chapters 12–14, the goal is to clarify the other sorts of knowledge and skills that are important. Chapter 12 examines what beginning readers must also learn about the nature of spoken language. Chapter 13 focuses on what they must learn about the structure and functions of print. Chapter 14 discusses the ways in which reading acquisition can be fostered through independent writing and spelling. Toward developing solid reading skills, the various instructional approaches reviewed are seen to complement both one another and the basic phonic curriculum.

On Teaching Phonics First

The reading process is driven by the visual recognition of individual letters in familiar ordered sequence and is critically supported by the translation of those strings of letters into their phonological correspondences. In view of this, I have suggested that activities requiring children to attend to the individual letters of words, their sequencing, and their phonological translations should be included in all beginning reading programs.

Because they are designed around these very activities, "phonics-first" curricula immediately spring to mind. Historically, however, there is another perspective on such curricula that has been far more influential in their widespread development, adoption, and advocacy.

We have long recognized that the task of reading for meaning is enormously complex, involving a host of visual, linguistic, and conceptual skills. To understand it, we have been compelled to find ways to break it down into tractable sets of subskills and to identify their interrelations.

The traditional approach to this problem begins with the ultimate goal of reading and then successively identifies its prerequisites. To have extracted the full meaning of a written text, readers must first have understood its individual sentences. To have understood its individual sentences, readers must first have correctly analyzed the clauses and phrases of those sentences. Whereas proper analysis of those phrases and clauses depends on having correctly recognized their component words, recognition of each word depends on having processed its spelling patterns or phonological translations. Finally, recognizing the spelling or phonological translation of a word depends on having processed the ordered array of individual letters that comprise it.

When analyzed in this way, the processes involved in reading appear to be organized hierarchically and rather strictly so. Whereas the reading of a written passage depends on the reading of its sentences, words, and letters, the dependency is in some sense unidirectional. An individual letter may be legible whether or not it is embedded in a word, a sentence, or a passage. Similarly, individual words and sentences are legible in the absence of any larger context.

Within this sort of hierarchical view of the process, the phonics-first approach to beginning reading instruction is nearly begged. Start at the bottom, with individual letter-sound correspondences and successively work up through the higher-level skills. Instruction is thus inherently staged in order of complexity, and each new level of complexity is introduced only after all of its component subskills have been established.

Indeed, within this hierarchical view, the phonics-first approach seems to offer the ideal in terms of rational instructional models. In combination with the apparent importance of direct instruction in letters, spelling patterns, and spelling-sound translations, one might expect this approach to produce superlative instructional results. Consistent with this, across the method comparison studies, programs involving early and systematic instruction in phonics have generally been found to produce better results than their various alternatives. On the other hand, these advantages were neither large nor universal. Why not?

Having developed and defended the potential strengths of providing instruction on spellings and sounds for beginners, I devote this chapter to discussion of its weaknesses and limitations.

Teaching Individual Letter-Sound Correspondences

Written English is fundamentally alphabetic. The purported advantage of an alphabetic script is that if one learns the speech sounds corresponding to each of its individual graphemes, one has the requisite knowledge to read and write any word in the language. And so, claimed Rudolph Flesch, "ever since 1500 B.C. people all over the world—wherever an alphabetic system of writing was used—learned to read and write by the simple process of memorizing the sound of each letter in their alphabet."[1]

In the 1986 reissue of his provocative book, *Why Johnny Can't Read,* Flesch reflects,

---

1. Flesch (1955, p. 4).

What I suggested was very simple: Go back to the ABC's. Teach children the 44 sounds of English and how they are spelled. They can sound out each word from left to right and read it off the page. . . .

With phonics-first, you teach a child to read the word fish by telling him about the sounds of f—'ff'—i—short i—and sh—'sh.' Then you tell him to blend the sounds from left to right to read the word: "fish." . . .

Independent studies have proved that the average child comes to school with a speaking and listening vocabulary of about 24,000 words. Learning to read is simply learning a system of notation for the language the child already knows.[2]

In principle, Flesch's approach seems elegantly simple and powerful: Teach the children individual letter-sound correspondences; teach them to read words by chaining these individual correspondences together; memorization of a score or so of elementary symbol-sound pairs yields mastery tens of thousands of words and uncountable sentences and ideas.

Yet, looking at the map and traveling the route are often very different. In practice, this seemingly smooth and direct route can be slow and tortuous, especially when one is working with students who are not well prepared for reading on school entry. Let us examine some of its complications.

The Right Amount of Practice

The first complication derives from the fact that both graphemes and their phonological correspondences are meaningless, perceptually sparse, and piecewise confusable. Because of this, letter-sound pairings are not very easy to remember, and they are very easy to forget or confuse.

Many children enter the classroom with lots of prior experience with print. For most of these children, the content of the symbol-sound lessons will consist more of review and clarification than of new information, and to that extent will be relatively easy. Furthermore, for most of these children, the purpose of the lessons will be clear and, to that extent, their motivation should be relatively high. For these children, symbol-sound lessons may proceed quite quickly.

Other children enter school with next to no relevant knowledge about print. Relative to their well-prepared peers, these children are likely to have less interest in these lessons and less appreciation of their point. We must therefore expect their learning to be slower and their patience to be slimmer. At the same time, however, mastery of the symbol-sound relations will

---

2. Cited by Ziegler (1986, pp. viii–ix).

require more study for these children. After all, some of them may still be having difficulty discriminating the letter shapes; their entering level of phonological awareness will be relatively low; and so, too, will be their prior knowledge of letter-sound relationships. Much of the content of these lessons will be new for these children in detail and concept. As a consequence, it will be more confusing and harder to consolidate. Finally, in order for all necessary symbol-sound pairs to be learned well, each must be allowed sufficient practice and opportunity for evaluation.[3] The implication, in short, is that the teaching of individual letter-sound correspondences cannot proceed quickly for these children. It must be spread over time.

How much time? For a first answer, we may look to published reading programs. We may assume that the teaching schedule they propose reflects their highly experienced estimates of the pace at which the first-grade consumer, for whom the programs were designed, can absorb these correspondences.

The data in table 11.1 are taken from an analysis by Isabel Beck and Ellen McCaslin of eight beginning reading programs.[4] Beck and McCaslin selected these eight programs specifically because each had been used with students designated for compensatory education; that is, each had been used with students entering school without high levels of literacy preparation. Although each of the eight programs includes phonic instruction, they differ in didactic philosophy. For the first four programs in the table the emphasis is on teaching symbol-sound relations; for the last four it is on engaging the students in the reading of meaningful whole words, sentences, and stories from the start.

---

3. More generally, "Abundant experimental research . . . has confirmed the proposition that prior learnings are not transferable to new learning tasks until they are first overlearned. Overlearning, in turn, requires an adequate number of adequately spaced repetitions and reviews, sufficient intratask repetitiveness prior to intra- and intertask diversification, and opportunity for differential practice of the more difficult components of a task. Frequent testing and provision of feedback, especially with test items demanding fine discrimination among alternatives varying in degree of correctness, also enhance consolidation by confirming, clarifying and correcting previous learnings" (Ausubel, 1967, p. 239).

4. Beck and McCaslin (1978). Note that, whereas basal series are generally revised every few years, the eight programs in this analysis were published in the mid-1970s. It is therefore inappropriate to draw conclusions about the merits and demerits of current products by these publishers on the basis of the data presented. The purpose instead is to present contrasts that will serve as undated food for thought in considerations of curriculum design variables.

Table 11.1

Number of grapheme-phoneme pairs presented in the first half of first grade for each of the eight programs analyzed by Beck and McCaslin (1978).

Program[a]	Short vowels	Long vowels	Vowel digraphs/ dipthongs	r and l controlled vowels	Single consonants	Double consonants	Initial consonant diagraphs	Final consonant digraphs	Total
Distar	4	4	4	--	13	8	2	2	37
Sullivan	3	--	--	--	16	6	4	2	31
Palo Alto	4	--	--	1	16	--	--	--	21
Merrill	2	--	--	--	19	--	--	--	21
Ginn	1	1	--	--	18	--	--	1	21
Houghton Mifflin	2	--	5	--	20	--	3	4	34
Bank Street	--	--	--	--	7	--	--	--	7
Open Highways	--	--	--	--	20	--	3	3	26

a. **Distar**: Engelmann and Bruner (1974); **Sullivan**: Buchanan (1973); **Merrill**: Otto, Rudolph, Smith, and Wilson (1975); **Palo Alto**: Glim (1973); **Houghton Mifflin**: Durr, LePere, and Aslin (1976); **Ginn**: Clymer, Christenson, and Brown (1976); **Bank Street**: Bank Street College of Education (1973); **Open Highways**: Scott, Foresman and Company (1974).

The data in table 11.1 indicate that across the first semester of first grade, the number of grapheme-phoneme correspondences taught in these programs ranges from seven to thirty-seven, with a median of twenty-three or twenty-four. Given that there are roughly eighteen weeks in a school semester, the pace of these programs ranges from two weeks per correspondence to two correspondences per week. Even throwing a few weeks away for beginning-of-the-year adjustment time and so on, it is clear that, averaged over the semester, none of these programs is designed to introduce more than two or three symbol-sound pairs per week.

Is that an encouragingly fast pace or a discouragingly slow one? Let us reserve judgment while we examine a few more dimensions of the issue.

How Many Pairs Must Be Learned?

If English were perfectly alphabet—if each letter corresponded to exactly one phoneme and vice-versa—then the number of grapheme-phoneme pairs to be learned would equal twenty-six. It is the case, however, that our letters and phonemes do not correspond one to one with each other. Instead, a number of the letters can symbolize several distinct phonemes; a number of the phonemes can be symbolized by each of several different letters; and some of the phonemes are symbolized by pairs of letters, each of which, when separated from one another, has its own independent and distinct phonemic values.

Since the correspondence is not consistently one to one, but often one to several in both directions, there are many more than twenty-six grapheme-phoneme pairs to be learned. Exactly how many are in fact involved? A number of studies have been undertaken on this issue.

Just to represent the spelling-sound mappings of a good majority (80 to 90 percent) of English words—that is, ignoring true exceptions—it is generally found that hundreds of correspondences are involved.[5] Even in a study where concern was restricted to one- and two-syllable words found in reading materials of six to nine year olds, the number of relevant spelling-sound correspondences was found to be 211.[6]

Against a grand total of hundreds of correspondences, the pace of even the most aggressive of the programs analyzed by Beck and

---

5. Dewey (1970, cited in Beck and McCaslin, 1978); Hanna et al. (1966); Wijk (1966).

6. Berdiansky, Cronnell, and Koehler (1969, cited in Smith, 1973).

McCaslin may seem disturbingly slow. On the other hand, not all of the nameable correspondences are equally useful. Not all are required with equal frequency. Not all need to be learned in the first grade. And not all that will eventually be learned by the maturing reader need be explicitly taught. With concern toward sound curriculum design, we might better ask which correspondences should be taught than how many.

Which Correspondences Should Be Taught?

Across all eight programs analyzed by Beck and McCaslin, the number of different correspondences explicitly taught by the end of the second grade totaled 170.[7] Program by program, the totals ranged from 65 to 135, with a median of 93.5.

By compiling the overlap between these programs, can we establish the correspondences that are most important to teach? The list of correspondences explicitly taught by all eight programs is shown in table 11.2. The most surprising feature of this list is that it contains only thirty-five graphemic units.

Unanimously the programs agree to teach the dominant phonemic mappings of the twenty-one consonants (including the consonantal use of the letter *y*) as well as the "short" pronunciations of the five primary vowels. Moreover, the assertion that these twenty-six elementary letter-sound correspondences should eventually be covered in any course of phonic instruction seems inarguable. Just as inarguably, however, the teaching of these twenty-six correspondences is not enough to empower young learners to read many words. What else should be taught?

The nine other graphemic units presented by all of Beck and McCaslin's eight programs are spread across six other classes of correspondences. And the remaining 135 correspondences—those that are seen to warrant explicit attention by at least one but not all of the programs—are spread across these categories plus four more: double consonants, final consonant clusters, vowel variants, and "other" (which includes, for example, *y* as in *cry*; *y* as in *penny*; *-igh* as in *night*; final syllable *-el* and *-le*; and the suffixes *-sion* and *-tion*).

---

7. Beck and McCaslin (1978) included explicit teaching of initial (e.g., *slap*) and final (e.g., *fast*) consonant clusters in their count. If one excludes consonant clusters that are derivable from their component consonants, the total number of different grapheme-phoneme correspondences found across these programs is reduced from 170 to approximately 110.

Table 11.2

The thirty-five graphemic units taught by the end of the second grade within all eight programs analyzed by Beck and McCaslin.

Single consonants

b	bat
l	lap
r	ran
h	hat
j	jam
c	cat
f	fan
y	yard
n	not
d	did
qu	quite
t	tap
v	van
m	man
s	sit
w	wag
p	pat
z	zip
g	gun
k	kiss
x	six

Short vowels

a	man
e	get
i	sit
o	cot
u	cup

Long vowels

a-e	made
i-e	nice

Vowel digraphs and dipthongs

ee	seem

r and l controlled vowels

all	ball

Initial consonant clusters

sl	slap
br	bring

Initial consonant digraphs

sh	ship
ch	chin

Final consonant digraphs

ck	back

There are, of course, many other beginning reading programs besides these eight; however, if we counted the correspondences in these too, the conclusion would be the same. Beyond the most basic of basics and despite its long history and broad use, the various renditions of the phonic method contain little in the way of consensual recommendations as to the best set of grapheme-phoneme pairs to teach explicitly to our students. What we need are some principles to guide our choices and their orderings, and a number exist for our reflection.

The Teaching of Individual Grapheme-Phoneme Correspondences

The structure of instructional programs on grapheme-phoneme correspondences is, by and large, based on principles. A major reason for the disagreement among programs as to methods and schedules of instruction is that these principles are incompatible with one another. In this section, I have divided instructional issues into categories. We shall see that even within categories, the principles and their instructional implications often conflict with one another. When we back off to examine the implications across categories, the situation becomes even more complex.

Establish the Alphabetic Principle

Perhaps the most important goal, in the interest of giving students a productive knowledge of grapheme-phoneme correspondences, is to convey to them the basic alphabetic principle. Very early in the course of instruction, one wants the students to understand that all twenty-six of those strange little symbols that comprise the alphabet are worth learning and discriminating one from the other because each stands for one of the sounds that occur in spoken words. Written language is a "cipher," as Gough and Hillinger put it, and the alphabetic principle is its key.[8]

As it happens, novel, abstract concepts cannot be explained well, to children or anyone else. Such ideas must be illustrated. One must show the students that letters do represent speech sounds. One must persuade them that this is true not of one letter or even of a few but, much more, that it is the core principle of our writing system.

So how might one best illustrate this rule? Most obviously, it is through the consonants. With gratifying frequency, the mapping

---

8. Gough and Hillinger (1980).

from single consonants to phonemes tends to be one to one. In word-initial position and in short (two- and three-letter) words, this is all the more true, making the consonants all the more appealing for beginning instruction. Introducing the letters *y* and *w* as word-initial consonants allows one to address the significance of twenty-one of the twenty-six letters through this approach. Alternate pronunciation(s) of *y* and *w*, as well as those few true consonants that do misbehave (e.g., *c* as in *city* instead of *cat*, *g* as in *giant* instead of *got*, *s* as in *sure* instead of *sun*, and *h* as in *hour* instead of *hat*), are postponed until after the alphabetic principle has (presumably) been established.

Thus we see from table 11.1 that in each of the eight programs evaluated by Beck and McCaslin, the majority of early phonic lessons are devoted to single consonants. This is also true of the vast majority of phonic and code-emphasis programs reviewed in Robert Aukerman's books.[9]

In contrast to the consonants, the vowels are rampantly irregular in our writing system. Yet, five of the letters in the English alphabet can be treated only as vowels, and they too must be introduced. Fortunately when vowels occur singly in three-letter words, they most often take on a regular, "short" pronunciation.

Thus of the programs analyzed by Beck and McCaslin, it is the category of "short" vowels that is given the second most attention in the initial phase of reading instruction (see table 11.1). Furthermore, by the end of the second grade, this is the only vowel category that is treated completely by all of the programs analyzed by Beck and McCaslin (see table 11.2). Most of the phonic and code-emphasis programs reviewed by Aukerman give similar emphasis to the "short" vowels early in instruction.[10]

---

9. Aukerman (1971, 1984). In fact, most words begin with consonants, and many programs and experts offer this as an additional motivation for teaching the consonants first. The rationale is that if the children understand the context and can sound out the initial consonant, they can guess the identity of the word. However, as will become clear later in this chapter, encouraging this word identification strategy among beginning readers is probably not wise.

10. Aukerman (1971, 1984). In contrast, an analysis of three of the major meaning-emphasis programs indicates that they include relatively little instruction on vowels and that even that which they include tends to be deferred until later in the school year (Meyer, Greer, and Crummey, 1987).

Phonemic Accessibility

To establish the link between a letter and a sound, the learner must first establish a clear image of each. Toward this end, the individual letters, quite amenably, consist of discrete, self-contained, visual patterns. We can print or point to them one by one. The phonemes, in contrast, are more elusive. In normal oral production, their images are fleeting. Moreover, they do not correspond to discrete segments in spoken language. Instead their features overlap in time such that their sounds are inextricably blended with one another in the acoustic stream. In view of this, it is not surprising that a number of the principles guiding initial phonic instruction are directed toward making the phonemic side of the letter-sound relationship as salient as possible.

Perhaps the most widespread technique in this category consists of beginning with letters whose sounds can be pronounced in isolation with least distortion. Among the consonants, the most popular in this category are *f*, *m*, and *s*. The sounds of each of these letters can be flourished both in isolation (*/f-f-f/*, */m-m-m/*, */s-s-s-s/*) and in the words in which they occur (e.g., *s-s-s-snake*). When concern is focused on helping the children to recognize that the sounds that will be paired with each letters are the subsounds of words, the potential value of these attributes should be clear.[11]

Reflecting different approaches toward this same goal, a few programs advocate presenting the vowels first. All vowels have the attribute of being pronounceable in isolation. In addition, they are the most frequent letters in our script.

Several programs, moreover, advocate presentation of the "long" vowels before the "short" ones. And here again the rationale is well motivated: "Long" vowels have the special advantage of sounding like their names. For children who know the letters' names, what better clue could be provided as to the relation between letter identities and speech sounds?

A major problem to teaching the "long" vowels first is that in most words, the "long" sound of a vowel is signaled by relatively complex but only semireliable spelling clues (such as adjacent vowels and word-final *e*'s). Thus if one wishes to exercise the lesson in real word contexts, one quickly runs up against spelling

---

11. Other consonants with these attributes are *l*, *n*, *r*, *v*, and *z*. These letters are also among the first taught by many programs, though somewhat less often for reasons of, for example, their frequency in print or their ease of segmentation and proper enunciation by children. Note that in contrast to such "continuant" consonants, the distinctive features of the "stop" consonants (e.g., *b*, *d*, *p*, *t*) cannot be elongated; indeed, they cannot even be spoken without the support of a vowel sound.

pattern issues that might best be saved for later. A problem to teaching the "short" vowels first is that, relative to the sounds of other letters, those of the "short" vowels seem to be especially difficult to learn.[12]

The problem with focusing on either the "long" or the "short" vowels to the exclusion of the other is that both types occur in many high-frequency words. Thus, whichever of these two categories is chosen as the initial set of vowel correspondences to be taught, one is setting the students up to encounter exceptions very early in the game.

The problem with postponing all vowels and teaching the consonants first is that no words can be spelled without vowels. While one postpones the vowels, one is caught in a dilemma: Expose the children to words with untaught correspondences or to no words at all.

In view of these difficulties, many programs introduce at least one (typically "short") vowel early in the letter-sound correspondence lessons. This approach abates the problem in quantity but not quality. Whatever subset of spelling-sound correspondences one chooses to teach first, problems of how to deal with the exceptions to every rule, as well as the as-yet-untaught correspondences, will not go away.

Referential Clarity

Solid knowledge of the nature and identity of phonemes is crucial to an appreciation of the alphabetic principle. We thus seek not only to let children know that there are such units but to let them know, with no shadow of confusion, precisely what they are. About what types of confusion shall we worry most?

The sounds of phonemes are similar to but different from letter names. In the interest of stressing that it is phonemes that are at issue and of preventing confusion between them and letter names, some programs choose to avoid or minimize use of letter names in their instruction. On the other side, having taught the sounds of the letters *b*, *a*, and *t*, one hopes the child will be able to produce /*bat*/, not /*buh*/-/*ah*/-/*tuh*/. In recognition of these sorts of problems, some programs avoid or limit the use of isolated phonemes in their instruction.

Most programs that avoid or minimize the use of letter names in instruction do rely on oral production of isolated phonemes.

---

12. Carnine and Silbert (1979); Coleman (1970); Williams and Knafle (1977).

Sometimes they do so with a warning to the teacher to take care to say, for example, just /b/ and not /buh/ or /bih/ (as if that were possible). Often the sounds of the letters are introduced by way of example or so-called word mediation. To introduce the "short" sound of the letter *i*, for example, the teacher might point out that it is the sound that is represented by the first letter of the words *is*, *in*, *imp*, and *igloo*. Most programs attempt to reinforce the letter sounds by having the children repeat and rehearse them in various ways.

Some programs attempt to minimize phonemic distortions by requiring only the teacher, and not the children, to speak the sounds in isolation, but this is probably a mistake. Phonemes are not defined by the way in which they sound. The sound of a phoneme varies greatly with the spoken context (or lack thereof) in which it occurs. That which defines a phoneme is the voicing or aspiration with which it should be produced together with the "target" or ideal position of the mouth, lips, and tongue while producing it. From this perspective alone, having children produce letter sounds may be invaluable toward helping them to understand and learn what is in reference in these lessons.[13]

In grapheme-phoneme instruction, one often has need to refer to the letter as distinct from its sound. It is extremely hard to conduct a discussion of grapheme-phoneme correspondences without some label for the letter. Most of the programs that avoid letter names therefore resort to some alternate system of letter labels, e.g., vowels, consonants, letters with breath sounds, nasal sounds, or voiced sounds, diphthongs, digraphs, and unglided vowels.

In contrast, programs that seek to minimize use of isolated phonemes almost have to use letter names. On the other hand, these programs face an analogous referential problem with respect to phonemes: There is often need to refer to the sound of a particular letter as distinct from the sound of the whole word in which it occurs. The most frequent solution again is to develop a terminology that permits such reference: "the short vowel sound of the letter *e*," and so on.

In addition or as an alternative to such substitute labeling, the teacher be may provided with rather detailed guidance on what to say. The following example was originally cited in a paper by Walter MacGinitie:

---

13. The Lindamoods (1975), on the observation that some poor readers have never realized that their mouths provide clues about phonemes and phonology, include explicit instruction on articulatory monitoring in their program for remedial reading and spelling.

The teacher is instructed to write the word *girls* on the board. The teacher then says, "You can find out what this word is. With what consonant does it begin? With what consonant does it end? You know the sounds that *g* and *r* and *l* and *s* stand for. I am going to say something and leave out this word at the end. When I stop, think of a word that begins with a sound *g* stands for, ends with the sounds *r* and *l* and *s* stand for and makes sense with what I said."[14]

This instruction may sound quite clear, even overspecified, to our adult minds. Yet, MacGinitie vivified its relational complexity by replacing the grapheme-phoneme correspondences with color-shape pairings. Thus, the last sentence of this instruction was translated as:

[When I stop,] find the row that begins with the color that goes with rectangle, ends with the colors that go with triangle, diamond, and square, and that has a wavy line under it.[15]

To document the comprehensibility of such instructions, MacGinitie presented them to a group of young readers. In distinction from the true phonic task, the children were not asked to construct the appropriate response but only to choose from several rows of colored shapes that were set before them. Not surprisingly, they could not do it.

As yet one more path around such problems, programs may defer their solution to the teacher, as in the following example:

Help the children to understand that the underlined letter in the word *fish* is a symbol for the vowel sound heard in the word *fish*.

Imagine that you are the teacher: How might you go about doing this? Remember that you're working with a bunch of six year olds. Remember that the challenge of extracting the vowel from a syllable is among the most difficult of phonemic segmentation tasks. And remember that you are not supposed to voice the sound of the phoneme in isolation.[16]

There are occasional programs that try to limit use of both letter names and isolated phonemes. Although the motivation for doing so is clear, the referential difficulties that result are outstanding. Here, for example, is an instructional quote from one such program:

---

14. MacGinitie (1976, p. 372 [boldface added]).
15. MacGinitie (1976, p. 372).
16. The example and the point are owed to Beck and McCaslin (1978).

Refer to the CVC pattern and explain that . . . when the vowel letter *i* is between two consonant letters, the corresponding vowel sound is usually unglided.[17]

There are two drawbacks to the use of special terminology in instructional dialogues. The first is probably obvious: Special terminology is sometimes hard to understand. The second is that the purpose of such terminology is easily misperceived. In particular, students tend to think of the content of the lesson as an illustration of the special term instead of thinking about the special term as a label or direction for what they are to notice in the content. Thus, they tend to treat "The Highwayman" as a vehicle for learning the definition of *alliteration*—instead of using the term *alliteration* as a lens for examining the structure of the poem; they tend to treat Greek plays as vehicles for learning the term *hubris*—instead of contemplating the term *hubris* as a label for a syndrome to be contemplated more generally and an entry to the larger message of the plays; and so on.

In the same vein, use of special terminology may subvert the goal of beginning reading lessons. As illustrated, the resulting instruction is rarely transparent. Furthermore, the goal is not to have children study words such as *fish* to learn the denotation of *unglided vowel*. Rather, it is to find a term through which we can successfully direct their attention to the spelling and sound structures of words such as *fish*.

In the interest of referential ease and clarity, use of both letter names and isolated phonemes seems reasonable, and most programs do seem to use both. To use both while minimizing confusions between them, we must observe two principles. First, both cannot be introduced to the children at the same time. Either the letter names should be thoroughly overlearned before the sounds are introduced, or vice-versa. Second, we must remember that the goal of letter-sound instruction is to help the children to acquire the relations between printed letters and speech sounds. The names of the letters are neither; they are labels, and care should be taken to avoid blurring their status as such.

As an example, exercises requiring the children to respond with the phoneme /e/ when the teacher orally produces the name of the letter *e* surely do not represent the best use of instructional time. Such exercises might well increase rather than reduce any confusions a child might have with respect to which is the name and which is the phoneme. Further, if the goal is to establish

---

17. "CVC" stands for consonant-vowel-consonant. Examples of CVC patterns are *bid*, *bud*, and *mud*.

linkages between *printed* letters and their phonemic correspondences, this is, at best, an indirect way to go about it.

In contrast, exercises requiring the students to generate the phoneme /ə/ in response to the printed letter *e* (or vice-versa) would seem well directed. And provided that it is done so as to avoid confusions, it would seem entirely acceptable to use the letter's name, as referentially convenient, in the instructions or discussion of such exercises.

Inasmuch as the debate over the merits and demerits of using letter names or isolated letter sounds has sharpened our sensitivity to important dimensions of referential clarity, it has been useful. Yet, the whole debate seems one step removed from the larger issue that motivated it: how best to help the students to perceive the nature of phonemes and their relation to letters.

Graphemes with Multiple Sounds

The correspondences typically taught first are the "short" sounds of the five primary vowels and the word-initial consonant sounds of the other twenty-one letters. Maybe these twenty-six simple grapheme-to-phoneme correspondences are fine for starters. However, written English is estimated to consist of fifty or so graphemic units,[18] and spoken English is estimated to include forty or so phonemes.[19] To read, the twenty-six simple correspondences are not enough.

On the other hand, the twenty-six simple correspondences use up all twenty-six letters. One is thus left with three (partly overlapping) classes of potentially confusing correspondences to teach. The first consists of multiletter graphemic units (such as *ch*, *sh*, *th*) and various vowel digraphs (such as *au*, *ea*, and *oo*) whose pronunciations differ from what could be deduced from the pronunciations of their component letters. The second consists of single letters or digraphs with multiple pronunciations, such as *c*, *g*, *h*, *gh*, and the vowels. The third consists of phonemes that can be represented by more than one graphemic unit, such as /s/ as in *sit* and *city*.

To learn any of these correspondences, the students must be disabused of any notion that English alphabetic notation is simple and direct. Yet, we do not want to disabuse them of the

---

18. For example, the number of major spelling units counted by Venezky (1967) is 52: 32 for the consonants and 20 for the vowels.

19. Although the phoneme counts for English vary somewhat, this is a representative number.

notion that the system is alphabetic. How can such instruction proceed for maximum progress and minimum confusion? Which should we teach and when?

With respect to the issue of when, two principles can be offered. Under the first, instruction on alternate letter-sound correspondences should be well separated in time. Under the second, alternate letter-sound correspondences should be presented closely in time.

At least two arguments can be offered for separating the instruction of alternate letter-sound correspondences. The first is that introducing messy grapheme-phoneme mappings early in instruction makes it more difficult for the students to appreciate the alphabetic principle; to establish this principle, the students should begin by thoroughly learning one single phonemic response to each letter. The second is that introducing alternate letter-sound relations closely in time increases the likelihood that students will confuse one with the other.

At least two arguments can also be offered for introducing alternate correspondences closely in time. The first is that it is misleading to present too clean a vision of our symbol-sound system; to do so will cause trouble later. The second is that separating the introduction of alternate letter-sound relations widely in time increases the likelihood that the learning of the first will block or interfere with the learning of the second.

Thus, not only are these two guiding principles diametrically opposed to one another; so are their justifications. Moreover, the empirical evidence on this issue is scanty and hard to interpret. The existing data support both sides: Close presentation of alternate letter-sound correspondences seems to produce confusion; widely separated presentation interferes with the learning of the second.[20]

After reviewing each of these alternatives and their supporting arguments, Beck and McCaslin suggest that the best solution lies in between: Do not teach alternate correspondences too closely together, but do not wait too long between them either.[21] Exactly what is the right amount of time to wait between lessons? An answer can only be given in principle: The first alternative should receive sufficient exercise to be clearly and comfortably established but not so much that it is preemptively locked in.

---

20. See Beck and McCaslin (1978).
21. Beck and McCaslin (1978). See also Carnine and Silbert (1979).

To apply this principle sensitively, we should perhaps remind ourselves that confusion and interference of this nature are general features of human memory. For example, when we move to a new home, it is hard to learn our new telephone number. The old, overlearned response seems to keep the new one from sticking. This sort of interference is analogous to the difficulties of waiting too long before trying to learn an alternate letter-sound correspondence.

It is also hard for us to learn two or three telephone numbers or names at the same time. When we have to, we know just what to do: We practice one until it is settled; then we turn to the next; then we go back to the first and practice it some more. To turn to the second too soon is wholly counterproductive. To turn to it much too late is inefficient. Fortunately, any of a range of durations in between seems to work fine.

While we can escape from this dilemma by applying principles of human memory and sensitively monitoring the progress of students, we might avoid it altogether by using a revised orthography. If the grapheme-phoneme correspondence of the revised orthography were truly one to one, the response conflicts of concern would never arise.

But revised orthographies can carry a negative side as well—especially given that the goal of reading instruction is to teach children to read conventional orthography. Most important, proficient word reading is a perceptual skill. It depends on overlearned and thus effortless *visual* recognition of letters, words, and frequent spelling patterns. To the extent that revised orthographies use wholly novel graphemes and noncanonical spellings, they cannot exercise the visual pattern recognition through which skillful word reading grows.

On the other hand, the use of minor visual cues and diacritical marks that do not distort the basic shapes of letters or spelling patterns of words may be quite helpful to students. As such cues signal the particular behavior of a letter, they may reduce the trial, error, and confusion involved in mastering our complex orthography. In so doing, they may genuinely reduce the time required to consolidate the orthographic patterns and conditions that determine the phonemic significance of the letters.

Examples of such minimally altered type conventions are offered by the Distar program: "Silent" *e*s initially appear in half-size print, the letters of common digraphs, such as *th*, are squeezed together, and "long" vowels are diacritically marked. Theory suggests that such minimally altered type conventions are worthy of more serious consideration by researchers and publishers.

Summary: Teaching Individual Letter-Sound Relationships

Ideas that appear to be elegantly simple and powerful from the vantage point of the armchair often lose their gleam under the close lens of implementation. Letter-sound instruction seems to be a case in point.

First, the correspondences between letters and sounds are not one to one. Instead they are one to several in both directions, spoiling the tidiness or simplicity of the "hierarchy." Second, this diminution in the simplicity of the system brings with it a diminution in its power. Where once the goal was (glibly) cast as one of teaching the children the correct sound for each letter, it turns out to be one of teaching them a whole set of possible sounds for each letter. Obviously this changes the nature of the task quantitatively, but it changes it qualitatively as well. Specifically the goal is not to condition the children to come up with one of many or even with all appropriate phonemic translations of any given letter when they see it. It is to develop in them the ability to come up with the appropriate phonemic translation for each letter in each word they read. The task thus cannot be conceived as one of stimulus-response training. To master it, the children must learn to think about not just the letters and their sounds; rather, they must understand the basic nature and purpose of the system and reflectively use that understanding to contextualize the letter-sound pairings productively.

This brings us to the third problem with phonics-first instruction: Letter-sound correspondences are not the basics of literacy knowledge; they do not lie at the bottom of the reading hierarchy (or, more accurately, lattice). Acquisition of letter-sound relations depends, first, on solid visual familiarity with the individual letters. Unless the relevant letters are already firmly represented in memory, such instruction cannot be anchored. Just as critically, it depends on the students' awareness of phonemes—on their understanding that the little sounds paired with each letter are the subsounds of words. This again requires an understanding of the essential nature and purpose of print. Thus it seems that the true basics on which productive acquisition of letter-sound correspondences depend include prior learning about higher- as well as lower-order strata of the system.

Finally, we may profitably consider the results of Great Britain's large-scale experiment on the relative effectiveness of using the initial teaching alphabet (i/t/a) versus traditional orthography in beginning reading instruction. Across a variety of measures of print and linguistic development, the children whose initial instruction had been with the i/t/a were found to exhibit a significantly lower failure rate than those who worked with the traditional orthography from the start, and this advantage persisted at least through the fifth grade.[22]

In reviewing these results, John Downing suggested that they were due, most of all, to the consistency of the grapheme-phoneme pairings within the i/t/a system. As one strong benefit of such consistency, he cited its potential for hastening the child's conception of individual phonemes. But even while stressing the importance of such phonemic awareness, he extended his interpretation of the i/t/a's successes one step further.

The most valuable aspect of such grapheme-phoneme consistency, Downing argued, is that it helps the children to *understand* the fundamental nature of the alphabetic system. It helps them to *understand* the nature of the relationship under study. The long-term benefits of the i/t/a, he argued, derive not just from the children's early consolidation of this understanding but, moreover, from its support of the general and invaluable attitude that what one learns is meant to be understood.

The pedagogical difficulties surrounding effective letter-sound instruction are primarily difficulties for children who enter school with relatively little prior literacy preparation. This is partly because much of the content of the letter-sound lessons is already familiar to the well-prepared child. At least as important, however, it is because the well-prepared child faces these lessons with the basics that they presuppose—prior understanding of their nature and purpose.

Phonic Generalizations

Learning that many letters symbolize more than one phoneme and that many phonemes are symbolized by more than one letter or group of letters is not enough. Both the phonemic significance of a letter and the graphemic representation of a phoneme depend on context. They depend on the letters or sounds that surround them and even on the words in which they occur.

We want our students to understand not simply that *g* can signal a hard or soft pronunciation but the conditions under which

---

22. See Downing (1979).

it is most likely to do one versus the other. We want them to appreciate not simply that /j/ can be spelled with *j, g,* or *dge* but the conditions under which one of these spellings is more likely than another. The internalization of such phonic generalizations is necessary for proficient reading and writing. However, they are complex, they are numerous, and almost none is 100 percent reliable.

Our sense of the utility of phonic generalizations has been strongly influenced by a study of Theodore Clymer's who, in turn, attributes the inspiration for his study to a young student named Kenneth:

Difficulties with Kenneth began as the class reviewed phonic generalizations at the start of the school year. Our procedures were like those used in many classrooms: Groups of words were presented, and the class analyzed their likeness and differences with a view toward deriving a generalization about relationships between certain letters and sounds or the position and pronunciation of vowels.

...While the class was busily engaged in developing the generalization, Kenneth had skimmed his dictionary, locating long lists of exceptions to the generalization. In fact he often located more exceptions that I could list applications. When I protested—somewhat weakly—that the dictionary contained many unusual words, Kenneth continued his role as an educational scientist. He turned to the basic reader word list in the back of his text and produced nearly similar results.[23]

With Kenneth as his provocateur, Clymer took on a more general investigation of the reliability of phonic generalizations. First, he extracted the to-be-taught phonic generalizations from the teacher's manuals of four widely used basal programs.[24] Through this process, he ended up with 121 generalizations, including fifty for vowels, fifteen for consonants, twenty-eight for word endings, and twenty-eight for syllabification. Surveying the list, Clymer notes that there was substantial disagreement between programs with respect to both which of these should be taught and when:

Of the 50 different vowel generalizations, only 11 were common to all four series. None of these 11 was presented initially at the same half-year grade level in all four series. Some series gave a much greater emphasis to the generalizations than did other series. One publisher introduced only 33 of the 121 generalizations, while another presented 68.[25]

---

23. Clymer (1963, p. 252).
24. The specific programs were not cited by Clymer.
25. Clymer (1963, p. 253).

Of the 121 generalizations thus found, Clymer selected forty-five that were stated with sufficient clarity to permit assessment of its applicability to whole words (though he adds that "the selection of these [forty-five generalizations] was somewhat arbitrary"). As a database against which to assess the generalizations, he put together a list of 2,600 words. These included each distinct word in each of the four basal series from which the generalizations were drawn, plus all of the words from the Gates Reading Vocabulary for the Primary Grades.

For each of the forty-five generalizations, Clymer and his colleagues counted all of the words to which it pertained and, of those, all of the ones with which it properly conformed according to Webster's *New Collegiate Dictionary* (edition uncited). To quantify the reliability of each generalization, he divided the number of words with which it conformed by the total number of words to which it could be applied. His resulting table of phonic generalizations is reproduced in table 11.3. I have changed it only by regrouping the generalizations by functional category and, within category, ranking them in order of the total number of words (conforming plus exceptions) to which each was found to pertain.

The point that Clymer drew from this table is that the generality of most of these generalizations is disturbingly low. Those that work reliably (have the highest percentage of utility) often pertain to relatively infrequent spelling patterns. Those that pertain to the most frequent spelling patterns are often relatively unreliable. In Clymer's words: "In evaluating this initial venture in testing the utility of phonic generalizations, it seems quite clear that many generalizations which are commonly taught are of limited value."[26]

I am sure that I was taught some "silent-*e* rule" quite similar to generalization 6 in Clymer's table. And, although I am fully aware of a number of exceptions, my feeling was that it really does work better than indicated by Clymer's statistics. Perhaps because others were similarly surprised by these results, the study has been repeated in kind, over and over again. Each time the statistical results have also been replicated in kind.[27]

Yet the data in Clymer's table extend well beyond the numbers and so do the pedagogical points the data should raise. Specifically, the utility (or lack thereof) of a phonic

---

26. Clymer (1963, p. 255).

27. Bailey (1967); Burmeister (1968); Emans (1967); Sorenson (1983, cited in Searfoss and Readence, 1985).

Table 11.3
Clymer's summary table of the utility of forty-five phonic generalizations.

Generalization	Number of words conforming	Number of exceptions	Percentage utility

Pronunciation of vowels

Generalization	Number of words conforming	Number of exceptions	Percentage utility
1. One vowel letter in an accented syllable has its short sound.	547 *city*	356 *lady*	61
2. When a word has only one vowel letter, the vowel sound is likely to be short.	433 *hid*	322 *kind*	57
3. When there are two vowels side by side, the long sound of the first one is heard and the second is usually silent.	309 *bead*	377 *chief*	45
4. When a vowel is in the middle of a one-syllable word, the vowel is short.	408	249	62
a. Middle letter.	191 *dress*	84 *scold*	6
b. One of the middle two letters in a word of four.	191 *rest*	135 *told*	59
c. One vowel within a word of more than four letters.	26 *splash*	30 *light*	46
5. The *r* gives the preceding vowel a sound that is neither long nor short.	184 *horn*	134 *wire*	78
6. When there are two vowels, one of which is final *e*, the first vowel is long and the *e* is silent.	180 *bone*	108 *done*	63

Generalization	Number of words conforming	Number of exceptions	Percentage utility
7. The first vowel is usually long and the second silent in the digraphs *ai, ea, oa,* and *ui.*	179	92	66
a. *ai*	43 *nail*	24 *said*	64
b. *ea*	101 *bead*	51 *head*	66
c. *oa*	34 *boat*	1 *cupboard*	97
d. *ui*	1 *suit*	16 *build*	6
8. When words end with silent *e,* the preceding *a* or *i* is long.	164 *cake*	108 *have*	60
9. When *y* is the final letter in a word, it usually has a vowel sound.	169 *dry*	32 *tray*	84
10. When *y* is used as a vowel in words, it sometimes has the sound of long *i.*	29 *fly*	170 *funny*	15
11. When *y* or *ey* is seen in the last syllable that is not accented, the long sound of *e* is heard.	0	157 *baby*	0
12. The letter *a* has the same sound (*o*) when followed by *l, w,* and *u.*	61 *all*	65 *canal*	48
13. *W* is sometimes a vowel and follows the vowel digraph rule.	50 *crow*	75 *threw*	40
14. When there is one *e* in a word that ends in a consonant, the *e* usually has a short sound.	85 *leg*	27 *blew*	76

Generalization	Number of words conforming	Number of exceptions	Percentage utility
15. In many two- and three-syllable words, the final *e* lengthens the vowel in the last syllable.	52 *invite*	62 *gasoline*	46
16. Words having double *e* usually have the long *e* sound.	85 *seem*	2 *been*	98
17. The two letters *ow* make the long *o* sound.	50 *own*	35 *down*	59
18. When *a* follows *w* in a word, it usually has the sound *a* as in *was*.	15 *watch*	32 *swam*	32
19. In the phonogram *ie*, the *i* is silent and the *e* has a long sound.	8 *field*	39 *friend*	17
20. In *ay* the *y* is silent and gives *a* its long sound.	36 *play*	10 *always*	78
21. If the only vowel letter is at the end of a word, the letter usually stands for a long sound.	23 *he*	8 *to*	74
22. When *e* is followed by *w*, the vowel sound is the same as represented by *oo*.	9 *blew*	17 *sew*	35
23. When *a* is followed by *r* and final *e*, we expect to hear the sound heard in *care*.	9 *dare*	1 *are*	90

Generalization	Number of words conforming	Number of exceptions	Percentage utility

Vowel/consonant combination

Generalization	Number of words conforming	Number of exceptions	Percentage utility
24. When the letter *i* is followed by *gh*, the letters the *i* usually stands for its long sound and the *gh* is silent.	22 *high*	9 *neighbor*	71

Pronunciation of consonants

Generalization	Number of words conforming	Number of exceptions	Percentage utility
25. When two of the same consonants are side by side only one is heard.	334 *carry*	3 *suggest*	99
26. When the letter *c* is followed by *o* or *a*, the sound of *k* is likely to be heard.	143 *camp*	0	100
27. *Ch* is usually pronounced as it is in *kitchen*, *catch*, and *chair*, not like *sh*.	99 *catch*	5 *machine*	95
28. When *c* and *h* are next to each other, they make only one sound.	103 *peach*	0	100
29. The letter *g* often has a sound similar to that of *j* in *jump* when it precedes the letter *i* or *e*.	49 *engine*	28 *give*	64
30. When *c* is followed by *e* or *i*, the sound of *s* is likely to be heard.	66 *cent*	3 *ocean*	96
31. When a word ends in *ck*, it has the same last sound as in *look*.	46 *brick*	0	100

Generalization	Number of words conforming	Number of exceptions	Percentage utility
32. When *ght* is seen in a word, *gh* is silent.	30 *fight*	0	100
33. When a word begins *kn*, the *k* is silent.	10 *knife*	0	100
34. When a word begins with *wr*, the *w* is silent.	8 *write*	0	100

Division of syllables

35. If the first vowel sound in a word is followed by two consonants, the first syllable usually ends with the first of the two consonants.	404 *bullet*	159 *singer*	72
36. If the first vowel sound in a word is followed by a single consonant, that consonant usually begins the second syllable.	190 *over*	237 *oven*	44
37. In a word of more than one syllable, the letter *v* usually goes with the preceding vowel to form a syllable.	53 *cover*	20 *clover*	73
38. If the last syllable of a word ends in *le*, the consonant preceding the *le* usually begins the last syllable.	62 *tumble*	2 *buckle*	97
39. When the first vowel element in a word is followed by *th*, *ch*, or *sh*, these symbols are not broken when the word is divided into syllables may go with either the first and or second syllable.	30 *dishes*	0	100

Generalization	**Number of words conforming**	**Number of exceptions**	**Percentage utility**

Accentuation of syllables

Generalization	**Number of words conforming**		**Number of exceptions**		**Percentage utility**
40. In most two-syllable words, the first syllable is accented.	828	*famous*	143	*polite*	85
41. When the last syllable is the sound *r*, it is unaccented.	188	*butter*	9	*appear*	95
42. In most two-syllable words that end in a consonant followed by *y*, the first syllable is accented and the last is unaccented.	101	*baby*	4	*supply*	96
43. If *a*, *in*, *re*, *ex*, *de*, or *be* is the first syllable in a word, it is usually un-accented.	86	*belong*	13	*insect*	87
44. When *tion* is the final syllable in a word, it is unaccented.	5	*station*	0		100
45. When *ture* is the final syllable in a word, it is unaccented.	4	*picture*	0		100

generalization depends on much more than the frequency or reliability of its applicability.

Evaluating Phonic Generalizations

Psychologically, whatever we may call them and however unreliable they may be, phonic generalizations are essentially rules. As such, they cannot substitute for direct familiarity with the patterns to which they apply. Nevertheless, there remain at least two wholly reasonable motivations for presenting them.

The first is to direct students' attention to a particular orthographic structure and its behavior. Generalizations presented under this motivation need not be memorized; their purpose instead is to sharpen the students' memory for the patterns to which they apply.

The other motivation is to provide the students with some cognitive recourse for dealing with recognition difficulties—with some consciously mediated guidance for constructing and trying out alternative responses. Although memorization of useful generalizations in this category is worthwhile, there are stronger constraints on what makes generalizations in this category useful.

First, remember that such generalizations operate only through conscious recourse. This means that it is critical that they be expressed and elaborated or otherwise taught in a way that they can be productively understood and applied. Second, it is only when the recognition network has failed to yield an acceptable response that conscious resort to such generalizations will be attempted. By implication the kind of guidance that such generalizations can usefully provide is that which is somehow incompatible with or foreign to the current knowledge or structure of the reader's recognition system.

Having set this second group of generalizations off as different in kind from the first, I must now point out that, for any given generalization, the distinction is temporary. Thus when a child is perceptually insensitive to the difference between *b* and *d*, some consciously mediated heuristic, such as to imagine the shape of a **bed**, may be quite helpful. With experience, however, the distinction between these letters will find representation in the letter recognition network—perforce explicit knowledge of the **bed** heuristic will then be superfluous. And the same holds for any other relation that might once have required conscious thought—be it the "final-*e* rule," that *data* takes a plural verb, or when to use *which* and when to use *that*. Gradually, as these relations become more and more broadly instantiated in our memories, we find we deliberate on their application less and less. From that point on, errors in their application need only be pointed out. No one need explain to us the rule, and we need not memorize their explanation if they do.

With these motivations and conditions in mind, let us examine Clymer's generalizations a bit more closely, category by category. We will do so in order of their overall percentage utility. Moreover, since almost any relation may be worth articulating or bringing to a child's attention at some point, our concern will be with which of them meet the criteria for conscious memorization.

Pronunciation of Consonants

In general, the consonant generalizations (numbers 25-34) seem exceptionally reliable. On the other hand, for any child who has so far learned only a unique sound for their individual letters, they do represent exceptions to an established response. Early in a child's acquisition of phonics, therefore, it might well be helpful to let her or him learn some appropriate rendition of such generalizations (e.g., "Remember? When *c* and *h* are together like that, they make a special sound. Do you remember what that is?").

On the other hand, most of these generalizations are not only highly reliable but pertain to specific pairs of adjacent letters.[28] Because of these qualities, the letter recognition network should be able to acquire them especially early and easily. It follows that rather than asking for their explicit memorization, it may be at least as effective to just exercise them, expressing each generalization only as necessary to explain or remind the children of its nature.

Accentuation of Syllables

In terms of their percentage of utility, the six generalizations within this category appear nearly as successful as those on consonants. They nevertheless seem somewhat less useful.

To the extent that a child has special difficulty with any of the last four (42–45), it may be worth expressing them. On the other hand, as each of these generalizations pertains to a specific

---

28. The exceptions here are the generalizations pertaining to the "soft" sounds of *c* and *g*. Because the conditions of application for these rules are a little more complicated, they may be more broadly appropriate for explicit memorization.

spelling pattern, they, too, might better be instilled through guided practice than through memorization of their descriptions.

It might be noted, moreover, that generalizations 43–45 are tacitly about the accentuation of affixes. If one wished to have the students memorize a generalization that captured these relationships, it might be more productive and efficient to present these syllables as affixes, exploring their functions as well as their accentuation. To a large extent, generalizations 41 and 42 would also be covered through such treatment of affixes. To the extent that they were not, however, they are less extensive than, but wholly redundant with, the first generalization in this group, 40.

Generalization 40 states: "In most two-syllable words, the first syllable is accented." Both the number of words to which it pertains and its percentage of utility are relatively high. So is it useful? Not very. Research indicates that it is the exceptions to this generalization that cause the most trouble—that the accentuation of two-syllable words is most problematic when the accent falls on the second syllable, as in *canal* and *propel*.[29]

Thus, whether or not generalization 40 is worth explicit presentation, its memorization is not expected to improve word recognition performance. More useful would be generalizations that highlighted the conditions under which accentuation belongs on the second syllable. For example, one might point out that if there is only one consonant at the syllable boundary, it is worth trying the accent on the second syllable. To complement this point, it might be useful to point out that most of its exceptions are verbs.[30]

Division of Syllables

The capacity to break long words into syllables is critical for decoding them. Viewed as procedural guidance, generalization 35 ("If the first vowel sound in a word is followed by two consonants, the first syllable usually ends with the first of the two consonants") seems useful in spirit, if not optimally expressed for generality, usability, or understandability by children. For purposes of decomposing a word into syllables, students should minimally appreciate that when separated by one or more

---

29. P. Smith (1980).

30. Accentuation of the first syllable is found to hold for 89 to 94 percent of two-syllable nouns, but only 31 to 46 percent of two-syllable verbs (Kelly, 1988).

consonants, two vowels must belong to different syllables. Attempting to divide such syllables between consonants seems a reasonably useful strategy.

Similarly, generalization 36 ("If the first vowel sound in a word is followed by a single consonant, that consonant usually begins the second syllable") seems somewhat useful in spirit—at least in view of the fact that those vowels that it stipulates as syllable-final have a special tendency to take on their "long" sounds.[31]

In contrast, generalizations 37–39 are too specific. They beg presentation of scores more generalizations at their level, and, more than that, syllable boundaries cannot be reliably defined at the level of individual letters. Observe that even in the dictionary, the hyphenation in the entry words often conflicts with the hyphenation in their pronunciation keys. Further, the issues defining exactly where the boundaries between spoken syllables do fall are recognized by speech scientists as both complicated and unresolved.

Finally, we may question the very value of trying to teach the precise, dictionary-defined locations of the syllable boundaries in printed words. If you are responsible for setting type, this is information you (or your machine) should have. If you are not a typesetter, however, the effort required to memorize dictionary-defined syllable boundaries outweighs the benefits.

For purposes of sounding out a polysyllabic word, it matters little, for example, whether you attempt *simple* as *simp-le* or *sim-ple*. What is important is that every parsed unit be pronounceable and that unitized spelling patterns be left intact regardless of their letter-by-letter composition (consider *fathead*, *mishap*, and *preeminent*). Respect of these constraints depends not on memorization of rules but on possessing and applying appropriate sensitivity to the orthographic and morphemic constraints of our script and the semantic constraints of the text.

---

31. This generalization similarly falls into the category of "perhaps useful in spirit but unreliable." Among two-syllable words with two or more consonants at their syllable boundary, the first vowel is almost always short (*hundred, pocket, nickel*); however, among two-syllable words with just one consonant at their syllable boundaries, the first vowel is often long (*famous, open, tiger*) but not always (*canal, pedal, magic*). In words of three or more syllables, *u* and *o* are usually long only when they are syllable-final (i.e., when they precede a separately voiced vowel or a single consonant), but *i* (in American English) tends to be short in any case, and *a* and *e* have customs of their own.

Note that the percentage utility that Clymer gives this generalization must be traced to his use of the dictionary as a syllabification reference.

Pronunciation of Vowels

Slightly more than half the generalizations in Clymer's table belong in this category, and in general their performance is dismal: Only four of the twenty-three were found to work in as many as four out of five cases. But there is something else even more discouraging about the list of vowel generalizations: Across the twenty-three, all but two represent various ways and levels of describing only six basic classes of spelling-sound patterns.

The first of these classes (1, 2, 4, and 14) is about the idea that single unmarked vowels that are surrounded by consonants usually take a "short" sound. The second (3, 7, 16, 17, 20) is about the idea that "when two vowels go walking, the first does the talking." The third (6, 8, 15, 23) is about the "silent-*e* rule." The fourth (9, 10, 11, 20) is about the behavior of *y* when it is acting like a vowel. The fifth (13, 17, 22) is about the behavior of *w* when it is acting like a vowel. And the sixth (5, 12, 18) is about *r*-, *l*-, and *w*-controlled vowels.

At a global level, it is worth reflecting on the prominent attention generally given to *r*-, *l*-, and *w*-controlled vowels in phonic programs. The reason that we pronounce, for example, the *a* in *war* a little differently is not because its spelling starts with a *w* and ends with an *r*. It is because we have lazy mouth. While we are producing the *w*, our mouths are getting ready for the *r*. Meanwhile, the *a*, because it is temporally sandwiched between these two sounds, gets modified by both; the shape of our mouth while saying the *a* is a compromise between the three distinct shapes needed for the *w*, the *a*, and the *r*. Try pronouncing *war* with the same *a* as is heard in *wham*: It can be done, but the result is nasal, and it is much more work to produce. Over rapidly repeated attempts, you may find either that the sound of the *a* tends toward its *w*- and *r*-controlled value or that your enunciation of the *r* begins to deteriorate, or both.

Lazy mouth (or, more kindly, anticipatory mouth) can generally explain the distributions of *schwa* and of voiced and unvoiced *th* and *s* as well.[32] In some cases (e.g., *war*), this

---

32. In fact, the distinction between voiced and unvoiced *s* or *th* is sometimes phonemically significant. (Compare, e.g., *either*/*ether* and *his*/*hiss*.) On the other hand, substitution of an unvoiced *s* or *th* in context rarely disguises the identity of the intended word. Note too that with little loss in intelligibility, such voiced-unvoiced distinctions are regularly abused by many speakers of English as a second language. The problem for these foreign-born speakers is that they do not anticipate the speech stream in the same way as a native would. In the same way, Americans have trouble, for example, rolling the *r*s in such Spanish words as *marron*:

phenomenon significantly distorts the spelling-sound translation. To this extent, it surely warrants explicit attention. However, I am skeptical about the amount of time and energy it is accorded by so many programs. Would a confusion between a voiced and unvoiced *s* block your ability to recognize the word *is*? Doesn't the *s* in the word *is* wander between these alternatives in connected speech anyhow? Would a confusion between voiced and unvoiced *th* block your ability to recognize the words *the*, *these*, and *this*? Can you pronounce the *u*, *i*, and *e* in *nurse*, *birch*, and *terse* in a way that is *not* *r*-controlled? And it has been demonstrated that even where the unstressed vowels of polysyllabic words are normally sounded as *schwa*, children who are taught to pronounce them instead as they are printed learn more about the words' spellings.[33]

The criterion for how much priority to assign any given spelling-sound pattern should depend not on whether the pattern has been identified by speech scientists or lexicographers, but on how much reading leverage the teaching of that pattern brings to the children. And, remember, the goal of these lessons is not to teach the phonology of English, but to use the phonology of English to help the children learn spelling patterns as they relate to words.[34]

The major problem with the remainder of the vowel generalizations is that despite the multiple renditions of each, they basically do not work. The exceptions are had only for those entries that seem uselessly general (9) or discouragingly specific (7c, 16, 23). Is it a hopeless notion that the phonemic translations of vowels can be adequately specified through some reasonably small but broadly applicable set of generalizations? Maybe. But then memorization of such generalizations will not result in proficient word recognition, anyhow. Proficient word recognition depends on the perceptual learning of spelling patterns and the direct linkage of these patterns in memory to the speech patterns and meanings to which they pertain.

They have not become fluent enough to prepare their mouths for the *rs* while producing the *m*.

33. Drake and Ehri (1984).

34. Related to this, Chomsky and Halle (1968) have argued that the "optimal orthography" will not explicitly represent that which the phonology takes care of on its own.

Summary: Phonic Generalizations

Backing away from the specific generalizations in Clymer's study, we may reflect on several more general points.

One of these is that care should be taken not to misuse the dictionary. Dictionary pronunciation keys are based no more on rigid, universal, or scientifically established truths about the pronunciation of words than on the thoughtful analysis of the dictionary's lexicographers. The pronunciation keys do not specify the way words ought to be said but the way that their lexicographers believe they typically are said.[35] Dictionary syllabification is even more arbitrary, reflecting customs owed mostly to one man, Noah Webster, and may have been built more often on considerations of orthography than of speech.

A second point that warrants reflection is that no phonic generalization can be useful unless it is understandable by the person who is supposed to use it. Although this seems obvious, the majority of generalizations excerpted by Clymer are remarkably presumptuous of their students' vocabulary, syntactic competence, and even their basic conceptual level. As an example of the latter, consider generalization 14: "When there is one *e* in a word that ends in a consonant, the *e* usually has a short sound." The exception cited is *blew*. Now, you or I might object that the *w* in *blew* is actually a vowel. But can we expect a child to think of that?

A third point is that the helpfulness of a generalization cannot be indexed by the reliability or percentage of utility with which it applies. The sorts of generalizations discussed in this section may equally be described as conditional exceptions. The helpfulness of presenting any one of them depends on whether the conditions of its application are worthy of appreciation. It also depends on whether the generalization is presented—neither too soon nor too late—but within that interval in the reader's development during which she or he is just ready to appreciate it.

---

35. As a case in point, consider generalization 11 which states, "When *y* or *ey* is seen in the last syllable that is not accented, the long sound of *e* is heard." The purpose of this generalization is presumably to give children a means of distinguishing words like *penny* and *monkey* from ones like *rely* and *supply*. This rule is somewhat circular in the sense that the final syllable of these words automatically gains stress when the *y* is given the sound of the long *i*. Regardless of whether you find the particular statement of the generalization helpful, it does seem to capture the distinction at issue. Yet, Clymer gave it 0 percent utility — which is to say that he found zero words to which it applied. The reason is that in the older editions of *Webster's New Collegiate Dictionary* which Clymer must have used, the *y* in such words as *baby* was transcoded as a short *i*.

The most important point underlying this discussion is that one cannot become a skillful decoder by virtue of either hearing or memorizing generalizations. For the learner, such generalizations can be usefully interpreted only with reference to the words to which they apply. For the fluent reader, they are operative only as they are implicitly captured directly within the representations of the words and spelling patterns to which they apply. For neither the expert nor the novice can rote knowledge of an abstract rule, in and of itself, make any difference.

Reading Connected Text

The goal of teaching phonics is to develop students' ability to read connected text independently. For students, however, the strongest functional connection between these two skills may run in the reverse direction. It is only the nature of reading that can make the content of phonic lessons seem sensible; it is only the prospect of reading that can make them seem worthwhile. And, certainly, we hope that such instruction will seem both sensible and worthwhile to students.

Because of this, we are faced with yet another dilemma, perhaps the most serious of all for cogent phonic instruction. Should our policy be to withhold connected text from students until after they have mastered all relevant grapheme-phoneme correspondences? Or should we expose them to and challenge them with meaningful, interesting text from the start, regardless of the extent to which the demands of its wording go beyond their word attack skills to date? In their extremes, both proposals are preposterous. But the concerns are the same, if easier to overlook, for any position in between.

Let us begin with the option of withholding connected text until phonic instruction has been completed. Assuming the teaching of two or three correspondences per week and even assuming perfect learning, it would take many years to cover all possible spelling-sound translations. Without the rewards of reading, what child would sit still for such instruction? Without the imminent challenge of reading, what could make it worthwhile? How would the child practice and extend that which had already been taught?

One seemingly reasonable compromise would be to wait until some critical mass of grapheme-phoneme correspondences and phonic generalizations has been taught. But again this strategy leaves us in a quandary about the right moment. Obviously, we do not want to wait until the students have been taught about the *oo* in *oogenesis* and *oology* or the *oe* in *synaloepha* and *onomatopoeia*. Rather the optimal moment would seem to be as soon as the variety of explicitly taught correspondences and generalizations is sufficient to permit the generation of meaningful text from them.

How soon might that be? In table 11.4, I have listed the 150 most frequent words in schoolbook English according to Carroll, Davies, and Richman's count.[36] Of these, 35 (those that are italicized) can be sounded out as some sequence of the basic single-consonant and single-short-vowel correspondences that are most often taught first. I tried to be liberal in selecting these words. Provided that their letter-sound correspondences were otherwise more or less as defined, I have included as "soundable" those words that end in doubled consonants (e.g., *will, off*); those that involve consonant blends (e.g., *and, must*); those with *r*-controlled vowels (e.g., *her, first, word*); and even those that end with voiced instead of unvoiced *s* (e.g., *is, his*). If I had discounted all such iffy words (including *get*, which follows the rules but should not), the number of soundable words on the list would be reduced from 35 to only 14 out of 150.

The unitalicized words in table 11.4 represent a variety of different spelling-sound complexities:

- Some contain consonant digraphs (e.g., *them, which, back, long*).
- Some have two or more syllables (e.g., *after, different, number*).
- Some look as if they should have two or more syllables but do not (e.g., *called, used*).
- Some involve vowel sounds that are not "short" (e.g., *to, be, all, was*).
- Some involve vowel digraphs (e.g., *see, years, out, too*).
- Some involve *y* or *w* as vowels instead of consonants (e.g., *by, day, many, down, new*).
- Some involve complex but "regular" spelling patterns that signal alterations in the phonemic significance of the vowels or consonants (e.g., *time, made, could, would, right, little*).
- Some belong to families of relatively frequent but "rule-breaking" spelling patterns (e.g., *look, find, most, old, through*).
- Some are just plain irregular (e.g., *one, two, said, does*).

In view of this, I ask you to reflect on three questions: (1) Examining the distributions of complications, which

---

36. Carroll, Davies, and Richman (1971).

Table 11.4

The 150 most frequent words in printed school English according to the American Heritage *Word Frequency Book.* "Soundable" words are italicized.

the	*but*	into	long	also
of	what	*has*	little	around
and	all	more	very	another
a	were	*her*	after	came
to	when	two	words	come
in	we	like	called	*work*
is	there	*him*	*just*	three
you	*can*	see	where	*word*
that	*an*	time	most	*must*
it	your	could	know	because
he	which	no	*get*	does
for	their	make	through	part
was	said	than	back	even
on	*if*	*first*	much	place
are	do	been	before	*well*
as	*will*	*its*	go	such
with	each	who	good	here
his	about	now	new	take
they	how	people	write	why
at	*up*	my	our	things
be	out	made	used	*help*
this	them	over	me	put
from	then	*did*	*man*	years
I	she	down	too	different
have	many	only	any	away
or	some	way	day	again
by	so	find	same	*off*
one	these	use	right	*went*
had	would	may	look	old
not	other	water	think	number

correspondence or phonic generalization would you teach next? (2) How long would it take to establish all of them? (3) How many interesting, meaningful stories could you write without any of the complicated words on this list? And, bear in mind, that even the "soundable" words on this list would need await the end of the first semester at least.

For children who enter school with solid literacy preparation and with the desire to read, the drawbacks of postponing reading too long in favor of drill are clear. For children who enter school without such preparation, the drawbacks are potentially even greater.

These children may be lacking in basic print awareness. They may not know that reading has its rewards of entertainment and information. They may not know that all writing is comprised of letters. They may not be aware of the format of books. They may not know that print reads left to right or that those clusters of print separated by spaces are words. In all probability, these children have little in the way of phonemic awareness on entering school. To gain such awareness through phonic instruction, they must appreciate that the sounds being taught are the sounds of meaningful, spoken words. Yet, they may not have had the insight that words are independently speakable and meaningful units. As we exercise these children on *fin*, *tin*, and *bin* in isolation, they may not notice that these syllables are meaningful words at all. They may not, in short, know why phonic lessons are useful or important to them. We want to expose these children to meaningful written text as soon as possible so that they will begin to notice and have an interest in all of the things around them that there are to read. We want these children to sense the utility of their phonic lessons as soon as possible.

Thus, many and perhaps most reading programs engage their students in connected reading from the start. All but universally, the solution for those high-frequency (or otherwise contextually necessary) words that extend beyond expected phonics-to-date, is to use them in the children's texts anyway. In view of the trade-offs, this compromise is wholly understandable. Whether it is reasonable depends on the constraint with which it is exercised.

Working with eleven classrooms in three schools, Connie Juel and Diane Roper/Schneider examined the impact of such connected text on children's word recognition skills.[37] In the school

---

37. Juel and Roper/Schneider (1985).

district in which their study was situated, phonic instruction was tightly standardized across classrooms. All teachers were required to spend the first twenty to thirty minutes of each one-hour reading period instructing the whole class on synthetic phonics. Further, the phonic lessons were scripted such that the material taught, as well as the form and sequence of delivery, were controlled across classrooms. Observation in the classrooms confirmed that the teachers used the district's procedures and materials and that they rarely supplemented them with outside materials.

The balance of the reading period was spent with one of two sets of basal materials in reading group activities. One of these basal series emphasized phonics, and the core vocabulary of its three initial or "preprimer" texts stressed words with regular, decodable spelling patterns. The other series was not phonic oriented, and the word selection in its preprimers stressed frequent words instead. (There is, of course, solid rationale for stressing frequent instead of graphophonemically regular words in beginning texts. It is the very frequent words that are most likely to be in the child's speaking vocabularies, that are most likely to be encountered in uncontrolled print experiences, that the children will most often want to write when they write, and so on.)

The core content words in the phonic-oriented preprimers tended to be somewhat less frequent, shorter in letter length and number of syllables, more regular in letter-sound correspondence, and repeated more often than those in the other series. At the same time, the balance of orthographically regular versus irregular words in the preprimers of the two series was nearly equal. Thus the major difference between the two sets of preprimers was not in the number of potentially decodable words introduced. It was in the extent to which those decodable words were clustered, repeated, and otherwise presented in a way that emphasized and exercised their decodability.

In terms of word characteristics, the later books of the two series—the primers and readers—were much more comparable. (As a potentially significant exception, the series differed in total number of different words each presented over the course of the year. While the phonic-oriented series contained 1,560 different words, the other contained only 1,286 or 17 percent fewer.)

Juel and Roper/Schneider obtained performance measures from the children five times during the year:

- In the beginning of September the children were given some graded word lists and informal reading inventories along with the Metropolitan Reading Readiness Test. Only children who scored above the fortieth percentile on the Metropolitan and placed in the middle reading group were included in the study. (The final sample included ninety-three children: Sixty-one were Anglo Americans; most of the others were Mexican-Americans.) The children assigned to one of the basal series versus the other were quite comparable in their entering levels of reading readiness.

- In late November and early December when the children had completed the preprimers, they were tested on the words identified by the respective basal publishers as core vocabulary. To assess the children's decoding skills, they were also tested on a graded list of fifty rule-governed pseudowords.[38]

- In February when the children had completed their respective primers, they were tested on the publisher-designated core vocabulary of the primers and given the list of pseudowords again.

- In April the children received the list of pseudowords once more, this time in temporal conjunction with the Iowa Test of Basic Skills, which was administered by the school district.

- In May after completing their first readers, the children were tested on all of the publisher-designated core vocabulary from their own readers, primers, and preprimers and on the words that were unique to the three core lists of the other series.

In addition, on completion of each book (except the first preprimer), the children were asked to read passages from the book and were scored on their pronunciation of each word. This was intended to assess differences in the children's ability to use contextual cues in word recognition.

When the children were tested on the core vocabulary items from their own books, performance was generally indifferent to which of the series they had used. Furthermore, assessments of the children's abilities to read passages from their books indicated that the two series produced no differences in the tendency to exploit contextual clues in recognizing words. On the other hand, the growth of the children's decoding skills was significantly influenced by their basals at each testing opportunity.

In November, after completion of only the preprimers, the children in the phonic-oriented basal program were already significantly better able than their peers to read the list of pseudowords. Furthermore, for the children who had used the phonic-oriented basals, pseudoword performance was a strong predictor of core vocabulary recognition; for the children in the other program, it was not.

---

38. N. Bryant (1975).

This finding was extended through analyses of the influence of word and text characteristics on the children's core vocabulary recognition. For children who had used the phonic-oriented basal, core vocabulary recognition was most strongly influenced by the simplicity and predictability of the words' spelling-sound mappings. For the children in the other program, it was most strongly influenced by the number of letters and syllables in the words.[39]

Closer analyses of the data collected in November turned up other revealing patterns of performance. For both groups of children, recognition of core vocabulary words was sensitive to the number of different words in which the sequences of letters within them had appeared. However, for children who had used the phonic-oriented preprimers, performance was better if these sequences had appeared in many different words; for children in the other program, performance was better if the sequences had appeared in only one or a few different words. Additionally considering the latter groups' strong sensitivity to word length, the suggestion is that they were identifying their core words more on the basis of visual distinctiveness than on the basis of spelling-sound cues.

Still more provocative was the pattern of errors on the pseudoword list. At the time of first testing, the children in both groups had covered the sounds of the initial and final consonants and the "short" vowels in their phonic lessons. Demonstrating that they had learned their phonic lessons equally well, performance on these correspondences did not significantly differ between groups. On the other hand, the children who had used the phonic-oriented preprimers were far more successful in decoding pseudowords whose spelling-sound correspondences had not been explicitly taught. The suggestion is that early in the year, the children in the phonic-oriented basal program had developed a more general appreciation of—and a more general reliance on—spelling-sound relations than had their peers in the other program. As we hope all children will, they were already spontaneously extending their repertoire of spelling-sound relations beyond those that had been explicitly taught.

In February the children who had just completed the phonic-oriented primers maintained their superiority on the pseudoword list. But at this point, the ease and simplicity of the core words'

---

39. The number of times that the test words had been repeated in the children's books was also significantly influential for both groups at every testing opportunity.

spelling-sound correspondences proved by far to be the strongest influence of word recognition for both groups. Others, too, have observed such deferential attention to graphophonemic cues in the middle of first grade.[40]

At the end of the year, when the children were asked to read the nonoverlapping core words from the program they had not used, those who had used the phonic-oriented books were significantly more successful. Ease and simplicity of spelling-sound correspondences was still the best determinant of core word recognition for the children in the phonic-oriented basal program. For the children in the other program, this variable had been overtaken by the number of times the words had been repeated in their books. And as in the November test, the presence of letter sequences that appear in many words proved a significant benefit to the children who had used the phonic-oriented program.[41] For the other children, it was again distinctive letter sequences— sequences more or less unique to particular words in their experience—that were most helpful; for these children, it seemed that visual cue strategies were regaining precedence over spelling-sound strategies.

In the end, despite their common and standardized phonic instruction, the children's decoding proficiency (as measured by performance on the pseudoword list) was significantly influenced by two variables: their entering scores on the Metropolitan Reading Readiness Test and the basal series that they had used. And, most important, regardless of these variables, the children who read best at the end of the year were those who were most proficient at decoding (as measured by performance on the pseudoword list). Performance on the last pseudoword test of the year correlated 0.77 with recognition of the core words from the children's own basal, 0.72 with recognition of the core words from the other basal, and 0.55 with their scores on the Iowa Test of Basic Skills.

In summarizing their study, Juel and Roper/Schneider conclude that

the selection of text used very early in first grade may, at least in part, determine the strategies and cues children learn to use, and persist in using, in subsequent word identification. . . . In particular, emphasis on a

---

40. Biemiller (1970); Weber (1970).

41. However, the influence of bigram "versatility," as it is termed by Juel and Roper/Schneider, was less apparent for words that had been repeated many times. The suggestion is that these very frequent words had come to be recognized as wholes.

phonics method seems to make little sense if children are given initial texts to read where the words do not follow regular letter-sound correspondence generalizations. Results of the current study suggest that the types of words which appear in beginning reading texts may well exert a more powerful influence in shaping children's word identification strategies than the method of reading instruction.[42]

When reading a report such as Juel and Roper/Schneider's, one inevitably pauses to wonder whether it is representative. After all, in recent years, the basals have been applauded by some for increasing their attention to phonic instruction.[43] One might wonder whether Juel and Roper/Schneider chose an extreme case, an outlier, in order to make their results more forceful. Or perhaps if the teachers had been using the phonic lessons from the basal itself rather than that prescribed by their school district, the mismatch would not have been so marked.

In fact, Juel and Roper/Schneider's other basal series—the one that was not phonic oriented—was the market leader by a healthy margin. Moreover, such mismatch between phonic lessons and text samples is common among basals that are not phonic oriented, even when compared to their own phonic lessons. Table 11.5, compiled by Beck, shows the percentage of decodable words found in reading books accompanying each of eight different beginning reading programs through the first third of the first grade.[44]

The first four programs in table 11.5, which Beck terms "code programs," belong to the same class as Juel and Roper/Schneider's phonic-oriented series. The second four, which Beck terms "basal programs" and describes as meaning oriented, belong to the same class as Juel and Roper/Schneider's "other" program.[45] As is clear from the table, a mismatch between their own instruction on phonic principles and the opportunity to exercise those principles in connected reading was common among these meaning-oriented programs.[46] Notably just two of these meaning-oriented programs represent 40 percent of the beginning reading market; they are by far the programs used most often in our schools.

42. Juel and Roper/Schneider (1985, pp. 150-151).

43. For example, Chall (1979); Popp (1975).

44. Beck (1981).

45. And include Juel and Roper/Schneider's other program.

46. Similar discrepancy in meaning-emphasis programs has been documented by Meyer, Greer, and Crummey (1987) and Willows, Borwick, and Hayvren (1981).

Table 11.5
Percentage of decodable words in the first third of first grade in eight beginning reading programs.

Program[a]	Percentage of decodable words
Code programs	
Distar	100
Sullivan	93
Merrill	79
Palo Alto	69
Basal programs	
Houghton Mifflin	13
Ginn	3
Bank Street	0
Open Highways	0

a. References for these programs are given in table 11.1.

In concurrence with Juel and Roper/Schneider's conclusions, the National Academy of Education's Commission on Reading has strongly urged publishers to bring the structure and wording of their earliest reading books into coordination with their phonic instruction.[47] To do so may significantly increase the effectiveness of their series. Knowing that, and knowing that we care and are watching, these publishers must also know that such an investment is worthwhile.

Recall that Juel and Roper/Schneider's study included only students who were assigned to the middle reading group and who scored above 40 percent on the Metropolitan Reading Readiness Test that they took on entering the first grade. Properly, then, their results pertain only to children in the middle of the readiness distribution. These children apparently tend not to use or internalize the point of their phonic lessons unless the lessons are applicable in their day-to-day reading. What about the children at either end of the readiness distribution?

First let us consider the children who enter school with high literacy preparation. It makes little sense to withhold connected text from these children in wait of phonic lessons. For these children, virtually all of the information in the basic phonic lessons—beginning consonants and "short" vowels—will be familiar already. Indeed most of the phonic lessons taught through the first year of school may consist more of review and refinement than new information for these children, and the same may well be true of their second-grade phonic lessons by the time they get there.[48]

---

47. Commission on Reading, National Academy of Education (1985).

48. My grandfather, who was in education, helped me learn to read before I got to school. He must have known it was against the rules because he never offered information but only helped when I had questions. Still, it was clear to me that he was fiercely proud of my initiative and progress, and that is surely what kept me going. Much after that (he died when I was four), I remember sitting before a paper easel in first grade. Each page of the easel was devoted to one lowercase letter. On the first line, it was written with its uppercase twin. Then on the next few lines, it was written over and over, all by itself. Our job was to say, for example, "puh, puh, puh, puh, . . . " as the teacher pointed to each token of the letter. I remember feeling embarrassed and uncomfortable during this activity. I also remember wondering why the teacher thought we could read the various reading materials she gave us if she thought we did not know that *p* said "puh." As I sat still for this activity, I diverted myself by watching my classmates. I remember finding it quite interesting and mysterious that some of them just did not get it.

Many first-grade teachers give their students homework: Read the following story at home tonight, and we will read it together in our reading circle tomorrow. How are the children expected to manage such assignments? With help from their parents. Although many parents are initially surprised at the presumptions implicit in such homework assignments—and at what these presumptions imply about their school system—those from literacy-oriented homes nevertheless help their child as needed. As a consequence, these children get two lessons on each story: one at home and one at school.

If these children are so well on their way, need we be concerned with the extent to which their earliest texts support the learning of phonic correspondences and generalizations? In my opinion, yes. These children will have already learned to recognize a number of words, and they will also have some repertoire of sounding-out heuristics. However, few, if any of them, will have received any coherent presentation of the symbol-sound system of our orthography. More likely their parents helped them with words and correspondences as opportunities arose, and tradebooks—the fodder of preschool text exploration—are rarely worded with an eye toward exercising families of spelling-sound regularities.[49] These children are ready to learn, and the text in their schoolbooks, if structured properly, offers a superlative medium for helping them to do so.

Now let us consider the children at the other extreme: those who enter school with little literacy preparation. Many of these children will not yet be comfortable with the distinctive visual forms of the letters, especially the lowercase letters. For them, the basic letter-sound correspondences will be new in concept as well as content. Excepting salient environmental print in context, they are unlikely to be capable, or even marginally capable, of recognizing many words by sight.

In view of their relative lack of print, word, and phonemic awareness, it is a good idea to expose these children to connected text as soon as possible. But how can we do that in a reasonable way? We cannot expect to solve the problem by sending the stories home with the children for prereading or rereading with their parents. If their parents were inclined or able to invest much time in such activities, few of these children would have had such low readiness scores in the first place. (Remember the home literacy situations that Heath described.[50] Remember Feitelson and

---

49. There are exceptions, such as Dr. Seuss's *Hop on Pop*.
50. Heath (1983).

Goldstein's finding that 60 percent of the kindergartners in neighborhoods where children tend to do poorly in school did not own a single book.[51] Remember that most of the children observed by Teale had experienced almost no home storybook reading in their entire lives.[52])

Imagine that you are such a child and that, so far, you are an earnest student. You have learned more or less to recognize all of the letters. (To assist your imagination, I have substituted the letters of the alphabet with symbols that should, similarly, be more or less familiar to you.) You have also attended to and understood your phonic lessons although you are still dependent on the keyword charts for recalling, or at least confirming, which sound goes with each of the letters. (To assist your imagination, I have provided the key words for each of the symbols below; the sound that each is supposed to symbolize is enlarged in its keyword.)

~	**b**all	#	**m**oose	—	fo**x**
!	**c**at	±	**n**est	≠	**y**ard
%	**d**og	+	**p**ig	π	**z**oo
)	**f**lower	=	**q**uiet	}	b**a**t
^	**g**oo	?	**r**un	√	b**e**d
$	**h**at	¢	**s**un	≈	m**i**tt
@	**j**uice	∞	**t**ongue	¿	p**o**t
&	**k**ite	÷	**v**eil	§	tu**b**
*	**l**emon	«	**w**and		

Now, with all of this relevant knowledge and support to assist you, imagine that your teacher asks you to read five pages from your primer. Maybe she asks you to take it home, maybe she asks you to read it quietly at your seat; maybe she asks you to read it in circle with the other children in your group. Here is the title of the story and the first two paragraphs of the first page. Do your best.[53]

---

51. Feitelson and Goldstein (1986).

52. Teale (1986).

53. Note that this exercise also provides a reasonably compelling demonstration of the importance to comprehension of speed and automaticity of spelling-sound translations.

¢¿#√∞$≈±^ +?√∞∞∞≠
#¿∞$√? ¢}≈%, "*¿¿&, *¿¿&.
¢√√ ∞$≈¢."
"¿$, ¿$," ¢}≈% ¢}**≠.
"≈∞ ≈¢ +?√∞∞∞≠."54

To my imagination, this is not only a tedious exercise: It is also frustrating and relatively unrewarding. Even if the letter-sound correspondences in this story matched those in my keywords, the task would severely tax my imagined six-year-old capabilities. Even if I could figure out the identity of each word, I do not think I would have the patience and discipline to do it again and again such that I could understand the story.

Already this would seem to be an insuperable challenge for most six year olds. But to make matters worse, it turns out that only one, single word in this excerpt is wholly decodable on the basis of the phonic correspondences illustrated by the keywords.

What, in view of this whole situation, would I, as a six year old, do? I might pretend that everything was okay; I might cry; I might decide that I was stupid; I might decide that the kids who could do it were stupid; I might decide that reading was stupid; I might decide that school was stupid. I suspect that the more often my teacher put me in this situation, the more likely I would be to adopt one of these self-destructive, if self-protective, stances.

Summary: Phonics and Connected Reading

On scrutiny, the notion of phonics first turns into a pedagogical morass. Beyond the issues of what, when, and how to teach individual grapheme-phoneme correspondences and families of exceptions, it begs the larger question of how best to communicate with the children about phonic points and procedures. The referential difficulties associated with using letter names, letter sounds, and special terminology have already been discussed. But there are other difficulties within this domain as well. How, for example, can you explain to a child that letters should be sounded

---

54. This passage is from page 21 of the primer, *The New Fun with Dick and Jane* (Gray et al., 1956, cited in Chall 1967). In letters, it reads:

Something Pretty
Mother said, "Look, look.
See this."
"Oh, oh," said Sally.
"It is pretty."

out from left to right? How can you explain what is meant by segmenting or blending to a child with little phonemic awareness?

And still, the most serious problem confronting phonics-first methods remains that of how to introduce the reading of meaningful, connected text. All of us have found ourselves in the situation where we could do the arithmetic in our math books but not the word problems. Just as word problems do for arithmetic, connected reading provides the meaningful exercise necessary for linking the spelling patterns to the rest of the cognitive system, for ensuring that they are understood and learned in a way that is useful and usable toward the tasks for which they were taught. Like arithmetic without application, phonics without connected reading amounts to useless mechanics. And like the arithmetic that we never did understand well enough to do the word problems, it is easily forgotten altogether.

It is not for lack of thought, care, or effort that such disarray exists. There exist scores of beginning reading programs whose primary purpose is to instill in their students the nature of the spelling-sound correspondences of our writing system. Within each of these programs and many times over across them, we know that experts have invested enormous effort in finding the most coherent and teachable way to do so. Yet chaos prevails.

Looking with an academic eye, we find this situation dismaying. But how must it appear from the teachers' point of view? The teachers are responsible for teaching this mess: How do they manage it? Several naturalistic studies of classroom instruction suggest, not surprisingly, that they do so with difficulty. Knowing that reading itself is the goal, there is even some tendency to finesse the phonic lessons quite drastically. From a study of fifteen first-grade classrooms in six schools, Barr and Dreeben reported:

More phonic instruction [than connected reading] occurs as seatwork and supervised instruction is rare. . . . Teachers allocate more time to basal reading (43 minutes) and supervise a substantial portion of that time (33 minutes). By contrast, less time is spent on phonics each day (31 minutes) and considerably less of it is supervised (8 minutes).[55]

And, similarly, from a study of reading in special education classrooms:

The teachers in this study spent only 16 minutes per day in . . . direct instructional contacts, and of that time, 14 minutes were used to give general reading instructions, 1 minute per day was spent waiting while a

55. Barr and Dreeben (1983, p. 120; cited in Calfee and Drum, 1981).

student completed a reading task, and only 1 minute per day was used to explain or model correct elements in reading.[56]

The downplaying of phonic instruction reflects a compromise. For the teacher, the choice is surely not just one of limited classroom time but of limited classroom time against a choice of two activities that differ in manageability, apparent pertinence, and evident progress.[57]

When teaching word attack skills in the context of connected reading, their applicability is immediate. The challenge is pertinent to the story at hand. Its relevance to the greater goal of reading connected text is self-evident. Moreover, the course of instruction is given: Go to the next sentence, turn the page, or start a new story. And it is easy to keep track of progress: How far have we gotten in the basal?

In contrast, the pertinence of phonic instruction may be more difficult to convey to students, especially when it mismatches the word identification challenges in their basal reader. It may be more difficult to understand by the teachers, especially when it mismatches the word identification requirements of the basal. Its pace may seem excruciatingly slow, especially when it lags behind the word identification demands of the basal. And given the diffuse and complex nature of English spelling-sound translations, there is no obvious path through the phonic correspondences and generalizations; along that path, there are no obvious landmarks to let teacher or student know which way it will turn next or how much headway has been made toward its end.

To lead an activity effectively, most people need a comfortable understanding of what they are doing, why they are doing it, where the activity is going, how far its going, and how far they have gotten. A teacher may well find that the pages, stories, and books of the basal series provide a sense of purpose, direction, and achievement that is both clearer than and incompatible with that defined by the schedule and progression of phonic lessons.

Cursory treatment of phonic instruction may also be traced to simpler, logistical considerations. In the classroom, the amount of time to be spent on reading is limited; there are other lessons and activities that must be covered. Clearly, oral reading requires supervision. At the same time, many workbook activities are

---

56. Leinhardt, Zigmond, and Cooley (1981, p. 358, cited in Calfee and Drum, 1986).

57. For discussions of the social etiology of this situation, see Chall (1989); Shannon (1987); Williams (1987).

available on phonics. Thus, one possible escape from this squeeze, from the viewpoint of the teacher, is to relegate the bulk of phonic exercise to seatwork.

Even for very well prepared students—those who are ready to read with comprehension and who already know considerable phonics—this may not be the optimal solution. For the rest of the children, however, this routine may be a big mistake.

Investigators have repeatedly found that the degree of engagement or attention that students invest in their schoolwork is directly related to the learning that results.[58] Whereas seatwork is associated with lower levels of engagement and achievement, high levels of student engagement and classroom achievement are associated with teacher-led activities.[59] Furthermore, in the early grades, the amount of time for which students are engaged in instruction on phonics per se is found to be a strong predictor of their reading achievement.[60]

The dilemma here is tragic. We strive to teach the children phonics. With good reason, we argue that we do so to enable them to recognize the words of connected text independently and with sufficient ease that their attention and interest can be focused on its meaning. At the same time, we provide them with connected text. With good reason, we argue that we do so to enable them to understand the purpose and value of the phonics to enable them to learn and practice it in its appropriate context of application. In practice, however, it seems that we often lose sight of the goals beneath our plans such that those initial exercises in connected reading tend to compete with or even to displace the word recognition skills that we hoped they would develop.

Clearly we are all aware of the inanity of expecting the cart to pull the horse. Just as clearly, we are highly susceptible to such backwards expectations or we would not have so familiar an expression for describing them. Yet, another factor may be at work

---

58. For a review, see Rosenshine and Stevens (1984).

59. For a review, see Rosenshine and Stevens (1984).

60. Fisher et al. (1978, cited in Rosenshine and Stevens, 1984). This analysis was part of a larger effort to identify how classroom time is actually spent and how it might be most effectively spent. The statistics are from second-grade classrooms. The phonic instruction evaluated was subcategorized as (1) decoding blends and long vowels, (2) decoding variant consonants, and (3) decoding complex patterns and spelling. It included, in other words, those more complex levels of spelling-sound correspondences about which least agreement and guidance is found among experts and curricula.

here: The very structure of the basal instructional series may lead us down this path.

In the fifteen first-grade classrooms that Barr and Dreeben observed, the primary determinant of lesson level and pace was the students' ability to read their basal stories aloud. In other words, students who read poorly were started at lower levels of the basal series so that they would be faced with easier stories. Similarly, students who read more slowly and laboriously progressed through the story sequence more slowly.[61]

By itself this makes perfect sense. We must bear in mind, however, that the basal series and their accompanying materials, guidebooks, and worksheets, are intended to provide the teacher with a core program of reading instruction. If the teacher is relying on the basal series to prescribe instructional content and activities that are to accompany each story—and most teachers do[62]—then progress on all aspects of the reading program is tied to the children's progress through the stories.

The result is that the more poorly prepared a student is on entry, the less she or he will be taught about letter-sound correspondences and spelling patterns. Yet, the less a student has internalized about letter-sound correspondences and spelling patterns, the less fluent and able she or he will be in deciphering connected text. (The earlier %√#¿±¢∞?}∞≈¿± was intended to convince you of that.)[63]

This situation is counterproductive whichever way you view it. The amount students learn through connected reading is tightly bound to the amount of difficulty they experience in reading it. High error rates are negatively correlated with achievement; low error rates are positively correlated with achievement. It has been estimated that for maximum achievement, the responses of the average student should be correct 70 percent of the time; those of the slower student should be correct 80 percent of the time.[64]

The teacher of the low-readiness student is thus caught in a bind: She can speed progress through the stories only by accepting higher error rates or by skipping stories. Although the statistics imply that stories read with high error rates might as well be skipped, the realities are not that simple. Across the lessons of the basals, visual vocabulary and readability are built up, story

---

61. Barr and Dreeben (1983).

62. Yarington (1978, cited in Lapp and Flood, 1983) estimates that 95 percent do.

63. That is, "demonstration."

64. For a review, see Rosenshine and Stevens (1984).

by story. The teacher cannot skip stories without accepting an accelerated increase in difficulty between those that are read. Where the motivation for skipping the next story is precisely that the children had so much trouble with the last one, this trade-off is also unacceptable. As yet one more alternative, the teacher could move the children more quickly through the phonic than through the reading components of the basal, but this creates management problems.

In many ways, the compromise of moving through the lesson sequence more slowly seems not unreasonable. By spending more time on each story, the teacher can bring the children to a level of 80 percent correct responding. The only cost is that of diluting the lesson's supporting activities, including its word analysis activities; this may consist of omitting some, making short shrift some, or spreading the material across extra classroom days. But even this has its advantages: It leaves more instructional time per day for working on the connected reading—and do note that basal coverage is itself a good predictor of first-grade reading achievement.

The only major disadvantage to this option may be that the children receive less explicit instruction and exercise in phonics and word analysis skills. But this is a very serious disadvantage. The best differentiator between good and poor readers is repeatedly found to be their knowledge of spelling patterns and their proficiency with spelling-sound translations. Phonic mastery is not only highly correlated with phonic coverage, but for low-readiness children—for those who lack it most—it is strongly and directly dependent on it. Barr and Dreeben's analyses indicate that

In the low aptitude subsample, phonics learning is not related to basal learning. . . . Among these children, who are the least ready to read, the acquisition of phonics skills does not occur derivatively from basal reading or in conjunction with it, but more narrowly reflects the pace of phonics instruction. In short, the low aptitude children learn the phonics they are taught and do not pick it up as a by-product of more general reading.[65]

Reflecting upon all of this, we may demur that if only the basal stories and basal phonic instruction were consistently and carefully designed in support of one another, these conflicts might disappear.

---

65.   Barr and Dreeben (1983, p. 148).

Although I believe that such coordination would significantly improve the situation, it would not provide a total cure. There is a deeper problem: As material to be taught or learned, individual letter-sound correspondences and phonic generalizations are inherently intractable when divorced from the rest of the reading situation. They are abstract, piecewise, unorderable, unreliable, barely numerable, and sometimes mutually incompatible. Moreover, to be useful, any given individual letter-sound correspondence or phonic generalization must not merely be learned; it must be overlearned such that it is instantly and effortlessly available to the reader. But overlearning requires lots of exercise and review and therefore lots of time.

If low-readiness students learn only what they are taught, how are we ever to teach them enough, quickly enough, and thoroughly enough, to make reading a rewarding activity before they have had enough? And if we could find more effective ways of instructing the low-readiness student, wouldn't they also be more effective with those who come better prepared?

The touted importance of spelling-sound relationships seems not to be an illusion. As we have examined each of a number of domains of study—program comparisons, research on prereader skills, the knowledge and performance of skilled readers, theory on the nature of learning—each has pointed toward the conclusion that skillful word reading depends critically on the deep and thorough acquisition of these relationships.

On the other hand, the hierarchical model of reading appears to be psychologically faulty. At the most global level, its problem seems to be with the initial assumption that reading is the process of extracting information from text. In the reading situation, as in any effective communication situation, the message or text provides but one of the critical sources of information. The rest must come from the readers' own prior knowledge. That knowledge does not function hierarchically from the bottom up but meets the printed information from all levels at once, interactively and in parallel. Whether to support learning or fluent performance, it must.

Again, productive phonic instruction is far less tricky for students who enter school with solid literacy preparation. Earlier I suggested that one reason for this disparity is that, for well-prepared children, such instruction consists as much of review and clarification as it does of new content.

Surely that is true but, just as surely, it is only a fraction of the picture. To gain proper registration, phonic instruction must articulate with the understanding and expectations of the learners, with both lower- and higher-order information in their memories. Many children enter first grade prepared with much of the understanding, expectations, and prior knowledge required by their lessons. On that basis, they can more or less fill in many of the presumptions, exceptions, and contingencies that are omitted or postponed in lesson delivery.

Other children begin first grade without such preparation. In the extreme, these children will come to know only what we have helped them to learn and only as we have helped them to learn it. The chapters to come are addressed to the issue of what else these beginners need in order to master print. If we want our students to learn to read, we must make reading learnable for them.

Phonological Prerequisites: Becoming Aware of Spoken Words, Syllables, and Phonemes

Across this book, I have argued that proficient reading depends on an automatic capacity to recognize frequent spelling patterns visually and to translate them phonologically. Differences in this capacity are principal separators of good from poor readers. Only those prereaders who acquire awareness of phonemes (the sounds to which graphemic units map), learn to read successfully. Programs explicitly designed to develop sounding and blending skills produce better word readers than those that do not. I have even argued that synthetic phonics is of special value for young readers. Yet, on top of all that I have just argued that the basic phonic curriculum is inherently intractable, slow, inefficient, and worse: Except for students who essentially know how to read before it is begun, it is also likely to be ineffective.

Are we stuck? Not at all. The basic motivation for this book was that too many children do not learn to read as well as they should, and that has been true of children in phonic as well as nonphonic programs. Moreover, the basic argument against phonic programs has always been that they are often boring, ineffective, inefficient, and too much removed and abstracted from the real task of reading.

We are now in a far better position to respond to each of these issues. We now know what must be learned for proficient word recognition. We know a lot about the mental architecture and processing that must be involved in the acquisition of word recognition skills. The issue is how best to couch phonic instruction, how to build to it, from it, and around it in ways that best ensure the ease and productivity of its acquisition. The issue is how to make instruction on word recognition skills a self-engendering, motivating, and meaningful experience for the students and a manageable one for their teachers.

In this and the remaining chapters of this part, I shall examine some other approaches to developing the knowledge and skills that support word recognition proficiency. Interestingly, each of these promising approaches has, at one time or another by one group or another, been a strongly advocated component of the reading and language curriculum. Reexamined in light of recent theory and research, however, the respective strengths of each and the ways in which each might best be used to complement each other and the basic phonic curriculum become much more clear.

Levels of Linguistic Awareness

In one way or another, virtually all modern writing systems are parasitic on language. But this was not always true: In the earliest writing systems, meaning was depicted directly. Linguistic mediation of visual communication evolved gradually in both time and levels of abstraction—first words, then syllables, then phonemes. Interestingly, the ease and order with which cultures have become aware of these levels of abstraction in history and exploited them as units of writing is mirrored in the ease and order with which children become aware of them developmentally.[1]

The obstacle to such linguistic awareness seems to be the limited capacity of our active attention. In speaking and listening, our attention is focused on the task of comprehending—of making sense out of the collective, ordered stream of words. To focus instead on each individual word, syllable, or phoneme would be counterproductive. Even ignoring issues of comprehension, it would be too time-consuming; we would quickly lose track of the rest of the spoken stream.[2] For purposes of listening to language, therefore, it is fortunate that the processing of subunits— phonemes, syllables, and words—is automatic.

For purposes of learning to read or write, however, these subunits must be dug out of their normal, subattentional status. Children must push their attention down from the level of

---

1. Gleitman and Rozin (1977); Rozin and Gleitman (1977).

2. You may have experienced the difficulty and mental exhaustion that comes with too much listening to a marginally familiar foreign language. This is presumably the source. Alternatively, one of the most convincing proofs of speech scientists in this context is that if phonemes arrived as discrete acoustical segments, the speed of their arrival (eight to thirty segments per second) would exceed the temporal resolving power of the human ear. Speech would sound like an unanalyzable buzz (Liberman, Shankweiler, Cooper, and Studdert-Kennedy, 1967).

comprehension at which it normally works. Not surprisingly, the deeper into the system they must push, the harder it is to do. Thus awareness of clauses or propositions develops earlier and more easily than awareness of words. Awareness of words develops earlier and more easily than awareness of syllables. And awareness of syllables develops earlier and more easily than awareness of phonemes.

When degree of awareness of (or performance on a task that requires direct attention to) each of these units is compared with beginners' reading achievement, phonemic tasks produce the highest correlations by a wide margin. Syllabic tasks generally produce significant but weaker correlations. And the results with word tasks are only sometimes significant. Moreover, sophisticated statistical analyses indicate that performance on all such linguistic awareness tasks generally reflects a single pool of underlying ability rather than any independent lineup of unrelated skills.[3]

These results invite misinterpretation. To the statistically uninitiated, they almost beg the conclusion that phonemic awareness is the single most important skill to develop among prereaders. After all, it might be reasoned, if all of these awarenesses reflect the same basic ability, why waste time on any but the one that relates most strongly to reading?

Though seductive, this conclusion is patently unwarranted. A strong correlation between two measures depends on two conditions. First, the scores on the two measures must predict one another: The children who perform worse on one measure should generally be the same as those who perform worse on the other, and similarly for those whose performance is good or in between. Because it is precisely to find this kind of relationship that we usually undertake correlational analyses, the strength or weakness of the results is usually interpreted as the evidence for the presence or absence thereof. Tasks with zero correlation are typically interpreted as being unrelated.

We must not, however, overlook the second condition on which a strong correlation depends. Specifically, performance on each measure must range broadly: There must be some people who get high scores on each measure, and some who get low scores.[4] For

---

3. Stanovich, Cunningham, and Cramer (1984); Wagner and Torgeson (1987).

4. In addition, for the resulting correlation to be a good index of the relationship between the two tasks, it is important that the performance of a representative group of children with in-between ability also be measured.

example, across all children, the correlation between reading ability and number of years of schooling should be quite strong. Reading ability may range from none to great proficiency; years of schooling may range from one to twelve or more; and in general children with more schooling do read better. In contrast, no significant correlation is expected between reading ability and letter-naming accuracy among college students. The reason is that the students' letter naming scores should be all but identical—in this case, perfect.[5] Unless both sets of scores range in value, no "corelation" between the values in one and the values in the other can be statistically detected.

Despite the nil correlation between letter naming accuracy and reading ability among college students, normal reading is strongly dependent on facile letter recognition.[6] By the same logic, the lower correlations between reading achievement and measures of word and syllable awareness do not negate their importance. They may indicate only that these are abilities that the majority of youngsters can quickly acquire or bring forth when the situation pointedly requires it.

The relative magnitudes of the correlations between children's reading acquisition and their awareness of spoken phonemes, syllables, and words are consistent with the evidence that each is more difficult and attained later in development than the next. They are uninterpretable with respect to the relative importance of these skills to reading. In fact, each is critically important.

Becoming Aware of Spoken Words

Words seem so obvious and accessible a unit of speech to us. They are fundamental units of meaning. We use them all the time in speaking to children, and they to us. Much of the linguistic growth of the preschooler consists of learning new, individual words. And just a few years before, their speech began with single

---

5. Even second graders are found to be so uniformly capable of naming individual letters that this task ceases to be a useful index of their reading ability (Walsh, Price, and Gillingham, 1988).

6. Actually, if all of the students we studied had exactly the same letter-naming scores, the correlation between letter-naming speed and reading ability would be undefined. For any correlation to obtain, there must be some variance in both scores. Insignificant or near-zero correlations would result if the difference between the letter-naming accuracy of the most and least able readers were slight compared to the range of accuracy obtained by those whose reading abilities fell in between.

word utterances. What kind of a child could be unaware of the status of words?

The seminal study on word awareness was reported by Karpova in 1955.[7] Working with normal children, aged three to seven years, Karpova began by training them to count pictures and unrelated spoken words. After that task had been mastered, Karpova asked the children to repeat several sentences and to count the words and identify the first, second, third, . . . word in each. When the words were presented in meaningful sentences, the children could not break them apart.

Karpova's youngest children focused on the number of propositions or idea units that each sentence conveyed. A typical response to the sentence "Galya and Vova went walking" was that it contained two words: *Galya went walking*, and *Vova went walking*.

At the next stage, children began to segment the propositions into subject and predicate terms. Thus, a sentence like "Misha ran quickly" would be said to contain two words: *Misha* and *ran quickly*. Alternatively the child might restrict focus to the just one of the clauses and count the phrases in it: "Galya and Vova went walking" might be said to contain two words: *Galya* and *Vova*.

Only at the third level, did children begin to break the sentences into individual words. Even then, they occasionally mistook syllables for words and generally failed to split prepositions away from content words or to count conjunctions.[8]

Variations and refinements on Karpova's studies have been undertaken by a number of investigators. Perhaps children really do know what words are but do not understand the word *word*. Perhaps the requirement of counting is just too much for them. Perhaps the sentences were too long, and that is why they bunched words together in their responses. Perhaps it was the prosodics (patterns of pitch and timing) of the spoken sentences

---

7. Karpova (1955, abstracted in Slobin, 1966).

8. An argument might be made that such function words contribute to the meaning of oral language as much through the rhythmic nuances they insert in the speech flow as through their phonemic or lexical status. Both of my children went through a period in their language development where they regularly included prepositions but pronounced them distinctly and uniformly as "uh." They would say, for example, "Give it uh me," or "This is uh you, Mommy." Along the same theme, many times I have received notes from well-educated adults that included such constructions as "should *of* [asked]" and "must *of* [been]." The occurrence of such errors among adults prompts the hypothesis that resolution of such functors comes partly from writing, as opposed to listening, experiences.

that induced them to respond to whole phrases rather than individual words.

In fact, many young children do not understand the word *word*,[9] but the same pattern of results is obtained when testing procedures are designed around this problem. The same pattern of results is also obtained when the children are asked to tap the table or to push out a poker chip for each word instead of counting them.[10] It is obtained whether or not the sentences are spoken in a monotone.[11] And it is even obtained when the sentences are only two words in length.[12] Furthermore, when real, familiar words and spoken pseudowords are presented one by one to kindergarten-aged children, they are largely unable to discriminate which are meaningful and which are not.[13]

Surprising as it may seem, the evidence concurs that children are not naturally prepared either to conceive of spoken language as a string of individual words or to treat words as individual units of meaning. What they listen for is the full meaning of an utterance, and that comes only after the meanings of the individual words have been combined—automatically and without their attention. More picturesquely:

During this period, the word may be used but not noticed by the child, and frequently it presents things seemingly like a glass, through which the child looks at the surrounding world, not making the word itself the object of awareness, and not suspecting that it has its own existence, it own aspects of construction.[14]

Early reading instruction begins with the assumption that words are individually codable units of language. The concept of a word and the ability to recognize otherwise familiar words when examined one at a time are taken for granted. Moreover, the word *word* is nearly unavoidable in instructional delivery. To make any sense whatsoever out of their classroom activities, children must already understand or quickly catch on to the idea of what a word is.

Fortunately, words lie relatively close to interpretations within the system. It should therefore be fairly easy to induce children to attend to them—and indeed this is so. Researchers

---

9. Downing (1970a, 1970b); Francis (1973); Reid (1966).

10. Ehri (1975); Holden and MacGinitie (1972).

11. Ehri (1975).

12. Huttenlocher (1964).

13. Downing and Oliver (1973–1974); Ehri (1977, cited in Ehri, 1979).

14. Attributed to A. R. Luria by Downing (1979, p. 27).

have shown that even in a single sitting, young children can make great progress in segmenting sentences into individual words[15] (although they are extremely resistant to conceding word status to function words and prepositions).

Of course, the number of children who learn about words through such experiments is extremely small. How do the rest of them do it? Ehri argues persuasively that many learn through exposure to print.[16] In speaking, we do not emit words one by one. We do not pause between them. Instead we produce whole clauses or sentences in one single continuous breath. In print there are spaces between the words. Each is discretely represented. As children become aware of the one-by-oneness of words in print, they begin to notice and isolate the words in speech. Apparently this insight requires no great amount of reading sophistication, for Ehri has shown that word awareness increases dramatically along with the earliest signs of emerging reading ability.[17]

Becoming Aware of Spoken Syllables

Unlike words (excepting single-syllable words) or phonemes, individual syllables are distinctly marked in the speech stream. By definition, every syllable contains a vocalic nucleus (roughly, a period of free voicing or a vowel sound). In speech, these vocalic nuclei correspond to peaks of acoustic energy or loudness, providing physical cues by which the listener may distinguish one spoken syllable from the next.[18] Very roughly, the peaks of loudness correspond to the centers of syllables, and the troughs in between to their boundaries.[19] On the other side, for the speaker, the vowel-consonant cycles of syllables correspond to the opening and

---

15. Engelmann (1969); Fox and Routh (1975); Kirk (1979, cited in Blachman, 1984).

16. Ehri (1976); Ehri (1979).

17. Ehri (1979).

18. Fletcher (1929, cited in Liberman, 1973).

19. The question of exactly where each syllable of a multisyllable word begins or ends is hotly debated among scholars on the topic. Certainly the syllable boundaries specified in dictionaries are to be taken loosely; they reflect principles taken more from Noah Webster than from linguistics or psychology. The same factors that make it difficult for scholars to resolve the boundaries between syllables of individual words must also make it difficult for the prereader to resolve the boundaries between whole words in continuous speech.

closing cycles of the jaw.[20] Syllables are, moreover, the smallest unit of speech that can be produced in isolation. (Free-standing vowels are technically syllables.)

To the extent that syllables are physically distinguishable from one another, we might expect the acquisition of syllabic awareness to come relatively easily. In keeping with this, research has shown that even people with little or no reading ability can generally learn to direct their attention to syllabic units with reasonable ease and success. This has been found true, for example, with preschool children,[21] illiterate and barely literate adults,[22] and slow beginners from inner-city first grades.[23]

On the other hand, compared with words, syllables are still deeper in the system, still further removed from meaning, and still closer to phonemes. This suggests that their conscious appreciation might be more difficult and more strongly related to reading acquisition than that of words. Consistent with this, the ability to detect syllables in speech or to segment syllables from speech has been shown to predict future reading,[24] to correlate with the reading progress of beginners,[25] and to differentiate older disabled or "dyslexic" readers from normal first graders.[26]

In view of these findings, it is somewhat puzzling that when the task is not one of detecting or counting syllables but instead of manipulating (e.g., deleting or reversing them), the relationships to reading ability seem to be weaker.[27] What, then, are we to make of syllabic awareness? Why is it a good predictor in easier than in more rigorously demanding tasks?

For good syllabic counting and detection performance, one might argue that conscious, cognitive awareness of syllabic units is unnecessary; after all, syllables are acoustically and articulatorily distinct. To perform well on syllabic counting and detection tasks, one need not think of syllables as representing any particular class of speech units. For segmentation, it is sufficient merely to listen for those peaks of loudness; one need not even

---

20. Gleitman and Rozin (1977).

21. Liberman, Shankweiler, Fischer, and Carter (1974); Mann and Liberman (1984).

22. Morais, Bertelson, Cary, and Alegria (1986).

23. Treiman and Baron (1981).

24. Lundberg, Olofsson, and Wall (1980); Mann and Liberman (1984).

25. Morais, Bertelson, Cary, and Alegria (1986); Treiman and Baron (1981).

26. Morais, Cluytens, Alegria, and Content (1984).

27. Mann (1984, 1986); Morais, Bertelson, Cary, and Alegria (1986).

think about their particular sound, their articulatory cause, or how they relate to the rest of the syllable. For detection, one need only listen for the repetition of a sound that the experimenter has presented; the idea that this sound has the special status of a syllable is immaterial. In contrast, syllable deletion and reversal tasks require identification and conscious manipulation of the syllable as a whole. Isn't it strange that the tasks that do not require precise identification and isolation of syllables do correlate with reading ability while the tasks that do require it often do not?

One possible explanation for this paradox is that we have misconstrued the value of syllable detection and segmentation tasks. Perhaps they most usefully assess awareness of the sound structure of speech rather than any specific awareness of syllables as such. Inasmuch as people's ability to attend to the sound as opposed to the meaning of speech must precede their ability to appreciate the alphabetic principle, this explanation seems quite palatable.

But an even better, more direct measure of people's sensitivity to the sound structure of words ought to be had through rhyme detection tasks, and, spoiling our tentative explanation, performance on rhyme and syllable tasks seems somewhat unrelated.[28] Working with adult illiterates, for example, Morais and his colleagues found some whose performance was excellent with rhymes but extremely poor on syllable segmentation; at the same time, the performance of others was excellent on syllable segmentation but extremely poor on rhyme detection.[29]

An alternative interpretation of the seemingly backward disparity between rudimentary and rigorous syllabic awareness tasks is that it makes sense. Perhaps there is a fundamental importance to syllabic awareness that, though distinct from the importance of attending to the sound structure of words, does not extend to the capacities to transpose or delete syllables. Perhaps the most important level of syllabic awareness is something close to that which is demanded by the syllable counting and detection tasks.

---

28. For example, see Lundberg, Frost, and Petersen (1988); Morais, Bertelson, Cary, and Alegria (1986); Stanovich, Cunningham, and Cramer (1984). Note also that the relative weakness of the statistical relation between these tasks may be misleading. It may be solely due to the fact that the variability in people's performance on rhyming tasks is relatively constrained because most find rhyming tasks to be relatively easy.

29. Morais, Bertelson, Cary, and Alegria (1986).

Three lines of argument can be offered to support this conjecture. The first line of argument addresses the reason that one might expect the more sophisticated syllabic awareness tasks to be poor predictors of beginning reading success. The second two offer explanation for why the simpler abilities to count and detect syllables might be adequate and important components of beginning reading success.

First, why might one discount the predictive utility of the syllable deletion and transformation tasks? The use of syllabic units in printed word perception is a late-emerging skill among normal readers. It does not appear until they are in the fourth grade.[30] Moreover, its appearance appears to be governed not by the children's level of phonological sophistication but their level of orthographic sophistication—by their *visual* responsiveness to multiletter spelling patterns. And beyond the fact that beginners are generally incapable of undertaking syllabic analysis of long words is the fact that they are rarely required to do so: Most of their reading vocabulary consists of short single-syllable words. To the extent that the capacity for conscious, methodical syllabic isolation is neither apparent among nor required of beginning readers, it seems a stretch to expect it to predict their success.

Why might the level of syllabic awareness required for detection and counting be important? One promising explanation is that although the capacity to manipulate and isolate syllables is not required of the beginner, the capacity to know when one does (or does not) have a good, familiar syllable is. Indeed this capacity may be an essential mediator of the child's ability to sound out visually unfamiliar words.

The remaining and perhaps most forceful explanation is that, to use letters, children must gain conscious access to phonemes. Yet, the sounds of individual phonemes are not physically dissectable from the speech stream, but are thoroughly blended together within the syllable.[31] Whether to extract spelling from speech or to translate spelling to speech, therefore, it is the syllable with which one must start.

The suggestion, in short, is that syllabic awareness constitutes an essential link between that seemingly easy-to-acquire ability

---

30. Friedrich, Schadler, and Juola (1979).
31. Liberman (1970).

underlying our sensitivity to sound similarity and rhyme[32] and that hard-to-acquire capacity to recognize individual phonemes.[33]

To boost this argument, we might consider some results obtained by Blachman with a group of low-readiness kindergartners and first graders.[34] Among the kindergartners, the ability to tap out syllables was a uniquely strong, positive correlate of their familiarity with letter-to-sound associations.[35] (Significantly, these were children who knew very little about printed language. They could recognize so few printed letters that Blachman had to discard their performance on a letter-naming task from her analyses.)

In contrast, among the first graders, the correlation between the syllable task and letter-sound facility was no longer significant. On the other hand, though the correlation between rhyme production and phonemic segmentation was close to zero, both were strongly correlated with the children's syllable tapping performance.

The predictive strength of the syllable segmentation task for Blachman's kindergartners is consistent with the suggestion that it is an important reading ability. Its dissipation as an index of reading progress among Blachman's first graders is consistent with the suggestion that the ability to attend to syllables is a rudimentary and early developing skill. Its resilient correlation with both rhyme production and phoneme segmentation is consistent with the suggestion that syllabic awareness is an important mediator between children's attention to the sound structure of English and its relationship to spelling.

Becoming Aware of Phonemes

To learn letter-sound correspondences, children must become aware of phonemes. In the reading-as-paired-associate game, the proper responses to individual graphemes are individual phonemes. Moreover, the system is set up to give the reader a double-or-nothing return on phonemic knowledge. To the extent that children have learned to "hear" phonemes as individual and

---

32. See Morais, Bertelson, Cary, and Alegria (1986); Yopp (1988).

33. See Lundberg, Frost, and Petersen (1988); Morais, Bertelson, Cary, and Alegria (1986); and Read, Yun-Fei, Hong-Yin, and Bao-Qing (1986).

34. Blachman (1984a).

35. Phonemic segmentation was not measured among the kindergarteners.

separable speech sounds, the system will, through the associative network, strengthen their ability to remember or "see" individual letters and spelling patterns. To the extent that they have not learned to "hear" the phonemes, the network cannot help their learning of individual letters and may even work against the efficient learning of spelling patterns.

It is from this perspective that we finally get an aha! experience from those earlier reported findings about the special magic of learning letters and their sounds together. On one hand, we saw that teaching children to recognize letters produced little reading benefit unless the children were also taught the letters' sounds.[36] On the other, we saw that training phonemic awareness produced little reading benefit unless children were also taught the printed letters by which each phoneme was represented.[37] Functional understanding of the alphabetic principle depends equally on knowledge of letters and on explicit awareness of phonemes because it depends integrally on the association between them.

The nature and importance of phonemic awareness has already been treated in detail.[38] In view of this, the present discussion will focus less on the questions of what it is, when it develops, or why it is important than on the question of how it might develop.

Faced with an alphabetic script, the child's level of phonemic awareness on entering school may be the single most powerful determinant of the success she or he will experience in learning to read and of the likelihood that she or he will fail. Measures of preschoolers' level of phonemic awareness strongly predict their future success in learning to read, and this has been demonstrated not only for English,[39] but also for Swedish,[40] Spanish,[41] French,[42] Italian,[43] and Russian.[44] Measures of schoolchildren's ability to attend to and manipulate phonemes strongly correlate with their

---

36. Ohnmacht (1969).

37. Bradley and Bryant (1983).

38. See chapter 4.

39. See chapter 4.

40. Lundberg, Olofsson, and Wall (1980).

41. deManrique and Gramigna (1984, cited in Liberman, 1987).

42. Alegria, Pignot, and Morais (1982).

43. Cossu, Shankweiler, Liberman, Tola, and Katz (1988, cited in Liberman, 1987).

44. Elkonin (1973).

reading success all the way through the twelfth grade.[45] Poorly developed phonemic awareness distinguishes economically disadvantaged preschoolers from their more advantaged peers.[46] It is characteristic of adults with literacy problems in America,[47] Portugal,[48] England,[49] and Australia.[50] And it may be the most important core and causal factor separating normal and disabled readers.[51]

As crucial as phonemic awareness is to the process of learning to read, it is also difficult to acquire. Children have a highly developed knowledge of phonemes long before learning to read; if they did not, they could neither produce nor understand oral language. But, again, this is working knowledge, not conscious knowledge. It is deeply embedded in the subattentional switches, sensors, and gears of their oral language machinery.[52]

Unlike people's sensitivity to rhyme, the tendency to attend to individual phonemes is not triggered through mere exposure. Unless it is explicitly taught, and it can be,[53] it seems to develop only with the successful acquisition of an alphabetic script.[54] The development of phonemic awareness seems to depend on finding oneself in a situation in which phonemic awareness is inescapably required.

Unlike the relatively crude awareness of syllables that is required, the useful awareness of phonemes includes not just a rough sense of what and where they are. Instead, it extends to the

---

45. See chapter 4.

46. Wallach, Wallach, Dozier, and Kaplan (1977).

47. Liberman, Rubin, Duques, and Carlisle (1985).

48. Morais, Cary, Alegria, and Bertelson (1979).

49. Marcel (1980).

50. Byrne and Ledez (1983, cited in Liberman, 1987).

51. Stanovich (1986); Stanovich (1989, in press); Juel (1988).

52. If you are still having difficulty with the idea that people can quite thoroughly possess and regularly use knowledge without explicitly knowing that they know it, think about how you might explain to a child why we say "cute little bunny," but not "little cute bunny." Once you have explained that, compare it to "little blue car" versus "blue little car." The point here is not about whether we can explain such linguistic "rules" but that, whether or not we can, we readily use and, therefore, must deeply know them at some level.

53. Bradley and Bryant (1983); Elkonin (1973); Lundberg, Frost, and Petersen (1988); Wallach and Wallach (1979).

54. Liberman, Rubin, Duqués, and Carlisle (1985); Morais, Cary, Alegria, and Bertelson (1979); Read, Yun-Fei, Hong-Yin, and Bao-Qing (1986); but also see Mann (1986).

abilities to segment, rearrange, and substitute them one for the other.[55]

Furthermore, unlike people's capacity to attend to words and syllables, the capacity to attend to phonemes is not easily attained. Whereas conscious awareness of words or syllables may not be natural, it is relatively easy to teach and to learn. The same cannot be said of phonemic awareness.

Normal readers' ability to count the phonemes in a word or syllable is only beginning to stabilize by the end of first grade.[56] Their ability to delete, transpose, or add phonemes to a syllable continues to develop at least through high school.[57] And successful efforts to increase phonemic awareness through training have involved many, many sessions worth of lessons.[58]

In view of the extreme importance of phonemic awareness, the difficulty of instilling it is disturbing. Moreover, the difference in the difficulty of establishing awareness of phonemes versus syllables seems far too great.[59] One can hardly help but ask whether there anything in between. And it seems that there is.

Between Syllables and Phonemes: Onsets and Rimes

Psychology versus Acoustics

Acoustically, the syllable is an unanalyzable spoken unit. Yet psychologically, it is obviously analyzable. The syllable is psychologically analyzable into phonemes, and this is obvious to us because (and perhaps only because) we have learned an alphabetic script.

Importantly, our alphabetic script did not cause us to invent phonemes. To the contrary, it was their prior psychological reality that enabled us to invent the alphabet. Psychologically, phonemes were there all along, waiting to be discovered.

It is the phonemes' psychological reality combined with the salience of their printed correspondents—graphemes—that enables accomplished readers to be so confident of their nature

---

55. See chapter 4.

56. Blachman (1984); Liberman, Shankweiler, Fischer, and Carter (1974).

57. Calfee, Lindamood, and Lindamood (1973).

58. Bradley and Bryant (1983); Lundberg, Frost, and Petersen (1988); Wallach and Wallach (1979); Williams (1979). Note, too, that some *unsuccessful* efforts to train phonemic awareness have also involved many months of training sessions (e.g., Rosner, 1974).

59. See, e.g., Rosner (1974) and Rozin and Gleitman (1977).

and status. Yet phonemes are not the only psychological units mediating the transformation of acoustics to speech. Scientists have long been aware that phonemes themselves are composites of still smaller units, corresponding to the place, manner, and voicing with which we produce them. To illustrate each:

Place: The consonants /b/, /p/, /m/, and /w/ are made with our lips while /t/, /d/, /s/, /z/, /n/, /l/, and /r/ are made by placement of the tongue on or near the ridge of gum behind our teeth.

Manner: "Stop" consonants, /p/, /b/, /t/, /d/, /k/, and /g/, are produced by momentarily but completely obstructing the flow of wind from our mouths at their places of articulation. "Fricatives," /f/, /v/, /th/, /s/, /z/, /sh/, /zh/, and /h/, are produced by forcing a controlled leak of air through their place of articulation. "Nasals," /n/, /m/, and /ng/, are produced by forcing the air out through the nose.

Voicing: Some of our consonant sounds are all wind, and others include vocal accompaniment. To see this, place your fingertips on your Adam's apple while you pronounce the following, otherwise matched, voiceless versus voiced pairs of phonemes:

/p/ - /b/
/t/ - /d/
/f/ - /v/
/s/ - /z/.

Most of us gain awareness of these subphonemic features only in school or by reading a text like this one. Conscious awareness of them, after all, is necessary for neither listening, speaking, reading, nor writing. Despite this, the psychological reality of subphonemic features became everywhere noticeable once we had thought to notice it. In particular, our minds seem to master or mess up phonemes not holistically but in a feature-by-feature manner. This is apparent in the listening confusions and articulatory errors of adults,[60] in the order in which babies, world around, learn the phonemes of their own language,[61] and even in the learning of letter sounds by schoolchildren.[62]

By extension, if someone would just point it out to us, mightn't there be some psychologically real level of analysis that sits between the syllable and the phoneme? Not too long ago, some

---

60. See Clark and Clark (1977).

61. Jakobson (1968).

62. Treiman and Baron (1981).

linguists and psycholinguists began to propose that there is.[63] Shortly thereafter, a psychologist, Rebecca Treiman, picked up on this proposal. Since then, considerable data and argument have been amassed on its behalf.

What Are Onsets and Rimes?

According to these proposals, the syllable divides into two primary parts: the *onset* and the *rime*.[64] The rime is the obligatory part of the syllable: It consists of its vowel and any consonant sounds that come after it. The onset, if it is there, consists of any consonant sounds that precede the vowel. To clarify, here are some words divided into onsets and rimes:

Word	Onset	Rime
I	—	I
it	—	it
itch	—	itch
sit	s–	–it
spit	sp–	–it
split	spl–	–it
splint	spl–	–int
spline	spl–	–ine
spilt	sp–	–ilt
spoil	sp–	–oil
pie	p–	–ie
spy	sp–	–y

The theory is that the onset and rime of a syllable are separate but internally coherent psychological units. While it is relatively easy to break the onset away from the rime, it is relatively difficult to break either the onset or the rime into its phonemic components.

Evidence for the Psychological Reality of Onsets and Rimes

Toward this theory, there have long been hints floating around in the literature. For example, many researchers have noticed that when given monosyllabic words or pseudowords to read, beginners

---

63. Cairns and Feinstein (1982); Fudge 1969); Halle and Vergnaud (1980); Hockett (1967/1973); MacKay (1972); Selkirk (1982).

64. This is not a typo. As will become clear, *rimes* are intimately related to but distinct from *rhymes*.

make significantly more errors on the final consonants than on the initial ones.[65] If the letters are to be translated one by one into phonemes, this difference is a little difficult to explain. After all, if the child knows that *p* says /p/ in *pat*, why would she or he fail to realize that it said /p/ in *tap?*

By itself, of course, this observation is not very convincing. It could be, for example, that children simply devote more attention (or have more attention to devote) to the beginnings than to the endings of words. Surely the ends of words are less informative once the beginning has been decoded. And for any of a variety of reasons, the precise pronunciation of the end of a word might be less salient or noticeable.

But here is another hint: Children make far more errors in reading the vowels of words than the consonants.[66] This cannot be due to the positions of the vowels in the word: When Liberman and her colleagues gave children three-letter, single-syllable words, they found that the likelihood of misreading a vowel was independent of whether it was in the first, second, or third position.[67] And regardless of position, the vowels were misread more often than the consonants. Nor can it be that vowel sounds generally go unnoticed in speech: Vowel errors in oral repetition are infrequent in general and far less frequent than consonant errors.[68]

Besides that, the presence of the vowel is the key to syllable perception which is relatively easy for young children. Yet here is another mystery: When children are asked to tap out the phonemes of a syllable, they are far more likely to miss its vowel than its consonants.[69]

Liberman tried out several explanations for children's difficulties with vowels.[70] Maybe, she suggested, it is related to the greater irregularity of their spelling-to-sound correspondences—though her preliminary data provided no support for this hypothesis. Alternatively, she suggested, it might be due to the greater variability of any given vowel sound

---

65. Daniels and Diack (1956, cited in Liberman, 1973); Fowler, Liberman, and Shankweiler (1977); Liberman (1973); Shankweiler and Liberman (1972); Treiman and Baron (1981); Weber (1970).

66. Monroe (1932, cited in Liberman, 1973); Shankweiler and Liberman (1972); Weber (1970).

67. Liberman (1973).

68. Shankweiler and Liberman (1972).

69. Liberman (1973).

70. Liberman (1973).

across individual speech samples and dialects—though that doesn't quite balance with the fact that children have no trouble in accurately repeating vowels.

Treiman (who, interestingly, was an undergraduate honors student of the Libermans) has since offered a different explanation: The final consonant of a syllable and its vowel, wherever it occurs, are not easily perceived as isolable phonemes for they are integral parts of the syllable's rime. In contrast, the initial consonant is easily broken away as the onset of the syllable—at least if it is a singleton.

To assess whether onsets and rimes really do govern children's ability to penetrate a syllable, Treiman introduced a group of five year olds to two puppets.[71] Each puppet had a favorite sound and responded gleefully whenever it heard a word that started with its favorite sound. But it responded with great disappointment when it heard a word that did not.

After the task had been explained, demonstrated, and practiced, the puppet was passed to the child. The child was to repeat each of a taped series of syllables, and make the puppet "say" whether or not it began with its favorite sound.[72]

For the puppet used in two of the sessions, the favorite sound was /s/; for the puppet used in the other session, the favorite sound was /f/.[73] None of the "disappointing" items began with either /s/ or /f/. However—and this is the important part—some of the "favorite" consonants were followed immediately by a vowel sound (e.g., /sa/ and /sap/ or /fa/ and /fal/) whereas the rest were followed by another consonant (e.g., /sme/ and /ski/ or /fla/ and /fru/).

What Treiman wanted to know was whether the children's ability to recognize the initial consonant would depend on whether it was the single member of the syllable's onset. It did. When the "favorite" consonants were singletons (as in /sa/ and /sap/), the children succeeded in recognizing roughly 87 percent of them. When the "favorite" consonants were joined with another (as in /smi/ and /ski/), the children succeeded in recognizing only

---

71. Treiman (1985a).

72. If a repetition was erroneous, the tape was rewound and replayed until the child got it right.

73. These sounds were chosen because they can be produced in isolation, thus making the instructions easier.

72 percent of them. In contrast, the children judged only 13 percent of the "disappointing" syllables to be pleasing to the puppet.[74]

Note that whether the syllables began with one consonant or two, the "favorite" one always came first, if at all. This fact lends extra credence to Treiman's hypothesis that children have special difficulty dissolving initial consonant clusters into individual phonemes.

Pushing her prediction one step further, Treiman then asked first and second graders to read aloud a set of pseudowords consisting of such pairs as *smoo* and *soom*. Her reasoning was that if children generally map letters to individual phonemes, one by one and left to right, then the *s* and the *m* should be read correctly at least as often in *smoo* as in *soom*. If, on the other hand, children are less attuned to individual phonemes than they are to onsets and rimes, they should find the consonants in *smoo* especially hard to read.

Both the first and second graders behaved in accordance with Treiman's onset-rime hypothesis. Indeed, the first graders made nearly twice the consonant-reading errors with the *smoo* items (64 percent) than with the *soom* items (36 percent).

The nature of the children's misreadings was also consistent with the idea that it was the complexity of the onset that was causing the difficulty. Among first graders' errors with *smoo* items, the syllable's onset was reduced to a single consonant in 65 percent of the cases. In 15 percent of the cases, the second and third phonemes were reversed—for example, changing *smoo* to *soom*. And in 20 percent of the cases, the children created an extra syllable—for example, changing *smoo* to *somo*. In each of these cases, the children conquered the complex onset by simplifying it.[75]

So far the evidence is consistent with Treiman's tenet that the awareness of syllable onsets is a different and simpler challenge than awareness of individual phonemes. Yet, an alternative explanation is that youngsters have special difficulties with the interior sounds or letters of a word.

To test this hypothesis, Treiman went back to preschool with her puppets. This time the contrasts of interest were items such as

---

74. Though not quite significant, erroneously accepted items tended to share more subphonemic features with /s/ or /f/ than correctly rejected ones.

75. This pattern of misreadings has also been documented by Miller and Limber (1985).

smi versus *ami*.[76] Thus, for both types of "likeable" items, the "favorite" sound—in this case, /m/—was the second in the string. However, for items like *smi*, it was part of a complex onset; for items like *ami* it was the simple onset of a second syllable.

Overall the children's error rate was high: 30 percent of the "disappointing" items were accepted. And the differences were relatively small: 50 percent of the *smi* items, while 60 percent of the *ami* items were accepted. But the pattern of results was once again consistent with the hypothesis that children are better attuned to syllable onsets than to individual phonemes.

Another line of evidence for the psychological reality of onsets and rimes comes from the kinds of phoneme awareness tasks whose very difficulty prompted their investigation. As one example, Treiman cites an effort by Barton, Miller, and Macken to train four and five year olds on a syllable-splitting task.[77] For the first phase of training, the words to be split began with single consonants, such as *mouse*. The children mastered this challenge with a minimum of training. In the next phase, the children were given words that began with two or more consonants such as *swing* and *train*. Again, about one-third of them had no trouble, consistently splitting just the first consonant sound away from the word. On the other hand, another 20 to 40 percent of the children consistently produced the entire consonant cluster, insisting, for example, that the first sound of *swing* was /sw/. The rest of the children vacillated between singleton and cluster responses.

Miller and Limber have since extended this study in an intriguing direction.[78] Working this time with nonsense words that began with either one or two consonant sounds (e.g., *keeg* and *dreeb*), twenty-one kindergartners were first asked to spell the nonsense words—to write them down "the way they thought the words sounded."[79] After each of the syllables had been spelled, they were presented once more. This time the children were asked to say the first sound (consonant) of each. When they erred— which happened most often when they produced two consonants instead of just one—they were asked to try again. Finally, after correctly producing the initial consonant in isolation, they were asked to say the rest of the word with that single consonant deleted.

---

76. Recall that children's phoneme recognition performance is generally better with nonwords than with familiar words (McNeil and Stone, 1965).

77. Barton, Miller, and Macken (1980, cited in Treiman, 1988b, in press).

78. Miller and Limber (1985).

79. Miller and Limber (1985, p. 4).

The children had no trouble spelling or deleting the single consonant onsets. In contrast, in both the spelling and the delete-initial-consonant tasks, the children omitted the second consonant of the onset cluster approximately 50 percent of the time. The correlation between their omissions of the second consonant across the two tasks was 0.64.

Most interesting of all, Miller and Limber adduce that the pattern of second consonant omission reflected in these data closely mirrors the articulatory simplifications commonly observed in the speech of one- and two-year old children. Through earlier work, Limber had confirmed that toddlers go through a stage of regularly simplifying the onsets of words—of saying, for example, /*tuck*/ for *truck* and /*cock*/ for *clock*. Why should it be, asked Miller and Limber, that "in putting their speech on paper, [the children would] fail to represent just those segments apparently deleted four years earlier in their speech?"[80] Their tentative answer was that there is something fundamentally unanalyzable about initial consonant clusters.

Treiman, too, has recognized phoneme manipulation tasks as ideal means for assessing the onset-rime hypothesis and has explored a host of variations on this theme. In some experiments, she has simply asked adults to combine two syllables into one, using the beginning of one and the end of the other however they might please. Examples of the starting pairs and their acceptable responses follow.[81] (As you look at these, bear in mind that both the stimulus items and the responses were not written but spoken in all cases.)

Stimulus Items		Acceptable Responses				
pab	gafe	*pafe*	paf			
mab	nafe	*mafe*	maf			
wab	yafe	*wafe*	waf			
splee	skraw	*splaw*	spraw	spaw	sraw	saw
skree	sploo	*skroo*	skloo	skoo	sloo	soo
frail	slat	flat	*frat*	freight		
blame	freed	breed	*bleed*	blade		
packed	nuts	pats	*putts*	packs		
billed	guns	bins	*buns*	bills		

---

80. Miller and Limber (1985, p. 4).

81. Treiman (1986).

The preferred response to each stimulus pair, generally by an overwhelming margin, is printed in bold italics. In each case, the preferred response consists of the entire initial consonant cluster from the first stimulus syllable plus the vowel and final consonants from the second. Treiman's adults, in short, uniformly preferred to keep the onsets and rimes of the stimulus words intact. Moreover, Treiman has found this to be true regardless of the nature of the consonant in the onset (stop, fricative, nasal, liquid, glide), of the number of consonants in the onset (one, two, or three), or of whether the items to be combined were words or nonwords. It is even true when the subjects could have opted to split the words at their morphemic boundaries instead.

The contrast between people's respect for onsets and rimes versus morphemes is illustrated in the last two examples in the list. To my intuitions, preservation of the morphemes (such that *pack-ed* plus *nut-s* would yield *packs*) seems easily the more intelligent and compelling strategy. Intuitions notwithstanding, Treiman's subjects preferred onset-rime combination, such as *putts*, to morphemic combinations, such as *packs*, at a ratio well over a hundred to one.

Looking over these results one might protest that what people most often do is not the cleanest index of what they can do. (Just think about that one for a moment.) While the foregoing is consistent with the notion that onsets and rimes are psychologically real units of analysis, it is still not compelling. Toward clarifying this issue, Treiman has also tried training people to play the syllable combination game by other rules. Yet, even with training, eight year olds[82] as well as adults[83] have difficulty splitting syllables anywhere but between their onsets and rimes.

Sensitivity to Onsets and Rimes: Nature versus Experience

It is occasionally speculated that the onset and rime are linguistic universals.[84] In the jargon, this is to say that they are natural units in any human language and to suggest that they are units to which the child is innately predisposed.[85] The appearance of

---

82. Treiman (1985).

83. Treiman (1983, 1985, 1986).

84. For citations, see: Treiman (1988a, in press, 1988b, in press).

85. The classic reference on the biological bases for human language is Lenneberg (1967). However, an accessible and balanced discussion of the issue is presented in Clark and Clark (1977).

onset simplification errors in babies' language acquisition certainly tempts this hypothesis. Nevertheless, another, more mechanical explanation can be offered.

To understand this, we must back up a bit. Within any given language, there are a few strong rules governing the sound structure of both onsets and rimes; within each, only certain sequences of sounds are allowed. Thus, in English, *str* can begin a syllable, but it cannot end one; similarly the sequence *rst* can end a syllable but not begin one. For rimes, there are also restrictions on what kinds of vowel sounds can (or ever do) precede each otherwise permissible final consonant cluster: The word *glĭmpse* (short *i*) is okay, but the syllable *glīmpse* (long *i*) is unacceptable. On the other hand, there are very few constraints between the onset and the rime. The combination of almost any legal onset with any legal rime results in a linguistically acceptable English syllable.[86]

The rules as to what is and is not acceptable in a language are the work of linguists. The way in which the rules are generated is essentially by reflecting on the frequencies with which the different kinds of sequences occur in a language. Where some sequences occur frequently and others not at all, there results a rule. Where no such pattern exists, there results none.

The linguists' early evidence for the distinction between onsets and rimes was, in other words, purely distributional. It was based on the relative frequencies of various sound patterns in the spoken language. Yet, in order to respond holistically to patterns that occur frequently and to dissociate patterns that do not, we do not need innate, response-specific sensors. The associational architecture of our minds is set up precisely to cluster and sort our perceptions on this sort of distributional data.

To illustrate, imagine how our recognition apparatus would respond to the word *drink*. In all probability, the initial /d/-/r/ sequence would be recognized as a familiar and tightly associated pattern, /dr/. After all, /r/ is virtually the only consonant sound that can follow an initial /d/, and it does so quite frequently.[87] Similarly, the syllable-final /ink/ should be remembered as a familiar, well-integrated pattern, as it too is both common and distinctive.

---

86. See Treiman (1988a, in press).

87. More generally, there are relatively few sequences of consonant sounds that can occur in syllable-initial position (e.g., *bl, br, cl, cr, dr, fr*), and each such sequence that can occur, does occur relatively frequently (Mayzner and Tresselt, 1965).

But what about the link between /dr/ and /ink/? The sound patterns that can follow /dr/ include many besides /ink/: *drain, drag, dream, dress, drip, drop, drove, drool, dry,* and *drown.* Similarly, the rime, /ink/, is preceded by many patterns besides /dr/: *stink, think, blink, rink, sink, mink, wink,* and *pink.* In view of this, the associative link between /dr/ and /ink/ cannot be preemptively strong; these units cannot hold together in any domineering way. No matter which way you traverse the link, the competitors are too many, too diverse, and too frequent.[88]

More generally, the linguists' basic observations that

1. there are only certain legal onsets,

2. there are only certain legal rimes, and

3. that virtually any legal onset can precede any legal rime,

probabilistically ensure that

1. the links among the sounds (or letters) of onsets will be sufficiently unique and strong to cause them to behave more or less as units,

2. the links among the sounds (or letters) of rimes will be sufficiently unique and strong to cause them to behave more or less as units, and

3. the links between onsets and rimes will be sufficiently diffuse to allow them to break apart easily, or relatively so.[89]

---

88. This argument, in obverse, could be offered for children's tendency to omit the second (and third) consonants of complex onsets. The fact is that with very few exceptions, the sequel to every initial consonant is more likely to be *any* vowel than even the most likely consonant. For this reason, one might expect a tendency for the indirect excitation passed between an initial consonant and its following vowel (or, equivalently, the relative strength of the association between the initial consonant and its following vowel) to dominate or override its link to any consonant that lies in between.

89. Of special interest here, Seidenberg and McClelland (1988) trained a computer simulation of their model to learn to read words through nothing more than repeated pairings of a large number of words and their pronunciations. In the training regimen, the computer was given no guidance as to how it should go about building useful associations among the letter units. It was instead given nothing more than ample associative potential and a simple learning rule: Increase strength when you see it, decrease otherwise. Nevertheless, as evidenced by both posttraining analyses of the its learned associations among letter units and its performance on pronunciation tests with novel pseudowords, the computer had become particularly attuned to the correspondence between spelling patterns and phonological rimes.

Naturalistic Evidence for Onsets and Rimes

Enough of my theoretical ruminations.[90] And for now at least, enough with the laboratory data as well. As expected—and as with those other "psychologically real" units, the phonemes and the subphonemic features—now that we know to look for onsets and rimes, their presence and influence are everywhere apparent.

In slips of the tongue, we swap onsets and rimes but leave each in itself intact. For example, stumbling over their words, people have been caught (by linguists) producing *carpsihord* for *harpsichord*, *aminal* for *animal*, *coat thrutting* for *throat cutting*, and *clamage dame* for *damage claim*.[91] Waiting too long to decide whether the better word is *solely* or *totally*, they produce *sotally*. Similarly they get *hinpede* from *hinder* and *impede*, *symblem* from *symbol* and *emblem*, and *shell* from *shout* and *yell*.[92] In none of these cases has the error broken an onset or a rime. More generally, MacKay, through an analysis of naturally occurring speech errors of this sort, has shown that it very rarely does.[93]

For purposes of abbreviating words, we tend to leave out *l*s and *r*s when they are part of a rime and noninitial vowels in general.[94] We also tend to append the word's terminal consonant, if it has one, to the end. Beyond that, however, we apparently to prefer to use whole syllables or whole onsets. Thus, we have *abb.* for *abbot* but *abbr.* for *abbreviation*; *Apr.* for *April* but *appl.* for *applied*, *chem.* for *chemistry* but *chm.* for *chairman*, *cap.* for *capital* and *capt.* for *captain*, and for *France, Greece, Spain* and *Sweden*, we have *Fr., Gr., Sp., Sw.* And wasn't it irritating when the U.S. Post Office changed the official abbreviations for all of the states?

When speaking Pig Latin, we tend to ick-stay together whole onsets rather than plit-say them.

Last, but hardly least, there is rhyme. If it were not for the salience and perceptual integrity of rimes, why should we respond so much more strongly to the similarities in *sassed, massed, last,* and *blast* than in, say, *sassed* and *missed, sand,* or *sauced*?

---

90. Although I do hope to convince you that our various perceptual systems are commonly organized in a powerful, efficient, and consistently understandable way.

91. These examples are taken from Clark and Clark (1977).

92. These examples are taken from MacKay (1972).

93. MacKay (1972).

94. Treiman (1984) has shown that *r*s and *l*s often behave more like vowels than consonants in the psychological structure of rimes.

Indeed, while sensitivity to rhyme seems to develop relatively early and easily,[95] sensitivity to onsets or alliteration does not.[96] The latter is especially interesting in view of the fact that productive use of phonemes (e.g., in blending and sounding out) seems, to the contrary, to begin with initial consonants.

Putting the evidence all together, it is tempting to speculate about the course through which phonemic awareness might most easily develop. It seems plausible that awareness of rimes might come from one's awareness of syllables and rhymes, that awareness of onsets might then come from awareness that there is more to syllables than rimes, and that awareness of onsets might be the key to awareness of phonemes.

The Instructional Prospects of Onsets and Rimes

And that brings us back to the major topic at hand. Onsets and rimes do indeed appear to be real psychological units, and that is exciting news toward the refinement of reading instruction. Exploitation of onsets and rimes could well provide the key to unlocking phonemic awareness (as opposed to prying it open, as we seem, at best, to do now). Onsets and rimes seem relatively accessible to preschoolers. By making them a focus of explicit attention, that critical step of isolating and recognizing phonemes might ensue much more tractably.

Treiman describes how this approach might proceed. After children had been taught to divide spoken words into syllables (and presumably spoken sentences into words), instruction on sound awareness would be coupled with spelling. Children would work first with words with simple and orthographically regular onsets and rhymes. More specifically, instructional modules might be organized around words with similarly spelled rimes, such as *bell*, *tell*, *sell*, and *fell*. Working, for example, with the word *bell*, the children would be led first to divide it into its onset, /b/, and its rime, /el/. They would then be helped to learn that the initial /b/ is spelled *b* while the final /el/ is spelled *ell*. More generally, rimes and onsets would be introduced as units, separable from each other but integral in themselves. Explaining the rationale, Treiman states:

Just as children in traditional phonics programs are not expected to deduce that *oy* is pronounced as /oi/ based on knowledge about the

---

95. Maclean, Bryant, and Bradley (1987); Morais, Bertelson, Cary, and Alegria (1986).

96. Stanovich, Cunningham, and Cramer (1984).

sounds of *o* and *y* (even though such a deduction is theoretically possible, given that /*oi*/ is a diphthong), children at this stage of the onset rime program are not expected to deduce that *ell* is pronounced as /*el*/.[97]

Because this argument applies equally to complex onsets, such as /*bl*/ and /*str*/, the children would be given explicit help in analyzing those as well. Finally, she suggests, correspondences between individual letters and phonemes would be developed only later and would proceed by having the children compare and contrast the onsets and rimes that they had already mastered.

Though offered from a new perspective, this is in many ways not a new proposal. The pedagogical utility of onsets and rimes has long been implicitly recognized. For example, the importance of affording direct attention and exercise to complex onsets is implicitly acknowledged in many of the consonant blending activities that appear in instructional materials and practices. Furthermore, sets of words with matching rimes, such as *bell, tell, sell*, and *fell*, are nothing more or less than "phonograms" or "word families." They have long been central components of a variety of approaches to instruction on word recognition.

The Visual Salience of Onsets and Rimes

Although our attention to the perceptual salience of onsets and rimes has thus far been focused on its implications for the acquisition of phonemic awareness, evidence suggests that these units may be equally influential in the acquisition and operation of printed word recognition skills.[98]

For example, in both word-nonword decision tasks and anagram tasks, adult readers have been shown to recognize one-syllable words more easily when the words are divided between their onsets and rimes than when they are divided elsewhere.[99] Santa has reported evidence that this is true even among second graders.[100] Further, as described earlier, Treiman found first and second graders to experience significantly more difficulty in sounding out printed pseudowords with complex onsets, like *smoo*, than ones composed of the same letters but simple onsets, like *soom* or *somo*.[101] And, most provocative of all in this domain may be a recent report by Goswami that low-readiness five and six

---

97. Treiman (1988b, p. 54).
98. And spelling skills too, as will be discussed in chapter 14.
99. Treiman and Chafetz (1987).
100. Santa (1976–1977).
101. Treiman (1985a).

year olds can occasionally, with no further instruction, induce the pronunciation of new words by analogy to another with the same rime (e.g., they could read *beak* given *peak*); these children could not, in contrast, make any use of matching spellings and sounds that did not correspond to rimes (e.g., they could not read *beak* given *bean*).[102]

More generally, rimes have been shown to be especially accessible in studies of children's decoding skills. Working with 230 children who were just finishing the first grade, Wylie and Durrell administered a multiple choice test, wherein the printed choices consisted of five rimes such as the following:

ack   ick   ock   eck   uck

In one condition, the children were instructed, for example, to "circle the one that says *ock*." In another condition, the children were instructed to "circle the one that has an /o/ in it." The children were far more successful in identifying the spellings of whole rimes than of individual vowel sounds.[103]

The Utility of Rimes in the Development of Vowel Generalizations

As we have seen, phonic generalizations about the pronunciations of individual vowels and vowel digraphs are frustratingly unreliable.[104] As it turns out, however, vowel sounds are generally quite stable within particular rimes. Even the "irregular" behaviors of vowel spellings are relatively rime specific; for example, the vowel digraph *ea* is quite consistently pronounced as long *e*, except in the rimes *-ear*, *-ead*, and *-eaf*.

In this context we may recall that, independent of any plan of its creators, the vowel pronunciations of Seidenberg and McClelland's computer simulation of word learning turned out to be highly sensitive to the spellings of rimes, but less so to onsets.[105] More important, the same seems true of children. Zinna, Liberman, and Shankweiler have shown that third graders' pronunciations of the vowel or vowels in monosyllabic pseudowords are strongly influenced by the identities of the syllable-final consonants—that is, by the rime as a whole. In

---

102. Goswami (1988, in press).
103. Wylie and Durrell (1970).
104. Clymer (1963).
105. Seidenberg and McClelland (1988); reviewed in chapter 6.

contrast, the children's vowel pronunciations were much less influenced by the spellings of the onsets that preceded them.[106]

The suggestion is that, in operation, memory depends on rimes for the phonological translation of vowels. This raises the question of whether rimes might provide a good vehicle for teaching children about such translations as well.

In support of this idea, Wylie and Durrell reported that children generally find it easy to learn to read words by use of "rhyming phonograms."[107] Indeed, in contrast to the difficulties and complexities of teaching vowel readings through individual spelling-sound correspondences and phonic generalizations, the children they studied seemed easily to learn phonograms, almost regardless of the nature of the vowels they contain. For example:

- Phonograms containing long vowels were learned as easily as phonograms containing short vowels.

- Long vowel phonograms spelled with "silent e" were not more difficult to learn than long vowel phonograms containing vowel digraphs.

- Phonograms containing vowel variants, including r-, l-, and w-controlled vowels, vowel digraphs, and vowel diphthongs, were nearly as easy to learn as those containing long and short vowel sounds.

- Phonograms containing just one syllable-final consonant were easier to learn than phonograms ending in consonant blends.

In further support of the utility of phonograms for beginning reading instruction, Wylie and Durrell pointed to their generalizability. More specifically, they reported that of a list of 286 rimes that appear in primary grade texts, the vowels in 272 (95 percent) are pronounced in the same way in every word in which they are found.[108] Moreover, these 272 stable rimes are contained in 1,437 of the words in Murphy's inventory of the speaking vocabularies of primary grade children.[109] Finally, Wiley and Durrell point out that nearly 500 primary grade words can be derived from a set of only 37 rimes:

–ack	–ail	–ain	–ake	–ale	–ame	–an
–ank	–ap	–ash	–at	–ate	–aw	–ay
–eat	–ell	–est	–ice	–ick	–ide	–ight
–ill	–in	–ine	–ing	–ink	–p	–ir

---

106. Zinna, Liberman, and Shankweiler (1986).
107. Wylie and Durrell (1970).
108. Durrell (1963, cited in Wylie and Durrell, 1970).
109. Murphy (1957).

–ock	*–oke*	*–op*	*–ore*	*–or*	*–uck*	*–ug*
–ump	*–unk*					

To appreciate the promise in these statistics more fully, we may compare them to the discouragingly low percentage utility of the vowel generalizations summarized by Clymer.[110] And again, whereas vowels, even single short vowels, are found to be especially difficult for children to decode in words,[111] the vowel sounds of phonograms are apparently relatively easy to learn to read—whether long, short, regular, "variant," or complex.

Other Instructional Considerations

The instructional implications and potential utilities of onsets and rimes extend beyond vowel generalizations. At the same time, as with any other instructional construct, onsets and rimes can be overdone and misused. Let us turn our attention to some of the other issues related to their implementation.

First, the very mention of phonograms or word families will, for some, raise memories of the so-called "linguistic" programs for beginning reading and of such notorious text offerings as:

The pan is on the van. The cat can bat the pan. Dan can pat the cat. . . .[112]

The motivation for including such text in primers has been to reinforce, through repetition, the spelling patterns and contrasts that it contains. Yet, even while applauding this motivation, we may criticize its realization.

In particular, exercise of phonograms can be overdone in connected text. When minimal contrast and repetition is carried to such extremes, the effect seems not to be one of strengthening the patterns of the individual words but of allowing them to break apart and become confused with one another in the reader's mind.[113] Research has shown that text that is composed of high proportions of orthographically and phonologically similar words is inordinately difficult to process.[114] Even when read silently by skillful readers, such texts produce the disruptiveness of tongue twisters.

---

110. Clymer (1963).

111. Liberman (1973).

112. From Fries, Fries, Wilson, and Rudolph (1966, cited in Chall, 1967).

113. Petrick and Potter (1979, cited in Perfetti, 1985).

114. Baddeley and Lewis (1981); Perfetti and McCutcheon (1982, cited in Perfetti, 1985).

A second reservation toward the linguistic programs relates to their oft-taken stance that spelling-sound correspondences and phonic generalizations are best acquired through induction—that sufficient repetition of any particular spelling pattern is enough to establish the phonemic significance of its letters.[115] To the contrary, for the child who is having trouble segmenting the sounds of words, some explicit guidance and instruction is invaluable. Moreover, word families and phonograms offer certain definite advantages toward providing the same.

For example, we have seen that children experience extra difficulty in sounding final, as compared with initial, consonants of syllables.[116] We have also seen that in programs of individual letter-sound instruction, final consonant sounds are given but secondary attention. In contrast, instruction that is methodically structured about onsets and rimes should inherently distinguish initial from final sounds and spellings of consonants and consonant clusters.

As another example, young readers' special difficulties with blending have been underscored in our reviews of children's phonological awareness and decoding difficulties[117] and will arise again when we examine their spelling errors.[118] Meanwhile, the value of direct instruction on blending was pointed up in our reviews of program comparison studies.[119] As the literature on onsets and rimes helps us to understand the nature of these difficulties, it also gives us guidance toward helping children to conquer them.

More specifically, the research on onsets and rimes divides blending difficulties into three different categories, corresponding to (1) the psychological difficulty of analyzing rimes into their component phonemes, (2) the awareness that different onsets can be spliced onto the same rime to make different words, and (3) the psychological difficulty of analyzing complex onsets into individual phonemes. As Treiman suggested, phonograms offer a means of methodically approaching each of these problems.

Refining her suggestion, one might want to begin with an onset-free rime composed of a single short vowel and a single final consonant. For illustration, let us choose *at*. With *at* on display, it might be explained that the *a* says /a/ and the *t* says /t/, and the

---

115. See Aukerman (1971; 1984).

116. Daniels and Diack (1956); Liberman (1973); Weber (1970).

117. See this chapter and chapter 4.

118. See chapter 14.

119. See chapter 3.

children would be encouraged to produce these individual sounds and blend them together to the teacher's choreography.

Next, a consonant would be added to the beginning of the syllable, say *s*. The children would learn first to sound and then to blend the new consonant with the rime of the phonogram, producing *sat*. Repeating the process with a sampling of single consonant onsets, the children might eventually be led to read or write *at, sat, fat, rat, mat, hat, pat, bat, that*. Each new word might thus be discovered by sounding the onset and then the rime, in sequence. Only after such patterns had been comfortably mastered would instruction be extended to the sounding and blending of initial consonant clusters—the observant instructor may be surprised at how difficult *scat* and *brat* are even given solid knowledge of *cat* and *bat*.

Where children have difficulty with an onset, they may initially pause before producing its rime. However, if they are to pause within a syllable, this may be an optimal place to do it: As coherent psychological units in themselves, the onset and rime are relatively easy to remember and to splice back together.

Yet another advantage of exploiting phonograms in decoding instruction is that they provide a means of introducing and exercising many printed words with relative efficiency, and this, as we have seen, is in marked contrast to the slowness with which words can be developed through individual letter-sound correspondences. Again, this advantage has long been recognized in many instructional programs.

In table 12.1, listed in order from top to bottom, are the first forty-eight words presented in each of four different "code-emphasis" reading programs. Within each program, the majority of the words presented are phonograms of at least one other word on the list. In discussing this pattern, Willows, Borwick, and Hayvren point out:

Because symbol-sound correspondences are paramount in code-emphasis programs, these correspondences should require repetition rather than any particular words, the mastery of symbol-sound correspondences being better served by the use of a wide variety of words [in which these correspondences occur].[120]

In other words, a prevalence of phonograms may be expected within code-emphasis curricula regardless of whether phonograms are otherwise methodically exercised or even explicitly acknowledged within their instructional agenda. The determining

---

120. Willows, Borwick, and Hayvren (1981, p. 102).

Table 12.1

First words presented in four code-emphasis programs.

Program A[a]	Program B[a]	Program C[b]	Program D[b]
cat	Sam	an	am
fat	sit	Ann	I
Nat	Tim	ran	ran
is	this	Dan	mat
a	is	dad	the
sat	Matt	add	that
on	it	and	see
mat	mitt	run	and
Pat	at	mud	at
the	bat	mad	Sam
hat	Jim	man	tam
not	hit	am	sat
look	Tam	ram	rat
at	has	drum	look
bat	the	Pam	saw
man	Tip	pan	said
ran	habit	pad	Al
Dan	a	up	Sal
fan	Pam	pup	tan
to	stamp	map	an
pan	jam	nap	ant
van	mat	rap	fat
lap	bath	pump	fan
nap	Pat	ramp	Bob
cap	rat	the	bat
tap	Miss	did	bam
map	Smith	in	rob
bad	ham	rid	not
he	that	mid	on
had	bit	rip	lot
Dad	trap	dip	Tom
sad	Nan	dim	man
mad	Tab	rim	hat
Sam	man	pin	hal
in	in	drip	do
ham	snap	Sid	is
am	spit	sip	yes
jam	hat	sad	has
bag	nap	Sam	hog
tag	mast	sun	log
and	his	sand	fog
wag	pants	us	bog
rag	rip	Russ	this
dig	Cam	miss	In
bit	camp	pass	Tag
fit	path	is	rag
for	trap	as	bag
it	rabbit	runs	so

a. From Willows et al. (1981, p. 101).
b. From Carnine and Silbert (1979, p. 166).

Table 12.2
First words presented in five meaning-emphasis programs.

Program E[a]	Program F[a]	Program G[a]	Program H[b]	Program I[b]
is	Bill	girl	funny	Mr.
in	Lad	man	face	Mugs
the	runs	dog	the	Pat
will	hides	horse	Mother	Curt
go	Jill	the	look	Mommy
I	and	is	in	Daddy
to	go	on	mirror	look
on	I	not	make	a
and	am	boy	a	jet
it	rides	puppy	Father	here
not	run	and	at	come
you	hide	find	lunch	it
get	can	likes	girl	my
Jill	this	baby	want	pet
Andy	yes	sandwich	lemon	I
help	no	thumb	for	can
cat	is	man	is	surprise
truck	here	cake	not	Tiger
can	not	pie	good	is
see	duck	cherries	gum	dog
come	get	bed	fox	love
stop	Ben	eating	ate	see
here	Ted	shells	made	thank
where	Nan	people	monkey	you
its	look	look	goat	for
rocket	at	car	red	on
are	said	cat	boot	run
bus	park	sun	rain	fast
tiger	the	rainbow	boy	get
have	will	red	his	ball
this	like	apples	under	what
me	to	horse	bed	forget
with	we	duck	one	play
tigers	help	pig	rug	Jan
zoo	are	saw	has	oh
want	stop	ran	two	turtle
can't	heres	house	put	the
real	it	children	on	raccoon
going	eat	woman	now	and
am	you	orange	can	frog
I'm	can't	tree	go	like
wants	helps	lots	out	this
fish	me	of	seed	pretty
school	with	got	I	fun
sick	we'll	ate	have	outdoors
fishing	I'll	big	six	green
day	what	little	ten	Mrs.
today	come	potato	here	White

a. From Carnine and Silbert (1979, p. 166).
b. From Willows et al. (1981, p. 101).

advantage, continue Willows, Borwick, and Hayvren, is that introduction of words with similar spelling-sound correspondences allows for more unique whole words to be introduced more rapidly "since, in the [code-emphasis programs], words are grouped according to phonemic patterns and thus (it is assumed) would not have to be learned individually."[121]

For comparison, the first forty-eight words from several meaning-emphasis programs are displayed in table 12.2. In each of these lists we see a broad variety of spelling-sound correspondences, and phonograms appear more as the exception than the rule. Willow, Borwick, and Hayvren suggest again that this is to be expected:

The vocabularies of these programs are selected to be "high frequency words and words that are likely to be in the child's experiential store" (Beck, 1981) and they are not constrained by spelling-sound correspondences.

But they continue:

Since the vocabulary in basal programs is selected with little or no concern for symbol-sound correspondences, the usefulness of "phonics cues" (irrespective of how much instructional emphasis is placed on them) will be quite limited and the child will be forced to rely on less dependable cues such as word shapes, initial letters, and pictures. As a consequence, one might expect that in basal programs children would have to learn many words through sheer memorization of the visual form, and thus, repetition of the same words would seem to be essential for this learning to occur.[122]

Roswell and Natchez place work with phonograms in the category of "rudimentary phonics."[123] As they point out, it affords only limited independence in word analysis. Nevertheless, through their work on the diagnosis and treatment of children with reading difficulties, they have found phonograms to provide a useful bridge toward the levels of phonemic and orthographic awareness upon which skillful reading depends. And that, after all, is what we were looking for.

Phonograms offer a means of helping children not just to analyze the sounds of syllables but to work from syllables to phonemes in a psychologically stepwise and thus more supportive, manner. They offer a means of teaching children not just letter-

---

121. Willows, Borwick, and Hayvren (1981, p. 102).

122. Willows, Borwick, and Hayvren (1981, p. 102).

123. Roswell and Natchez (1971).

sound correspondences but letter-sound correspondences as conditioned by the letter's position in a syllable and its larger orthographic environment. They offer a means of teaching children not just spelling patterns but spelling patterns that correspond to frequent, coherent, syllabic units. As argued throughout this book, syllable-level spelling patterns are extremely important for the Orthographic processor to acquire.

Moreover, toward developing skillful word recognition, the establishment of phonemic awareness and spelling-sound mappings are among the most critical and nettlesome challenges. Although the final verdict awaits further research, onsets and rimes may well offer easier paths toward both. Through explicit attention to these units, we might simultaneously improve teaching methods, increase our understanding of our teaching methods, and support and extend our students' linguistic intuitions and learning strategies in invaluable ways.

Putting It All Together

The basic units of representation in text are printed words and graphemes. Before children can acquire a productive understanding of the significance of these units, they must acquire an awareness of their oral correspondents: spoken words and phonemes. Yet it seems that awareness of neither comes naturally.

Though not natural, awareness of words seems to come quite easily. Several researchers have suggested that the key to the development of word awareness may lie in the child's exposure to print.[124] More specifically, it may derive from the observation that written words are represented as discrete units—as wholes unto themselves and physically separate from each other.[125]

In contrast, the development of phonemic awareness is often slow and difficult. Among those children who will successfully learn to read but are not sensitive to phonemes before reading instruction is begun, phonemic awareness seems to develop alongside their word recognition skills.[126] On the other hand, an absence or lack of phonemic awareness appears to be characteristic of children who are failing or have failed to learn to read.[127]

---

124.   Ehri (1976); Lomax and McGee (1987).
125.   Ehri (1976).
126.   Tunmer and Nesdale (1985).
127.   Rozin, Poritzky, & Sotsky (1971); Stanovich (1986, 1988).

Although phonemic awareness is not spontaneously acquired, it can be successfully taught. Furthermore, when reading instruction is methodically coupled with such training, the success rates are dramatic. Some examples worthy of special attention include Michael and Lise Wallach's program with low-readiness first graders from Chicago's South Side,[128] Joanna Williams's program with Title I students from Harlem and the Lower East Side of New York City,[129] and Benita Blachman's program in two inner city schools in New Haven, Connecticut.[130]

Blachman's data are particularly inspiring. Instead of setting up matched groups of experimental and control students, she redesigned the reading curricula for two whole schools. Through workshops, the teachers were led to consider the importance of helping the children to understand the relationships between speech and orthography, with special emphasis on the difficulties and importance of phonemes. In addition, with Blachman's guidance, they worked out a series of thirty-minute lesson plans designed to develop the children's awareness of individual words, syllables, and phonemes and to build their knowledge of print on that understanding.[131]

In one school, the program was administered to one half of all children in grades 1 and 2, extending to those in grade 3 "if needed." In the second school, it was administered to all children in grades 1 and 2. Regular classroom teachers, reading teachers, and special education teachers were all involved in this project, and all three groups reportedly found that, "in speaking the same language" to each other and the students, their partnerships, effectiveness, and efficiency felt much improved.[132]

At the same time, there resulted an enormous improvement in the children's reading proficiency. Before Blachman intervened, fourth-grade achievement scores in the first of these schools were seven months below national norms; in the second of the schools, they were a full year below national norms. In contrast, when the first cohorts of Blachman's students reached fourth grade, they were reading seven and six months above national norms, respectively.

---

128. Wallach and Wallach (1979).

129. Williams (1979, 1980).

130. Blachman (1987).

131. Many of these activities are described in Liberman and Shankweiler (1979); Liberman, Shankweiler, Blachman, Camp, and Werfelman (1980).

132. Blachman (1987, p. 53).

Follow-up data from the second school (the one that had had worse reading problems before intervention) showed that in the fifth grade, reading achievement scores were still nearly a year above national norms. Furthermore, compared with other schools in the New Haven system, the overall reading achievement of this school had moved from a rank of 17.5 out of 24 before intervention to a rank of 5 out of 24. The reading scores and school rank for the next year's class were similar. Indeed, the only schools that ranked higher in reading achievement were those that also ranked at the top of the city's socioeconomic status distribution.

Now, in each of Blachman's, Williams's, and the Wallachs' programs, instruction on linguistic awareness was coupled with instruction on reading. It could be, therefore, that their results reflect something special about their reading instruction rather than their emphasis on analyzing the sound structure of spoken language.

Although there were certain outstanding aspects of each of these reading programs and their implementations, this seems not be the entire explanation. Lundberg, Frost, and Petersen have recently reported the results of a program to develop phonological awareness among preschool children.[133] Over the course of the school year, these children were engaged in a variety of games and activities involving nursery rhymes, rhymed stories, and rhyme production; segmentation of sentences into individual words and investigations of word length; clapping and dancing to syllabic rhythms and solving puzzles posed by a "troll" who could speak only in a syllable-by-syllable manner; and, finally, isolation and identification of word-initial phonemes and then of word-final and -internal phonemes. (Again we see the onset-rime intuition at work.)

This program was not about reading, writing, or language comprehension. Its purpose was to develop phonological awareness. Consistent with this, year-end (May) measures showed the children who participated in the program to be indistinguishable from a control group in either letter knowledge or higher-order language comprehension. On the other hand, the experimental children were significantly superior to their controls on a battery of tests designed to assess sensitivity to rhymes, syllables, phonemes, and word lengths. Within this battery, it was differences in phonemic awareness that were most pronounced.

---

133. Lundberg, Frost, and Petersen (1988).

The experimental and control children were again compared in grade one, but this time on printed word recognition, spelling, mathematics, and a nonverbal IQ test (Raven's Progressive Matrices).[134] The control children slightly outperformed the experimentals on both the math and IQ tests.[135] However, the experimental children outperformed the controls on both the word recognition and the spelling test. Retesting in the second grade showed further that the experimental children's advantage over the controls by these measures remained as great or even increased.[136]

The evidence is compelling: Toward the goal of efficient and effective reading instruction, explicit training of phonemic awareness is invaluable. The path to phonemic awareness is stepwise, beginning with children's awareness of spoken words, then syllables, and the next best steps may well be rimes and onsets. More direct research on the predictive and instructional utility of onsets and rimes will no doubt be forthcoming very soon.

To this high point, I must still add a note of caution. A new trend is developing amid many well-intentioned school communities in our country. Kindergartners are being given tests of phonemic awareness, and those who flunk are being held back from first grade. This trend is disturbing on two points.

First, the key to phonemic awareness seems to lie more in training than in age or maturation. If these children have not received the proper exposure to print and sound in either their homes or their kindergarten classrooms by age five and a half, what is there to suggest that they will by the time they are six and a half?

Second, short of its explicit training, the activities that seem to lead most strongly to the development of phonemic awareness are those involved in learning how to read and spell. Thus, in keeping a child back to "wait" for phonemic awareness to develop, we hold them back from what may be, to that point in their lives, the best opportunity to allow it to develop. On the other side of this coin, of course, is the risk these children may be

---

134. Remember that the phonological awareness program had terminated in May of the preceding year.

135. The school system in which the control children were enrolled had historically outscored that of experimental children on standardized tests in general.

136. Although the difference in the children's spelling scores was significant in both first and second grade, the difference in word recognition scores did not reach statistical significance until the second grade.

too underprepared to catch on in the course of normal first-grade reading instruction. By evidence, if they do not catch on to the concept and nature of phonemes, they will fail at reading—and that is too great a tragedy to gamble with.

Yet there would seem to be an easy escape from this dilemma: Specifically, why not suggest that all of our schools incorporate linguistic awareness games and activities into the standard kindergarten and preschool curricula?[137]

---

137. Such as those developed by Elkonin (1973), Liberman, Shankweiler, Blachman, Camp, and Werfelman (1980), and Lundberg, Frost, and Petersen (1988).

13

Learning about Print:
The First Steps

We have seen again and again that skillful reading depends
critically on the speed and completeness with which words can be
identified from their visual forms. Yet, for the beginning reader,
it is visual word recognition skills, it is the knowledge that
makes the Orthographic processor work and links it to the rest of
the system, that are uniquely absent.

Acquisition of these skills depends in part on the child's
conscious awareness of the phonological structure of speech. It
depends equally on conscious awareness of the nature of print. No
matter the child's level of phonemic awareness, to make use of it
she or he must learn the visual identities of the individual
letters. No matter the child's sureness with individual letters or
their sounds, such knowledge can be productive only given an
awareness that words consist of strings of letters and print of
strings of words. But not even word awareness is enough. Linking
up the system as a whole, building both to it and from it, depends
on the child's possessing certain expectations and understandings
about the basic structure and functions of print.

Becoming Aware of the Nature of Print

As it is used in the literature, "print awareness" is sometimes
extended to include phonological awareness, letter recognition,
word recognition, and various levels of sound-symbol appreciation.
These sorts of relatively sophisticated and analytical knowledge
about print are discussed under their own headings. What is at
issue here are certain basic insights and observations about the
forms and functions of print.

From the Child's Vantage Point

Little ones seem spontaneously to do things that amuse us and make us proud, such as intuiting that an occasion calls for an especially pretty dress or politely shaking hands and saying, "It's nice to meet you," to their grandmother's friends. And they seem spontaneously to know things that drive us crazy, such as what kinds of packages are likely to contain candy—even kinds of candy we know they have never seen before.

Of course, none of this is really spontaneous; young children are shrewd observers. They watch, they learn, they make generalizations and distinctions with respect to just about everything in their worlds. And for children who grow up in a print-rich environment, that includes print. What are some of the things they seem to learn about print?

At some point, children must gain the insight that *print is categorically different from other kinds of visual patterns in their environment*. In some vague but characteristic way, it is visually distinct from other sorts of pictures and patterns. On each occurrence, what it looks like, more than anything else, is other print. And though it seems iconically inscrutable—it contains no familiar, legible pictorial information—adults, quite mysteriously, can extract meaning from it.

However it works, *print is print across any of a variety of physical media*. It can appear on paper, fabric, television screens, signs, boxes, and walls. It can be colorful or black and white; there can be lots and lots or just a little; it can be accompanied with lots of pictures or none at all. It can be formed of ink or paint, plastic letters, electronic lights, or finger marks in dirt. Sometimes it is made by hand, sometimes obviously not. However it is made and wherever it occurs, it still seems to be print.

Once you notice it, *print seems to be all over the place*—not just in books and on newspapers, but on storefronts, trucks, envelopes, cookies, coins, tickets, boxes, bottles, cans, signs, and household appliances. It appears at the beginnings and ends of your television shows (that is how you know they are over) and on the ads in between (that is when you are afraid they are over). It is inside your clothes and outside your shoes. It is even stamped on the backs of your dolls' necks and on the tops of your blocks.

Different samples of print are used by adults in different ways. They read picture books aloud to you but newspapers and no-picture books to themselves. They read signs, labels, and tags in stores, and they announce decisions when they are done. And there is lots of print that they seem to ignore, but they will tell you what it says if you ask them to. And someplace in here, the child must induce that *print symbolizes language.*

There appear, moreover, to be different categories of printed materials, each with their own characteristic appearances and uses. Besides books, magazines, and newspapers, there are signs, labels, instructions, telephone books, lists, price tags, and menus. There is print of the outsides of envelopes and print on the insides: party invitations, cards from your grandparents, and who-knows-what in the grown-ups' envelopes.

And *print holds information:* the stories in your books, the grocery list, the instructions to your toys, the flavors of ice cream that can be had, the messages on your cards, your friend's telephone number, the time of the movie, whether there is anything good on TV, whether you have to take a sweater, and the note from your teacher (when you were so glad that she didn't say anything before you left).

Finally, *print can be produced by anyone.* There are pencils, pens, crayons, and markers that you can do it with, though it is strongly preferred that you do it on paper. Grown-ups are pleased when you write, though they can't always read it. There seems to be more to producing it than might appear.

From Our Vantage Point

In a print-rich environment, children quite visibly acquire such insights about print. Many little ones go through a stage of gleefully pointing out "ABC's" wherever they see letters. They sit with books, often upside down, leafing through the pages as they talk aloud. They make you feel silly as they imitate the exaggerated intonation and funny voices with which you read stories to them. You nail them for bouncing off the walls at an inappropriate time or place, and they disarm you with some semiliterary retort like, "I was just running away with my imagination."

They eagerly participate in turning the pages while you are reading aloud and forever desist from turning them too early when only once you've barked at them. They tease you by putting their hand over the print while you are reading—but not too many times because they don't want you to stop. In just a few years, they become quite sophisticated about storybooks. To your relief and gratification, they become quite reliable at choosing a *short* book when you insist. To your sometimes disgruntlement, they also become quite good at noticing when you have cheated and skipped a page while reading.

They ask you to read things that open, like menus, and things with pictures, like catalogs, brochures, and cartoons in the funny paper. They want to open envelopes for you to see if there is anything good inside. They insist that you read the instructions for their toys, even when you tell them that you did and that the information was not there. They argue with their friends about what print "says." They tell you, with firm authority, that it's a diplodocus and not a brontosaurus because their preschool teacher showed them in a *book*.

They scribble and make letterlike forms and tell you what it "says." They want to use your pens instead of their crayons. They are delighted to make letters with a typewriter or a computer. They learn that letters and numbers are different from each other. They arduously but proudly try to learn to print.

Summary: Print Awareness

Beginning with Dolores Durkin's classic study of early readers,[1] there exist a number of case studies, chronologies and descriptions of prereaders' growing understanding of the nature and uses of print.[2] Each of these works is reflective, insightful, very engaging, and comes wholly recommended.

Stories about the blossoming of print awareness in preschool children are for many of us as familiar as they are enchanting. Such development, however, does not occur in a vacuum. It depends on growing up in an environment where print is important. It depends on an environment where interactions with print are a source of social and intellectual pleasure for the individual children and the people who surround them. It thrives on pride and affection and develops only through extensive experience.[3]

As discussed earlier, the typical American child enjoys many hundreds of hours of storybook reading and several thousand hours of overall literacy support during her or his preschool years.[4] But there are also pockets of children who receive only a few minutes of storybook reading per year. There are pockets of children who grow up with little tutelage in literacy or encouragement toward

---

1. Durkin (1966).

2. For example, see Baghban (1984); Bissex (1980); Snow (1983). In addition, a number of interesting papers on this topic have been collected in Teale and Sulzby (1986).

3. See, for example, Durkin (1966); Ferriero (1986); Flood (1977); Flood and Lapp (1981); McCormick and Mason (1986); Snow (1983); Wiseman (1980).

4. See chapter 4.

it, without exposure to grown-ups who like to read, without papers and pencils and books to fool with. How much will these children learn about print in their preschool years?

Research indicates that many youngsters approach school having learned very little. For example, they know not even what a letter or word is, much less how to read one. They know not even that print reads left to right, much less that it transcodes words and sentences. They know not even the front from the back of a book, much less that its print is meant to convey meaning.[5] Yet, the very prospect of learning or understanding in the classroom depends on prior establishment of the relationships that will be presumed and prior expectations about those that will need be constructed.

In discussing such difficulties, John Downing avers:

To an adult, this problem may seem so simple that it is hardly worth troubling about. Yet the research evidence leads to a quite contrary conclusion. Understanding of the functions of reading and writing is of crucial importance and it is not acquired easily. Probably the most important single fact about the process of reading is that the purpose of the reading act is inextricably interwoven in its technique. In other words, the ends are an integral part of the means.[6]

The importance of prereaders' awareness of print is more and more being recognized, thanks largely to the work and writings of Marie Clay and John Downing.[7] Such global awareness of the forms, functions, and uses of print provides not just the motivation but the basic conceptual backdrop against which reading and writing may best be learned.

Children's performance on tests designed to measure such print awareness[8] is found to predict future reading achievement[9] and to be strongly correlated with other, more traditional measures of reading readiness and achievement.[10] More than that, analyses of the interdependencies among measures of reading readiness and achievement indicate that such basic knowledge about print

---

5. Clay (1972, 1976); Downing, Ollila, and Oliver (1975, 1977); Reid (1966); Vygotsky (1962).

6. Downing (1979, p. 12).

7. See, for example, Clay (1972, 1979b); Downing (1979).

8. Among these tests are Downing, Ayers, and Schaeffer (1984), Blum, Evans, and Taylor (1980), and Clay (1979a).

9. Tunmer, Herriman, and Nesdale (1988); Wells (1985).

10. Clay (1979b); Johns (1980); Lomax and McGee (1987).

generally precedes and appears to serve as the very foundation on which orthographic and phonological skills are built.[11]

Becoming Aware of Words in Print

As discussed in the last chapter, conscious appreciation of the isolable existence of individual words seems not to arise spontaneously among children. Nor is it something that we regularly teach in any explicit or methodical way. Still, most children must catch on at some point, or they would never master print. The ability to recover words as individually speakable, printable, and understandable linguistic units is critical not just to learning spelling-sound correspondences but, even before that, to gaining any initial insight into how our written language works.

Indeed, it may well be through interest in print that most do catch on.[12] Given the ease with which children can learn to segment language into individual words when required to do so, this explanation seems quite credible. Print maps to speech, word by word, with little spaces in between. For many, awareness of this mapping may be all that is needed to provoke awareness of words.

Yet here may be a source of concern: When children are left to catch on to an idea by their own devices, who knows what parts of it they'll catch? Children, quite uncontrollably, think. Thus even for so simple a concept as this, their misunderstandings can be quite elaborate. For a child who has already had the insight that separate words are separable words, the function of that extra, blank space between them in print may well be self-evident.[13] For children who have not, however, that extra space may not be enough to tip them off.

Evidence in point has been provided by Meltzer and Herse.[14] The children with whom they worked had been in the first grade for only a few months. Although the idea that individual printed words are separated from each other by extra space had not been mentioned, the children had been reading connected text. Moreover, the emphasis of their reading program was on vocabulary and sentence control.

---

11. Lomax and McGee (1987).
12. Ehri (1976, 1979).
13. See Holden and MacGinitie (1972).
14. Meltzer and Herse (1969). See also Mickish (1974).

Had the children discovered the word boundary convention on their own? To find out, Meltzer and Herse printed up sentences on long strips of paper, purposefully exaggerating the amount of space between words. For each of these sentences, the children were asked to count and point to each of the words it contained. Then they were asked either to draw a circle around each separate word or to cut the sentence into single word pieces with a pair of scissors.

Some of the children seemed to misunderstand either the task or the concept of a word altogether, segmenting the sentences into individual letters. The behaviors of others, however, were more troubling. Some regularly formed groups of multiple letters but did so irrespective of the between-print spaces. Some usually broke the sentence at between-print spaces but not if the words were very short (in which case they were combined despite the space between them) or especially long (in which case they were divided despite the absence of any extra space between them). And some used a combination of between-print space and tall letters to place their boundaries.

It seems not that the children had not been thinking or paying attention during their reading lessons. For example, the notion that words should not be more than so many letters in length was entirely consistent with the sample of words they had been taught to read so far. Further, the "tall letter" heuristic appeared to reflect relatively keen inductive learning. On examining the children's primers, Meltzer and Herse found that many of the words began or ended with tall letters. Invariably, the first word of a sentence of connected text began with a tall (uppercase) letter. In many primers, the first word of each line of text begins with an uppercase letter, perhaps making this misleading correspondence between tall letters and word boundaries especially salient.

In the end, the nearly-but-not-quite-obvious nature and function of individual words seems more a reason to teach than not to teach it. Moreover, training of word awareness seems another ideal candidate for the kindergarten or preschool curriculum.

Lundberg, Frost, and Petersen included sentence segmentation games in the first month of their preschool curriculum.[15] Others have successfully used picture cards or, effectively, logograms, in training word awareness. Both problem readers and children as young as three years of age are quite readily able to "read"

---

15. Lundberg, Frost, and Petersen (1988). Note that because of the grade-school schedule in Denmark, their preschoolers were six years old.

sentences made from strings of picture cards.[16] Further, by playing with the orders and combinations of the cards—or, better yet, letting the children do so—the activity can be extended to explore the meanings and functions of words as well as their segmentability.[17]

Once the children have become attuned to words, it should be relatively easy to show them that those patches of ink between the spaces in print are the very units they have been isolating their speech. To ensure that the children understand that this convention of extra space between words is one that holds for print in general rather than, say, one that works only on the school blackboard, it is also probably a good idea to point to the words in their storybooks as you read them aloud.[18]

In their successful preschool program on linguistic awareness, Lundberg and his colleagues also included activities designed to allow investigation of word length.[19] Exploring and contrasting the lengths of printed words may serve several different purposes. First, it should help to clarify the difference between syllables and words and thereby perhaps to hasten the insight that a printed word, when recognized, should be meaningful. Second, it could help to seed awareness of those short function words whose status proves so elusive to children. Third, it might nip in the bud that common first-grade notion that all words should be about three to five letters in length. Finally, it is a way of showing the children that words that take longer to say, look longer in print; Rozin and his colleagues have pointed out that this correspondence in length reflects "the basic relationship between speech and [alphabetic or syllabic] writing."[20]

Rozin, Bressman, and Taft have shown that an awareness of this relation between the spoken and printed lengths of words is a strong separator of reading-ready and -unready youngsters.[21] The children in their study were shown printed pairs of very long and very short words such as *mow* and *motorcycle*. As they examined the word pairs, they were told, "One of these words is *mow*. The

---

16. Farnham-Diggory (1967); Hall, Salvi, Seggev, and Caldwell (1970).

17. For a description of this approach with low-readiness first graders, see Rozin and Gleitman (1977).

18. Clay (1966, cited in Calfee and Drum, 1978) found pointing to written words while reading to be a necessary step toward learning to match print to speech.

19. Lundberg , Frost, and Petersen (1988).

20. Rozin, Bressman, and Taft (1974).

21. Rozin, Bressman, and Taft (1974).

other one is *motorcycle."* Then they were asked,"Which one is *mow?'*

Among the suburban kindergartners who were tested, 43 percent chose correctly on at least seven of the eight pairs presented. In contrast, only 10 percent of a group of inner-city kindergartners reached this criterion. Even at the end of first grade, only 48 percent of the inner-city children could pass the test; at the end of second grade, only 60 percent of them could do so.

In passing, I point out that many of Dr. Seuss's books are ready-made for developing word awareness. Dr. Seuss has been so insightful as to "design" the print in some of his books rather than just typesetting it. In particular, it is often the very word that he has led the children to anticipate—the one that they can supply if you stop and request it—that he has made graphically distinct. If you give the kids time to voice these words, his print is ready to answer: There is the word; it is large, colorful, and right in the middle of the page. In addition, Dr. Seuss has a wonderful flair for playing with word length, e.g., "*Z* is for *zyzzer-zazzer-zuzz*," that seems unfailingly to tickle his young audience.[22] Although "Sesame Street" currently carries few modules to illustrate the importance of word length and between-word spaces, these topics seem like naturals for their animators and puppeteers; we may hope that they develop more such material in the near future.

Becoming Aware that Printed Words Consist of Letters

Children are surrounded by print in our society. It is not just inside their storybooks but in ways that are bigger, brighter, and often of more immediate interest, it is also stamped, blazoned, posted, and hung all over the ads and boxes for toys, the outsides of stores, and the labels for foods. Attention to such environmental print, it is argued, could well be the critical first step toward reading, the step that provides children with both the understanding and incentive necessary for approaching the decontextualized print of books.[23]

Preschoolers commonly do seem to recognize a variety of the environmental print that they encounter day to day. Goodman reports that when shown familiar environmental print, such as

---

22. From *Dr. Seuss's ABC*.

23. Hall (1987); Harste, Burke, and Woodward (1982); Goodman (1986); Goodman and Goodman (1979).

cereal boxes, toothpaste cartons, STOP signs, and soft drink logos, 60 percent of the three year olds tested could "read" it, as could 80 percent of the five year olds.[24] As another example, Masonheimer and her colleagues found that, shown a color photograph of a McDonald's™ restaurant, fully 92 percent of the two through five year olds they asked could "read" it.[25]

There is, of course, a big "but" that must be appended to these statistics. First, in neither of these studies were the children constrained to literal readings of the labels. It was counted as correct, for example, if they said "toothpaste" when shown a carton of Crest™, "crayons" when shown a box of Crayolas™, or even "Burger King™" when shown a picture of McDonald's™. Head counts, such as those described above, make clear that many children come to recognize such labels and logos, at least in terms of personal significance. Yet such labels and logos bring with them a complex array of visual and contextual cues. To what extent is their recognition influenced by the print they bear?

The answer, for most prereaders, seems to be "not much." When the print, complete with color and stylized type, is removed from its normal visual context—say, by cutting the word "Crest" off its box, the number of four and five year olds who can recognize it drops precipitously.[26] When, further, the characteristic shape and color of the print is replaced with neutral, manuscript type, signs of recognition may all but vanish.[27] If the characteristically colored and stylized print is placed in a misleading context, e.g., if *Coca Cola*™ is pasted on a Rice Krispies™ box, many preschoolers (nearly half of those tested) suggest that it says "Rice Krispies."[28]

All of the above suggests that in preschoolers' "reading" of environmental print, it is more the environment than the print that is providing the cues. Still, it is plausible that with repeated exposure to such print, along with the understanding that it is a label, children will learn to separate it from its nonprint context. Once having focused their attention on the words, it may well become obvious that each is composed of a string of individual characters. And turning their attention to these individual characters, the notational system should become

24. Goodman (1986).

25. Masonheimer, Drum, and Ehri (1984).

26. Goodman (1986).

27. Harste, Burke, and Woodward (1982).

28. Dewitz and Stammer (1980, cited in Masonheimer, Drum, and Ehri, 1984).

apparent through basic principles of learning. There are, after all, only twenty-six characters in all. Moreover, just a few of these twenty-six occur all but everywhere: The five primary vowels, *a, e, i, o,* and *u,* account for nearly four of every ten letters in text. If the child is attending to the print, then one might expect the learning of letters to ensue through their sheer repetition

The way to find out would be to gather a group of children who were very attentive to signs and labels and to assess their knowledge of the print on signs and labels that they knew well. To the extent that the hypothesis were true, most of these children should have learned something about the letters on at least some of the signs they had studied.

With this in mind, Masonheimer, Drum, and Ehri surveyed 228 children, aged two to five years, to establish a set of commonly known signs and labels and to identify the prereaders who knew them best.[29] From the 21 signs and labels in the survey, the researchers selected the 10 most widely known; and from the 228 children, they selected the 102 most widely knowing. Of these, 6 children passed a simple word reading test and were removed from the sample on that basis.

Each of the 96 remaining "prereaders" was asked to identify one of three versions of the 10 most familiar labels. In one version, the children were shown pictures of the labels in their full visual contexts; these were correctly recognized 81 percent of the time. In the second version, the children were given the print along with its logo; these labels were recognized 67 percent of the time. Finally, in the third version, the children were given only the print, typed in normal, upper- and lowercase manuscript type: These were recognized only 23 percent of the time. But what about that 23 percent? Had the children learned something about the spelling of the words through their experience with the signs and labels? Or were they just plain learning to read?

To ask this question, the researchers presented the labels plus logos to the children again, but this time one of the letters in the label had been replaced by a visually dissimilar letter—e.g,

---

29. Masonheimer, Drum, and Ehri (1984).

Despite the changes, the children displayed a strong tendency (74 percent of responses) to "read" the label as it would normally have been written. When they did so, they were then pointedly asked whether there was anything wrong with the display. Virtually none noticed the problem on this prompt. All of the children were then presented with the altered label and logo side by side with a correct version and asked if they could detect any difference; 65 percent of the time, they still failed to do so.

The children's failure to respond to the grossly altered spellings in this study is particularly disappointing. Perhaps they were unaware or in disbelief that the alteration of these little scritches in the middle of so obviously familiar a label might count as an important difference to a worldly adult. Perhaps the familiarity of the overall visual array detracted from their inclination to attend to the print. Consistent with this, the children were significantly more successful at detecting the misspellings when presented with black-and-white rather than normal, colored versions of the labels. And, interestingly, this is reminiscent of the experiments on scene recognition that were reviewed earlier. Remember? Even when people were told to study particular, identifiable objects in a complex scene, their ability to recognize the object depended on whether it was presented by itself or within the larger context of the scene.

Indeed, this takes us full circle, back to our analysis of the nature and structure of learning. The memory for a visual pattern is composed of interrelations among the familiar subpatterns that it contains. If a child is unfamiliar with the concept of letters, much less the particular letters in a pattern, they cannot be remembered as letters. At best, each such letter will be retained as an individually coherent pattern of visual features; at worst, its features will not be collected unto itself but only in broader association to the overall pattern of the print or the entire label.

But suppose someone points out to the child that the print is a special part of the label. Suppose someone points out that the print symbolizes words and that the discrete subpatterns of which it is comprised are special, that they are letters. The child would then know to examine the letters individually. Though a step removed from the most autonomous kind of inductive, "emergent" learning that we might initially have imagined, it is plausible that under these conditions, environmental print would support letter learning.

But it is barely plausible. After all, that which characterizes a good label or logo is its distinctiveness. The lettering used on one brand of soup is intended to be visually distinct from that used on any other. Just from compiling the visual similarities and differences of the characters on labels and logos, how long would it take to realize that, functionally speaking, there are just twenty-six different letters? (Note that, in contrast, books—including primers and preprimers—are generally printed in a relatively uniform typeface.)

More concretely, compare the visual differences across acceptable renditions of any given letter, for example:

G G G G G G G G G G G

with the visual similarities of two functionally distinct letters: e.g.,

G   C

When challenged to name these two letters, my daughter, now just three years old, looked me squarely in the eye and said firmly, "I call them both *C*." It is not that she could not discriminate their shapes: She regularly performs perfectly on an uppercase letter-matching game on the computer. Nor is she unaware that I like to call these letters by different names: Her answer was clearly intended to preempt the correction that she knew I would produce.

But she has a point. In what reasonable kind of world would people would agree to call both a dachshund and a St. Bernard "dogs" while calling one of these characters a "C" and the other a "G"? To us, the answer is obvious: in the kind of a world where people use *C*s and *G*s discriminately for reading and writing—which, of course, she does not yet do.[30]

In summary, then, how much letter knowledge *could* the prereader gain from exposure to environmental print? The answer

---

30. And this is a little girl who is highly attuned to similarities, producing one innocent metaphor after another in her free speech. "Excuse me while I find a parking space for my towel," she says at the wading pool. "The leaves are flagging in the wind," she says while gazing out the window. "I don't like wet pizza and little trees," she says while scowling at her lasagna and broccoli.

is that it depends. If the child concentrates on the print, processing it as a picture, responding to aspects of its length, shape, color, and even its internal pattern of line segments and curves, the answer is not much—or at least not much that would be assimilated by the Orthographic processor. In contrast, if the child perceives the print as a sequence of discrete, individual, and individually identifiable letters, then environmental print may contribute as much to orthographic growth as the most deliberate word-training exercise. But perceiving the print as a series of individual and identifiable letters depends on unitary recognition of the letters themselves, and the development of this skill is a separate issue.

Learning the Visual Identities of the Individual Letters

The Orthographic processor matures by building associations among the patterns representing each of the individual letters and among each of these letter patterns and the corresponding representations in the other processors.[31] The implication is that growth in orthographic competence depends integrally on visual recognition and discrimination of the individual letters, and this implication is consistent with the evidence that letter recognition facility is strongly and causally related to success in beginning reading.[32]

What is it about the visual forms of letters that makes them hard to master? How is visual letter recognition taught in the classroom? How is it learned outside the classroom? When and how might we best teach it? Each of these questions is addressed in this section.

What's Hard about Learning Letter Identities?

The hard part about learning the visual identities of letters is that they were not designed with an eye toward visual distinctiveness or memorability. They are graphically abstract, having no prior iconic significance—how much easier it would be

---

31. Of course, it should now be clear that memory is not literally comprised of a bank of separate processors but of clusters of knowledge that are more and less similar to each other and that may or may not be directly connected to particular input and output modalities, such as seeing, hearing, and speaking.

32. See chapter 4.

if an *a* in some way resembled an ant, a *b* a ball, and so on. They are graphically sparse, composed of rather minimal configurations of rather minimal visual features, simple arcs and line segments. They are highly confusable in terms of our normal visual recognition heuristics: A cup is a cup turned any whichway, but *d*, *b*, *p*, and *q* are distinctly different letters. They must be learned in such a way that they will be recognizable across a variety of hands and typefaces. And, in fact, there is not one set of twenty-six basic letters to be learned, but four, including both upper- and lowercases, in both manuscript and cursive. Learning the visual identities of letters is not a snap even for children who are interested in doing so. It takes time and practice and requires careful visual attention.

I have already mentioned that my three-year-old daughter has an "attitude" about letters. In contrast to her brother, this child is far less interested in learning for the sake of knowing than in doing for the sake of effect. As a baby, she was a good crawler, having started at six months, and, try as we might, we could not get her to show the slightest interest in walking—until her big brother had a birthday party. She crawled out, surveyed all that miniature bipodal activity, stood up, and walked. She never really went through the one- and two-word stage of language acquisition. Indeed we have never been able to interest her in playing the labeling game either with books or with real-world objects. Until she was able to produce five- and six-word sentences, she hardly spoke a word.

She loves storybooks but has never been interested in any of our alphabet books. On the other hand, she went through a period of insatiable interest in her number books, and she has had the concept and process of counting down since she was barely two. I had simply assumed that she knew her numerals until one night when we were trying to teach her a card game.[33]

As she persisted in audibly counting the spots on each of her cards, her father insisted that she stop and just look at the numeral in the corner. What ensued was very funny. If the value of the card was five or less, she would announce it immediately. Otherwise she would place her card down on the table and stare at it intently. Becoming impatient (partly because John was taking these opportunities to cheat), her father would say, "Well? Who wins?" And she, still staring at the card, but neither touching it nor uttering a sound, would reply with controlled

---

33. After all, children normally learn the names and shapes of the numerals well before they catch on to their meanings.

dignity, "Just a minute. I'm trying to decide." She was counting the spots to herself.

It is now abundantly clear that Jocelyn has not learned to recognize numerals—despite the fact that, because of her interest in numbers, she has had great opportunity to do so. But then, why should she have learned them? In every one of her number books and games, the numeral is printed side by side with that same number of countable things—and obviously it is the number of things, not the numeral, that matters.

The point is that exposure is not enough. In order to learn, children must pay attention, and in order for children to pay attention, they must *want* to pay attention. Jocelyn's world is full of letters and numerals, and—independent and willful as she is— she will eventually decide to learn their identities. But without the allure of stories, games, and sibling achievements, without the ever- and everywhere-waiting and self-empowering challenge of reading and writing on her own, she instead might not. Against the other things she has to think and learn about, she finds letters and numerals unattractive, uninteresting, and tedious. And I guess they are, except in their ultimate utility. In the opportunities for discovering this utility surely lies one of the great advantages of growing up in a print-rich environment.

Encoding the Characters

How does the visual system come to recognize these characters? One hypothesis is that it memorizes each as a holistic pattern. Under this hypothesis, when faced with a new character, the system compares it to each of the whole-letter patterns it has learned and recognizes it as the one that fits best. The alternate hypothesis is that the visual system analyzes each letter into its elementary visual features—its horizontal, vertical, and diagonal line segments and its arcs—and then encodes the letter's overall shape in terms of the relative positions, orientations, lengths, and sizes of these elements.

In many ways, the latter approach is inherently more powerful. It is, for example, set up to be indifferent to changes in the size, obliqueness, and orientation of the letter as a whole— what's important is the *relative* size, obliqueness, and orientation of its *parts*. Moreover, if the system knows about the relations between letter parts, it can accept visually salient but immaterial changes that a holistic letter recognizer would reject, and it can reject visually slight but significant changes that a holistic letter recognizer would accept.

By analogy, a recognition system that focused on elements and their permissible interrelations would easily recognize a living room whose couch had been moved to the other wall but reject one whose couch had been levitated by a foot and become translucent. In contrast, a holistic pattern recognizer would prefer the latter because it would be visually closer to its total image of what the room should look like.

Within the theory developed in part III, it is assumed that for skilled readers, individual letters are represented in memory as the interrelated sets of elementary visual features, and there exists considerable research to support this view.[34] Research further indicates that children, too, learn letters and letter-like patterns in this synthetic way.[35]

Over time and with increasing familiarity with the letters as a group, children also become sensitive to the classes of spatial relationships that do and do not distinguish one character from another. Thus, given a set of novel, letterlike characters to inspect, Eleanor Gibson and her colleagues have shown that even five years olds attend closely to gaps or openings between the features (as in the difference between *C* and *O; F* and *P;* and *A* and *H*).[36] By the time they are seven, most children are equally attentive to changes in rotation or orientation (as in the differences between *b, d, p,* and *q*). Although their attentiveness to whether a segment is curved or straight (as between *J* and *L*) starts off higher than their attentiveness to rotation and orientation, it has become less important by the time they are seven—quite plausibly this reflects their growing experience with handwriting and stylized fonts. By comparison, neither the youngest nor the oldest children in this study paid much attention to whether the overall forms of characters were squashed or slanted in one way or the other.

Poor readers are often reported to have special difficulties with letter orientation and reversals. Such errors were once widely interpreted as signs of neurological dysfunction, perhaps an immature or otherwise inappropriate balance in cerebral

---

34. McClelland and Rumelhart (1986). Note, too, that what is being posited is that the visual identities of letters are represented in memory in exact analogy to the way it represents printed words as interrelations among individual letters, spoken words as interrelations among their smaller phonemic elements and syllables, meanings as interrelations among primitive meaning units, and so on.

35. Odom, McIntyre, and Neale (1971); Pick (1965).

36. Gibson, Gibson, Pick, and Osser (1962).

dominance.[37] Yet careful analysis of the frequency and distribution of such errors suggests, instead, that they reflect nothing more than insufficient knowledge of letter shapes.[38] The latter conclusion fits readily with the idea that the system learns separately about the parts of a letter and about their spatial relations—all the more, given children's late maturing sensitivity to differences in rotation and orientation.[39] On a positive note, training children to attend to the relational contrasts between letters has been shown to hasten their ability to recognize and distinguish between them.[40]

How Are Letter Identities Taught in School?

To gain a global answer to this question, I read through the letter training components of the programs reviewed by Aukerman.[41] Surprisingly, a number of these beginning reading programs assume that entering students are already well versed in letter identification, providing no instructional guidance for helping those who are not and starting right in with exercises that require it.

The majority of the programs do provide exercise in letter recognition and discrimination and do so through one of two methods. Under one of these methods, the children are taught to *name* the letters as they learn to recognize them. Under the other, students are trained to respond to each letter with the *sound* it makes in print (e.g., *m* says /*m*/), and the names of the letters are avoided.

Programs that teach students to name the letters tend to introduce them in alphabetical order, but then move on to randomly ordered presentations to ensure that students know their independent identities. Typically such programs are designed to teach their students to recognize all of the letters with confidence before getting involved in phonic or word-reading instruction.

Programs that avoid letter names and instead teach their students to respond with the letters' sounds tend not to introduce the letters in alphabetical order, deferring instead to some phonic principle or word-learning goal. Nearly all of the programs that refrain from teaching letter names rely heavily on pictured

---

37. Orton (1937).
38. Liberman, Shankweiler, Orlando, Harris, and Berti (1971).
39. Gibson, Gibson, Pick, and Osser (1962).
40. Samuels (1970a, cited in Gibson and Levin (1975).
41. Aukerman (1971, 1984).

keywords—that is, on displays that include the letter, one or more words that illustrate its phonemic significance, and distinctive pictures of each of these example words.[42]

Finally, a number of the programs in each category engage the children in copying or tracing the letters and, regardless of approach, there are differences in the order in which upper- and lowercase letters are taught.

Bear in mind that the issue with which we are currently grappling is that of how children may best be taught to recognize and discriminate the *visual* shapes of letters. In theory, this skill could be taught without the use of letter names, letter sounds, or writing. Yet this is impractical. First, without coupling recognition to some observable response, how could one ever tell whether the children were learning? Second, because of the linkages between the processors, the types of responses that are coupled to a perceptual event really do influence its learning. For this reason, we shall examine each of these approaches more closely.

Teaching Visual Recognition with the Help of Letter Names

One motive for teaching letter names first is that, through history, that is what has most often been done.[43] Thus, there are precedence, well-known methods (e.g., the ABC song), ample material (ABC books and posters), and often generational support for this practice.

A second rationale for this approach is that it is pedagogically convenient to have a label for a to-be-learned concept. Clearly, it is easier to say, "Point to the *a*," than to say "Point to the letter that says /æ/ (or /ä/ or /ā/ or /uh/)."

The third rationale may be both more influential and less fully appreciated. There is, in itself, pedagogical power in having a label for a to-be-learned concept.

Specifically, in memory, the label provides a means of bonding together all of one's experiences with a to-be-learned concept. In doing so, it can only hasten the recognition of the similarities of the concept across its occurrences. They will overwrite and reinforce each other.[44]

---

42. There are also some that do not. As examples, *The Writing Road to Reading,* or Spalding method, develops letter knowledge principally through handwriting; the Michigan Language Program employs visual discrimination exercises plus tracing and printing of letters.

43. Mathews (1966).

44. See discussion of labels and "acquired equivalence" in chapter 9.

Labels will also hasten the child's sensitivity to critical differences in the features of different letters. The difference between a *C* and a *G* will not lie on an otherwise unmarked continuum of variation. Instead as the label "C" collects together all and only all the *C*s it has labeled, and the label "G" collects together all and only all of the *G*s it has labeled, the presence or absence of a bar on the lower mouth of the letter will accrue as a central and distinctive feature of each of these separate bundles.[45]

Furthermore, whenever a concept occurs with its label, the system will unerringly find, arouse, and add to the same interconnected constellation of units in the Orthographic, Phonological, and Meaning processors. In this way, it will hasten the consolidation of the entire distribution of tokens to which the label has been applied. And in so doing it will also hasten development of an imaginal prototype of the letter, as defined by the center of that complex of visual features by which the letter has most often been represented. Research indicates that the provision of a distinctive and uniform label for a concept is especially important—perhaps critically so—for the attainment of concepts whose context and superficial expression varies across occurrences.[46] It is not hard to argue that printed letters tend toward this category.

Finally, a fourth rationale for teaching letter names is that the names of most letters contain clues to their phonemic significance.[47] As examples, the name of the letter *a* captures one of the sounds that an *a* makes in print; the name of the letter *b* contains the phoneme /*b*/, and so on.

But herein also lies the principal argument against teaching letter names: The names and phonemic translations of letters differ, and sometimes greatly, from one another. Eventually the reader must learn to respond automatically to each letter with its phonemic translation. That being the goal, why confuse the child's Phonological processor by first teaching it to respond with the letters' names?

Teaching Letters through Sounds Instead

The rationale for introducing letters with their sounds instead of their names has been given. Inasmuch as we have already seen that the speed of the Phonological processor's responding

---

45. See discussion of labels and "acquired distinctiveness" in chapter 9.
46. Gick and Holyoak (1983).
47. Durrell (1980).

decreases with the number of appropriate responses it has learned, this rationale also seems sound.

But for purposes of developing a useful visual memory for letters, there are weaknesses to this approach too. In particular, in the standard orthography, any given letter may correspond to more than one sound. As a consequence, a letter's sounds provide weaker guidance toward its consolidation in memory.[48] Until the Orthographic processor learns to recognize the letter completely and unerringly across its occurrences, such consolidation must depend heavily on the letter's perceived sound(s). Yet if the sound of the letter is not reliably categorized by the student (or if more than one is presented), consolidation will take longer. Further, without a unique label, there is nothing but complete and unerring visual perception of the letter to link its multiple sounds together.

There is, in other words, a significant mnemonic disadvantage to trying to develop the visual identities of letters without giving each a unique and perceptually distinct label. For a child with no prior familiarity of the shape or sound of a letter, the expectations of this situation may amount to something like the cart pulling the cart.

It is surely in tacit recognition of this that the sound-only programs rely so prominently on keyword charts. As keyword charts couple each letter's form and sound with meaningful words and salient graphics, they create an entry for the letter in all three processors. Further, by providing a prototypical pronunciation of the letter, they must also help to regulate or focus the "sound" response in the Phonological processor.[49]

In short, when names are avoided in letter instruction, good keyword charts should and, indeed do, provide significant instructional support. However, as with the supportive graphics of environmental print, keyword charts involve a risk: The children may learn to depend on the whole, complex design of the

---

48. Note that where the orthography of instruction has been altered such that each different sound of a letter is represented by a visually distinct symbol, this problem disappears.

49. Capturing this spirit, in the Northern Semitic and Phoenician alphabet from which the English alphabet was derived, the name of each letter was the name of a familiar word that began with its sound. For example, the Semitic word for *house* — *beth* — was the "name" of the letter representing the phoneme /b/; the Semitic word for *door* — *daleth* — was the "name" of the letter representing the phoneme /d/; and so on. (Balmuth, 1982).

chart, such that when the letter is presented alone with the chart no longer in sight, their erstwhile progress vanishes.[50]

If the letter shape is presented as a central, salient component of the keyword's picture,[51] as illustrated below, this risk is diminished:

F as in flower[52]

With both prereaders and troubled beginners, Ehri and her colleagues found that such integrated letter/keyword/picture support resulted in better retention of letter-sound associations than side-by-side presentations of the picture or keyword with the letter.[53] Displays of this sort help to ensure that when children see the letter in isolation, they will automatically be reminded of its pictured keyword which will, in turn, evoke its sound and reinforce its shape.

A final drawback to teaching the visual identities of letters through their sounds is that such instruction progresses relatively slowly. Most programs spend considerable time instilling each letter-sound correspondence, and indeed they should. But the topic in focus in this section is not the learning of letter-sound correspondences; it is the learning of the visual forms of the letters.

If learning of letter discrimination awaits letter-sound instruction, then word reading is limited to the number of letter-sound pairs that have been taught. Yet, many of the words children may want to read—indeed, many of the words in many beginning texts—contain spellings that have not been covered in the children's letter-sound instruction.[54] If the children can readily recognize and name the component letters, they may be able to identify the words despite their untaught letter-sound

---

50. Marsh and Desberg (1978).

51. This technique is used in a number of commercially available programs including Harrison and McKee (1971) and Laubach, Kirk, and Laubach (1969).

52. Taken from Ehri, Deffner, and Wilce (1984).

53. Ehri, Deffner, and Wilce (1984).

54. Beck (1981); Meyer, Greer, and Crummey (1987).

correspondences. If they can neither recognize nor name the letters, they hardly have a chance.

Learning Letters through Writing, Copying, and Tracing

A number of programs engage the students in writing, copying, and tracing the letters as they learn them. Do these activities assist the children's ability to recognize the letter visually?

By conjecture, independently writing the letters should. After all, the writing of a letter and the checking of one's product depend not only on thinking about its visual image but on thinking about it in an active and critical way that is not required for mere recognition. Further, printing is such a slow process for the beginner that it is typically supported by the "articulatory loop": It is common for children to voice the sound or name of each letter as they print it. In this way, the exercise of printing should help bind the visual, motor, and phonological images of the letter together at once.

Augmenting such value, programs that emphasize the proper formation of letters, implicitly direct children's attention to their distinctive features. Some programs do so by categorizing the letter shapes: These letters have arcs that start and stop here; these letters have horizontal or vertical lines that start and stop here; for these letters the vertical line is drawn before (to the left of) the arc; for these the line or "tail" is drawn after (to the right of) the arc; and so on.[55] Others do so by setting up "motor patterns" for each letter, defining the order and direction of "strokes" for each and exercising the patterns—for example, by having the children write letters in the air with their fingers or trace and copy letter templates that are appropriately marked with numbers (to indicate sequential pencil placements) and arrows (to indicate the proper direction of the pencil stroke).[56]

Copying should also help to consolidate the child's knowledge of the letter's form. However, because copying can be done without thinking about either the letter's sound or its name, much less the ways in which it is distinctively different from any other letter, it is expected to facilitate letter recognition less than independent writing. By extension, because tracing can be done without thinking about the letter's overall form, function, *or* identity, it may add very little to the child's letter recognition facility.

---

55. See, for example, Spalding and Spalding (1986).

56. See, for example, Engelmann and Bruner (1968); McMahon (1968).

Although there is little research on these issues, what exists is consistent. Working with kindergartners, Williams found tracing and copying letterlike symbols to be a less effective means of improving later recognition than was visual discrimination training that involved no copying or tracing but forced attention to the subtle yet distinctive differences between them.[57] In a subsequent study, Williams found that whereas visual discrimination training produced positive transfer toward the learning of novel letterlike symbols, training on copying did not.[58] Gates and Taylor found that giving preschoolers practice in copying letters resulted in better letter writing skills than giving them practice in tracing letters.[59] And Pryzwansky found that training in printing produced significant improvement in children's scores on a standardized reading readiness test.[60] Finally, in program comparison studies, a general advantage is found for those that engage the students in independent writing from the start.[61]

In this context, it is worth reemphasizing the modularity of these training alternatives. Just as the sheer copying of letters does not efficiently foster visual discrimination, training on the visual discrimination of letters does not particularly improve children's ability to copy them. Furthermore, practice in copying results in significant improvement only on the letters that have been practiced. In summarizing these findings, Williams advises:

The implications for instruction, especially for reading and writing, seem clear. One cannot rely on transfer from training on one task to another, even though both deal with the same content (alphabet letters). Rather, the perceptual learning involved in the development of the ability to differentiate between letters and the acquisition of the ability to copy letters must be considered in terms of optimal curriculum development as separate tasks.

Presumably, whatever is learned in the training of letter discrimination—the ability to identify and contrast the distinctive features according to Gibson (1970)—will transfer when the child is faced with novel letters. But the letter-formation training to be pursued in the development of good handwriting must focus on all the letters; improvement on novel, untrained forms cannot be expected.[62]

---

57. Williams (1969).

58. Williams (1975).

59. Gates and Taylor (1923, cited in Feitelson, 1988).

60. Pryzwansky (1972).

61. Bond and Dykstra (1967); Chall (1967); Evans and Carr (1985).

62. Williams (1975).

Although letter tracing and copying activities would not seem to constitute robust means of developing visual letter recognition, the message here is not that they should be cast from the classroom. Each may contribute valuably toward the development of those fine motor skills that determine the willingness as well as the ability to write. Moreover, there is every reason to believe that engaging students in the independent writing of letters is a thoroughly worthwhile activity toward developing necessary skills for reading as well as writing.[63]

Uppercase and Lowercase Letters

Eventually the child must learn to recognize both uppercase and lowercase letters, so at some point each must be taught. The best answer to the question of which to teach first probably depends on when one is teaching.

Research suggests that uppercase letters are more discriminable from one another.[64] In addition, whatever letter knowledge a prereader already has is most likely to be about uppercase letters.[65] Thus, if working with preschool children, uppercase letters are probably the better bet.

On the other hand, the ability to recognize the lowercase letters is more important for reading text. Thus, if working with first graders, it is probably wise to concentrate on them.

The question of how best to deal with confusable forms becomes acute when working with lowercase letters, most notably *b, d, p,* and *q.* One idea that springs to mind is to present the confusable letters simultaneously, such that they are available for direct comparison and contrast. As with confusable sounds, however, this idea sounds better than it works. Laboratory evidence indicates that discrimination of visually *dissimilar* letters is hastened under such simultaneous presentation conditions; on the other hand, discrimination of visually *similar* or confusable letters seems to proceed more quickly, and perhaps more robustly, when the letters are studied one at a time.[66] Evidence from the classroom also suggests that to minimize confusion between visually similar letters, especially *b* and *d,* it is best to separate

---

63. See chapter 14.

64. Tinker (1931).

65. McCormick and Mason (1986); Smythe, Stennett, Hardy, and Wilson (1970–1971).

66. Williams and Ackerman (1971).

their introduction in time such that the first is thoroughly familiar before the second is presented.[67]

With respect to teaching uppercase and lowercase letters, the theory holds only one strong suggestion. If you are working with a child with little or no letter recognition facility, do not try to teach both versions of all twenty-six of them at the same time. Early in its visual learning, the features and featural interrelations of a pattern are fragilely held together. To try simultaneously to teach two visually distinct forms with identical responses amidst fifty other sometimes confusable forms with independently but equally confusable sounds and labels will almost guarantee visual confusion and slower learning of each.

This very practice was quite common in the olden days when print-rich home environments and preschool literati were relatively rare. Observing it, Charles Hoole remarked that while some "ripe witted" children did somehow succeed, others

have been thus learning a whole year together (and though they have been much chid, and beaten too for want of heed) could scarcely tell six of their letters at twelve months' end.[68]

We must bear in mind that, in our times, the issue of how best to teach visual letter recognition in school is primarily an issue for those children who, not unlike their typical classmate of yesteryear, come to us with little home preparation and print-poor environments.

How Are Letter Identities Most Often Learned?

Research indicates that, before entering school, most children have learned to name most of the letters of the alphabet[69]—or, at least, most of the uppercase letters.[70] Further, as reviewed in chapter 4, children's facility in naming letters has repeatedly been shown to be a powerful predictor of their reading achievement. More specifically, it has been shown that the

---

67. Beck and McCaslin (1979); Carnine and Silbert (1969).

68. Hoole (1660/1912, cited in Feitelson, 1988).

69. Durrell and Catterson (1980, cited in Chall, 1983b); Mason (1980); McCormick and Mason (1986); Nurss (1979). This too varies culturally. For example, Masonheimer (1982, cited in Ehri, 1986) found that by age five, English-speaking children in California could name most (71 percent) uppercase letters correctly. In contrast, Spanish-speaking children could name very few (4 percent).

70. Lowercase letters are less likely to be well known (McCormick and Mason, 1986; Smythe, Stennett, Hardy, and Wilson, 1970-71).

learning of letter names frequently turns spontaneously, or at least easily, into interest in their sounds and in the spellings of words;[71] that knowing letter names is strongly correlated with the ability to remember the forms of written words and the tendency to treat them as ordered sequences of letters rather than holistic patterns;[72] and that *not* knowing letter names is coupled with extreme difficulty in learning letter sounds[73] and word recognition.[74]

How can we reconcile these demonstrated benefits of letter name knowledge with the logical argument that such knowledge should confuse the learning of letter sounds? The answer may lie in the manner in which the knowledge is acquired.

Studies of preschoolers indicate that they often learn to recite the names of the letters very early, and that the way in which they very often learn them is through the Alphabet Song ("A, B, C, D, ..." to the tune of "Twinkle, Twinkle Little Star"). Typically, it is only after a child has learned all of the names of the letters that parents begin to help her or him with their shapes. Interest and development in the writing of letters, in the sounds of letters, and in the spellings of words comes next.[75]

There are a couple of important points lurking in this progression. First, it indicates that the ability to name and recognize letters is, in general, not established through showing the children the letters and then teaching them the names. That's backwards. Most children are taught the letters only after they know their names. By thoroughly learning the names first, the child has a solid mnemonic peg to which the percept of the letter can be connected as it is built. By thoroughly teaching the names first, the teacher can methodically exploit them toward developing the child's sense of the functionally equivalent and distinctive differences between characters.

Second, it is significant that the initial ability to recite the alphabet is so often achieved through the Alphabet Song. Because the Phonological processor is highly attuned to patterns of rhyme, rhythm, and pitch, songs are much easier to learn than unintoned lists. Moreover, teaching the letter names in such a context of rhyme, rhythm, and tune is mnemonically analogous to introducing their shapes as an integral part of a picture that

---

71. Chomsky (1979); Mason (1980); Read (1971).

72. Ehri (1986, 1987); Ehri and Wilce (1985).

73. Ehri and Wilce (1979).

74. Mason (1980).

75. Mason (1980); Sulzby (1983).

reflects their sounds. That is, the names of the letters are likely to be recalled by the song, and the song by the names of even a few letters.[76]

Third, the longitudinal studies consistently indicate that the learning of the letter names comes well before the learning of their sounds, and this carries two advantages.[77] First, it means that, in general, the children know the names of the letters very well before being introduced to the sounds. Their solid, overlearned familiarity with the letter names will, in itself, protect them from confusions. Second, it means that the children will know that the letter names are in fact *names*.[78] In short, such separation in time must play a significant role in allowing the children to learn the letter sounds with only the help and not the hindrance that may be had from their names.

Fourth, among children in these studies, letter recitation or the Alphabet Song was typically learned well before they were four years old and often before they were three. With such an enormous headstart, the teaching of letter shapes may proceed very gradually: first maybe *A*, *B*, and *C*, or maybe *O*, *X*, and *Z*; then maybe forget about identifying individual letters for a while and just play with letter jigsaw puzzles; then maybe help the child with the letters in his or her first name; meanwhile point out words and their letters in books and environmental print from time to time, join the child in participatory watching of "Sesame Street," and so on.

From a pedagogical standpoint, leisure is a wonderful thing. The progression of lessons can be determined strictly on the basis of interest and mutually amenable opportunity, and always with thorough deference to prior mastery. It can proceed nonthreateningly, without pressure, and heedless of first-grade milestone charts. These children have two to four years to master the letter shapes before it is time for them to enter school.

---

76. Although, for me at least, the likelihood with which the tune recalls the letters depends on whether I am thinking of it as "The ABC Song" rather than "Twinkle, Twinkle Little Star" or "Baa Baa Black Sheep." I find this sort of a cute demonstration of how even identical, or nearly identical, patterns can become mnemonically distinct depending on the contexts and responses to which they have been associated.

77. Mason (1980); Sulzby (1983).

78. Note also that children are generally quite young when they make the categorical distinction between the names of animals and the sounds they make.

Summary: Learning Letters

Solid familiarity with the visual shapes of the individual letters is an absolute prerequisite for learning to read. To make this assertion more vivid, we may compare two "word"-learning studies, one by Pieter Reitsma and one by Lee Brooks.[79]

Reitsma's study was undertaken with twenty-nine normal, second-grade Dutch children. He presented each child with a list of ten pseudowords, four to seven letters in length, and printed on cards. Flipping through the cards, he gave each child four or eight tries, with feedback, at reading each of the pseudowords.

Three days later, Reitsma measured the speed and accuracy with which the children could read these same pseudowords, using two sets of control items for comparison. One set of control items consisted of homophonic pseudowords, spelled identically to the trained words with the exception of one single (often visually confusable) letter. The other set consisted of unrelated and previously unseen pseudowords whose pronunciations the children had repeated during training.

Those who three days earlier had been given just four practice trials read both the trained pseudowords and their homophonic contrasts significantly faster than the unrelated controls. Those who had practiced eight times read the trained pseudowords faster than either the homophonic or unrelated controls. None of the children made many errors.

Reitsma then extended this study using a set of unfamiliar real (Dutch) words, four to ten letters long, with eighteen normal first-grade children. The words were again printed on cards but this time embedded in meaningful sentences. The training sentences and, thus, the test words they contained, were read two, four, or six times by each child.

Three days later, the training words, along with sets of homophonic and unrelated control words, were presented in isolation on a computer screen, and the children were timed as they read each aloud. After only two practice trials, both the trained words and their homophones were read significantly faster than the unrelated controls. After only four practice trials, the trained words were read significantly faster than either their homophonic or their unrelated controls.

Against this remarkably spongelike word acquisition of Reitsma's young children, we may compare the performance of a group of college students trained by Brooks.[80] Brooks's adult

---

79. Brooks (1977); Reitsma (1983).
80. Brooks (1977).

subjects were given twelve monosyllabic, four "letter" pseudowords
to learn. The spellings of six of the pseudowords reflected frequent
English spelling-to-sound rules. The spellings of the other six did
not and therefore had to be learned as "whole word patterns." (In
fact, Brooks's purpose in conducting this experiment was to
compare the speed of phonic versus whole word learning.)

The two types of words were trained in separate blocks of
trials so that there should have been little confusion as to which
were and which were not alphabetically decodable. With respect
to differences in the learnability of the two types of pseudowords,
the alphabetic items showed a slight disadvantage early in
training and a slight advantage later in training. However, the
point here is that, after 200 practice trials with each of the
twelve items, the adults were still having trouble recognizing
them. Their learning curves were still not close to asymptote.

Two trials for the children versus hundreds for the adults: To
what can we attribute this contrast? Whereas Reitsma's items
were spelled with normal familiar letters, Brooks's were spelled
with an invented alphabet. Brooks's characters were exceedingly
simple— ∞, $\vee$, $-$, $|||$, $\cap$, $\sqcup$; there were only six of them; and the
subjects were given ten minutes of practice just on the individual
letter-sound correspondences before training began. Nevertheless,
Brooks's adults, in contrast with Reitsma's children, had to learn
to recognize—and to recognize easily—not just the sequences of
characters of which each item was comprised but also the
characters themselves.

The Orthographic processor cannot begin to learn spellings until
its has learned to recognize the letters from which they must be
built. The Phonological processor cannot usefully learn letter
sounds until the Orthographic processor has learned to
discriminate the individual letters with which they must be
linked. Yet the visual forms of the individual letters are abstract
and highly confusable.

In view of this, I urge that instruction in letter recognition be
begun long before children get to school. The goal is to ensure that
the letter shapes are highly familiar and discriminable to the
children before they are faced with the tasks of learning the
letters' sounds or, more generally, of learning to read words. After
children have become thoroughly familiar with the letters and
their names, reading and writing activities follow far more
easily.

Many preschoolers become familiar with letters through a
common sequence of activities. First, they learn the alphabet song.
Then they learn the shapes that go with each of the letter names

they have learned. In both of these challenges, they may gain both motivation and guidance from "Sesame Street," especially if it is treated as a participatory program rather than passively watched. More generally, there is no substitute for the attention and praise of a real person in any enrichment activity.

For children who enter school *with* such background, there would seem to be little argument for avoiding careful use of letter names in the classroom. For children who enter school *without* it, however, this issue is more difficult. For these children, there is good reason for concern that distinctions between the names and sounds of letters will be confused if they are taught at the same time.

Both theory and data suggest that instruction on neither the sounds of letters nor the recognition of whole words should be earnestly undertaken until the child has become confident and quick at recognizing individual letters.[81] While *every* aspect of reading growth depends on the speed and accuracy of letter perception, learning to recognize and discriminate printed letters is just too big, too hard, and too fussy a task to be mastered incidentally, in tandem with some other hard and fussy task, or without an adult's focused attention to its progress and difficulties. Succinctly, what a waste to correct the pronunciation of a letter sound or word if the child's confusion was really in the visual identity of the letter.

Thus, even for poorly prepared children, I would be tempted to begin with the Alphabet Song. I would exploit the letter names it teaches along with any other kinds of appropriately challenging and interesting activities toward helping them learn the letters' shapes. Only after I was very sure that the children's learning of letter shapes was well under way, would I begin serious instruction in spelling-sound relations or word recognition.

It also seems like a good idea to exercise children's ability to print individual letters from the start. This is not only because of its potential for enhancing individual letter recognition but, further, because it will allow them to write words as soon as they are introduced—and, as we shall see, writing seems a solidly productive activity for the young reader.[82]

---

81. This is not to say that, before this, one should avoid showing printed words to children and helping them to appreciate that they symbolize spoken words, that they are comprised of individual letters, and that the letters correspond to the sounds of the corresponding words. This sort of exposure and the "print appreciation" it supports are key steps toward reading readiness.

82. See chapter 14.

In the initial introduction of a letter shape, and otherwise to assist development of fine motor skills, tracing may be used. Tracing exercises may be more effective if the stencils are coded to encourage a uniform sequence of motor patterns for each letter (e.g., for the letter *b*, first trace the vertical bar from top to bottom, then draw the circle). This is both because control develops through repetition and because it enhances the chances that the child will attend to the individual features of the letters and their interrelations. (Note that the basis of this recommendation is orthogonal to any puritanical notions about the hygiene of penpersonship. After the children have thoroughly learned the letters, it is okay if they want to write them in a mirror, with their toes, while standing on their heads.)

Copying, of course, must be used; it is a necessary step toward the independent printing of a letter. But it appears that neither tracing nor copying, but independent printing holds the greatest leverage for perceptual and motor learning of letter shapes. It will be obvious when a child needs a model to produce a letter—that is, it will be obvious when reversion to copying is necessary. In such cases, copying should be encouraged and coupled with guidance about those aspects of the letter with which the child is having difficulty.

It also seems that whenever letter-sound instruction is begun, it is a good idea to present integrated letter/keyword/ picture displays. These may be charts to be hung on the classroom wall or pictures in an alphabet book. In whatever showcase, such displays provide mnemonic assistance for letter shapes, letter sounds, and their couplings, at once.

Finally, given that the notion that letters spell words is so very critical, one wonders why more preschool trade books and preprimers and are not produced in ways that make their print more salient. In tradebooks, at least, the possibilities of graphically or stylistically enhancing print are myriad. Again, some of Dr. Seuss's books provide good models. Further, one wonders why so very few preschool tradebooks and preprimers are printed in uppercase type. Inasmuch as children generally learn uppercase letters first, this might provide a good early clue that letters are related to language and print.

The Value of Pictures

At the turn of this century, in reviewing "present-day methods and texts in elementary reading," Edmund Burke Huey remarked:

Concerning texts, manuals, and specific systems for teaching children to read, the writer has recently examined with some care more than a hundred, representing the best that could be found in the modern literature of the subject. . . . In working over the primers and first readers, one is impressed with the fact that the artistic side has had far more attention and a far greater development than has the side of method and reading content. The books are often superbly illustrated, in colors or with fine photographs, and the covers and typography are most attractive. . . . It is a matter of gratification that we now have books that are so attractive and that set before the child high standards of beauty. . . . It is a question, anyway, how much reading owes to his aesthestic development, when pictures are needed rather to assist with natural child interpretaion of what is read.[83]

With the passage of time, Huey's observations seem no less appropriate.

First, the quantity of artwork in basals has continued to increase. Examining one series of basal readers while writing *The Great Debate*, Chall found 0.9 picture per 100 running words of text in the 1920 edition, 1.3 in the 1930 edition, 1.4 in the 1940 edition, 1.6 in the 1956 edition, and 1.7 in the 1962 edition.[84] Examining the 1978 edition of the same series, Willows, Borwick, and Hayvren found that the count had risen to 6.5 pictures per 100 running words.[85]

Second, the quality of the artwork has remained high. Examining the highest-level first-grade readers of three different basal series, Willows, Borwick, and Hayvren found each averaged at least one illustration per page. The pictures were most often stylized, complex, brightly colored, maximally eye catching, and, whether above, below, or beside the text, were most often placed in the center of the page.

And third, the quantity and quality of the artwork in the children's texts seem still to be largely driven by aesthetic considerations. What kinds of pedagogical motivations can be offered? Willows and colleagues offer two: (1) Pictures may provide cues for identifying words that are otherwise hard to recognize, and (2) pictures may stimulate interest in reading the text and promote a better understanding of textual information.

---

83. Huey (1908/1968, pp. 276–278).

84. Chall (1967).

85. These researchers examined only the highest levels (Level C) of first-grade readers. Observing that the number of words per page was substantially higher than in the lower levels, they point out that their count commensurately underestimates the amount of artwork in the series as wholes (Willows, Borwick, and Hayvren, 1981).

Pictures as Aids for Word Recognition

It used to be, explain Willows, Borwick, and Hayvren, that the practice of presenting an identifying picture along with each new sight word was common in basal reader programs.

> The assumption is essentially that the picture-word pairing procedure will cause paired-associate learning to take place. That is, by looking at the sight word along with an identifying picture the child will learn to associate the picture with the word. Then when the child encounters the word on its own, he/she will remember the picture that went with it and, through that association, be able to identify the word.[86]

Against this assumption, S. Jay Samuels offered the hypothesis that the presence of identifying pictures might actually interfere with printed word learning.[87] After all, if the children are deriving their response from the picture, shouldn't that displace or at least detract from the attention they might otherwise accord to the print?

To test this hypothesis, Samuels examined the influence of pictures on the speed with which kindergarten children would learn to read four new words.[88] On learning trials, the to-be-read words were pronounced aloud by the experimenter whenever a child's response was slow or in error. In addition, for some of the children, the words were accompanied by pictures and, for others, they were not. To discern whether the children were responding to the picture or the print, each set of four learning trials was alternated with four test trials in which each of the words was presented without pictures and no feedback was given.

The children who studied the words alongside the pictures made significantly more correct responses during the learning trials than those who studied the words without pictures. This, of course, is consistent with the premise that pictures should help cue the desired response. However, on the pictureless test trials, the performance of the children who had studied the words with pictures was worse than that of the children who had studied the words without. This is consistent with Samuels' hypothesis: The helpfulness of the pictures seemed derived at the cost of attentiveness to the print.

Across replications of this study, the message seems clear. If the goal is to help children to respond to an unfamiliar, isolated word, accompanying pictures may be helpful. If the goal is to

---

86. Willows, Borwick, and Hayvren (1981, p. 147).

87. Samuels (1967, 1970b).

88. Samuels (1967).

induce the children to attend to and learn about details of the print, accompanying pictures may be diversionary.[89]

Given the prevalence of illustrations in tradebooks and textbooks alike, the more important question is probably whether the presence of pictures helps or hurts children's tendency to learn about the words of connected text. The research on this issue is sparse, but—so far at least—the answer on balance seems to be neither.[90]

Pictures as Support for Comprehension and Interest

In their examination of basal guidebooks, Willows, Borwick, and Hayvren found that all occasionally used the pictures as means of preparing the children for the text.[91] Alluding to the pictures, teachers are to ask such questions as "What is going on in the picture?" and "What do you think will happen?" The children are then to read the text and find out.

The intention of such exercises, argue Willows and colleagues, is to promote the children's interest in and understanding of the accompanying text. The presumption, they argue, is that the children will transfer this questioning approach to their own independent reading.

Consistent with this, children are found to take more time with illustrated than unillustrated texts when reading silently. They are also found to pay more attention to the pictures when the text is relatively difficult for them. The suggestion is that they do attend to the pictures when left to their own devices. But do they do so in a way that is constructive?

Again, the evidence is sparse,[92] but there is none to argue to the contrary. In general, information that is illustrated tends to be better remembered, particularly at the level of details. In addition, illustrations appear to be an effective means of inserting information that is consistent with but supplementary to the text (though incongruous illustrations can, conversely, disrupt memory for text). And, importantly, the presence of illustrations seems not to diminish comprehension for unillustrated sections of text.

---

89. Willows, Borwick, and Hayvren (1981) review a number of studies that have re-examined and supported this conclusion, including Braun (1969), Harris (1967), Hartley (1970–71), Harzem, Lee, and Miles (1976), and Singer, Samuels, and Spiroff (1973–74).

90. Willows, Borwick, and Hayvren (1981).

91. Willows, Borwick, and Hayvren (1981).

92. And there is virtually none on beginning readers.

In short, research provides no compelling argument against the presence of compatible illustrations in meaningful text.[93] On the other hand, toward the goal of instilling the most positive attitudes towards text, one can think of lots of arguments for making children's books as enticingly attractive as possible.

For little ones who are not yet reading themselves, intuitions suggest that pictures often provide an important and pleasing means of comprehension support. Extending such intuitions, research indicates that, in both quantity and quality, parent-child discussions of pictures are key to the appreciation of language and literature that grows from picture-book reading.[94]

I add as a note that, until recently, both of my children have steadfastly refused books that were low on pictures (or even books with what, in their opinion, were ugly pictures). On the other hand, I just finished reading a pictureless version of George MacDonald's *The Princess and the Goblins* to my son, now five; he listened with great engagement and fine visual imagery—and asked for another when we were done. While this clearly demarcates a new level of sophistication with language and literacy on John's part, it in no way reflects a diminution in his appreciation of pictures. In the same period of time, he has, for example, discovered D.C. Comics with great glee.

Fostering Awareness of Print

Appreciation of the pictures in a book is functional. Familiarity with letters and awareness of words is critical. But these are only pieces of the puzzle. Children need more. They need to understand how such components piece together in the interwoven fabric of useful, meaningful text.

In preschool and kindergarten programs, enhancement of children's print awareness should be a central goal. The classroom should be print-rich, and the print should be varied, functional, and significant to the children. In addition to displays of, for example, current activity themes and the children's names and birthdays, logistically useful print can be made salient. Newsletters and notices can be transmitted through the children, the names of those who will be absent can be visibly posted such

---

93. Although Willows, Borwick, and Hayvren (1981) caution that there may be important individual differences in the productivity with which children attend to illustrations.

94. Snow and Ninio (1986).

that the others can ask about them, cubbies and coat hooks can be labeled, sign-up lists can be posted for optional activities, and so on. When possible, visits to the school or public library are well worth the hassle. And the research everywhere indicates the value of reading books with them.[95]

Sharing Books with Children

Books should be read in such a way that the children can examine the pictures, discuss all aspects of meaning, and become aware of the format and function of the print. Books should be kept in such a way that they are invitingly available for direct examination by the children.

To this end, the use of "big books," as proposed by Don Holdaway, offers many opportunities.[96] "Big books" are nothing more than large-sized books. As such, however, they offer the opportunity for sharing print with a whole group of children as visibly and interactively as one might share a normal-sized or "little book" with just a few. Through the reading of big books, children can be engaged not just in listening to the language of books but also in the collective exploration of their visual and thematic composition. Big books, in short, allow a classroom equivalent of bedtime stories and, like bedtime stories, they are meant to be read over and over, as often as they are enchanting.

The goal in reading big books is to elicit the children's participation in unlocking all aspects of their message. Favorite candidates include "The Gingerbread Man" and "The Three Billy Goats Gruff." The semirepetitive schemes of these books invite prediction of events. Moreover, the repetitive refrains invite prediction of and, thus, engagement in their wording.

In reading a big book aloud to children, Holdaway strongly suggests that the teacher point to each word as it is read. This serves at once to illustrate that text proceeds from top to bottom and left to right and to introduce the status of printed words.[97]

Repeated words may be hunted down and thus soon acquired as sight words. Conveniently such oft-repeated words tend to be those unavoidable but metacognitively elusive function words. Further, repeated readings and repetitive texts set the stage for acquisition of a broader sight vocabulary. To this we might add the observation that early acquisition of a few sight words is

---

95. For reviews see Goldfield and Snow (1984); Johns (1984); Teale (1984).
96. Holdaway (1979).
97. Following Clay (1972).

surely beneficial. As it arms the child with the knowledge that a given word is represented by the same spelling all the time, it promotes that invaluable (if not quite valid) insight that a given spelling represents the same word all the time.

As the children become more familiar with the nature of texts, such word exploration can become more methodical. For example, the reading situations can be used to lead children to discover the visual differences between one word and two words or between long words and short words. Rhyming texts may be ideal for introducing the basic concept of spelling-sound correspondences. Poetry, Holdaway suggests further, offers superlative opportunity for exercising children's ability to think about both context and phonology in predicting words.

For focused discussions of orthography, he recommends methodical use of cardboard masks.[98] By exposing just one word or letter through the center of the mask, one can direct the children's attention to that one word or letter. By progressively unmasking the letters of a word as they are read, one can help the children to understand that letters, too, proceed left to right. Moreover, having secured the children's eagerness to predict and participate, one may thereby lead them to discover how, left to right, letters encode sound—and how they sometimes do not (or at least not as initially expected).

Where teachers construct their own big books, even their "homemade" quality can be turned to advantage. The print can be made more eye-catching through variations in color and design—obeisant, of course, to the emotions of the text. The illustrations can be added by the children themselves. And the very flaws and imperfections of the homemade big books spur the children to scrutinize their commercial little book cousins most carefully—which, of course, should be constantly available for independent "rereading" and borrowing.

The advantages of such book sharing go beyond print exploration. The participatory forum is ideal for engaging the children in discussions of character and plot. It is, moreover, ideal for engaging children in predicting, accommodating, and more generally thinking about the forms, uses, and messages of written text—and, again, it is thinking most of all that supports learning. At best, such sharing of books provides a way of delighting the children both in texts and in their own capacity to explore and learn from and about texts.

---

98. As he points out, these activities may be still easier with an overhead projector than with a big book.

Language Experience Activities

As important as books are, there is a more basic message to be conveyed about written text. Specifically, text is language.

The language experience approach was designed to convey this point in the most self-evident manner imaginable: Let the students see that print is "talk written down."[99] In this way, a natural bridge can be created from their oral language knowledge to their literacy challenge. The objective, succinctly summarized and in classic dialectic form, is to create the understanding that

What I can think about, I can talk about.
What I can say, I can write.
What I can write, I can read.
I can read what I write and what other people can write for me to read.[100]

The canonical method of the language experience approach thus consists of writing down the children's own oral language and then leading them to appreciate that what has been written is what they have said.[101] As the teacher transcribes the child's contribution, she or he carefully enunciates each word, emphasizing the pauses between the spoken words and the spaces between their written renditions.

The variety of classroom opportunities for capturing talk in writing is limited only by imagination. Even with very young children, one may print labels or captions on artwork or notes on holiday cards to be sent home. Students may be helped to author their own books, to be shared with one another. The method can be usefully deployed for cognitively preparing a class activity or, afterward, for summarizing it. Before a unit on spiders, for example, the teacher can make a poster listing a comment from each child on the nature of spiders; afterward, another poster may be made, eliciting new knowledge from each. The intellectual growth it may foster can thus extend well beyond print awareness.

In managing such discussions, the teacher may be tempted to paraphrase a child's contribution or to summarize those of the

---

99. As I had always believed this to be an especially British method, I was interested to note that Edmund Burke Huey (1908/1968) attributes its suggestion to John Amos Comenius (1592–1670) and its popularization to George Farnham (1887), superintendent of the Binghamton, New York, schools.

100. Allen (1976, cited in Lapp and Flood, 1983).

101. In the interest of maximizing the relevance and fidelity of the "talk written down"—and, thus, of maximizing the personal involvement of the learner, many feel that the method is most powerfully used with individual children rather than with groups.

group. To do so, however, runs awry of the spirit of the approach. Although the teacher may profitably take the opportunity to help students to refine the syntax of a contribution, the words that are written should be the words that the children feel that they themselves have produced. Not just the personal involvement of each learner but, more important, the very "Aha!" experience that the approach is intended to produce depend on the children's seeing that the print represents their very own words. [102]

Beyond supporting the insight that what is said can be written, the approach provides a natural medium for clarifying the referent of the word *word*, for pointing out that individual words are separated by spaces in print, and for making such points as that print is written from left to right and top to bottom, and that the end of a line is not always the end of a thought. [103] Toward developing writing and inducing the children to scrutinize the visual structure of words, one may also ask them to trace or copy their dictated text.

It has additionally been argued that because comprehension is not a problem with such self-produced materials and, moreover, since the message is familiar before it is read, language experience products offer certain distinct opportunities for conveying information about the sound-symbol structure of print. Specifically the children may be led to notice that every time a particular word is written, it looks the same; that the reason this word always looks the same is that it is always comprised of the same ordered set of letters; that, in fact, all words are made up of letters; that the difference between words is only in the particular number, selection, and ordering of letters they contain. From there, the child might be led to notice that "each letter of the alphabet stands for one or more sounds that I make when I talk." [104] Moreover, the next logical step, to phonic and spelling instruction proper, would seem to follow naturally.

Complementing these activities, the children may be helped to develop their own inventory of sight words. For example, any word of special interest to a child may be printed on a card to be taken home. [105] Alternatively, each child may accrue a file of such cards, available for admiration or augmentation at any time. As a useful and entertaining twist on this theme, Holdaway

---

102. Feitelson (1988).

103. See Durkin (1988).

104. Allen (1976, p. 54).

105. Ashton-Warner (1963).

suggests occasionally shuffling together the cards from a group of children and then laying all of them out on the floor.[106] The children must then find their own cards and read each aloud to the group before returning it to their personal pile. The words that are recognized by no one are left on the floor and discarded. Meanwhile the pile that is retrieved by each child holds a growing trove of words that are truly being learned.

Of course, the idea that written language is a special and invaluable channel of communication extends beyond the basic idea that what we think can be written. One would also like the children to discover that other people's thoughts are often useful or pleasurable to read. One would like the children to appreciate that what they do not know can be read and that what can be read can be known.

In view of this, language experience proponents frequently advocate that the texts under study be progressively expanded from transcripts of the children's own speech to, for example, informational placards at the zoo, manuals of driving rules and regulations, or, more generally, "any noncommercial text that deals with the interests and experiences of an individual or a particular group."[107]

The stipulation that the texts be "noncommercial" probably should not be taken literally. Rather, I interpret it as shorthand for the idea that the texts be ecologically valid and, more important, that their content be of personal relevance and interest to the students.[108] Focal attention is thus given to the idea that people more willingly try to read that which they are interested in reading. This is a point that no teacher or curriculum designer should overlook.

Given its strengths and possibilities, it is not surprising that the language experience approach has sometimes been used as the central vehicle for reading instruction proper. Yet there are drawbacks to this idea. Whereas texts that the children produce themselves may reflect too little in the way of new linguistic challenges, texts that are selected for interest value may contain too much. Furthermore, the orthographic structure of the words contained in either may be all over the map. Perhaps for these reasons, research on the effectiveness of relying heavily on the

---

106. Holdaway (1979).

107. Durkin (1988, p. 374).

108. In particular, Durkin (1988) stresses that language experience texts should be used to supplement, not replace basal instruction.

language experience approach for reading instruction itself has shown it, on balance, to be suboptimal.[109]

Nevertheless, the potential of the language experience approach for developing basic print awareness is outstanding. For purposes of conveying and refining the relation between print and language, what better means could there be than giving the child permanent, admirable, and holdable written displays of her or his own spoken thoughts? In keeping with this, research indicates that language experience activities are of special value toward the goal of enhancing reading readiness.[110]

Summary: Print Preliminaries

Along with phonological awareness, basic print awareness, word awareness, and letter recognition are capacities that we should seek to develop in kindergarten and preschool—well before first-grade. Collectively, the research suggests that if we could do so universally, we would enormously reduce the rate of primary school failures.[111] Research also indicates that children whom we cannot help to succeed in the primary grades are likely to fail in school forever.[112]

Earnest commitment to preschool literacy support may be the soundest investment we can make in the future productivity of our country and the future well-being of our people. Such preschool activities are valuable for any group of children. Yet, they may be invaluable for children from print-poor home environments. We as educators, psychologists, and policy-makers must do whatever we can to ensure that all of our children are headed toward the futures they deserve—not locked into the ones their parents got.

---

109. See especially Stahl and Miller (1989, in press).

110. Stahl and Miller (1989, in press).

111. Minimally it would seem that diagnostic testing for and responsive remediation of such print basics should be of paramount importance in designing reading programs for entering first-graders. See Clay (1979); Downing (1979); McCormick and Mason (1986)

112. Carter (1984); Juel (1988).

14

To Reading from Writing

Chances are good that the very first person who invented speech, did not do so because she or he was itching to hear someone else hold forth. Similarly, it is a good bet that the person who invented written language did not do so because she or he was yearning for a good book. There would seem to be something fundamentally human about the desire to communicate. Why not capitalize on this desire in beginning instruction on written language? Although this is not at all a new idea, it is worth examining anew in context.[1]

In support of this foray, research indicates that children's achievements in reading and writing are generally quite strongly and positively related.[2] Further, across evaluations of beginning reading programs, emphasis on writing activities is repeatedly shown to result in special gains in reading achievement.[3] Although the supportive relations between reading and writing surely run in both directions, we will concentrate in this chapter on those that run *from* writing *to* reading.

Early Spelling and Phonemic Awareness

In an increasing number of classrooms in the United States, children are being encouraged to write even before they receive much instruction in reading. Although the idea of "write first,

---

1. Indeed, it has recently become a topic of intense interest among reading and language educators. For anthologies see, e.g., Jensen (1984); Squire (1987).

2. Chall and Jacobs (1983); Hammill and McNutt (1980); Stotsky (1983).

3. See, e.g., Aukerman (1971, 1984); Bond and Dykstra (1967); Chall (1967); Evans and Carr (1985).

read later" was long promoted by Maria Montessori,[4] writing was, until recently, generally postponed in our classrooms until after reading was well under way.

In her classic study of youngsters who learn to read well before entering school, Durkin observed that, for many, writing came first. For many, she reflected, the "ability to read seemed almost like a by-product of [the] ability to print and spell."[5]

Just a few years later, Carol Chomsky and Charles Read came out with seminal papers specifically on the nature and development of such early writing behavior.[6] Not knowing how to read, the spellings that such children produce are often incorrect by conventional standards. Instead, using their knowledge of letter names and sounds, the children spell each word as it sounds to them. And, as shown by their spellings, these children quickly develop an impressive appreciation of the phonemic structure of our language.

The educational interest in such children centers on the prospect that their phonemic awareness developed as a consequence of their phonetic spelling. This, in turn, prompts two questions. Can phonemic awareness be effectively fostered by teaching children how to spell phonetically (as contrasted with correctly)? Or does it accrue through the process of figuring out sound-to-spelling translations on one's own? Little hard evidence exists on these issues. Let us first consider the value of teaching children to spell phonetically.

Teaching Phonetic Spellings to Children

Hohn and Ehri asked whether pairing sounds to letters would result in superior phonemic segmentation skills.[7] The items to be segmented during training were nonsense syllables, each comprised of two or three phonemes from a total set of eight. As each nonsense syllable was pronounced aloud by the experimenter, one group of kindergartners was trained to push out a bingo marker for each phoneme—a standard procedure in the testing and training of phonemic awareness.[8] Another group was trained to select from among eight markers the one exhibiting the correct letter for each

---

4. Montessori (1966).
5. Durkin (1966, p. 137).
6. Chomsky (1971a, 1971b); Read (1971).
7. Hohn and Ehri (1983).
8. Elkonin (1973).

phoneme in the syllable. A third group received no training at all.

After training had been completed, all of the children were presented with a new set of syllables to segment. When the test syllables were comprised of novel two- and three- phoneme combinations of the phonemes used during training, the group trained with the letters outperformed both of the others. However, when one of the two or three phonemes in the test syllable was novel, the advantage of the children who had learned the letters disappeared (though both trained groups did better than the untrained group). Hohn and Ehri also found that none of the children could fully segment test syllables comprised of four phonemes, /blōt/, /māts/, and /slēm/, and this was despite the fact that these four-phoneme syllables were made up of the very same phonemes that were used during training. The suggestion is that learning letters promotes phonemic awareness better than straight segmentation training—but only awareness of the particular phonemes whose spelling has been learned and, even then, not if they occur in a blend.

In another study, Ehri and Wilce taught one group of children to spell phonemically transparent syllables while they taught another to match letters to isolated phonemes.[9] The training regimen was extensive for both groups. The children in the spelling group had to spell 147 nonsense syllables to perfection; the children in the isolated letter-sound group had to produce 436 letter responses to isolated phonemes.

Afterward, the children were given a set of four posttests. Two of these demonstrated that the children who had been taught to spell could spell or recognize the spellings of the training syllables better than the children who had only been trained on isolated letter-sound correspondences. A third demonstrated that the children who had been taught to spell could segment the training syllables better than those who had been taught isolated letter-sound correspondences.

Only in the remaining posttest (which was actually the first to be administered) was any attempt made to assess the extent to which the spelling training might transfer. For this test, the children were asked to read twelve untrained, monosyllabic words, each comprised of novel combinations of the trained

---

9. Ehri and Wilce (1987). The syllables were not orthographically regular in the sense that vowels, in whatever spellings, were given long pronunciations.

phonemes.[10] In fact, this word-reading test was repeated as many as seven times over, with feedback on each word each time it was read. The children who had received spelling training were significantly more successful than the others. Nevertheless, after seven passes through the list, even they read only half the words correctly. Interestingly, almost all of the spelling-trained children eventually mastered the three-letter words. It was the four-letter words—the ones that contained consonant clusters—that persisted in giving them difficulty.

These studies, in short, yield limited support for the idea that phonemic awareness will be fostered by teaching youngsters how to spell phonetically. On balance, it does not look like a very promising idea. In view of the specificity of what the children seem to have learned in these studies, it is probably a better idea to teach correct spellings when spellings are taught. Meanwhile, from both of these studies comes the suggestion that children have special difficulty in perceiving the phonemic structure of consonant clusters. Remember this suggestion; we will return to it later.

Letting Children Invent Spellings

The remaining question is whether the challenge of inventing one's own spellings promotes phonemic awareness. Although direct evidence on this issue is scant, an answer can be obliquely sought by examining the spellings that children produce. The potential utility of this approach derives from the fact that the invented spellings of different children have long been recognized to exhibit a number of common features.

Chomsky summarizes these commonalities as follows.[11] Often the children incorporate whole letter names into their spellings:[12] YL (while), THAQ (thank you), NHR (nature), PPL (people). More generally, the consonants tend to contribute the most salient fraction of their names—though sometimes unconventionally: KAN (can), JRIV (drive). Long vowels generally speak for themselves: BOT (boat), STA (stay), AGRE (angry). Short vowels come as close as they can: BAD (bed), OL (all), LUKS (looks); or are omitted altogether: TST (test). Postvocalic liquids and nasals tend to lose

---

10. The spellings of the words was simplified to match the trained correspondences, e.g., *stone* was spelled *stōn*.

11. Chomsky (1979) attributes these observations to Read (1975).

12. Note that children who invent spelling at home, prior to entering school, generally write in uppercase letters.

their vowels: *GRL* (girl), *KLR* (color), *PKN* (picking). And nasals before stops often go unrepresented: *WOT* (won't), *PLAT* (plant).

Chomsky thus puts her finger on one explanation for the peculiarities of children's invented spellings: In deciding how to represent a word, they tend to exploit the names of the letters rather than a direct image of the sounds they formally represent. Yet the extent to which this explanation can account for the range of peculiarities commonly found in the children's spellings is not clear. Also unclear is the extent to which their spelling patterns are not alternatively attributable to an incomplete sensitivity to the phonemic structure of words.

To investigate this issue more rigorously, Treiman[13] computerized a sample of 6000 spellings produced by 43 children in a first-grade classroom in Indianapolis, Indiana. Over the course of their first-grade year, the children received instruction with "standard reading and phonics materials." In addition, their teacher had set aside about half an hour every morning for writing.

For purposes of analysis, Treiman divided the children's spellings into four categories:

- Correct spellings
- Orthographically legal substitution errors
- Orthographically illegal substitution errors
- Omitted phonemes

Regression analyses of the *correct spellings* indicated that they were influenced by at least four factors. Concurring with earlier analyses, one of these factors was the letters' names: The spelling of a phoneme was more likely to be correct if the name of the correct letter contained its sound. A second factor was related to the dominance or simplicity of a letter-sound correspondence such that, for example, /j/ was more likely to be spelled with a *j* than a *g*. A third factor was the likelihood of the correct spelling relative to the total number of ways that a phoneme could be spelled. For example, since /b/ can be correctly spelled in only two ways, *b* and *bb*, the children were quite likely to spell it correctly; in contrast, since /k/ can be spelled in an number of ways, *k, c, ck, cc*, . . . , the children misspelled it quite often. The fourth factor was the number of letters in a phoneme's spelling; in particular, children had more trouble with digraphs than single-letter graphemes.

---

13. Treiman (1987).

The children's *orthographically legal substitution errors* also seemed governed by these four factors. For example, deferring to the sounds of letter names, the *ay* in "haystack" was spelled with just an *a* while the *oo* in "balloon" was spelled with a *u*. Choosing the dominant or simpler representations for a sound, they spelled the *gu* in "guessed" with a *g*; the *ck* in "haystack" with a *k*; and—quite often—voiced *s*, as in "cheese," with a *z*. Moreover, their greater difficulty in spelling vowels as compared with consonants was largely explainable by the fact that the spellings of vowel sounds are more numerous. Finally, where morphemic and phonemic spelling implications conflicted, the children were more likely to respect the phonemic implications, for example, spelling *-ed* as *t* in "guessed" but *d* in "hemmed."

Among the children's *legal substitution errors*, Treiman also observed a growing respect for some of the more subtle constraints of our system. One such example is the spelling of "he" as *hy*. Note that *y* usually says /ē/ in final position while *e* does not. On the other hand, children did not use *y* to represent the long *e* sound in word-initial positions; they did not, for example, spell "eat" as *yt*. As another example, children did sometimes represent /k/ inappropriately as *ck*, as in *mrckut* ("market"). However, as orthographically appropriate, *ck* showed up only in medial or final positions; spellings with word-initial *ck*, such as *ckup* (for "cup"), were not produced.

The children's *orthographically illegal substitution errors* generally fell into one of three classes. The first class corresponded to partial knowledge of correct spellings and was principally constituted of digraph misspellings. Digraphs were most often represented by just their first letter, as in *cez* for "cheese." Because the names of the letters in digraphs generally do not capture the sounds that they represent, such spellings were attributed to orthographic memory—albeit incomplete orthographic memory. The second class consisted of orthographic violations that were phonemically appropriate given the actual sounds of the words and included, for example, substitutions of *d* for *t* in words like "water," of *g* for *k* in words like "sky," and *ch* for *t* before *r* as in *chrap* ("trap").[14] The third class consisted of the substitution of one phoneme by another that was highly similar at the level of phonemic features, as in the use of *t* for initial *ch* and a number of short vowel errors.

---

14. Note also that these phonemes differ from each other by a single feature (see chapters 2 and 13).

Altogether the children's correct spellings, as well as their orthographically legal and illegal substitution errors, indicate astute attention to the phonemic structure of words. When errors occurred, they generally reflected either insufficient familiarity of spelling conventions or hearings of the sounds of individual phonemes that were occasionally imperfect but, as often, more veridical than the hearings that good spellers give them. Yet, there remains one more category of errors to be considered: *omission errors*.

Whenever a phoneme was not distinctly represented in the children's spellings, Treiman categorized it as an *omission error*. The omission errors, in turn, were divided into those that involved vowel sounds and those that involved consonant sounds.

Distinct representation of vowel sounds was frequently missing in unstressed syllables, as in *blun* ("balloon"), *wodr* ("water"), and *tekn* ("chicken"). In addition, separate letters for vowels were frequently omitted when their sounds were part of the name of an adjacent consonant, as in *bab* ("baby"), *lfunt* ("elephant"), and *mrckut* ("market"). Note that the names of *l*, *r*, and *n*—the final letters of the unstressed syllables cited by Treiman—all begin with a vowel sound (as do *f*, *m*, *s*, and *x*). In view of this, one wonders whether the observed tendencies to omit vowels in unstressed syllables and prior to liquids and nasals might be commonly explained by the presence of the vowel's sound in the name of the succeeding consonant.

In any case, the extent to which omissions of vowel sounds in the children's spellings reflected failures to recognize these sounds as separate phonemes as opposed to confusions about how the grapheme system works, is unclear. Biasing us toward the latter explanation, however, is the fact that vowel sounds generally do gain explicit representation when they are stressed and when the shorthand strategy of conveying them through the names of adjacent consonants will not work. Moreover, children's representations of diphthongs indicate considerable sensitivity to the separate sounds of vowels, e.g., *boe* ("boy") and *sgie* ("sky").

In contrast, and uniquely so, the children's omissions of consonant sounds seem to reflect a weak spot in their phonemic awareness, per se. Omitted consonant sounds were very often members of a syllable-initial consonant cluster.

To understand this tendency better, Treiman computed frequencies of consonant omissions as a function of the syllabic structure in which they occurred.[15] The first consonant of a

---

15. Treiman (1985b).

syllable was rarely omitted, whether it was a singleton (0.9 percent of opportunities) or the first consonant of a cluster (2 percent of opportunities). In contrast, subsequent consonants of initial clusters were omitted quite frequently: 23.3 percent for the second consonant of a cluster, and 22.7 percent for the third. (In Treiman's database, the third consonant of a cluster was always an *r*; in syllable-initial positions, *r* was omitted on only 3.8 percent of opportunities.)

In fact, not all consonant sounds can occur as the second in a cluster. Maybe it was just that the children had special difficulty with these particular sounds. To assess this possibility, Treiman examined omission frequencies for the phonemes /p/, /t/, and /k/, which can be either the first (e.g., *pram*, *tram*, and *clam*) or second (e.g., *spar*, *star*, and *scar*) sounds in a syllable-initial consonant cluster. When these sounds were the first of a cluster, they were omitted on only 1.3 percent of opportunities; when they were the second, they were omitted on 36.1 percent of opportunities.

Nor could the difference be explained in terms of the letters' position in their words. When a consonant was the second phoneme of a word but the first of a syllable (e.g., *along*), it was only omitted on 2.7 percent of opportunities. Furthermore, when consonant sequences occurred not in syllable-initial position but across syllable boundaries (e.g., as in *bedroom* instead of *dress*), both consonants were but always represented. Treiman's explanation for this pattern of results is, quite compellingly, that children's difficulties with syllable-initial consonant clusters reflect a basic difficulty in analyzing the phonemic structures of complex syllable onsets. The spellings and sounds of consonant clusters require special attention.

Pedagogical Issues

The means by which invented spelling is encouraged in the classroom is generally quite simple. Children are given regular opportunity to express themselves on paper, as the students in Treiman's study were given one half-hour each day. Initially, the centerpieces of their products are typically illustrations. With encouragement, both from their teacher and from watching their classmates, the children begin first to caption and then to write stories about the pictures that they have drawn. Teachers report that they provide little explicit instruction on exactly how to go about inventing spellings: "Just spell it the way it sounds. I'll be able to read it."

The major reservation to promoting invented spelling in the classroom relates to the concern that the spellings that children invent are frequently incorrect. Will their practice of and attention to such incorrect spellings impede their learning of correct spellings? A study on this issue has recently been conducted by Clarke.[16]

The 102 middle-class students in Clarke's study were drawn from four first-grade classrooms in Ottawa, Canada. Children in all four classrooms received reading instruction through a basal reading program along with supplementary phonics activities. In addition, all were regularly engaged in creative writing sessions for eighty to one hundred minutes each week. However, children in two of the four classrooms were encouraged to invent their spellings while writing; the children in the other two classrooms were encouraged to spell correctly.

More specifically, reports Clarke, during writing sessions in the classrooms in which invented spellings were encouraged:

Teachers circulated throughout the class encouraging effort, discussing ideas that might be developed and discouraging erasing ("just cross it out"). Teachers did not spell. Children were told to sound out the words and print the letters they heard. The teachers emphasized that children were not always going to be right in their letter choices, but that that did not matter just now.

In contrast, when children in the classrooms emphasizing traditional spellings were ready to write:

They immediately got out their dictionaries or personal word lists. As soon as they wanted to write a word they were not sure of, they searched for the spelling. Children frequently consulted with friends on the beginning sounds in words as help in finding the word in the dictionary or for confirmation on how a word should be spelled. . . . Teachers printed words on the chalkboard, on the children's story pages, or on their personal word lists, as well as spelled words aloud while children printed the letters. . . . Teachers also circulated ensuring that specific children known to have difficulty were able to write something. In the beginning months this entailed having each child experiencing difficulty dictate his/her story and then copy the teacher's printing.

Examinations of writing samples collected from the four classrooms between November and March indicated that the children using traditional spelling wrote with slightly more sophisticated vocabulary and more complex syntax. In addition, they committed many fewer spelling errors (6 percent) than those

---

16. Clarke (1989, in press).

using invented spellings (34 percent). On the other hand, the children using traditional spelling tended to write much shorter stories. In March, when virtually all of the children were composing on their own (as opposed to dictating), the stories of the traditional spelling group averaged thirteen words in length while those of the invented spelling children averaged forty words in length.

Given the difference in the classroom emphases for these two groups, one wonders about the extent to which the differences in the children's spelling accuracy reflected differences in knowledge as opposed to behavior. To assess this, Clarke administered a battery of spelling tests in March. Both groups displayed considerable but comparable difficulty in spelling high-frequency but orthographically irregular words. However, in contrast to the evidence available from the writing samples, the children in the invented spelling group were significantly more successful with both a list of lower-frequency regularly spelled words and with the words on the Level 1 Spelling Subtest of the Wide Range Achievement Test.

To see whether the children would also differ in their reading proficiency, Clarke administered a battery of reading tests in March, too. Whereas the performance of the two groups was quite comparable on a reading comprehension test, it differed significantly on several tests of word recognition skill. The classrooms who had relied on invented spelling significantly outperformed the others on nonsense words from the Woodcock Reading Mastery Tests, on untimed reading of two word lists from the Durrell Word Recognition Test, and on two lists developed by Baron and Treiman[17] consisting, respectively, of high-frequency irregular and lower-frequency regular words. In contrast, there was (albeit not consistent) evidence that the children who had used traditional spelling were more successful at recognizing words under speeded or "flash card" conditions.

On balance, Clarke's results seem to indicate a definite advantage for the invented over the traditional spelling groups. And yet, one wonders why. True, the children in the invented spelling group wrote more, but their evident attentiveness to correct spelling during writing seemed so much less. For example, in the writing samples that Clarke analyzed, spelling accuracy increased from 88 percent to 95 percent for the traditional spellers between November and March; for the inventive spellers it decreased from 66 percent to 58 percent.

---

17. Baron and Treiman (1980).

Staring at Clarke's statistical tables, one notices that, though the mean performance of the traditional spellers was often lower than that of the inventors, the variance—the range of scores— was often greater. That is, the benefits of emphasizing correct spelling appeared to be far less even across students. Indeed, on close examination of her data, Clarke confirmed this suspicion.

On the basis of pretests administered at the beginning of the year, Clarke selected a matched set of high-readiness students— twelve from the invented spelling classes and twelve from the traditional spelling classes—and another matched set—twelve and twelve—of low-readiness students.[18] For the two groups of high-readiness students, she found no significant differences on any of the posttests. For the low-readiness children, those who had been in the invented spelling classrooms significantly outperformed their traditionally instructed peers on the majority of spelling and word recognition posttests.

The tempting conclusion here is that the difference between the performance of these children arose from the differences in the way they were encouraged to confront holes in their knowledge. Whereas the traditional spellers dictated their earliest stories, the inventive spellers were on their own from the start. Whereas the traditional spellers were given correct models to trace, copy, and reference, the inventive spellers had to figure the system out by themselves. The tempting conclusion is, in other words, that the advantage of the low-readiness invented spellers reflected a better developed sense of the phonemic and phonetic relations between spoken and written words—a sense that had grown from their own, necessarily thoughtful and active efforts to spell.

In keeping with this, Carol Chomsky suggests:

Learning to read, or at first to identify printed words, surely involves forming hypotheses about the relations (direct and indirect) of spelling to pronunciation, changing these hypotheses as new evidence is added, and eventually arriving at a system of interpretation that is in accord with the facts. This hypothesis construction is an active process, taking the child far beyond the "rules" that can be offered by the best of patterned, programmed, or linguistic approaches. The more the children are prepared to do for themselves, the better off they are. Piaget (1972) has said, "Children should be able to do their own experimenting. . . . In order for a child to understand something, he must construct it himself, he must reinvent it. Every time we teach a child something, we keep him from inventing it himself [p. 27]." This view applies quite well to learning

---

18. The selection was based on the three pretests that best predicted posttest performance: the ability to print the lowercase alphabet, to spell words, and to recognize words on the Boder list under time pressure.

to read. The printed word "belongs" to the spontaneous speller far more directly than to children who have experienced it only ready made. For once you have invented your own spelling system, dealing with the standard system comes easy. A considerable amount of the intellectual work has already been done.[19]

Independent spellers, she reports, soon develop an avid curiosity about the print around them, what it says, and how it is spelled. While their efforts to spell words seem to foster this interest, their experience in spelling the words incorrectly does not seem to impede their progress. In part, she suggests, this independence may be due to the fact that in the course of inventing spellings, children "appear to be more interested in the activity than the product." "Often," she adds, "they cannot read back what they have written, nor are they interested in doing so."

Examining the products of another group of children who had been encouraged to write and spell creatively in class, Ehri observed that, for many, spelling development was quite gradual.[20] The earliest spellings often captured but a sampling of the phonemes of the word of interest, and not always correctly. For one particular little boy whom she describes in detail, the spellings invented for particular words were highly unstable throughout the first grade. Furthermore, phonemically complete spellings were not in the majority until he had been experimenting with the system for a whole year. Very soon after that point, however, the majority of his spellings shifted from phonemically correct to literally correct. It seems, just as Chomsky suggested, that once the child has understood and learned the principles of spelling, "dealing with the standard system comes easy."[21]

In overview, classroom encouragement of invented spellings and independent writing from the start seems a promising approach toward the development of literacy skills. Beyond all that was mentioned above and whether the children are directing their efforts toward good descriptions or imaginative stories, this approach appears incomparable for purposes of developing their abilities to reflect on their own thoughts, to elaborate and organize their ideas, and to express themselves in print.

---

19. Chomsky (1979, p. 49).

20. Ehri (1988).

21. Note, however, that this level of understanding that allows standard spellings to "come easy" is acquired only gradually, requires considerable time and effort, and exhibits similar developmental patterns among "spontaneous" and tutored spellers alike. See, for example: Baghban (1984); Beers (1980); Beers and Henderson (1977); Bissex (1980); Clay (1975); Ehri (1986); Gentry (1978, 1981).

Moreover, whether viewed at the level of text generation, sentence generation, or word generation, it is an activity that inherently requires children to think actively—and such activities are both invaluable and hard to come by in the classroom.[22]

Restricting concern to the issue of learning to read words, note that the process of inventing spellings is essentially a process of phonics. Not surprisingly, then, the phonetic appropriateness of prereaders' invented spellings is found to be predicted by their level of phonemic awareness[23] and to predict their later success in learning to read words.[24] Note further that, whereas the children in those early studies of Durkin, Chomsky, and Read, may have been linguistically exceptional,[25] the children whom Clarke, Treiman, and Ehri studied were just convenient collections of first graders.[26] For each group, however, the practice of inventing spellings was coupled with impressive awareness of and attention to the phonemic structure of words.

The evidence that invented spelling activity simultaneously develops phonemic awareness and promotes understanding of the alphabetic principle is extremely promising, especially in view of the difficulty with which children are found to acquire these insights through other methods of teaching.[27] Equally inspiring are the reports that early writing activities promote children's interest in learning about what words say and how they are spelled. Yet these are only starting points. Exercise in writing and invented spelling may significantly enhance children's attitudinal and linguistic readiness for reading. As such, it may invaluably complement instruction in reading.

But exercise in writing cannot supplant instruction and practice in reading and word recognition. All of the children discussed above were receiving instruction in reading and word recognition alongside their exercise in writing, and their progress in the two cannot be decoupled. Treiman's analysis strongly implies that direct instruction in word analysis and consonant blending is a necessary complement to children's independent orthographic

---

22. See Adams (1989).
23. Liberman, Rubin, Duques, and Carlisle (1985); Morris (1981).
24. Mann, Tobin, and Wilson (1987); Morris and Perney (1984).
25. Chomsky (1971b); Durkin (1966); Read (1971).
26. Clarke (1989, in press); Ehri (1988); Treiman (1985b, 1987) .
27. See chapters 2 and 12.

intuitions.[28] Moreover, in order for children's interest in how words actually are spelled to be functional, they must be exposed to properly written text. In order for children to learn how words actually are spelled, they must also learn to read.

But this raises one of the sticky points among advocates of invented spelling. When or how should we teach children about correct spellings? Chomsky and Clay suggest that parents and teachers should take care to provide correct spellings whenever a child asks.[29] In contrast, the invented spelling teachers whom Clarke studied not only refused the answer but actively discouraged the question.[30] Going one more step, we might argue that in the coming world of word processors, letter-perfect spelling will be as obsolete a skill as using logarithmic tables to multiply. But let us not be hasty.

Learning How to Spell Correctly

Prior to this century—in fact, for thousands of years prior to this century—spelling drill was the principal means of teaching children to read. The reasons for this emphasis on spelling surely included many that are of little interest to us now: the relative availability of chalk tablets versus books, the appropriateness within other eras of drill and rote recitation, the classroom exigencies of the one-room schoolhouse, . . . or, try this: Noah Webster is said to have held that spelling was the proper way to teach reading because, at the earliest instructional levels, the child's mind was not ready to deal with word meanings.[31] However remote these reasons may be from today's modal educational philosophies and processes, there must also have been one more: For the method to have prevailed for thousands of years, people must have felt that it worked.

Despite our heritage, the word *spelling* can hardly be found in the indexes of contemporary reading education textbooks. In 1980, Richard Venezky wrote that

Neither spelling instruction nor spelling reform occupy central roles today in education or in public life. No major funding agency in the last 25 years has included among its highest priorities the improvement of

---

28. Treiman (1987).
29. Chomsky (1979); Clay (1975).
30. Clarke (1989). See descriptive quote above.
31. Venezky (1980).

spelling instruction. . . . Few cognitive psychologists have confessed an interest in spelling processes and only a handful in the last decade have even suggested that this topic was worthy of serious investigation. Similarly, the public schools exhibit limited enthusiasm for spelling. Some have no systematic spelling instruction at all while the average class offers perhaps two or three 15-minute periods for it each week.[32]

Be that as it may, this quotation is taken from the first page of the first chapter of a book entitled *Cognitive Processes in Spelling*,[33] which in its very publication heralded renewed interest in the topic.

The Relation between Reading and Spelling Skills

Beyond being a trendsetter, this book is quite interesting in its own right. In particular, its chapters are topically organized like high drama, sequentially running from setting, to climax, to denouement and conclusion.

In the first part of the book, amidst reviews of the history of spelling instruction and reform and analyses of the nature and origins of English spellings, the plot becomes clear: Good spelling cannot be a direct derivative of phonological knowledge.

First, the ability to learn standard spellings seems uninfluenced by mismatches between spoken dialect and standard pronunciations.[34] Second, and more persuasively, spelling-to-sound rules just plain do not work in reverse. For example, Berdiansky and colleagues identified 166 spelling-to-sound correspondences that successfully generated pronunciations for 90 percent of the one- and two-syllable words in their spoken corpus for six to nine year olds.[35] Applying those rules in reverse, however, Cronnell found that they generated correct sound-to-spelling translations for fewer than half of the words in the corpus.[36] Similarly, with the 300 rules developed by Hanna and colleagues[37] fewer than 50 percent of the 17,000 words in their corpus were spelled correctly.[38] That's a lot of rules. Even ignoring issues of complexity, it is probably more than one could expect the average fourth grader to have usefully memorized. Yet, in a spelling bee

---

32. Venezky (1980, p. 9).
33. Frith (1980a).
34. Desberg, Elliott, and Marsh (1980).
35. Berdiansky, Cronnell, and Koehler (1969); see chapter 11.
36. Cited in Desberg, Elliott, and Marsh (1980).
37. Hanna et al (1966).
38. Cronnell (1970, cited in Desberg, Elliott, and Marsh, 1980).

between fourth graders and a computer that had been programmed with these rules, the fourth graders handily won out.[39]

The problem, more specifically, seems to be that there is considerably more entropy in sound-to-spelling than in spelling-to-sound translations. For example, the letter *f* quite reliably symbolizes the phoneme /*f*/. In contrast, the phoneme /*f*/ can be spelled as *f, ff, ph,* or *gh.* Nor will resort to morphemic rules solve the problem. Nonphonemic spellings may help the reader to perceive the morphemic relation between word cousins, as in *sign–signature, bomb–bombard,* and *muscle–muscular.*[40] But they are less helpful for the speller. Why, for example, isn't *procedure* spelled as *proceedure, holistic* as *wholistic,* or *spatial* as *spacial?* If *reception* is the reason for the *p* in *receipt,* then why is there no *p* in *conceit* or *deceit?* If the *i* was left in *receipt* because of *receive,* then how come a *percept* isn't a *perceipt?* And the problems extend in the reverse direction, too. For years, I spelled *hierarchy* as *heirarchy* because I thought it came from *heir.*

The intrigue climaxes in the center sections of the book. There we learn that for a variety of clinical cases and special populations, spelling skills appear perplexingly dissociated from receptive and productive language capacities as well as reading capacities. Still more provocative are the contrasting patterns of behaviors found among normal children who are good versus poor spellers.

Early in the course of spelling development, children tend to spell words in ways that are neither correct, phonologically acceptable, nor even stable from trial to trial.[41] Beyond that stage, however, the spellings of both young spellers and older, poorer spellers tend to reflect a relatively strict and stable respect of letter-sound correspondences. Their spellings of irregular words tend to be "regularized"[42] while their spellings of pseudowords tend to reflect sequential sound-to-grapheme translations.[43] Good spellers, in contrast, usually spell real words correctly regardless of their letter-to-sound irregularities,[44] while they tend to spell pseudowords in analogy with similarly sounded real words regardless of the phonemic transparency of the spellings that

39. Simon and Simon (1973, cited in Desberg, Elliott, and Marsh, 1980).

40. See Chomsky and Halle (1968).

41. Bryant and Bradley (1980); Ehri (1980); Frith (1980b).

42. Barron (1980); Frith (1980b); Sloboda (1980).

43. Frith (1980b); Marsh, Friedman, Welch, and Desberg (1980).

44. Barron (1980); Baron, Treiman, Wilf, and Kellman (1980); Sloboda (1980).

result[45] (e.g., *wength* in analogy to *length* or *jation* in analogy to *nation*).[46]

But even while poor spellers seem to demonstrate more sensitivity to letter-sound correspondences than do good spellers while spelling, they demonstrate less while reading. As compared to good spellers, poorer spellers are shown to be more likely to compare syllables on the basis of global similarity than phonemic structure,[47] to be slower in assessing the phonemic significance of graphemic units,[48] to have more difficulty reading aloud,[49] to have more difficulty reading regularly spelled pseudowords,[50] and to be less slowed by irregular spelling-sound correspondences in reading real words.[51] They are also more likely to rely on the initial letters of words and to commit semantically related but phonologically discrepant substitution errors while reading.[52]

In short, whereas good spellers seem to spell visually and read phonetically, poorer spellers seem to spell phonetically and read visually. Is there a syndrome here? Perhaps crossed wires of some sort? Or is it an illusion? Little by little, the book leads us to the latter conclusion.

First, the knowledge and behaviors of the poor spellers are a bit oversimplified in this summary. Poor spellers are not oblivious to grapheme-phoneme correspondences while reading; they are just less sensitive to them than are good spellers. Nor are they completely dependent on sequential grapheme-phoneme correspondences while spelling, just more so than are good spellers. What can only be traces of literal, albeit incomplete, memory for spellings often occurs alongside the phonetic misconstruals—as examples: *coronel* or *colonial* for *colonel* (why not *curnle?*), *psychik* for *psychic* (why not *cyckik?*), *pnemonia* for *pneumonia* (why not *numonia?*).[53]

Furthermore, even in first grade, while deep in the stage of phonetic spelling and reading by initial letters plus context, the speed with which children name a picture of an object is

45. Frith (1980b); Marsh, Friedman, Welch, and Desberg (1980).
46. Marsh, Friedman, Welch, and Desberg (1980).
47. Baron, Treiman, Wilf, and Kellman (1980).
48. Baron, Treiman, Wilf, and Kellman (1980).
49. Frith (1980b).
50. Barron (1980); Frith (1980b).
51. Barron (1980); Marsh, Friedman, Welch, and Desberg (1980).
52. Baron, Treiman, Wilf, and Kellman (1980).
53. Baron, Treiman, Wilf, and Kellman (1980).

significantly hastened by simultaneous presentation of the complete, correct spelling of the object. In contrast, the presentation of strings that are appropriate in both shape and initial and final letters (e.g., *aggte* instead of *apple*) produces no such advantage.[54]

In like manner, the suggestion that good spellers spell visually is also too simple. Although good spellers seem especially sensitive to whether the spelling of a word "looks right,"[55] their ability to spell correctly seems to reflect something more than visual imagery. Sloboda demonstrates quite convincingly that although the capacity for visual imagery differs substantially among individuals, it is not responsible for good spellers' ability to avoid phonologically plausible mistakes.[56] His evidence suggests further that visual imaging is not involved in the generation of a word's spelling; it is instead applied optionally to the end-product.

And what about good readers' tendency to spell pseudowords "irregularly" (as in *wength* and *jation*)?[57] Although this tendency cannot be ascribed to application of any simple and sequential set of grapheme-phoneme correspondences, it cannot reflect literal memory for spellings either. The items, after all, were novel pseudowords, written to dictation. The suggestion is that skillful spellers do depend on their knowledge of spelling-sound relations but that this knowledge is more complex and better sensitized to its conditions of application than that of poor spellers.

These observations provoke an alternative hypothesis about the differences between good and poor spellers. Perhaps the reading and spelling behaviors of both are directly and causally linked after all. In particular, perhaps poor spellers' prominent display of visual and semantic strategies while reading reflects precisely the same deficit as does their prominent reliance on simple grapheme-phoneme correspondences in spelling. Perhaps both reflect an incompleteness in the knowledge they have acquired about spelling patterns and the relations of those patterns to meanings and phonology—an incompleteness in their basic orthographic knowledge.

From this perspective, to say that poor spellers read visually is misleading. To the contrary, the suggestion is that poor spellers do *not* visually recognize word spellings completely or quickly

54. Posnansky and Rayner (1977).

55. Sloboda (1980); Tenney (1980).

56. Sloboda (1980).

57. Frith (1980b); Marsh, Friedman, Welch, and Desberg (1980).

enough to use any but the simplest and most salient orthographic features in their identification. By extension, to say that good spellers read phonetically seems equally misleading. Although their reading may be phonetically appropriate, it is not because they are recognizing the words by way of sounding them out in any letter-by-letter manner. Instead it is because they visually recognize the spelling patterns and link them to their phonological translations effortlessly and accurately.

This hypothesis is consistent with the entire pattern of poor speller difficulties we have reviewed thus far, including the slowness of their oral reading, their greater reliance on context, their difficulties in reading pseudowords, and so on. Frith recognized that it also suggests certain other tasks that should differentiate poor from good spellers.[58]

More specifically, Frith reasoned, if this hypothesis were correct, then the reading performance of good spellers should be more sensitive than that of poor spellers to the graphophonemic details of text. To test this idea, she gathered a group of good and poor twelve-year-old spellers of comparable reading ability and asked them to read aloud sets of meaningful, connected text.

In one set of texts, Frith had altered the spellings of the words in ways that distorted their spellings and, therefore, their appearance, but nott thair foneemick translayshuns.[59] Her reasoning was that if poor spellers generally do not engage in phonological translations (or cannot do so efficiently) but are instead dependent on superficial visual cues, such as word length, shape, and the presence of particular letters, then these distortions should seriously impede their ability to read the passages. In contrast, if good spellers are facile at recognizing and phonologically translating legal spelling patterns, then they should be better able to read the passages despite the distortions. The results were consistent with these predictions.

For another set of texts, she diluted the graphophonemic cues by replacing some of the internal letters of the words with little triangles. Her reasoning was that if good spellers' reading generally involves attention to the complete spellings of words, then their performance would be significantly disrupted. In contrast, to the extent that poor spellers generally depend on such superficial visual cues as word length, word shape, and word-initial and word-final letters, their performance should be

58. Frith (1980b).

59. In contrast to the "Ladle Rat Rotten Hut" story, none of the distorted spellings were real words, and word boundaries were respected.

relatively indifferent to this set of distortions. Again the results were consistent with these predictions.

In the end, these studies of the relation between reading and spelling again corroborate theoretical work on the nature and importance of orthographic knowledge.[60] By reminder, theory holds that, for proficient readers, the recognition of a word proceeds through the complete visual processing of its individual letters. To the extent that the spelling patterns of the word are familiar, such visual processing is automatically accompanied by phonological translation. To the extent that the word itself is also familiar, the resulting orthographic and/or phonological image of the word automatically arouse its meaning, in turn.

In this context, the theory offers a corollary that is also relevant: The individual letters of a word cannot be visually processed in this rapid, complete, and relatively effortless manner unless its reader already possesses within her or his Orthographic processor a relatively complete representation of the spelling patterns it comprises.

A self-perpetuating syndrome is thus suggested. To the extent that the representation of a word in their Orthographic processor is incomplete, students cannot process the word with adequate speed except by glossing the unfamiliar parts of its spelling. Yet, to the extent that students do not process the complete spelling of a word they read, they cannot augment the representation of the word in their Orthographic processor.

Unless this syndrome can be broken—unless, somehow, students can be persuaded to attend more fully to less familiar orthographic patterns—neither their reading nor their spelling will improve. The spelling studies, moreover, give us a new and useful piece of information: Poor spelling is symptomatic of poor orthographic development. Following through on this sobering suggestion, Bryant and Bradley conclude their paper with the following observation:

We have . . . encountered children of 11 and 12 who read well but spell appallingly, and we believe that there is one other interesting thing to be said about them. In our informal experience these children often begin to experience serious reading difficulties too at around the age of 13 years or so. We suggest that this is due to their being introduced to new subjects such as science subjects and therefore new words and contexts. . . . They are faced with words which they cannot recognize in contexts which do not help . . . and as a result are quite at a loss.[61]

---

60. See chapters 6 and 8.
61. Bryant and Bradley (1980, p. 369).

Reflecting on this observation, we in turn may be reminded of the poor reading comprehension of our older school children in national and international assessments.

In all, the relation of spelling to the rest of the system seems best represented by the schematic in figure 14.1. In this figure, spelling is shown as an output channel, directly dependent on the orthographic processor.[62] In this relation, it is clear why spelling performance should be directly diagnostic of orthographic development. It is less clear, however, whether or how the act of spelling per se might contribute to orthographic development, and maybe it does not. On the other hand, the schematic suggests that the activities involved in learning or figuring out how to spell should contribute positively.

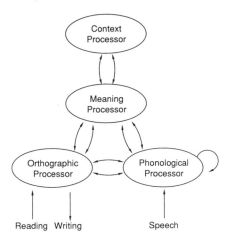

Figure 14.1
The relation between reading and writing.

Specifically, to memorize how a printed word is spelled, one must study its spelling. But theory holds that whenever information is entertained in memory, it also becomes registered or reinforced in memory. Whether one gets the spelling visually or aurally, it can only be passed to the spelling system by way of the Orthographic processor. As a consequence, the activity of attending to a word's spelling should strengthen a child's ability not only to write the word but also to read it. Further, by virtue of

---

62. This conception of spelling processor is also supported by studies of the dissolution of the spelling process under conditions of brain damage. See, e.g., Caramazza, Miceli, Villa, and Romani (1987).

the associations between processors, it should influence the child's phonological image of the word as well.

Similarly, to spell a never-seen word independently, the only option is to pass it from the meaning processor to the spelling system by way of, first, the Phonological processor and then the Orthographic processor. Minimally, then, the process of deducing spellings from sounds is expected to strengthen existing grapheme-phoneme associations. In addition, phonetically based spelling might be expected to foster phonemic segmentation skills. Each of these speculations is supported by research. Let us consider them in turn.

Directing Students' Attention to Spellings

One may ascertain the correct spelling of a word either by having somebody else spell it aloud or by looking at it in print. Research indicates that the experience of seeing a word in print is not just superior to hearing it spelled but is an extremely powerful and effective means of acquiring its spelling.[63] In addition, the experience of seeing or imagining a word's spelling, as contrasted with repeatedly hearing the word or even rehearsing it aloud, has been shown to be a superior means of remembering its pronunciation, even among first graders.[64]

One direct instructional implication of this evidence is that we should habitually encourage students to look at spelling patterns and vocabulary items that we want them to learn. We should write the words of interest on the board or point to them on the page. Spelling them aloud, relatively speaking, is a waste of time. A second implication of this evidence is that reading, since it requires children to look at words in print, should be a superlative means of learning the spellings of words. But as quickly as we recognize this point, we realize its limitations.

Where the purpose of reading is to comprehend, the process of word recognition is under considerable time pressure. As discussed in part III, the reader can invest extra time in identifying or sounding out letter sequences only at the expense of losing the meaning of the surrounding text. Yet unless the word is already orthographically familiar, the reader can fully process its letter sequences only through the time-consuming application of conscious effort and attention.

---

63. Henderson and Chard (1980).
64. Ehri and Wilce (1979).

The only way to process a troublesome word fully *and* comprehend the sentence to which it belongs, is by working out the word and then rereading the sentence. Although this is an excellent strategy for purposes of learning,[65] an easier alternative exists. Specifically, readers can finesse the orthographic difficulties of the word. Relying on whatever fragments of its spelling pattern they have perceived, along with contextual cues, they can just gloss over the fuzzier visual details. To a greater or lesser extent, this option is probably used by all readers, with the result that all readers can probably read more words than they can spell.

In contrast, if students are given isolated words to spell, there is no comprehension pressure to divert their attention. Moreover, research demonstrates that the process of copying new words significantly strengthens their visual perceptibility and does so rather enduringly.[66] Perhaps this should not be surprising: The writing of a word inherently forces attention to its full sequence of letters. For a student, the thought that somebody else might evaluate one's products may encourage such attention all the more.

The Influence of Spelling on the Perception of Phonology and Meaning

Adults' phonological intuitions are strongly influenced by their knowledge of spelling. Treiman has shown that when the actual sounds of syllables (e.g., /sbla/) are inconsistent with the phonemic structure implied by their imagined spellings (e.g., spla), adults tend to "hear" the spelled pattern.[67] Even when encouraged to listen harder and try something different, many had trouble hearing—indeed, could not hear—the phonetic structure of the syllables as they were spoken. They knew how such syllables should be spelled, and the phonemic implications of that knowledge prevailed.

This was true, moreover, even though Treiman's syllables were not real words. Her adult subjects could not have known how the sounds of the syllables actually were spelled. But they nevertheless had impressively strong ideas about how syllables that sounded that way ought to be spelled. In contrast to the

---

65. Dahl and Samuels (1979); Herman (1985); Samuels (1985).
66. Whittlesea (1987).
67. Treiman (1985d).

adults, Treiman found that kindergarten and first-grade listeners tended to hear and spell the sounds as spoken.[68]

Clearly, the possession of such bonds between subword phonological patterns and subword spelling patterns must be a tremendous asset. It must increase our ability to remember or figure out how a new word is spelled. It must increase our ability to recognize a printed rendition of a word once having heard it. And it must increase our ability to recognize a spoken rendition of a word once having seen it in print.

In contrast the absence of such bonds must be a handicap even for purposes of hearing unfamiliar words in one's oral language environment. Without expectations—be they phonological, semantic, or syntactic—running speech is basically unintelligible. To demonstrate this, Pollack and Pickett recorded several people in normal conversation.[69] Their individual words were then excised from the recording and played, in isolation, to other people for identification. The listeners could identify these isolated words only 47 percent of the time.

Much of the oral language children hear is, of course, normal conversation. On the other hand, maybe the conversation that Pollack and Pickett recorded was especially sloppy. To find out how intelligible the individual words of running speech could be, Pollack and Pickett asked another group of people to read passages into a tape recorder. Although this time the speech was generated with more deliberate and self-conscious diction, the intelligibility of its individual words was not greatly increased. When the passages had been read at normal rate, their isolated words were identified correctly 55 percent of the time. When the passages had been read quickly, accuracy fell to 41 percent.

Whether the purpose of voicing classroom words is to establish their identities or to hasten their reading, their individual intelligibility is very important. When classroom words are aurally unfamiliar, semantic expectations cannot suffice. Students must make the most of their phonological images. How, then, do such phonological images become established? Research suggests that it is very significantly through learning about spellings.

To assess this hypothesis, Ehri and Wilce examined second graders' perceptions of alveolar flaps in words like *glitter* and *cadillac.*[70] Alveolar flaps are produced by "flapping" the tongue against the alveolar ridge behind the teeth. Although they

---

68. See also Treiman (1985c).

69. Pollack and Pickett (1964).

70. Ehri and Wilce (1986).

typically are acoustically closer to /*d*/ in speech, they are sometimes spelled with a *d* and sometimes with a *t*. To find out how the children perceived the flaps, they were asked to select rhymes for the first syllable of each of a series of test words. As an example, the children were shown a picture of a *kid* and a picture of a *mitt* and asked which rhymed best with the first syllable of the word *glitter*. By inference, those who chose the picture of the *kid* must have perceived the flap in *glitter* as a /*d*/; those who chose the picture of the *mitt* must have perceived it as a /*t*/.

The second graders in this study were divided into two groups, matched for reading and spelling ability. On the first day of the experiment, the children were familiarized with the target words. To this end, the first group of children was asked to read each of the target words, name its letters, and listen to a recording of the word in a sentence. This procedure was repeated twice more, except that instead of listening to the sentence for each word, the children were asked to recall it. The familiarization procedure was similar for the second group of children except that they were neither shown nor asked to say the spellings of the words.

On the second day, the rhyming test was administered (twice to check on consistency). The children were then asked to listen to each word on tape and write it down.

Although half of the target words were actually spelled with *t*s and half with *d*s, the children who had not worked with the words' spellings were significantly more likely to perceive all of the flaps as /*d*/, as consistent with their acoustical structure. In contrast, with few exceptions, the children who had worked with the words' spellings perceived the phonemes as they were spelled: The *glit–* in *glitter* was seen to rhyme with *mitt* rather than *kid*, while the *cad–* in *cadillac* was seen to rhyme with *dad* rather than *hat*. In addition, these children were commensurately more likely to spell the flaps correctly than were their peers who had practiced the words without seeing or spelling them.

Ehri and Wilce had further hypothesized that the tendency to perceive these flaps as /*t*/ versus /*d*/ would be influenced by the children's morphemic knowledge. Recall that the rhyme task required separate pronunciation of the first syllables of the words. Thus, judgments of the flap in a word like *fatter* required pronunciation of its root, *fat*, which, if familiar, might induce the children to perceive the flap as a /*t*/. In contrast, for nonderived words like *pretty*, no such cues were available.

To test this hypothesis, Ehri and Wilce gave the first-syllable rhyme test to three more groups of children in the first, second, and fourth grades.[71] Fifteen of the tested words were derived (e.g., *fatter*), and fifteen were nonderived (e.g., *pretty*).[72] As in the other experiment, and consistent with the acoustical cues of the words, the children were inclined to perceive the flaps as /d/. With increasing age—and presumably spelling ability—this bias was increasingly supplanted by orthographically appropriate perceptions.

Nevertheless, perception of the flaps was wholly independent of whether the words were derived or nonderived. Among first graders for example, the *fat*– in *fatter* was no more likely to be "heard" with a /t/ than was the *pret*– in *pretty*. Among second graders, the *sit*– in *sitting* was no more likely to be "heard" with a /t/ than the *cent*– in *center*. And, averaged across words, this indifference held for every grade.

As an adult reader, I find it quite compelling that the *fat*– in *fatter*, *fattest*, and *fattening* are all spelled the same because they are all derived from the same root, *fat*. But this intuition is inconsistent with Ehri and Wilce's evidence that the morphemic structure of a word does not influence learners' image of its phonological structure or, by extension, its spelling. Instead their results invite the converse explanation: that morphemic appreciation derives from our knowledge of words' spellings and our image of their phonological structures.

Counterintuitive as this hypothesis may seem, it may be correct. Laboratory studies indicate that our knowledge of word spellings is automatically activated in the course of speech perception. Asking adults to listen to tape-recorded passages for the phoneme /b/, Rudnicky found that over half of their false identifications were to words like *comb* and *climb*, whose spellings include "silent" *b*s.[73] Along the same lines, Seidenberg and Tannenhaus found that adults are quicker to judge that two spoken words rhyme if their rhyming fragments are spelled similarly (e.g., *tie–pie*) than if they are spelled differently (e.g., *pie–rye*).[74]

---

71. Ehri and Wilce (1986).

72. As it happens, their set of nonderived words included a number whose first syllables, if not roots or related morphemes, were at least familiar and consistently spelled words. However, since they listed the proportion of incorrect responses to each word, it can be seen that their results held despite this confounding.

73. Rudnicky (1980, cited in Jakimik, Cole, and Rudnicky, 1985).

74. Seidenberg and Tannenhaus (1979).

Extending this line of research the crucial step further, Jakimik, Cole, and Rudnicky asked whether the spelling or pronunciation of a spoken word would influence adult listeners' ability to decide whether an ensuing syllable was or was not a word.[75] No facilitation was obtained when the items were related in spelling alone (e.g., *legislature–leg* and *tragic–trag*). Nor was facilitation obtained when the items were related in sound alone (e.g., *definite–deaf* and *precious–presh*). However, decisions were significantly faster when the items matched in both spelling and sound. Under this condition, words were accepted more quickly while nonwords were rejected more quickly.

The special pertinence of this finding derives from the fact that word-nonword judgments about pronounceable syllables depend heavily on considerations of meaning.[76] The matching spellings and sounds seem therefore to have preactivated the test words' meanings. Yet this was despite the fact that the matching fragments were not morphologically related, e.g., *message–mess*, *dignity–dig*, and *dollar–doll*. The hypothesis that morphological awareness derives from orthographic and phonological similarities follows readily.[77]

More generally, the theory of word recognition developed in part III implies that people's orthographic and phonological knowledge should be integrally tied in both directions and at all levels. In keeping with this, it is not just that knowledge of a word's spelling can influence the way in which people "hear" its sound but also the very likelihood that they will "hear" a sound at all.

To demonstrate this, Ehri and Wilce presented fourth graders with a series of words with phonetically ambiguous or misleading spellings such as *pitch, badge,* and *comb*.[78] The children's task was to segment the phonemes of each word by pushing out a bingo marker for each one. The question was whether they would push out an extra bingo marker for the acoustically indiscernible letters in these words. The answer was yes for words like *pitch* and *badge*, in which the central consonants (*t* and *d*) can be "heard," but not separately from the affricates (*–ch* and *–ge*) that follow. But the

---

75. Jakimik, Cole, and Rudnicky (1985).

76. Seidenberg and McClelland (1988).

77. This hypothesis is also provides motivation for the ways in which morphological relations are often preserved through nonphonetic spellings (e.g., *bomb–bombard; sign–signature; soft–soften*). See Chomsky and Halle (1968).

78. Ehri and Wilce (1980).

answer was no for *comb*, in which the extra consonant is truly silent.

Apparently where spellings can be mapped to sounds, they are, whether or not they are phonetically necessary. Furthermore, when spellings are mapped to sounds, they tend to shift our phonological perceptions toward their image. It may well be this very process that, over time, causes language groups to shift the pronunciation of words with incompatible spelling-sound correspondences such that they match their orthography.[79]

But what about truly silent letters? If they do not map directly onto phonology, is their presence harder to remember?

To ask this question, Ehri and Wilce gave a word imagery task to children in the second through fourth grade.[80] On each trail, the experimenter pronounced a word, and the children were instructed to envision it—to imagine how it would look if it were written down. Then the experimenter displayed a lowercase letter and asked the children whether or not it was one of the letters in the word they were imagining. The children were consistently more accurate in judging the presence of pronounced (e.g., *b* in *curb*) than of silent letters (e.g., *b* in *comb*). This result is compatible with the evidence that pronounced letters are directly represented in both orthographic and phonological memories and with the inference that "silent" letters should therefore be less memorable. Nevertheless, the situation seems more complicated than that.

After the letter judgment task had been completed, Ehri and Wilce gave the children a surprise recall task. Each of the test letters was presented once again, and the children were challenged to recall the word they had been imagining when it was presented earlier. Contrary to expectations, the children were significantly better able to recall the previously imagined words when presented with silent letters than when presented with pronounced letters.

The obvious, if uninteresting, explanation for this pattern of results is that the silent letters were better retrieval cues because the children had worked harder and thus more attentively at finding them in the judgment task. However, Ehri and Wilce offered a different hypothesis. The higher frequency of misses in the judgment task, they suggested, meant that silent letters were more often missing from the children's images of the words. In

---

79. Holender (1987). English examples of this phenomenon include *Detroit, Paris, Los Angeles, junta, guerilla, champagne, crayfish, petit fours, llama, sauna, minuet, Uranus*, ...

80. Ehri and Wilce (1982).

contrast, they continued, the better performance with silent letters in the recall task meant that, when present in an orthographic image, silent letters must somehow be more saliently marked than pronounced letters. Though tenuous, this explanation is not altogether implausible. It has also been found, for example, that when good spellers are asked to proofread text, they are significantly more likely to notice the omission of silent than pronounced letters.[81]

Why such salience? Although not pronounced themselves, the presence of silent letters in a word are often of key significance to its phonological translation. For example, silent vowels in two syllable words provide important cues about stress assignment: If there is a silent letter in one of the syllables, chances are that that syllable should be stressed. Using nonsense words, such as *nodude–nodud* and *geveste–gevest*, Philip Smith has shown that the stress assignments of adults and even second graders, though to a lesser degree, are sensitive to the presence or absence of silent letters in a syllable.[82] The implication is although such letters lack direct phonemic translations, they must nevertheless be well represented in the reader's system of phonological translations.

In keeping with this, Smith has also shown that, among skillful readers, the noticeability of silent *es* in connected text varies directly with their phonological or lexical import.[83] Silent *es* conveying either lexical distinctions (e.g., *please* versus *pleas* and *caste* versus *cast*) or phonological markings (e.g., *mate* versus *mat* and *cornice* versus *comic*)—or, more so, both—were significantly more likely to be noticed than silent *es* that were of orthographic import only (e.g., *freeze* and *give*). Silent letters, in short, seem very much present—if complexly so—in the skillful reader's representation of spelling-sound relations. It may well be the complexity of their representation that renders them differentially salient.

Finally, at least one more instructional practice begs review given the findings discussed in this section. In some commercial spelling programs, children are trained to translate dictionary pronunciation keys, such as *krum, boiz, eg·zakt', swich'·bord*, and *chok'·lət*, into correct spellings—in this case, *crumb, boys, exact, switchboard*, and *chocolate*. This procedure forces children to study spellings that: are not correct; involve illegal spelling sequences

---

81. Frith (1978).

82. Smith (1980).

83. To this end, Smith (1980) used a task in which people were to cross out all *es* while reading and comprehending meaningful text.

and characters that are not letters; drop silent letters; and often mask morphological segments.

Drake and Ehri reasoned that such phonetic spellings might well hinder rather than help children to learn correct spellings.[84] To assess this possibility, they compared the spelling performance of otherwise matched groups of fourth graders who had learned to spell words either by sounding out such dictionary keys or by sounding out correct spellings. As suspected, relative to their peers who had studied the dictionary keys, the children who had worked from the correct spellings succeeded in spelling more of the words correctly, in spelling more unstressed vowels correctly, in spelling more silent letters correctly, and in including fewer phonetically appropriate but orthographically inappropriate letters in their spellings. Moreover, these differences were especially pronounced among the children who were poorer spellers in the first place.

Summary: Learning How to Spell Correctly

The arguments for including spelling instruction as a major component of the reading and language program are strong. As learning about spelling serves to elaborate and reinforce knowledge in the Orthographic processor, it enhances reading proficiency. As it articulates with knowledge in the Phonological processor, it enhances children's ability not just to induce spellings and to render correct readings of unknown words but also to hear and pronounce words correctly in their oral language activities. Finally, learning about correct spellings may also be a key factor in children's development of morphemic awareness.

Beyond Spelling

Even among older students, the strongest measurable links between reading and writing abilities tend to cluster at the level of spelling and word recognition skills. But just as there is more to reading than word recognition, there is more to writing than spelling, and there is far more to the reading-writing connection than just reciprocal exercise with individual words.

Children's writing is strongly influenced by their reading. In reviewing the literature on this relationship, Stotsky makes the

---

84. Drake and Ehri (1984).

point that better writers tend to read more than poorer writers.[85] Moreover, she reports, in studies specifically designed to improve writing, the reading experiences in which the children were engaged were more beneficial than either grammar study or extra writing practice. Analyzing children's writing samples, researchers have documented a marked tendency to incorporate not just the content of material read just previously but also its orthographic, syntactic, and thematic structures.[86]

Even so, for young or uncertain readers, the potential contribution of writing to reading runs much deeper than any concern of form or style. In particular, as children become authors, as they struggle to express, refine, and reach audiences through their own writing, they actively come to grips with the most important reading insights of all.[87]

Through writing, children learn that text is not preordained or immutable truth. It is human voice. It is produced by people: people with their own personal and sometimes inappropriate sets of information and points of view; people with their own prior assumptions about who their readers will be and what those readers will already know and think; people who themselves have struggled and not always most fruitfully to find clear ways of expressing the ideas and information in their texts. Through writing, children learn that the purpose of text is not to be read but to be understood.

They learn that text does not contain meaning but is meaningful only to the extent that it is understood by its reader. They learn that different readers respond differently to the same text. They also learn that sometimes understanding comes only through hard work even for the best of readers. They learn that cogent writing may depend on consulting other sources (people or books), inviting the insight that cogent reading may too. They learn that text is written upon an underlying organization, inviting the insight that it may be productively read that way, too.

They learn, in short, that reading is about thinking and that lesson is critical. For the beginner, as we have seen, learning to read depends integrally on thinking and understanding. Yet more. The ultimate power of text is not from its understanding but from its broader interpretation, its critique, its extension through the

---

85. Stotsky (1984).

86. For a review, see Kucer (1987).

87. Donald Graves and his colleagues have been especially active and influential in promoting early writing from this perspective. An anthology of his papers is available in Graves (1983).

readers' own knowledge and thought and to the reader's own needs and interests. It is this power, most of all, that we want to give to all of our children.

VI
Summary and Conclusion

15

The Proper Place of Phonics

The purpose of writing is to record or convey meaning. The purpose of reading is to reconstruct and consider that meaning. Given an alphabetic script, the purpose of overlearning the spelling patterns and their phonological translations is to enable reading in its fullest sense; it is to enable the written word to flow quickly and effortlessly from print to meaning so that the reader's active, thoughtful attention can be devoted to the task of comprehension. The purpose of phonic instruction is to guide and expedite such learning.

The System in Review

The most salient characteristic of skillful readers is the speed and effortlessness with which they seem able to breeze through text. Over time, many hypotheses have been offered to explain this remarkable facility: Do skillful readers recognize words as wholes, relying on their overall patterns or shapes rather than any closer analysis of their spellings? Do they use context to anticipate the wording of the text, such that they can confine visual analysis to its most important or least predictable words? Do they use context to anticipate the meanings of the words they will see, such that their comprehension consists as much of confirmation as of interpretation? As appealing as each of these hypotheses may have been, none is correct. It turns out, instead, that skillful readers visually process virtually every individual letter of every word as they read, and this is true whether they are reading isolated words or meaningful, connected text.

Even while the individual letters of text are the basic perceptual data of reading, they are not perceived one by one, independently of each other. Instead, their efficient and productive perception depends additionally on ready knowledge of words—their spellings, meanings, and pronunciations—and on consideration of the contexts in which they occur. In the mind of the skillful reader, each such type of knowledge is represented by constellations of elementary units, connected in specific, learned relation to each other: Simple patterns are represented by interrelated clusters of units, more complex patterns by clusters of clusters of units, and so on such that the whole of any percept or idea is defined, at core, by the particular relations that hold among its parts. As examples, individual letters are represented as interconnected combinations of more elementary visual features while each familiar word is represented as a specific, interconnected combination of letters. Similarly, the meaning of a familiar word corresponds to some interconnected set of meaning elements, and its pronunciation to an interconnected complex of elementary speech sounds.

Because these types of knowledge are intricately connected to each other as well, skillful readers can recognize the spelling, sound, and meaning of a familiar word almost instantly and automatically, leaving their active attention free for critical and reflective thought. But herein lies a key point: Whereas the energy that any set of units can pass to any other depends strictly on the strength and completeness of the connections between them, the strength and completeness of the connections between them depends strictly on learning.

It is their overlearned knowledge about the sequences of letters comprising frequent words and spelling patterns that enables skillful readers to process the letters of a text so quickly and easily. As the reader fixates each word of text, the individual letters in focus are perceived almost instantly and effortlessly. Yet even as the letters are perceived, they are automatically clustered into familiar spelling patterns by virtue of the learned associations among them. Thus it is because of their deep knowledge about orthography that skillful readers look and feel as though they recognize words holistically. More subtly but just as importantly, this knowledge underlies the automaticity with which skillful readers are able to break long words into syllabic chunks and to rectify the sensory system's inherently unreliable transmission of letter order.

Our perceptual memory is well designed for learning about such relations among letters. Through its associative architecture, it comes to recognize a spelling pattern more quickly and completely every time its particular sequence of letters is attended. On the other hand, to the extent that the reader's attention is concentrated on the resolution of any single letter, it cannot be usefully distributed across the sequence as a whole. Worse still, to the extent that any letter cannot be solidly recognized, it prevents learning of the sequence as a whole. By implication, efficient growth of readers' orthographic facility depends critically on the ease and reliability with which they can recognize individual letters. It is extremely important that children embark on reading instruction with solid visual knowledge of the letters of the alphabet.

But knowledge of letters is of little value unless the child knows and is interested in their use: Correctly perceived and interpreted, print conveys information. In keeping with this, children's concepts about print are also strong predictors of the ease with which they will learn to read. Before formal instruction is begun, children should possess a broad, general appreciation of the nature of print. They should be aware of how text is formatted; that its basic meaningful units are specific, speakable words; and that its words are comprised of letters. Of equal importance, they should have a solid sense of its various functions—to entertain, inform, communicate, record—and the potential value of each such function to their own selves. All such awarenesses are powerfully fostered by reading aloud to children—by engaging them regularly and interactively in the enjoyment and exploration of print.

For many children, both letter recognition skills and basic print awareness are relatively well established even before entering school. Through storybook time and educational toys and games, through preschool activities and "Sesame Street," through life with adults who surround themselves with print, such children approach formal reading instruction with extensive knowledge and appreciation of text. But for each of these children, there are many others who reach school with relatively little exposure to the uses, methods, or pleasures of print. To learn to read, a child must learn first what it means to read and that she or he would like to be able to do so. Our classrooms, from preschool on up, must be designed with this in mind.

Although the ultimate goal of instruction on word recognition is to develop direct pathways from print to meaning, the growth of young readers' visual vocabularies depends integrally on knowledge of spelling-sound relations. As its most obvious benefit, such knowledge enables independent word learning: Printed words that are in the child's oral vocabulary can be discovered by sounding them out. Still more important to the learner, however, is the mnemonic support of spelling-sound relations. Visual knowledge of frequent words and spelling patterns consists, at core, of knowledge of the order and identities of their component letters. Through knowledge of spelling-sound relations, the sound sequence of a spoken word will lock into the visual sequence of its printed letters, thus serving to constrain and reinforce orthographic learning. Without such phonological support, acquisition of an adequate visual vocabulary would be difficult, if not impossible.

Consistent with this, children's awareness of the phonemic structure of spoken words is an extremely strong predictor of their success in learning to read. Because useful knowledge of spelling-sound correspondences depends on such phonemic awareness, children who fail to acquire it are severely handicapped in their ability to master print.

What is at issue here is not merely working knowledge of phonemes but *conscious* knowledge of them. Adequate working knowledge of phonemes is a concomitant of basic oral language capabilities. Yet, in the development of speaking and listening skills, phonemic knowledge becomes deeply embedded within subconscious layers of language system. Research indicates that regaining conscious awareness of the phonemic structure of speech is among the most difficult and critical steps toward becoming a reader. Importantly, research also indicates that children's awareness of phonemes can be hastened through appropriate training—and that such training produces significant acceleration in their acquisition of reading and writing skills.

In the course of perception, each word of the text automatically evokes the entire complex of meanings and experiences with which it has been associated. Clearly, were that the end-point of reading, the end-product would be mental chaos. But perception is only the first stage involved in comprehension.

To understand, the reader can focus on neither the broad distribution of meanings and experiences associated with each individual word nor on any preselected subset thereof. Instead the reader must work with combinations of words, searching the overlap in their meanings for textually acceptable relationships. This point is illustrated by the effortlessness with which context provokes contrastive interpretations of ambiguous words, as in *pig pens* versus *fountain pens*; *inaugural ball* versus *ping pong ball*; *lead singer* versus *lead pipe*; *wedding ring* versus *telephone ring*; *medium*-sized versus *broadcast medium*.

One might contend that we have, through experience, learned to respond to such phrases as wholes—that their disambiguation is more a matter of recall than of active interpretation. Familiar or not, however, the only way such phrases can be interpreted appropriately is by attending not to their individual words but to the relations between them. In the same manner, readers work with context to select (and, when necessary, reselect) the most appropriate meanings of words regardless of the predictability or familiarity of the phrase as a whole. Thus, while _does_ *eat oats, a* *wolf _does_ not;* and while *sometimes I wake up _grumpy_ in the morning, I* *prefer to let _him_ sleep.*

It is because the process of comprehension consists of actively searching the overlap among words for syntactic and semantic coherence that reading depends so critically on the speed and automaticity of word recognition. Although the words of a text necessarily arrive sequentially, the activation of each dwindles away quite rapidly once the eye has turned to the next. Hence the importance of speed: In order for each of a series of words to be aroused at once, all must be perceived in rapid sequence. The importance of automaticity relates to the fact that the search for coherence requires active, thoughtful attention. Where a reader is instead wrestling with the resolution of any particular word, syllable, or letter of the text, comprehension is necessarily forfeited. For it to be recovered, the phrase must be reread with fluency.

Fortunately, any word that is highly familiar will be mapped directly, instantly, and effortlessly from sight to meaning. Yet, this can happen only to the extent that the word's unique, ordered sequence of letters has been learned and overlearned through experience. Printed words vary enormously in their frequency of occurrence. By force of probabilities, they must range just as widely in their familiarity—even for skillful readers.

Analyses of the everyday reading matter of adults reveal that the vast majority of print consists of relatively few, very frequent words. Because each of these words should be highly familiar to the mature reader, each should be recognized quickly and easily. On the other hand, these oft-repeated words account for but a small fraction—about 5 percent—of the number of *different* words in text. Each of the remaining 95 percent of the distinct words occurs relatively infrequently—on average, just a few times within every million words of running print. By extension, the reader's visual familiarity with many of these words must be relatively weak and incomplete—often too weak and incomplete to support the perceptual speed and automaticity on which comprehension depends.

Word counts of schoolchildren's books reveal a similar pattern. Fifty percent of the print in such books is accounted for by only 109 different words; 90 percent by only 5,000 different words. It is reasonable to suppose that, not too far into their schooling, most children will have become quick to recognize most of these words by sight.[1] But how are they to cope with the remainder of the words they see? It will not do to skip such words or guess at their identities: Whereas the coherence of a text depends strongly on its frequent words—*it, that, this, and, because, when, while,* the information in a text derives disproportionately from its less frequent words—*doctor, fever, infection, medicine, penicillin, Alexander Fleming, melon, mold, poison, bacteria, antibiotic, protect, germs, disease.*

For skillful readers, automatic phonological translations provide a backup system for recognizing visually less familiar words. By virtue of the alphabetic principle, permissible syllables are represented by frequent spelling patterns. For the skillful reader, it follows that even where a word as a whole is not visually familiar, fragments of its spelling almost certainly will be. Courtesy of the reader's spelling-sound associations, these spelling patterns will be translated automatically to their phonological equivalents. As a result, even the occasional, never-before-seen word may be read off with little outward sign of difficulty. Just try it: *interfascicular, hypermetropical, hackmatack.*

Of still greater importance, however, the irrepressible automaticity of skillful readers' spelling-to-sound translations ensures that those many words of known meaning but marginal visual familiarity will be recognized with the ease and speed required for fluent reading comprehension. Further, as the phonological translations serve at once to turn on the word's meaning while maintaining activation of its spelling, each such encounter also results in a strengthening of the word's direct spelling-to-meaning connections.

Automatic phonological translation of the words in a text supports higher-order comprehension processes as well. We have seen that the basic perceptual data in reading are individual letters. Yet, the meaning of a text is several steps removed from its letter-by-letter composition. In order to make sense of the letters, the reader must collect them into words. But this is not enough, either. In language, the meanings of words are carefully interrelated through syntax and collected into sentences or basic idea units. In turn, the sentences are ordered so as to convey the larger message of the speaker or writer.

---

1. Remember that what really matters is not the frequency with which a word occurs in print but the frequency with which it has been encountered by the reader in question. Thus, any given child will also become familiar with a variety of personal favorites—*princess, dinosaur, ninja, Barbie, decepticon*—regardless of their length or normative statistical frequency.

Whether listening or reading, the procedure for interpreting the higher-order meaning of language is the same. The words of each sentence are perceived and remembered verbatim. Then, just as the speaker pauses at the end of each oral sentence, the skillful reader inserts a pause at the end of each printed sentence. During this pause, listeners or readers interpret the collective meaning of the chain of words in memory and its contribution to the overall meaning of the conversation or text. Having thus cleaned out their verbatim memory, they are ready to take in the next sentence.

As it happens, even skillful readers occasionally encounter a sentence in text that is too long or complex to be fit easily within their verbatim memory. Yet they have two means of overcoming this limitation. First, sensing an impending overload, the skillful reader may decide not to wait for the end of the sentence, pausing instead at some earlier point within it. Notably, not just any point will do for this purpose: To preserve the syntactic and semantic coherence of the words to be interpreted, such within-sentence pauses may be inserted only at major phrasal or clausal boundaries.

The second means by which skillful readers strive to maintain a complete and correctly ordered memory of the words between interpretive pauses is by exploiting their phonological translations. By thinking or speaking the words to themselves, they effectively renew their phonological activation, thus extending the longevity and holding capacity of their verbatim memory. Note that, in this case, the value of phonological translation extends beyond word identification per se. Preventing skillful readers from subvocalizing does not impair their ability to interpret single, familiar words or simple sentences. On the other hand, it severely disrupts their ability to remember or comprehend long or complex sentences.

With respect to young readers, there are two messages here. The first is that development of syntactic competence may be far more important than is generally recognized in reading instruction. Without the independent ability to recognize the within-sentence phrasal and clausal boundaries that permit interpretive recoding, the young reader has no rational option but to try to conquer whole sentences at a time. The second is that the capacity for sounding words out is at least as important when children are turned to informationally complex texts as it was when they were at the stage of mastering their basic visual vocabularies.

Importantly, full interpretation of a text at this level may require retrieval of particular facts or events that were presented many pages earlier. It may also require consideration of knowledge and construction of argument that are entirely extraneous to the text. And it certainly requires the critical and inferential activities necessary for putting such information together. It is, in short, this level of interpretation that we think of as true understanding.

But again, interpretation at this level unavoidably requires active attention and thought. It is not automatic or effortless. It will only be as fruitful as the discipline and effort that the reader invests in it. Yet, the effort and discipline that readers can invest in it depend, in turn, on the ease and completeness with which they have executed the levels that support it.

Phonics and Reading Instruction

In summary, deep and thorough knowledge of letters, spelling patterns, and words, and of the phonological translations of all three, are of inescapable importance to both skillful reading and its acquisition. By extension, instruction designed to develop children's sensitivity to spellings and their relations to pronunciations should be of paramount importance in the development of reading skills. This is, of course, precisely what is intended of good phonic instruction.

And so we are left with the question: Why is phonic instruction so often and so loudly protested? The answer would seem to lie in the typical realities of its implementation.

First let us consider the situation for those children who enter first grade with thousands of hours of literacy preparation behind them.[2] Many of these children will be on the brink of independent reading and writing, if not there already, and the basic phonic curriculum will generally consist less of new concepts and information than of review and clarification of things they already know. By extension, as sensed by many teachers, curricula that place elementary phonics first and foremost in time and emphasis are inappropriate. Systematic phonic instruction is no less important for these children. However, to be most productive, it may best be conceived as a support activity, carefully covered but largely subordinated to the reading and writing of connected text.

But what about those students who enter first grade with less literacy experience? Even among teachers of these students,

---

2. See chapter 4.

resistance to phonics is not uncommon. Such negative attitudes can again be traced to the prevailing realities of instructional delivery. To illustrate, let us consider the instructional treatment of at-risk students, as revealingly summarized by Richard Allington.[3]

As it happens, schools with high proportions of at-risk students tend to spend not more but less classroom time on reading instruction. Indeed, data from the most recent national evaluation of Chapter 1 programs indicate that schools with large numbers of students from low-income homes schedule nearly twenty minutes less reading instruction per day than comparison schools.[4]

Perhaps this disparity should not be surprising. Where many students are receiving individual reading instruction through support programs, one might reasonably conclude that less classroom time for reading is appropriate; there are, after all, other topics to be covered in a day. But not all of the students in a classroom receive supplemental instruction. And even of those who do, 90 percent miss at least some of the time scheduled for reading in their classrooms. In the end, not even these students gain any increase in the total amount of instructional time they receive.

The time allocated for reading instruction is no less telling than the ways in which it is spent. Characteristically, low achievers are given less classroom opportunity than their on-schedule peers to read text or to read text independently. When low achievers are asked to read, it tends to be orally, round-robin style, with the consequence that they are also asked to read far fewer words, stories, and books.

Furthermore, the emphasis during the round-robin sessions of low achievers tends to be on reading accuracy. While this emphasis no doubt reflects concern for their phonic development, it results in a large number of interruptions during reading. This reduces the number of words, stories, and books they will cover still further. But it also means that far less emphasis can be given to higher-order dimensions of their texts. Whether in their classrooms or their support programs, low-achieving readers are found to be given little encouragement or opportunity to examine the structure of their text, to reflect on aspects of its meaning, or to discuss its message. The focus of supervised reading is instead on words—and on relatively few of them.

---

3. Allington (1983, 1989a, in press, 1989b, in press).
4. Birman, Orland, Jung, Anson, Garcia, Moore, Funkhouser, Morrison, Turnbull, and Reiser (1987).

Still, while one group is reading with the teacher, the others must also be busy. How do students spend the time at their desks? Again a disparity is found between high and low achievers. Although the completion of skillsheets, workbooks and dittos accounts for the majority of all student seatwork, better readers are often engaged in silent reading or comprehension tasks. Low achievers rarely are.

Even within their support programs, the majority of the low achiever's time is spent on worksheets and especially on worksheets that emphasize letter-sound relations and word analysis skills. The motivation is clear. The worksheets are meant to develop the spelling and spelling-sound knowledge that these children lack.

Note that there is nothing wrong with giving students well-devised worksheets. To the contrary, if well designed and properly used, worksheets represent a valuable classroom resource. Beyond the fact that many children enjoy the sense of getting something done, independent seatwork affords an opportunity for exercising each on the knowledge and skills she or he needs most.

But opportunities aside, McGill-Franzen has found that such seatwork activities are rarely selected with an eye toward the student's individual needs.[5] She found that in both classrooms and pull-out sessions, all students are typically held accountable for the same seatwork. When pull-out children are returned to their classrooms, they are often required to complete seatwork despite having missed the relevant instruction. And in both classrooms and pull-out sessions, the seatwork of the low-achieving children is often completed only with a very high number of errors.

Seatwork should never be assigned unless the student understands its purpose and method and is expected to profit from its execution. Of equal concern, time spent on worksheets is time that cannot be spent in reading. And these children need desperately to read.

In the end, Allington observes, relative to their mainstream peers, low-achieving students enrolled in supplementary reading programs are typically confronted with twice as many vocabulary words and decoding "skills" but given less time for mastering either set. They are given less time for connected reading and independent writing. And during the time they do read text, they cover less material and are rarely challenged to think about its meaning or structure.[6]

---

5. McGill-Franzen (1988).
6. Allington (1989b).

Understandably, some may see phonic instruction as the problem with such programs for low-achievers. Yet, the problem is really not that the children are given phonic instruction, but that they are given a relative surfeit of phonic instruction and in suboptimal ways.

All students, whether their preschool reading preparation is high, low or in between, need to learn about spellings, sounds, and their relationships; few students will do so without conducive instructional guidance. Further, programs *can* be designed to provide an effective and sensitive balance of reading instruction. For the sake of concreteness, I describe one such program in some detail.

Marie Clay's Reading Recovery Program was designed to identify and "recover" students in need of extra help at the very outset of their formal schooling.[7] The program is initiated with a diagnostic survey, designed to assess the child's letter recognition abilities, knowledge of the structure and functions of print, word recognition abilities, passage comprehension ability, and writing skills.

During the first two weeks of tutoring, the teacher introduces nothing new for the child to learn. Instead, as based on the results of the diagnostic survey, the student and the teacher engage in what Clay terms "roaming around the known." So that the teacher can more fully observe and understand the knowledge, skills, and behaviors of the student, these introductory activities consist of finding different ways to exercise established skills fluently. So that child will understand the purpose of the tutoring, these activities are exclusively conducted with real texts and real writing (not isolated letters or words). In this way, the introductory sessions allow both the teacher and the student to develop their own separate but well-founded ideas of what they will be doing together.

When the first story is introduced, it is carefully chosen such that the child can read its words with at least 90 percent accuracy. The stories most often used with the Reading Recovery program are bound as separate little books. The illustrations are enchanting, the stories are delightful, and the language is full of rhyme and repetition as beginning books should be. A new book may be introduced each day, but the lesson always includes rereading of at least one more familiar one. Such rereading has been shown to be a superlative way of refining and reinforcing both word recognition and comprehension skills. In addition, it

---

7. Clay (1979).

provides a means of bolstering the child's sense of confidence and accomplishment.

Before, after, and sandwiched amidst the reading, the program includes a variety of other activities. Secure learning of letter identities is supported through key words, exercises with magnetic letters, verbal description, directed attention to similarities and differences, finger tracing, and printing. Letters may be labeled with their names, their sounds, or as the first sounds of a word, depending on which the child finds most comfortable.

The importance of phonological and linguistic awareness is also explicitly recognized. The child is asked to clap out syllables and to segment words into phonemes with bingo markers. In support of word awareness, the child is encouraged to point to each separate word while reading: Are there enough? Are there too many? What's wrong?

Writing is the principal vehicle for developing word analysis skills. As in the language experience method, writing may initially consist of dictation by the child to the teacher; however, independent writing is encouraged as soon as possible. In addition to asking the child to write independently, the teacher may give the child model words to copy and may even ask the child to write a word again and again so to know it thoroughly. The stories that the child writes may be typed but not edited by the teacher. They provide a major source of information about the student's growing mastery of orthography.

To encourage the understanding that print is print, writing is done in many different media—pens, chalk, magnetic letters. Similarly, word structures are also examined across a variety of media, including connected text.

To encourage attention to spelling patterns, a word in the text may be covered in part or in whole with a paper mask: What letter do you expect to see at the beginning? Alternatively, the child may be asked whether the word that has been "read" looks right, sounds right, or makes sense. Because new books are so carefully chosen to be just barely beyond the child's level of mastery and old books are reread so regularly, such attention to spelling and spelling-sound correspondences can proceed without detracting from pursuit of meaning—which is always foremost during connected reading.

While the child is reading, the teacher uses her own copy of the text to make a running record not just of words read correctly but also of, for example, misreadings, stumbles, impasses, appeals for help, repetitions, pauses, and directional difficulties. From these records, the teacher can learn much about how the child prioritizes and exploits the information and strategies available when reading. Over time, they also provide a detailed record of the child's progress.

The Reading Recovery Program has been methodically designed to establish and secure that whole complex of lower-order skills on which reading so integrally depends. But its goal extends much further. The program is intended to help the children learn to monitor their own reading; to develop the habit of rereading a word, phrase, or passage when unclear; to know not only that they can discover new words and meanings but also that they can cross-check their discoveries, confirming or correcting them on their own; and to develop a strong sense of how to search deliberately and methodically for information in letter sequences, word sequences, or meaning when needed. Its goal, in short, is to help the students understand the nature of text and reading—to understand that each is most to their benefit and within their control only as it is understood.

As fond as I am of the Reading Recovery Program, it is really quite similar, except in detail, to a number of others that have been developed including, for example, Jeanne Chall's Reading Laboratory at Harvard, the program at the Benchmark School in Philadelphia,[8] and the programs that Aukerman applauds under the heading "Total Language Arts and Eclectic Approaches."[9]

All of these programs are designed to develop thorough appreciation of phonics. Across this book, as we have examined each of a number of domains of study—program comparisons, research on prereader skills, the knowledge and performance of skilled readers, theory on the nature of learning—each has pointed toward the conclusion that skillful reading depends critically on the deep and thorough acquisition of spellings and spelling-sound relationships.

On the other hand, none of these programs treats phonics in a vacuum. Nor, to be learnable, can phonic skills be treated that way. Their proper acquisition depends on articulation with both lower- and higher-order knowledge about language and text.

Nor do good programs succumb to the simplistic hypotheses that letter-sound relations are the most basic of reading skills. Rather, with respect to the knowledge that is critical to reading, that which can be developed through phonic instruction

---

8. Gaskins, Downer, Anderson, Cunningham, Gaskins, Schommer, and the Teachers of the Benchmark School. (1988).
9. Aukerman (1984).

represents neither the top nor the bottom, but only a realm in between. Before children will learn to read, they must learn to recognize individual letters. They must become aware of the structure of language, from sentences and words to phonemes. And, most important, they must develop a basic understanding of the forms and functions of text and of its personal value to their own lives.

Finally, none of these programs embodies the misguided hypothesis that reading skills are best developed from the bottom up. In the reading situation, as in any effective communication situation, the message or text provides but one of the critical sources of information. The rest must come from the readers' own prior knowledge. Further, in the reading situation as in any other learning situation, the learnability of a pattern depends critically on the prior knowledge and higher-order relationships that it evokes. In both fluent reading and its acquisition, the reader's knowledge must be aroused interactively and in parallel. Neither understanding nor learning can proceed hierarchically from the bottom up. Phonological awareness, letter recognition facility, familiarity with spelling patterns, spelling-sound relations, and individual words must be developed in concert with real reading and real writing and with deliberate reflection on the forms, functions, and meanings of texts.

In fact, if we consider not what reading experts say but what they do, we quite commonly find this sort of pattern of activities. For example, Don Holdaway's model approach to "whole language" instruction is packed with activities for developing phonological awareness, orthographic knowledge, and spelling-sound relations.[10] And even treatises that are bitterly anti-phonics acknowledge the importance of teaching such skills "as needed."[11] On the other side, even Rudolph Flesch, while loudly touting basic, bottom-up phonics, explains on closer examination that before such instruction is begun, the child must acquire awareness of the phonological structure of words and ready familiarity with the visual forms of their component letters.[12] He assumes, moreover, that parents will have regularly read and enjoyed nursery rhymes, fairy tales, and other stimulating texts with their child from the earliest moment possible. He insists that reading should always be coupled with writing. And he asserts that it is through the reading and appreciation of classic

---

10. Holdaway (1979).
11. E.g., Carbo (1988).
12. Flesch (1955).

literature and informative text—not of individual words or texts controlled to vapidity—that the child's literacy competence is impelled.

With so much underlying agreement, why is there so much outward dispute? My best guess is that by virtue of human nature, people tend to conceive of some instructional activities as "key" and others as "support." But the process of reading cannot be divided into key and support activities. All of its component knowledge and skills must work together within a single integrated and interdependent system. And it is in that way that they must be acquired as well: It is not just eclecticism that makes a program of reading instruction effective; it is the way in which its pieces are fitted together to complement and support one another, always with full consideration of the needs and progress of the young readers with whom it will be used.

My objective in this book has not been to outline any particular universal, best method for teaching reading. I do not believe that a best method can be defined in outline. The effectiveness of a method depends too much on the details of its realization—its materials, its teachers, its students, and the compatibility of each with the other. By extension, there can be no such thing as a universal method. Toward the development of powerful curricula, I have tried instead to identify essential principles and goals and to clarify issues that should be considered along the way.

At the same time, efficient and effective implementation of a curriculum depends equally on solid understanding of the principles and goals upon which it is built. To make the most of a set of materials (or to make the most for a group of students), the teacher must understand *why* each activity is included. The teacher must understand the needs to which each activity was intended to respond so that its importance can be assessed with respect to the particular needs of her own students. The teacher must understand how the activities fit together in rationale, dependence and independence, and priority. The teacher must be able to separate purpose from materials, necessary achievements from recommended activities, necessary sequence from page numbers, desirable time and detail from number of pages, and so on.

With this in mind, it is for their relative silence with respect to principles and goals that I would most strongly fault the major reading curricula. Though they tend to be admirably eclectic, they tend to provide disappointingly little support as to the whys and wherefores of the activities they suggest. Perhaps this is our fault. Even if not labeled, activities, along with their rationale and sequels, will be recognized and applauded by their proponents. If labeled, however, they are more likely to be recognized and protested by their opponents.

It may be of comfort or at least interest to the reader that such divisiveness over code versus meaning emphasis in reading instruction rages the world around.[13] This is so even for orthographies such as Spanish that are far more lawfully alphabetic than ours and even in countries such as China and Japan whose writing systems are hardly alphabetic at all.

Written text has both method and purpose. It is time for us to stop bickering about which is more important. To read, children must master both, and we must help them. In the interest of developing not just their reading skills but their own personal intellectual and productive potential, we must further encourage them to read frequently, broadly, and thoughtfully.

---

13. Downing (1973).

Afterword

Dorothy Strickland
Bernice Cullinan

Beginning to Read: Thinking and Learning about Print *is a scholarly and at the same time readable book that is destined to have a major influence on the teaching of reading. Although the book was written by a single author, Marilyn Adams, it is a project of the Center for the Study of Reading. As the sponsor, the Center impaneled a group of scholars to advise Adams as she drafted the book. Adams carefully weighed all the advice she received. Nonetheless, she was unable to accommodate every criticism and suggestion to the satisfaction of those who offered them. In particular, two members of the advisory panel, Dorothy Strickland, Professor at Teachers College, Columbia University, and Bernice Cullinan, Professor Emeritus of New York University, worried that practitioners reading the book might not place phonics within a broader framework of literacy development.*

Phonics is the one topic in reading about which professionals are most likely to disagree. Our best hope for reaching a consensus about this difficult topic remains full and measured discussion in which every serious voice is heard. To this end, I invited Professors Cullinan and Strickland to write an afterword to this book. Their contribution follows.

Richard C. Anderson
Director
Center for the Study of Reading

Our primary purpose in writing this afterword is to alert teachers and policy makers that although we believe Adams does an admirable job of reporting on phonics, we do not agree totally with her selection of studies or with her interpretation of research data. We believe that the book is limited in presenting the total picture needed by practitioners to make sound instructional decisions.

First, let us say that we *do* believe in phonics; that is, we believe in providing opportunities for children to learn about letter-sound correspondences. We do *not* believe, however, that phonics should be taught in isolation from other aspects of a child's literacy development or that it is a precursor to reading development. The necessarily narrow focus of Adam's book puts its readers at risk of ignoring the way phonics instruction fits into a broader framework of language learning.

Second, we applaud Adams on the scope of her research and the skill she demonstrates in writing this book. It is highly readable, comprehensive, and comprehensible. It is a tribute to Adams's writing skill that she can make the details of experimental research so engaging and interesting to read about.

Third, we would like to emphasize that Adams professes the same developmental point of view as we do, although she sometimes draws conclusions that differ from those we draw. For example, in Chapter 4, after stating that reading is not an all-or-none skill, she describes her older child, John, approaching his fifth birthday. John recites the alphabet, recognizes all of the capital letters, prints words on his own, invents spellings, and teaches his three-year-old sister how to write. Despite these obvious signs of John's emerging literacy, Adams states that if he were evaluated according to her criteria, he would be classified as a nonreader or, in her terms, a prereader.

Terms such as "prereaders," "reading readiness," or "prerequisite skills" do not reflect the latest thinking on literacy development (Chapter 4, pp. 67–115). The term emergent literacy, coined by Marie Clay in her 1966 dissertation "Emergent Reading Behavior," is a more apt descriptor of children in the process of becoming literate. Research into young children's phonological development (Read, 1971), shows that writing does not wait on reading; there is a dynamic relation between the two, indicating that each influences the other in the course of development (Mason, 1980; Teale, 1987). Restricted views about what real literacy behavior includes and ignorance of the forms that early literacy behavior takes lead some to believe that the onset of literacy skills occurs more abruptly and much later than current research suggests (Schickedanz, 1986). The term "emergent" underscores the fact that young children are in a developmental process; there is no single point when literacy begins. Children's uses, motives, and functions associated with reading and writing in authentic situations, their knowledge about reading and writing, and their psycholinguistic processes are, to a surprising degree, similar to those of adults and older children (Heath, 1983; Sulzby, 1985; Taylor, 1983; Taylor and Dorsey-Gaines, 1987; Teale and Sulzby, 1986). The term "emergent literacy" is not a substitute for "beginning reading," which is associated with formal reading instruction; it should be thought of as literacy development and learning prior to formal instruction. The metaphor is clear: Children's literate acts *emerge* from their wealth of experience with oral language and their attempts to enter the rewarding world of print (Pearson, 1989).

The difference in terminology reflects a critical difference in our perspective. The process of becoming literate is developmental, and we use the term "emergent readers" to characterize the developmental nature of learning to read. Adams uses the term "prereader" for children who have not yet received any formal reading instruction. But even the persuasive evidence that Adams provides about her own children who are in the developmental process of learning to read does not convince her to abandon the term "prereaders."

We feel it is misleading to categorize a child as either a reader or a nonreader with no in-between. We prefer to trust the evidence that Adams provides about her own children as well as the careful observations of numerous researchers (Cochran-Smith, 1984; Bissex, 1980; Baghban, 1984) whose work suggests that literacy development starts early and is ongoing. Rather than classifying children as readers or nonreaders, we believe it is more accurate to consider their literacy development as being on a continuum of increasing competence.

Many of the studies Adams reviews focus on children's knowledge *about* literacy or their performance out of context—for example, whether children know letter names rather than what they can do with that knowledge— instead of on children's competence as readers and writers. The researchers Adams cites often assume that linguistic awareness is a precondition to reading and writing. Most of the studies that show a relation between knowledge of letter names and literacy development are correlational. The researchers use measures that diagnose a child's linguistic awareness—the result of which is not important in itself so much as it is a reflection of a broader knowledge about reading and language (Anderson, Hiebert, Scott and Wilkinson, 1985; Nurss, 1980). Moreover, this information does not provide a base to sort out any kind of temporal sequence nor does it imply that the best way for children to acquire linguistic awareness is through direct instruction. It may be that development in literacy *causes* growth in linguistic awareness. Ignoring recent observations about growth in literacy may lead us to lose sight of the fact that it is story reading, talking about stories and print, and attempts at writing that may influence the acquisition of phonics rather than the other way around.

Current naturalistic research strongly suggests that phonics is best learned in the context of reading and writing. If learning is to occur, we must give children good stories that intrigue and engage them; we must give them poetry that sings with the beauty of language; we must enchant them with language play; and we must give them opportunities to write. In short, we must surround them with literature that helps them understand their world and their ability to create meaning. We must read to children from the very beginning and read to them every day. We won't need to remind them when it's time for stories; they won't let us forget it! That's the magic of stories. In countless demonstrations of story reading and experimentation with writing, children develop the knowledge of the way print works.

In print-rich early learning environments, reading and writing are incorporated into every aspect of the day. Children are encouraged to explore print materials in the same enthusiastic manner that they approach sand, blocks, and outdoor games. They attempt to use literacy for their own purposes just as they see it being used by the adults around them. Because the learning is so joyful and natural, the development of specific skills may not be in evidence. Nevertheless, the skills, including phonics, are there.

Adults assist children in developing the skills of reading and writing through sharing books, notes, lists, and environmental print, as well as through the talk associated with that sharing. What are some of the skills they learn? Children learn that print conveys meaning; they learn that there is a certain directionality to the way we read. They learn terms such as "word," "letter," and "sound." They learn that the words we speak are mapped onto the print and that there are certain patterns in the speech-to-print match. They also learn the names of various letters and the sounds letters can represent. As children's experiences with print continue, they ask noticeably more specific questions about print, and they become substantially more sophisticated in their understanding and use of what they learn. Although as teachers and researchers we can talk about these skills as independent aspects of literacy, their acquisition and development is interdependent. Just as children's knowledge of concepts about print helps them learn phonics, phonics facilitates the exploration and experimentation with print. When the skills of written language are embedded in the very culture of the learning environment, reading and writing develop in much the same manner as oral language. In these settings, the skills are taught and attended to in the way that children learn best.

When the culture values literacy, we give children opportunities to make marks on paper so that they discern that those marks have meaning and that they can convey their own meanings through print. As children discover the relation between sounds and letters, they reveal to us what they know through their invented spellings, that is, their attempts to represent sounds with letters. Young children are active learners, they construct understandings about written language. Their invented spellings show us vividly that they are constructing knowledge about sound-symbol correspondences; at the same time, it shows us exactly how much phonics they know. As they continue to see conventional spellings in their books and in their environment, they learn to spell words in more traditional ways. The five-year-old who wrote the following on a computer is showing us that he knows a great deal about phonics. He is also showing us that he understands the playfulness and teasing that goes on within a family.

> My bruthr had the chicin pox.
> dad told him that hee is
> gowing to get a beec and litl wit
> fethrs growing awt of his armpits.
> and a litl red com wil grow awt of
> the top of his hed. hee got scard.
> I didnt get scard beecorz I noow hee
> wuz onleey teesing. Michael. (McDermott, 1989)

Children are not born smart; they learn how to become smart by being actively involved with the people around them. We teach them to think by engaging them in situations that involve thinking. Most often with young children, this thinking comes through narrative, a primary way we organize our minds. The primary role that parents and other caregivers play is to demonstrate literate behaviors—reading and writing print.

Children observe these demonstrations as they construct their own knowledge about the world of print.

Nearly all studies that Adams reviews examine children's performance in decontextualized situations with minute segments of language. Only a few of the studies she cites examine children's behavior in naturalistic settings that allow children to demonstrate what they know. In natural settings the environment encourages children to experiment with print (Schickedanz, 1986; Teale and Sulzby, 1989). In contrast, research based on preconceived notions of what literacy entails assumes that when children do not give an adultlike answer in a formal test situation, they do not know the answer.

Most researchers today attempt to study literacy learning from the child's point of view. They look for evidence of how children construct their own knowledge of reading and writing through experimentation and exploration with language. The observe children as they search for patterns in language and connect each new encounteer with print to what they have already learned from previous encounters. By using the child as informant, researchers have expanded our understanding about how phonics and other concepts about print come to be known and used by children in their attempts to become increasingly capable readers and writers. Unlike many early researchers, most contemporary researchers talk about what children *can* do rather than what they *cannot* do.

Our primary concern, however, lies not in the use of terminology nor in the criteria for selecting research studies but in the way the conclusions are portrayed to the practioner. Whether readers of this book take a readiness approach or an emergent literacy perspective will make a major difference in the learning environments they provide for children. The readiness approach leads one to believe that direct instruction in phonics is necessary for a child to become literate. In readiness programs, adults serve primarily as bearers and dispensers of information: What the child is to learn is predetermined by the adult and dispensed in discrete bits in a manner both prescribed and preordered. The emergent literacy perspective leads us to acknowledge that while much of the same information is critical, the responsibility for its access and use is shared between adult and child. Adults serve as facilitators and planners who take great care to structure the environment so that certain literacy experiences are apt to occur. They surround children with print and encourage them to use it for their own purposes.

Literacy learning proceeds naturally if the environment supports young children's experimentation with print (Schickedanz, 1986). Adults constantly monitor the learning; they use what they observe as the basis to intervene and to restructure the environment with direct and indirect instruction where needed. They are responsive to the child's efforts; they offer praise and affirmation of increasingly skilled attempts. They are also proactive, offering new ideas and new strategies that are developmentally appropriate for the child or group of children. We believe the different interpretation of the role of adults is an extremely important distinction.

Throughout the book, Adams does support a developmental, literature-based approach to reading instruction. She says "the single most important activity for building the knowledge and skills eventually required for reading is that of reading aloud to children," and "engaging children's active attention" when reading to them is important (Chapter 4, pp. 109–115). She says it is not just reading to children that makes the difference, it is enjoying the books with them and reflecting upon their form and content. It is encouraging children to examine the print. It is inviting discussions of the meanings of words and the relationship of the text's ideas to the world beyond the book. And it is showing children that we value and enjoy reading and that we hope they will, too.

Despite Adams's endorsement of features of a developmental, literature-based approach, she omits most of these elements in the final chapter of her book. Adams says that we should urge children to read and to read broadly, but she holds that that can only happen once their basic reading skills have been established. She overlooks numerous studies of children who figure out how to read by themselves and those who learn to read by seeing in print the predictable words they know by heart or have had read to them repeatedly (Baghban, 1984; Clark, 1976; Doake, 1985; Durkin, 1966). Throughout the book, she undervalues the learning that children discover on their own. The book gives the impression that only that which is explicitly taught is learned.

Adams acknowledges that it is a challenge to design initial reading texts that exercise the recommended phonogram patterns without, at the same time, presenting uninteresting texts or confronting children with too many words that cannot be decoded on the basis of the phonograms taught. She allows that, in connected text, exercise of phonograms can be overdone.

To Adams's credit, she suggests that children's very first texts be poems and that teachers read the beginnings of each line and the children read the ending words; she proposes that these exercises match their phonogram lessons. She recognizes the value of rhythm, repetition, and rereading, including the two-decade-old phenomena of Big Books and predictable books exemplified by Bill Martin, Jr.'s *Brown Bear, Brown Bear, What Do You See?*. She recognizes that whole language approaches are packed with activities for developing phonological awareness, orthographic knowledge, and spelling-sound relations. She points out that even Rudolph Flesch, who touted bottom-up phonics, wanted children to be read nursery rhymes and fairy tales from their earliest days; he also insisted that reading be coupled with writing. Further, Flesch believed that what impels children to literacy competence is reading classic literature and informative texts.

Adams states that learning how to translate sounds to spellings is only one of a complex of skills that need to be acquired by young readers. She allows that it seems a promising tactic to engage children in independent writing, encouraging them to invent spellings where they are not already known, although she cautions the reader to accept this with reservation since the data on its effectiveness are incomplete. A passing reference to the naturalistic data that Don Graves and his colleagues (Graves, 1981, 1983; Graves and Stuart, 1985) have amassed stresses that writers learn about deeper concerns of other writers—not the process of encoding.

All in all, Adams does a remarkable job of sifting through volumes of studies to deduce some reasonable statements about reading. She also draws some reasonable conclusions about what we know is required for learning to read and the nature of beginning reading materials. We want to point out these statements and conclusions to practitioners who tackle this volume. Therefore, we wrote this afterword to place the issue of phonics into a broader perspective. We sincerely hope that this book draws disparate groups in our profession together instead of providing further ammunition to continue the futile discussions of phonics or no phonics. We believe that the proponents of whole language can accommodate the essence of this book if phonics instruction is recognized as a part of an integrated approach to teaching.

In summary, Marilyn Jager Adams tackled an overwhelming body of research data, described it with style and grace, and deftly gleaned the essence of the reports. Although the perspective she presents differs from our perspective and leads her to some conclusions that diverge from ours, her scholarship is impeccable.

We believe the evidence supports a whole language and integrated language arts approach with some direct instruction, in context, on spelling-to-sound correspondences. Our chief concern lies in the way the book portrays conclusions to practitioners, the way it describes writing and its relationship to phonics and reading, and its need to draw upon research conducted in natural- istic, contextualized settings. Adams moves us closer to our goal of ending the phonics debate by leading us to ask not if, but how and when, spelling-sound information is made available to learners.

References

Anderson, R. C., Hiebert, E. H., Scott, J. A., and Wilkinson, I. A. G. (1985). *Becoming a nation of readers: The report of the commission on reading.* Champaign, IL: Center for the Study of Reading.

Baghban, M. (1984). *Our daughter learns to read and write: A case study from birth to three.* Newark, DE: International Reading Association.

Bissex, G. L. (1980). *GNYS AT WRK: A child learns to write and read.* Cambridge, MA: Harvard University Press.

Clark, M. M. (1976). *Young fluent readers.* London: Heinemann.

Clay, M. M. (1966). Emergent reading behavior. Doctoral dissertation, University of Auckland, New Zealand.

Cochran-Smith, M. (1984). *The making of a reader.* Norwood, NJ: Ablex.

Doake, D. B. (1985). Reading-like behavior: Its role in learning to read. In A. M. Jaggar and M. T. Smith-Burke (Eds.), *Observing the language learner.* Newark, DE: International Reading Association.

Durkin, D. (1966). *Children who read early.* New York: Teachers College Press.

Graves, D. H. (1983). *Writing: Children and teachers at work.* Portsmouth, NH: Heinemann.

Graves, D. H. (1981). *Donald Graves in Australia: Children want to write . . .* Portsmouth, NH: Heinemann.

Graves, D. H., and Stuart, V. (1985). *Write from the start.* New York: Dutton.

Heath, S. B. (1983). *Ways with words: Ethnography of communication, communities, and classrooms.* Cambridge: Cambridge University Press.

Mason, J. M. (1980). When do children begin to read: An exploration of four year old children's letter and word reading competencies. *Reading Research Quarterly, 15*(2), 203–227.

McDermott, V. (1989). The effects of daily self-generated writing, word processing and type of phonics instruction upon emergent literacy of kindergartners. Doctoral dissertation, New York University.

Nurss, J. (1980). Linguistic awareness and learning to read. *Young Children, 35*(4), 57–66.

Pearson, P. D. (1989). *Reading the whole language movement.* Manuscript in preparation.

Read, C. (1971). Preschool children's knowledge of English phonology. *Harvard Educational Review, 41,* 1–34.

Schickedanz, J. A. (1986). *More than the ABCs: The early stages of reading and writing.* Washington, DC: National Association for the Education of Young Children.

Sulzby, E. (1985). Children's emergent reading of favorite storybooks: A developmental study. *Reading Research Quarterly, 20*(4), 458–481.

Sulzby, E., and Teale, W. H. (1987). Young children's storybook reading: Longitudinal study of parent-child interaction and children's independent functioning. Final Report to the Spencer Foundation. Ann Arbor: University of Michigan.

Taylor, D. (1983). *Family literacy: Young children learning to read and write.* Portsmouth, NH: Heinemann.

Taylor, D., and Dorsey-Gaines, C. (1987). *Growing up literate: Learning from inner city families.* Portsmouth, NH: Heinemann.

Teale, W. H. (1987). Emergent literacy: Reading and writing development in early childhood. In *Research in literacy: Merging perspectives.* Thirty-sixth Yearbook of the National Reading Conference. Rochester, NY: National Reading Conference, Inc.

Teale, W. H., and Sulzby, E. (1986). *Emergent literacy: Writing and reading.* Norwood, NJ: Ablex.

Teale, W. H., and Sulzby, E. (1989). Emergent literacy: New perspectives. In D. S. Strickland and L. M. Morrow (Eds.), *Emerging literacy: Young children learn to read and write.* Newark, DE: International Reading Association.

References

Aaronson, D., and Scarborough, H. S. (1976). Performance theories for sentence coding: Some quantitative evidence. *Journal of Experimental Psychology: Human Perception and Performance, 2,* 56-70.

Adams, M. J. (1979a). Models of word recognition. *Cognitive Psychology, 11,* 133-176.

Adams, M. J. (1979b). Some differences between good and poor readers. In M. L. Kamil and A. J. Moe (eds.), *Reading research: Studies and applications,* 140-144. Clemson, SC: National Reading Conference.

Adams, M. J. (1980). Failures to comprehend and levels of processing in reading. In R. J. Spiro, B. C. Bruce, and W. F. Brewer (eds.), *Theoretical issues in reading comprehension,* 87-112. Hillsdale, NJ: Erlbaum Associates.

Adams, M. J. (1981). What good is orthographic redundancy? In O. J. L. Tzeng and H. Singer (eds.), *Perception of print: Reading research in experimental psychology,* 197-221. Hillsdale, NJ: Erlbaum Associates.

Adams, M. J. (1989). Thinking skills curricula: Their promise and progress *Educational Psychologist, 24,* 25-77.

Adams, M. J., and Bruce, B. C. (1982). Background knowledge and reading comprehension. In J. A. Langer and M. T. Smith-Burke (eds.), *Reader meets author/Bridging the gap,* 2-25. Newark, DE: International Reading Association.

Adams, M. J., and Huggins, A. W. F. (1985). The growth of children's sight vocabulary: A quick test with educational and theoretical implications. *Reading Research Quarterly, 20,* 262-281.

Adams, M. J., Huggins, A. W. F., Starr, B., Rollins, A., Zuckerman, L., Stevens, K., and Nickerson, R. (1980). *A prototype test of decoding skills.* BBN Report No. 4316. Bethesda, MD: National Institute of Child Health and Human Development.

Alegria, J., Pignot, E., and Morais, J. (1982). Phonetic analysis of speech and memory codes in beginning readers. *Memory and Cognition, 10,* 451-456.

Allen, R. V. (1961). *Report of the reading study project,* Monograph No. 1. San Diego, CA: Department of Education, San Diego County.

Allen, R. V. (1976). *Language experiences in communication.* Boston: Houghton Mifflin.

Allington, R. L. (1983). The reading instruction provided readers of different reading abilities. *Elementary School Journal, 83,* 95-107.

Allington, R. L. (1989a, in press). Coherence or chaos? Qualitiative dimensions of the literacy instruction provided low-achievement children. In A. Gartner and D. Lipsky (eds.), *Beyond separate education.* New York: Brookes.

Allington, R. L. (1989b, in press). How policy and regulation influence instruction for at-risk learners: Why poor readers rarely comprehend well. In B. F. Jones and L. Idol (eds.), *Dimensions of thinking and cognitive instruction.* Hillsdale, NJ: Erlbaum Associates.

Allington, R. L., and Fleming, J. T. (1978). The misreading of high-frequency words. *Journal of Special Education, 12,* 417-421.

Allington, R. L., and Strange, M. (1977). Effects of grapheme substitutions in connected text upon reading behaviors. *Visible Language, 11,* 285-297.

Allport, D. A., Antonis, B., and Reynolds, P. (1972). On the division of attention: A disproof of the single channel hypothesis. *Quarterly Journal of Experimental Psychology, 24,* 225-235.

Anderson, R. C., and Freebody, P. (1983). Reading comprehension and the assessment and acquisition of word knowledge. In B. Hutson (ed.), *Advances in reading/language research,* 231-256. Greenwich, CT: JAI Press.

Antes, J. R. (1974). The time course of picture viewing. *Journal of Experimental Psychology, 103,* 72-70.

Applebee, A. N., Langer, J. A., and Mullis, I. V. S. (1988). *Who reads best? Factors related to reading achievement in grades 3, 5, and 11.* Princeton, NJ: National Assessment of Educational Progress, Educational Testing Service.

Arlin, P. (1981). Piagetian tasks as predictors of reading and math readiness in Grades K-1. *Journal of Educational Psychology, 73,* 712-721.

Arter, J. A., and Jenkins, J. R. (1977). Examining the benefits and prevalence of modality considerations in special education. *Journal of Special Education, 11,* 281-298.

Arter, J. A., and Jenkins, J. R. (1979). Differential diagnosis—prescriptive teaching: A critical appraisal. *Review of Educational Research, 49,* 517-555.

Asche, S. E., and Nerlove, H. (1960). The development of double function terms in children. In B. Kaplan and S. Wapner (eds.), *Perspectives in psychological theory.* New York: International Universities Press.

Ashton-Warner, S. (1963). *Teacher.* New York: Simon & Schuster.

Aukerman, R. C. (1971). *Approaches to beginning reading.* New York: Wiley.

Aukerman, R.C. (1984). *Approaches to beginning reading* (2nd ed.). New York: Wiley.

Ausubel, D. P. (1967). A cognitive structure theory of school learning. In L. Siegel (ed.), *Instruction.* San Francisco: Chandler.

Backman, J., Bruck, M., Hèbert, M., and Seidenberg, M. S. (1984). Acquisition and use of spelling-sound information in reading. *Journal of Experimental Child Psychology, 38,* 114-133.

Baddeley, A. D. (1979). Working memory and reading. In P. Kolers, E. Wrolstad, and H. Bouma (eds.), *Processing of visible language, vol. 1.* New York: Plenum Press.

Baddeley, A. D. (1986). *Working memory.* New York: Oxford University Press.

Baddeley, A. D., and Lewis, V. (1981). Inner active processes in reading: The inner voice, the inner ear, and the inner eye. In C. A. Perfetti and A. M. Lesgold (eds.), *Interactive processes in reading,* 107-129. Hillsdale, NJ: Erbaum Associates.

Baddeley, A. D., Thomson, N., and Buchanan, M. (1975). Word length and the structure of short-term memory. *Journal of Verbal Learning and Verbal Behavior, 14,* 575-589.

Baddeley, A. D., Vallar, G., and Wilson, B. (1987). Sentence comprehension and phonological memory: Some neuropsychological evidence. In M. Coltheart (ed.), *Attention and performance XII: The psychology of reading,* 509-529. Hillsdale, NJ: Erlbaum Associates.

Baghban, M. (1984). *Our daughter learns to read and write: A case study from birth to three.* Newark, DE: International Reading Association.

Bailey, M. H. (1967). The utility of phonic generalizations in grades one through six. *Reading Teacher, 20,* 413-418.

Balmuth, M. (1982). *The roots of phonics.* New York: Teachers College Press.

Bank Street College of Education. (1973). *The Bank Street readers.* New York: Macmillan.

Baron, J. (1973). Phonemic stage not necessary for reading. *Quarterly Journal of Experimental Psychology, 25,* 241-246.

Baron, J., and Treiman, R. (1980a). Some problems in the study of differences in cognitive processes. *Memory and Cognition, 8,* 313-321.

Baron, J., and Treiman, R. (1980b). Use of orthography in reading and learning to read. In J. Kavanaugh and R. Venezky (eds.), *Orthography, reading and dyslexia.* Baltimore: University Park Press.

Baron, J., Treiman, R., Wilf, J. F., and Kellman, P. (1980). Spelling and reading by rules. In U. Frith (ed.), *Cognitive processes in spelling,* 159-194. New York: Academic Press.

Barr, R. (1984). Beginning reading instruction: From debate to reformation. In P. D. Pearson (ed.), *Handbook of reading research,* 545-581. New York: Longman.

Barr, R., and Dreeben, R., with Wiratchai, N. (1983). *How schools work.* Chicago: University of Chicago Press.

Barron, R. W. (1980). Visual and phonological strategies in reading and spelling. In U. Frith (ed.), *Cognitive processes in spelling,* 195-214. New York: Academic Press.

Barron, R. W. (1981a). Development of visual word recognition: A review. In G. E. MacKinnon and T. G. Waller (eds.), *Reading research: Advances in theory and practice, vol. 3*, 119-158. New York: Academic Press.

Barron, R. W. (1981b). Reading skill and reading strategies. In A. M. Lesgold and C. A. Perfetti (eds.), *Interactive processes in reading*, 299-328. Hillsdale, NJ: Erlbaum Associates.

Barron, R. W. (1986). Word recognition in early reading: A review of the direct and indirect access hypotheses. *Cognition, 24*, 93-119.

Barton, A. H., and Wilder, D. E. (1964). Research and practice in the teaching of reading: A progress report. In M. B. Miles (ed.), *Innovation in education*, 361-398. New York: Columbia University Teachers College Bureau of Publications.

Barton, D., Miller, R., and Macken, M. (1980). Do children treat clusters as one unit or two? *Papers and Reports on Child Language Development, 18*, 93-137.

Bateman, B. (1979). Teaching reading to learning disabled and other hard-to-teach children. In L. A. Resnick and P. A. Weaver (eds.), *Theory and practice of early reading, vol. 1*, 227-259. Hillsdale, NJ: Erlbaum Associates.

Beck, I. L. (1981). Reading problems and instructional practices. In G. E. MacKinnon and T. G. Waller (eds.), *Reading research: Advances in theory and practice, vol. 2*, 53-94. New York: Academic Press.

Beck, I. L., and McCaslin, E. S. (1978). *An analysis of dimensions that affect the development of code-breaking ability in eight beginning reading programs*. LRDC Report No. 1978/6. Pittsburgh: University of Pittsburgh Learning Research and Development Center.

Beck, I. L., Perfetti, C. A., and McKeown, M. G. (1982). Effects of long-term vocabulary instruction on lexical access and reading comprehension. *Journal of Educational Psychology, 74*, 506-521.

Becker, W. C., and Gersten, R. (1982). A follow-up of Follow Through: The later effects of the direct instruction model on children in fifth and sixth grades. *American Educational Research Journal, 19*, 75-92.

Beers, J. W. (1980). Developmental stragegies of spelling competence in primary school children. In E. H. Henderson and J. W. Beers (eds.), *Developmental and cognitive aspects of learning to spell*, 36-45. Newark, DE: International Reading Association.

Beers, J. W., and Henderson, E. H. (1977). A study of developing orthographic concepts among first graders. *Research in the Teaching of English, 11*, 133-148.

Berdiansky, B., Cronnell, B., and Koehler, J. (1969). *Spelling-sound relations and primary form-class descriptions for speech comprehension vocabularies of 6-9 year olds*. Technical Report No. 15. Los Alamitos, CA: Southwest Regional Laboratory for Educational Research and Development.

Bereiter, C., Hughes, A., and Anderson, V. (1986). *Catching on*. LaSalle Peru, IL: Open Court.

Biederman, I. (1972). Perceiving real-word scenes. *Science, 177*, 77-79.

Biederman, I., Rabinowitz, J. C., Glass, A. L., and Stacy, E. W. (1974). On the information extracted from a glance at a scene. *Journal of Experimental Psychology, 103,* 597-600.

Biemiller, A. (1970). The development of the use of graphic and contextual information as children learn to read. *Reading Research Quarterly, 6,* 75-96.

Biemiller, A. (1977-1978). Relationships between oral reading rates for letters, words, and simple text in the development of reading achievement. *Reading Research Quarterly, 13,* 223-253.

Birman, B. F., Orland, M. E., Jung, R. K., Anson, R. J., Garcia, G. N., Moore, M. T., Funkhouser, J. E., Morrison, D. R., Turnbull, B. J., and Reiser, E. R. (1987). *The current operation of the Chapter 1 program: Final report from the National Assessment of Chapter 1.* Washington, DC: Government Printing Office.

Bissex, G. L. (1980). *GNYS AT WRK: A child learns to write and read.* Cambridge, MA: Harvard University Press.

Blachman, B. A. (1984a). Relationship of rapid naming ability and language analysis skills to kindergarten and first-grade reading achievement. *Journal of Educational Psychology, 76,* 610-622.

Blachman, B. A. (1984b). Language analysis skills and early reading acquisition. In G. Wallach and K. Butler (eds.), *Language learning disabilities in school-age children,* 271-287. Baltimore: Williams and Wilkins.

Blachman, B. A. (1987). An alternative classroom reading program for learning disabled and other low-achieving children. In W. Ellis (ed.), *Intimacy with language: A forgotten basic in teacher education,* 49-55. Baltimore: Orton Dyslexia Society.

Blum, I. H., Evans, M., and Taylor, N. E. (1980). *BET: Written language awareness test.* Washington, DC: Catholic University.

Bond, G. L., and Dykstra, R. (1967). The cooperative research program in first-grade reading instruction. (1967). *Reading Research Quarterly, 2,* 5-142.

Bond, Z. S., and Garnes, S. (1980). Misperceptions of fluent speech. In R. Cole (ed.), *Perception and production of fluent speech, 1,* 15-132. Hillsdale, NJ: Erlbaum Associates.

Bradley, L., and Bryant, P. E. (1983). Categorizing sounds and learning to read—a causal connection. *Nature, 301,* 419-421.

Braun, C. (1969). Interest-loading and modality effects on textual response acquisition. *Reading Research Quarterly, 4,* 428-444.

Brill, L. (1974). *"What's so funny?" Children's understanding of puns.* Unpublished manuscript. Philadelphia: University of Pennsylvania.

Broadbent, D. E. (1967). Word-frequency effect and response bias. *Psychological Review, 74,* 1-15.

Brooks, L. (1977). Visual pattern in fluent word identification. In A. S. Reber and D. L. Scarborough (eds.), *Toward a psychology of reading,* 143-181. Hillsdale, NJ: Erlbaum Associates.

Brown, G. D. A. (1987). Resolving inconsistency: A computational model of word naming. *Journal of Memory and Language, 26,* 1-23.

Bruce, L. J. (1964). The analysis of word sounds by young children. *British Journal of Educational Psychology, 34,* 158-170.

Bruner, J. S. (1957). On perceptual readiness. *Psychological Review, 64,* 123-152.

Brunswik, E. (1955). Representative design and probabilistic theory in a functional psychology. *Psychological Review, 62,* 193-217.

Bryant, N. D. (1975). *Diagnostic test of basic decoding skills.* New York: Teachers College, Columbia University.

Bryant, P. E., and Bradley, L. (1980). Why children sometimes write words which they do not read. In U. Frith (ed.), *Cognitive processes in spelling,* 355-372. New York: Academic Press.

Buchanan, C. D. (1973). *Programmed reading: A Sullivan Associates program,* 3d ed. New York: McGraw-Hill.

Burmeister, L. E. (1968). Usefulness of phonic generalizations. *Reading Teacher, 21,* 349-356.

Buswell, G. T. (1935). *How people look at pictures.* Chicago: University of Chicago Press.

Byrne, B., and Ledez, J. (1983). Phonological awareness in reading disabled adults. *Australian Journal of Psychology, 35,* 185-197.

Cairns, C. E., and Feinstein, M. H. (1982). Markedness and the theory of syllable structure. *Linguistic Inquiry, 13,* 193-226.

Calfee, R. C. (1977). Assessment of independent reading skills: Basic research and practical applications. In A. S. Reber and D. L. Scarborough (eds.), *Toward a psychology of reading,* 289-323. Hillsdale, NJ: Erlbaum Associates.

Calfee, R. C., and Calfee, K. H. (1981). Interactive reading assessment system (IRAS). Unpublished manuscript. Stanford, CA: Stanford University.

Calfee, R. C., and Drum, P. (1986). Research on teaching reading. In M. C. Wittrock (ed.), *Handbook of research on teaching,* 804-849. New York: Macmillan.

Calfee, R. C., Lindamood, P. E., and Lindamood, C. H. (1973). Acoustic-phonetic skills and reading—kindergarten through 12th grade. *Journal of Educational Psychology, 64,* 293-298.

Caramazza, A., Miceli, G., Villa, G., and Romani, C. (1987). The role of the graphemic buffer in spelling: Evidence from a case of acquired dyslexia. *Cognition, 26,* 59-85.

Carbo, M. (1978). Teaching reading with talking books. *Reading Teacher, 32,* 267-273.

Carbo, M. (1988). Debunking the great phonics myth. *Phi Delta Kappan, 70,* 226-240.

Carlberg, C. G., Johnson, D. W., Johnson, R., Maruyama, G., Kavale, K., Kulik, C. C., Kulik, J., Lysakowski, R. S., Pflaum, S. W., and Walberg, H. J. (1984). Meta-analysis in education: A reply to Slavin. *Educational Researcher, 13*(10), 16-23.

Carnine, D., and Silbert, J. (1979). *Direct instruction reading.* Columbus, OH: Charles E. Merrill.

Carpenter, P. A., and Daneman, M. (1981). Lexical retrieval and error recovery in reading: A model based on eye fixations. *Journal of Verbal Learning and Verbal Behavior, 20,* 137-160.

Carpenter, P. A., and Just, M. A. (1981). Cognitive processes in reading: Models based on readers' eye fixations. In A. M. Lesgold and C. A. Perfetti (eds.), *Interactive processes in reading,* 177-213. Hillsdale, NJ: Erlbaum Associates.

Carr, H. A. (1935). *An introduction to space perception.* New York: Longmans Green.

Carr, T. H., and Pollatsek, A. (1985). Recognizing printed words: A look at current models. In D. Besner, T. G. Waller, and G. E. MacKinnon, *Reading research: Advances in theory and practice, vol. 5,* 1-82. Orlando, FL: Academic Press.

Carroll, J. B., Davies, P., and Richman, B. (1971). *Word frequency book.* Boston: Houghton Mifflin.

Carter, L. G. (1984). The sustaining effects study of compensatory and elementary education. *Educational Researcher,* 4-13.

Carver, R. P. (1985). How good are some of the world's best readers? *Reading Research Quarterly, 20,* 389-419.

Case, R., Kurland, M., and Goldberg, J. (1982). Operational efficiency and the growth of short-term memory span. *Journal of Experimental Child Psychology, 33,* 386-404.

Cattell, J. McK. (1885a). Ueber die Zeit der Erkennung und Benennung von Schriftzeichen, Bildern und Farben. *Philosophische Studien, 2,* 635-650. Reprinted in translation in A. T. Poffenberger (ed.). (1947). *James McKeen Cattell: Man of science.* York, PA: Science Press.

Cattell, J. McK. (1885b). The inertia of the eye and brain. *Brain, 8,* 295-312. Reprinted in A. T. Poffenberger (ed.). (1947). *James McKeen Cattell: Man of science.* York, PA: Science Press.

Cattell, J. McK. (1886). The time taken up by cerebral operations. *Mind, 11,* 220-242.

Chall, J. S. (1967). *Learning to read: The great debate.* New York: McGraw-Hill.

Chall, J. S. (1978). A decade of research on reading and learning disabilities. In S. J. Samuels (ed.), *What research has to say about reading instruction,* 31-42. Newark, DE: International Reading Association.

Chall, J. S. (1979). The great debate: Ten years later, with a modest proposal for reading stages. In L. B. Resnick and P. A. Weaver (eds.), *Theory and practice of early reading, vol. 1,* 29-55. Hillsdale, NJ: Erlbaum Associates.

Chall, J. S. (1983a). *Learning to read: The great debate.* Updated ed. New York: McGraw-Hill.

Chall, J. S. (1983b). *Stages of reading development.* New York: McGraw-Hill.

Chall, J. S. (1988). *Could the decline be real? Recent trends in reading instruction and support in the U.S.* Paper prepared for the

Subcommittee on the 1986 Reading data, NAEP Technical Review Panel. Cambridge, MA: Harvard University.

Chall, J. S. (1989). Learning to read: The great debate twenty years later. A response to "Debunking the great phonics myth." *Phi Delta Kappan, 71,* 521-538.

Chall, J. S. , and Jacobs, B. (1983). Writing and reading in the elementary grades: Developmental trends among low SES children. *Language Arts, 60,* 617-626.

Chall, J. S. , Roswell, F. G., and Blumenthal, S. H. (1963). Auditory blending ability: A factor in success in beginning reading. *Reading Teacher, 16,* 113-118.

Chang, F. R. (1980). Active memory processes in visual sentence comprehension: Clause effects and pronominal reference. *Memory and Cognition, 8,* 58-64.

Chao, Y-R. (1958). The non-uniqueness of phonemic solutions of phonetic systems. In M. Joos (ed.), *Readings in linguistics: The development of descriptive linguistics in America since 1925,* (2d ed.). New York: American Council of Learned Societies.

Chase, W. G., and Simon, H. A. (1973). The mind's eye in chess. In W. G. Chase (ed.), *Visual information processing,* 215-281. New York: Academic Press.

Cheng, P. W. (1985). Restructuring versus automaticity: Alternative accounts of skill acquisition. *Psychological Review, 92,* 414-423.

Chi, M. T. H. (1978). Knowledge structures and memory development. In R. Siegler (ed.), *Advances in the psychology of human intelligence, vol. 1,* 7-75. Hillsdale, NJ: Erlbaum Associates.

Chomsky, C. (1970). Reading, writing and phonology. *Harvard Educational Review, 40,* 287-309.

Chomsky, C. (1971a). Invented spelling in the open classroom. *Word, 27,* 499-518.

Chomsky, C. (1971b). Write first, read later. *Childhood Education, 41,* 296-299.

Chomsky, C. (1972). Stages in language development and reading exposure. *Harvard Educational Review, 42,* 1-33.

Chomsky, C. (1979). Approaching reading through invented spelling. In L. B. Resnick and P A. Weaver (eds.), *Theory and practice of early reading, vol. 2,* 43-65. Hillsdale, NJ: Erlbaum Associates.

Chomsky, N., and Halle, M. (1968). *The sound pattern of English.* New York: Harper & Row.

Clark, H. H., and Clark, E. V. (1977). *Psychology and language.* New York: Harcourt Brace Jovanovich.

Clarke, L. K. (1989, in press). Encouraging invented spelling in first graders' writing: Effects on learning to spell and read. *Research in the Teaching of English.*

Clay, M. M. (1966). *Emergent reading behavior.* Doctoral dissertion, University of Auckland.

Clay, M. M. (1972). *Reading: The patterning of complex behaviour.* Auckland, NZ: Heinemann.

Clay, M. M. (1975). *What did I write? Beginning writing behaviour.* Portsmouth, NH: Heinemann.

Clay, M. M. (1976). Early childhood and cultural diversity in New Zealand. *Reading Teacher, 29,* 333-342.

Clay, M. M. (1979a). *Stones—The concepts about print test.* Exeter, NH: Heinemann.

Clay, M. M. (1979b). *The early detection of reading difficulties,* (3d ed.). Portsmouth, NH: Heinemann.

Clements, F. (1587). *The Petie Schole.* London.

Clymer, T. (1963). The utility of phonic generalizations in the primary grades. *Reading Teacher, 16,* 252-258.

Clymer, T., Christenson, B., and Brown, V. (1976). *Ginn 720 reading program.* Lexington, MA: Ginn.

Cohen, J., and Cohen, P. (1975). *Applied multiple regression/correlation analysis for the behavioral sciences.* Hillsdale, NJ: Erlbaum Associates.

Cole, R. A., and Jakimik, J. (1980). A model of speech perception. In R. Cole (ed.), *Perception and production of fluent speech,* 133-163. Hillsdale, NJ: Erlbaum Associates.

Coleman, E. B. (1970). Collecting a data base for a reading technology. *Journal of Educational Psychology Monograph, 61* (4).

Coltheart, M., and Freeman, R. (1974). Case alternation impairs word identification. *Bulletin of the Psychonomic Society, 3,* 102-104.

Coltheart, M., Patterson, K., and Marshall, J. (eds.) (1980). *Deep dyslexia.* London: Routledge & Kegan Paul.

Commission on Reading, National Academy of Education. (1985). *Becoming a nation of readers.* Washington, DC: National Institute of Education.

Cossu, G., Shankweiler, D., Liberman, I. Y., Tola, G., and Katz, L. (1988). Awareness of phonological segments and reading ability in Italian children. *Applied Psycholinguistics.*

Cronbach, L. S., and Snow, R. E. (1977). *Aptitudes and instructional methods.* New York: Irvington.

Cronnell, B. A. (1970). *Spelling-to-sound correspondences for reading vs sound-to-spelling correspondences.* Technical Note TN2-70-15. Los Alamitos, CA: Southwest Regional Laboratory.

Cunningham, P. M. (1979). Investigating a synthesized theory of mediated word identification. *Reading Research Quarterly, 1975, 11,* 127-143.

Dahl, P. R., and Samuels, S. J. (1979). An experimental program for teaching high speed word recognition and comprehension skills In J. E. Button, T. C. Lovitt, and T. D. Rowland (eds.), *Communications research in learning disabilities and mental retardation.* Baltimore: University Park Press.

Daneman, M., and Carpenter, P. A. (1983). *Developmental differences in reading and detecting semantic inconsistencies.* Technical Report. Pittsburgh: Carnegie-Mellon University.

Daneman, M., and Tardif, T. (1987). Working memory and reading skill re-examined. In M. Coltheart (ed.), *Attention and performance XII: The psychology of reading*, 491-508. Hillsdale, NJ: Erlbaum Associates.

Daniels, J. C., and Diack, H. (1956). *Progress in reading*. Nottingham: University of Nottingham Institute of Education.

Deihl, W. A., and Mikulecky, L. (1980). The nature of reading at work. *Journal of Reading, 24*, 221-228.

deManrique, A. M. B., and Gramigna, S. (1984). La segmentación fonológica y silábica en niños de preescolar y primer grado. *Lectura y Vida, 5*, 4-13.

Dempster, F. N. (1981). Memory span: Sources of individual and developmental differences. *Psychological Bulletin, 89*, 63-100.

Denckla, M. B., and Rudel, R. G. (1976). Rapid automatized names (R.A.N.): Dyslexia differentiated from other learning disabilities. *Neuropsychologia, 14*, 471-479.

Dennis, I., Besner, D., and Davelaar, E. (1985). Phonology in visual word recognition: Their is more two this than meats the I. In D. Besner, T. G. Waller, and G. E. MacKinnon, *Reading research: Advances in theory and practice, vol. 5*, 167-197. Orlando, FL: Academic Press.

Desberg, P., Elliott, D. E., and Marsh, G. (1980). American Black English and spelling. In U. Frith (ed.), *Cognitive processes in spelling*, 69-84. New York: Academic Press.

Dewey, G. (1970). *Relative frequency of English spellings*. New York: Teachers College Press.

Dewitz, P., and Stammer, J. (1980). *The development of linguistic awareness in young children from label reading to word recognition.* Paper presented at the National Reading Conference, San Diego, CA.

Diringer, D. (1968). *The alphabet.* London: Hutchinson.

Doctor, E. A., and Coltheart, M. (1980). Children's use of phonological encoding when reading for meaning. *Memory and Cognition, 8*, 195-209.

Doehring, D. G. (1976). Acquisition of rapid reading responses. *Monograph of the Society for Research in Child Development, 41.*

Dolch, E., and Bloomster, M. Phonic readiness. (1937). *Elementary School Journal, 38*, 201-205.

Downing, J. (1970a). Children's concepts of language in learning to read. *Educational Research, 12*, 106-112.

Downing, J. (1970b). The development of linguistic concepts in children's thinking. *Research in the teaching of English, 4*, 5-19.

Downing, J. (1973). *Comparative reading.* New York: Macmillan.

Downing, J. (1979). *Reading and reasoning.* New York: Springer-Verlag.

Downing, J., and Oliver, P. (1973-1974). The child's conception of "a word." *Reading Research Quarterly, 9*, 568-582.

Downing, J., Ayers, D., and Schaeffer, B. (1984). *The linguistic awareness in reading readiness test.* Slough, England: NFER/Nelson.

Downing, J., Ollila, L., and Oliver, P. (1975). Cultural differences in children's concepts of reading and writing. *British Journal of Educational Psychology, 45*, 312-316.

Downing, J., Ollila, L., and Oliver, P. (1977). Concepts of language in children from differing socio-economic backgrounds. *Journal of Educational Research, 70,* 277-281.

Drake, D. A., and Ehri, L. C. (1984). Spelling acquisition: Effects of pronouncing words on memory for their spellings. *Cognition and Instruction, 1,* 297-320.

Durkin, D. (1966). *Children who read early: Two longitudinal studies.* New York: Teachers College Press.

Durkin, D. (1979). What classroom observations reveal about reading comprehension instruction. *Reading Research Quarterly, 14,* 481-533.

Durkin, D. (1988). *Teaching them to read,* (5th ed.). Boston: Allyn and Bacon.

Durr, W. K., LePere, J. M., and Aslin, M. L. (1976). *The Houghton Mifflin reading series.* Boston: Houghton Mifflin.

Durrell, D. D. (1963). *Phonograms in primary grade words.* Boston: Boston University.

Durrell, D. D. (1980). Commentary: Letter name values in reading and spelling. *Reading Research Quarterly, 16,* 159-163.

Durrell, D. D., and Catterson, J. H. (1980). *Manual of directions: Durrell Analysis of reading difficulty.* Rev. ed. New York: Psychological Corporation.

Dykstra, R. (1968). Summary of the second-grade phase of the Cooperative Reserach Program in primary reading instruction. *Reading Research Quarterly, 4,* 49-71.

Ehri, L. C. (1975). Word consciousness in readers and prereaders. *Journal of Educational Psychology, 67,* 204-212.

Ehri, L. C. (1976). Word learning in beginning readers and prereaders: Effects of form class and defining contexts. *Journal of Educational Psychology, 67,* 204-212.

Ehri, L. C. (1977). *Can readers distinguish single spoken words from pseudowords?* Unpublished manuscript. Davis, CA: University of California, Davis.

Ehri, L. C. (1979). Linguistic insight: Threshold of reading acquisition. In T. G. Waller and G. E. MacKinnon (eds.), *Reading research: Advances in theory and practice, vol. 1,* 63-111. New York: Academic Press.

Ehri, L. C. (1980). The development of orthographic images. In U. Frith (ed.), *Cognitive processes in spelling,* 311-338. New York: Academic Press.

Ehri, L. C. (1983a). A critique of five studies related to latter-name knowledge and learning to read. In L. M. Gentile, M. L. Kamil, and J. S. Blanchard (eds.), *Reading research revisited,* 143-153. Columbus, OH: Charles E. Merrill.

Ehri, L. C. (1983b). Summary of Dorothy C. Ohnmacht's study: The effects of letter knowledge on achievement in reading in the first grade. In L. M. Gentile, M. L. Kamil, and J. S. Blanchard (eds.), *Reading research revisited,* 141-142. Columbus, OH: Charles E. Merrill.

Ehri, L. C. (1986). Sources of difficulty in learning to spell and read. In M. L. Wolraich and D. Routh (eds.), *Advances in developmental and behavioral pediatrics, vol. 7*, 121-195. Greenwich, CT: JAI Press.

Ehri, L. C. (1987). Learning to read and spell words. *Journal of Reading Behavior, 19*, 5-31.

Ehri, L. C. (1988). Movement in word reading and spelling: How spelling contributes to reading. In J. Mason (ed.), *Reading and writing connections*. Newton, MA: Allyn and Bacon.

Ehri, L. C., and Wilce, L. S. (1979). The mnemonic value of orthography among beginning readers. *Journal of Educational Psychology, 71*, 26-40.

Ehri, L. C., and Wilce, L. S. (1980). The influence of orthography on readers' conceptualization of the phonemic structure of words. *Applied Psycholinguistics, 1*, 371-385.

Ehri, L. C., and Wilce, L. S. (1982). The salience of silent letters in children's memory for word spellings. *Memory and Cognition, 10*, 155-166.

Ehri, L. C., and Wilce, L. S. (1985). Movement into reading: Is the first stage of printed word learning visual or phonetic? *Reading Research Quarterly, 20*, 163-179.

Ehri, L. C., and Wilce, L. S. (1986). The influence of spellings on speech: Are alveolar flaps /d/ or /t/? In D. Yaden and S. Templeton (eds.), *Metalinguistic awareness and beginning literacy*, 101-114. Exeter, NH: Heinemann.

Ehri, L. C., and Wilce, L. S. (1987). Does learning to spell help beginners learn to read words? *Reading Research Quarterly, 22*, 47-65.

Ehri, L. C., Deffner, N. D., and Wilce, L. S. (1984). Pictorial mnemonics for phonics. *Journal of Educational Psychology, 76*, 880-893.

Eimas, P. D., Siqueland, E. R., Jusczyk, P., and Vigorito, J. (1971). Speech perception in infants. *Science, 171*, 303-306.

Elkonin, D. B. (1973). U.S.S.R. In J. Downing (ed.), *Comparative Reading*. New York: Macmillan.

Emans, R. (1967). The usefulness of phonic generalizations above the primary grades. *Reading Teacher, 20*, 419-425.

Engelmann, S. (1969). *Preventing failure in the primary grades*. Chicago: Science Research Associates.

Engelmann, S., and Bruner, E. (1968). *DISTAR*. Chicago: Science Research Associates.

Engelmann, S., and Bruner, E. C. (1974). *Distar Reading I: An instructional system*, 2d ed. Chicago: Science Research Associates.

Estes, W. K. (1977). On the interaction of perception and memory in reading. In D. LaBerge and S. J. Samuels (eds.), *Basic processes in reading*, 1-25. Hillsdale, NJ: Erlbaum Associates.

Evans, M. A., and Carr, T. H. (1985). Cognitive abilities, conditions of learning, and the early development of reading skill. *Reading Research Quarterly, 20*, 327-350.

Farnham, G. H. (1887). *The sentence method of teaching reading*. Syracuse, NY: C. W. Bardeen.

Farnham-Diggory, S. (1967). Symbol and synthesis in experimental "reading." *Child Development, 38,* 221-231.

Farnham-Diggory, S. (1984). Why reading? Because it's there. *Developmental Review, 1,* 58–60.

Farnham-Diggory, S. (1985). Commentary: Time, now, for a little serious complexity. In S. J. Cecil (ed.), *Handbook of cognitive social and neuropsychological aspects of learning disabilities, vol. 1.* Hillsdale, NJ: Erlbaum Associates.

Feitelson, D. (1988). Facts and fads in beginning reading: A cross-language perspective. Norwood, NJ: Ablex Publishing Corporation.

Feitelson, D., and Goldstein, Z. (1986). Patterns of book ownership and reading to young children in Israeli school-oriented and nonschool-oriented families. *Reading Teacher, 39,* 924-930.

Ferriero, E. (1986). The interplay between information and assimilation in beginning literacy. In Teale, W. H., and Sulzby, E. (eds.) (1986). *Emergent literacy: Writing and reading,* 15-49. Norwood, NJ: Ablex Publishing Corporation.

Fielding, L., Wilson, P., and Anderson, R. (1987). A new focus on free reading: The role of trade books in reading. In T. E. Raphael and R. Reynolds (eds.), *Contexts of literacy.* New York: Longman.

Finn, P. J. (1977-1978). Word frequency, information theory, and cloze performance: A transfer feature theory of processing in reading. *Reading Research Quarterly, 13,* 508-537.

Firth, I. (1972). *Components of reading disability.* Doctoral dissertation, University of South Wales.

Fischler, I., and Bloom, P. A. (1979). Automatic and attentional processes in the effects of sentence contexts on word recognition. *Journal of Verbal Learning and Verbal Behavior, 18,* 1-20.

Fisher, C. W., Filby, N. N., Marliave, R., Cahen, L. S., Dishaw, M. M., Moore, J. E., and Berliner, D. C. (1978). *Teaching behaviors, academic learning time, and student achievement: Final report of phase III-B, beginning teacher evaluation study.* San Francisco: Far West Educational Laboratory for Educational Research and Development.

Flesch, R. (1955). *Why Johnny can't read.* New York: Harper and Row.

Flesch, R. (1985). *Why Johnny can't read,* 2d ed. New York: Harper and Row.

Fletcher, H. (1929). *Speech and hearing.* New York: Van Nostrand Company.

Flood, J. (1977). Parental styles in reading episodes with young children. *Reading Teacher, 30,* 864-867.

Flood, J., and Lapp, D. (1981). *Language/reading instruction for the young child.* New York: Macmillan.

Flynn, J. R. (1987). Massive IQ gains in 14 nations: What IQ tests really measure. *Psychological Bulletin, 101,* 171-191.

Fowler, C. A., Liberman, I. Y., and Shankweiler, D. (1977). On interpreting the error pattern in beginning reading. *Language and Speech, 20,* 162-173.

Fowler, C. A., Napps, S., and Feldman, L. (1985). Relations among regular and irregular morphologically related words in the lexicon as revealed by repetition priming. *Journal of Experimental Psychology: Learning, Memory, and Cognition, 10,* 241-255.

Fox, B., and Routh, D. K. (1975). Analyzing spoken language into words, syllables, and phonemes: A developmental study. *Journal of Psycholinguistic Research, 4,* 331-342.

Francis, H. (1973). Children's experience of reading and notions of units in language. *British Journal of Educational Psychology, 43,* 17-23.

Frederiksen, J. R. (1978). Assessment of perceptual decoding and lexical skills and their relation to reading proficiency. In A. M. Lesgold, J. W. Pellegrini, S. E. Fokkems, and R. Glaser (eds.), *Cognitive psychology and instruction.* New York: Plenum Press.

Frederiksen, J. R. (1982). A componential theory of reading skills and their interactions. In R. Sternberg (ed.), *Advances in the psychology of human intelligence, vol. 1,* 125-180. Hillsdale, NJ: Erlbaum Associates.

Frederiksen, J. R. (1987). *Final report on the development of computer-based instructional systems for training essential components of reading.* Report No. 6465. Cambridge, MA: BBN Laboratories.

Frederiksen, J. R., Warren, B. M., and Rosebery, A. S. (1985a). A componential approach to training reading skills: Part 1. Perceptual units training. *Cognition and Instruction, 2,* 91-130.

Frederiksen, J. R., Warren, B. M., and Rosebery, A. S. (1985b). A componential approach to training reading skills: Part 2. Decoding and use of context. *Cognition and Instruction, 2,* 271-338.

Freebody, P., and Anderson, R. C. (1983). Effects on text comprehension of different proportions and locations of difficult vocabulary. *Journal of Reading Behavior, 15,* 19-39.

Friedrich, F. J., Schadler, M., and Juola, J. F. (1979). Developmental changes in units of processing in reading. *Journal of Experimental Child Psychology, 28,* 344-358.

Fries, C. C., Fries, A. C., Wilson, R. G., and Rudolph, M. K. (1966). *Merrill Linguistic readers: Reader 1.* Columbus, OH: Merrill Books.

Frith, U. (1978). From print to meaning and from print to sound, or how to read without knowing how to spell. *Visible Language, 12,* 43-54.

Frith, U. (ed.). (1980a). *Cognitive processes in spelling.* New York: Academic Press.

Frith, U. (1980b). Unexpected spelling problems. In U. Frith (ed.), *Cognitive processes in spelling,* 495-516. New York: Academic Press.

Fromkin, V. (1973). *Speech errors as linguistic evidence.* The Hague: Mouton Publishers.

Fudge, E. C. (1969). Syllables. *Journal of Linguistics, 5,* 253-286.

Gaskins, I. W., Downer, M. A., Anderson, R. C., Cunningham, P. M., Gaskins, R. W., Schommer, M, and the Teachers of the Benchmark School. (1988). A metacognitive approach to phonics: Using what you know to decode what you don't know. *Remedial and Special Education, 9.*

Gates, A. I., and Taylor, G. A., (1923). The acquisition of motor control and writing by pre-school children. *Teachers College Record, 24,* 459-468. Cited in Feitelson, 1988, *op. cit.*

Gelb, I. J. (1963). *A study of writing,* 2d ed. Chicago: University of Chicago Press.

Gentry, R. (1978). Early spelling strategies. *Elementary School Journal, 79,* 88-92.

Gentry, R. (1981). Learning to spell developmentally. *Reading Teacher, 34,* 378-381.

Gersten, R., and Keating, T. (1987). Long-term benefits from direct instruction. *Educational Leadership, 45,* 28-31.

Gerstman, L. (1967). Classification of self-normalized vowels. *IEEE Transactions on Audio and Electroacoustics, AU-16,* 78-80.

Gibson, E. J. (1969). *Principles of perceptual learning and development.* New York: Appleton-Century-Crofts.

Gibson, E. J., and Levin, H. (1975). *The psychology of reading.* Cambridge, MA: MIT Press.

Gibson, E. J., Gibson, J. J., Pick, A. D., and Osser, H. A. (1962). A developmental study of the discrimination of letter-like forms. *Journal of Comparative and Physiological Psychology, 55,* 897-906.

Gibson, E. J., Osser, H., and Pick, A. D. (1963). A study of the development of grapheme-phoneme correspondences. *Journal of Verbal Learning and Verbal Behavior, 2,* 142-146.

Gick, M. L., and Holyoak, K. J. (1983). Schema induction and analogical transfer. *Cognitive Psychology, 15,* 1-38.

Gigerenzer, G., and Murray, D. J. (1987). *Cognition as intuitive statistics.* Hillsdale, NJ: Erlbaum Associates.

Glaser, R. (1984). Education and thinking: The role of knowledge. *American Psychologist, 39,* 93-104.

Gleitman, L. R., and Rozin, P. (1977). The structure and acquisition of reading I: Relations between orthographies and the structure of language. In A. S. Reber and D. L. Scarborough (eds.), *Toward a psychology of reading,* 1-53. Hillsdale, NJ: Erlbaum Associates.

Glim, T. E. (1973). *The Palo Alto reading program,* 2d ed. *Sequential steps in reading.* New York: Harcourt Brace Jovanovich.

Glushko, R. J. (1979). The organization and activation of orthographic knowledge in reading aloud. *Journal of Experimental Psychology: Human Perception and Performance, 5,* 674-691.

Goldblum, N., and Frost, R. (1988). The crossword puzzle paradigm: The effectiveness of different word fragments as cues for the retrieval of words. *Memory and Cognition, 16,* 158-166.

Goldfield, B. A., and Snow, C. E. (1984). Reading books with children: The mechanics of parental influences on children's reading achievement. In J. Flood (ed.), *Understanding reading comprehension,* 204-215. Newark, DE: International Reading Association.

Goldman, S. R., Hogaboam, T. W., Bell, L. C., and Perfetti, C. A. (1980). Short-term retention of discourse during reading. *Journal of Educational Psychology, 68,* 680-688.

Goodman, K. (1972). Orthography in a theory of reading instruction. *Elementary English, 49,* 1254-1261.

Goodman, K. S., and Goodman, Y. M. (1979). Learning to read is natural. In L. B. Resnick and P. A. Weaver, *Theory and practice of early reading, vol. 1,* 137-154. Hillsdale, NJ: Erlbaum Associates.

Goodman, Y. M. (1986). Children coming to know literacy. In W. H. Teale and E. Sulzby (eds.), *Emergent literacy: Writing and reading,* 1-14. Norwood, NJ: Ablex Publishing Corporation.

Goodman, Y., and Watson, D. J. (1977). A reading program to live with: Focus on comprehension. *Language Arts, 53,* 868-879.

Goswami, U. (1988, in press). Orthographic analogies and reading development. *Quarterly Journal of Experimental Psychology.*

Gough, P. B., and Hillinger, M. L. (1980). Learning to read: An unnatural act. *Bulletin of the Orton Society, 30,* 179-196.

Graves, D. H. (ed.). (1983). *A researcher learns to write.* Portsmouth, NH: Heinemann.

Gray, W. S., et al. (1956). *The new basic reading program.* Chicago: Scott, Foresman.

Groff, P. (1975). Research in brief: Shapes as cues to word recognition. *Visible Language, 9,* 67-71.

Hall, N. (1987). *The emergence of literacy.* Portsmouth, NH: Heinemann.

Hall, V. C., Salvi, R., Seggev, L., and Caldwell, E. (1970). Cognitive synthesis, conservation, and task analysis. *Developmental Psychology, 2,* 423-428.

Halle, M., and Vergnaud, J.-R. (1980). Three-dimensional phonology. *Journal of Linguistic Research, 1,* 83-105.

Hammill, D. D., and McNutt, G. (1980). Language abilities and reading: A review of the literature on their relationship. *Elementary School Journal, 80,* 269-277.

Hanna, P. R. et al. (1966). *Phoneme-grapheme correspondences as cues to spelling improvement.* USOE Publication No. 32008. Washington, DC: Government Printing Office.

Harris, L. A. (1967). *A study of the rate of acquisition and retention of interest-loaded words by low socioeconomic children.* Doctoral dissertation, University of Minnesota.

Harrison, L., and McKee, P. (1971). *Getting ready to read.* Boston: Houghton Mifflin.

Harste, J. C., Burke, C. L., and Woodward, V. A. (1982). Children's language and world: Initial encounters with print. In J. A. Langer and M. T. Smith-Burke (eds.), *Reader meets author/Bridging the gap,* 105-131. Newark, DE: International Reading Association.

Hartley, R. N. (1970-1971). Effects of list types and cues on the learning of word lists. *Reading Research Quarterly, 6,* 97-121.

Harzem, P., Lee, I., and Miles, T. R. (1976). The effects of pictures on learning to read. *British Journal of Educational Psychology, 46*, 318-322.

Healy, A. F., and Drewnowski, A. (1983). Investigating the boundaries of reading units: Letter detection in misspelled words. *Journal of Experimental Psychology: Human Perception and Performance, 9*, 413-426.

Heath, S. B. (1983). *Ways with words.* Cambridge: Cambridge Univeristy Press.

Henderson, L., and Chard, J. (1980). The readers' implicit knowledge of orthographic structure. In U. Frith (ed.), *Cognitive processes in spelling*, 85-116. New York: Academic Press.

Herman, P. A. (1985). The effect of repeated readings on reading rate, speech pauses, and word recognition accuracy. *Reading Research Quarterly, 20*, 553-565.

Hinsley, D. A., Hayes, J. R., and Simon, H. A. (1977). From words to equations: Meaning and representation in algebra word problems. In M. A. Just and P. A. Carpenter (eds.), *Cognitive processes in comprehension*, 89-106. Hillsdale, NJ: Erlbaum Associates.

Hintzman, D. L. (1986). "Schema abstraction" in a multiple-trace memory model. *Psychological Review, 93*, 411-428.

Hockett, C. F. (1967). Where the tongue slips, there slip I. In *To honor Roman Jakobson: Essays on the occasion of his 70th birthday*, 910-935. The Hague: Mouton Publishers. (Reprinted in Fromkin, V. (ed.). (1973). *Speech errors as linguistic evidence*. The Hague: Mouton Publishers.)

Hohn, W. E., and Ehri, L. C. (1983). Do alphabet letters help prereaders acquire phonemic segmentation skill? *Journal of Educational Psychology, 75*, 752-762.

Holdaway, D. (1979). *The foundations of literacy.* Sydney, Australia: Ashton Scholastic.

Holden, M.H., and MacGinitie, W. II. (1972). Children's conceptions of word boundaries in speech and print. *Journal of Educational Psychology, 63*, 551-557.

Holender, D. (1987). Synchronic description of present-day writing systems: Some implications for reading research. In J. K. O'Regan and A. Levy-Schoen (eds.), *Eye movements: From physiology to cognition.* Amsterdam: Elsevier North Holland.

Hoole, C. (1660/1912). *A new discovery of the old art of teaching school.* Syracuse, NY.

Hooper, J. (1977). Word frequency in lexical diffusion and the source of morphological change. In W. Christie (ed.), *Current progress in historical linguistics.* Amsterdam: Elsevier.

Huey, E. B. (1908/1968). *The psychology and pedagogy of reading.* Cambridge, MA: MIT Press.

Huggins, A. W. F., and Adams, M. J. (1980). Syntactic aspects of reading comprehension. In R. J. Spiro, B. C. Bruce, and W. F. Brewer (eds.), *Theoretical issues in reading comprehension*, 87-112. Hillsdale, NJ: Erlbaum Associates.

Hull, C. L. (1943). *The principles of behavior.* New York: Appleton-Century-Crofts.

Humphreys, G. W., and Evett, L. J. (1985). Are there independent lexical and nonlexical routes in word processing? An evaluation of the dual-route theory of reading. *The Behavioral and Brain Sciences, 8,* 689-739.

Huttenlocher, J. (1964). Children's language: Word-phrase relationship. *Science, 143,* 264-265.

Ittelson, W. H. (1962). Perception and transactional psychology. In S. Koch (ed.), *Psychology: A study of a science, vol. IV,* 660-704. New York: McGraw-Hill.

Jakimik, J., Cole, R. A., and Rudnicky, A. I. (1985). Sound and spelling in spoken word recognition. *Journal of Memory and Language, 24,* 165-178.

Jakobson, R. (1968). *Child language, aphasia and phonological universals.* The Hague: Mouton Publishers.

Jensen, J. (ed.). (1984). *Composition and comprehending.* Urbana, IL: ERIC Clearinghouse on Reading and Communication Skills and National Conference on Research in English.

Johns, J. L. (1980). First graders' concepts about print. *Reading Research Quarterly, 15,* 529-549.

Johns, J. L. (1984). Students' perceptions of reading: Insights from research and pedagogical implications. In J. Downing and R. Valtin (eds.), *Language awareness and learning to read,* 57-77. New York: Springer-Verlag.

Johnson, D. D., and Bauman, J. F. (1984). Word identification. In P. D. Pearson, R. Barr, M. L. Kamil, and P. Mosenthal (eds.), *Handbook of reading research,* 583-608. New York: Longman.

Johnson, D. J., and Myklebust, H. R. (1967). *Learning disabilities.* New York: Grune and Stratton.

Johnston, J. C. (1978). A test of the sophisticated guessing theory of word perception. *Cognitive Psychology, 10,* 123-154.

Jorm, A. F., and Share, D. L. (1983). Phonological recoding and reading acquisition. *Applied Psycholinguistics, 4,* 103-147.

Juel, C. (1980). Comparison of word identification strategies with varying context, word type, and reader skill. *Reading Research Quarterly, 15,* 358-376.

Juel, C. (1983). The development and use of mediated word identification. *Reading Research Quarterly, 18,* 306-327.

Juel, C. (1988). Learning to read and write: A longitudinal study of fifty-four children from first through fourth grade. *Journal of Educational Psychology, 80,* 437–447.

Juel, C., and Roper/Schneider, D. (1985). The influence of basal readers on first grade reading. *Reading Research Quarterly, 20,* 134-152.

Juel, C., and Solso, R. L. (1981). The role of orthographic redundancy, versatility, and spelling-sound correspondences in word identification. In M. L. Kamil (ed.), *Directions in reading: Research and instruction,* 74-82. Washington, DC: National Reading Conference.

Juel, C., Griffith, P. L., and Gough, P. B. (1986). Acquisition of literacy: A longitudinal study of children in first and second grade. *Journal of Educational Psychology, 78*, 243-255.

Juola, J. F., Schadler, M., Chabot, R. J., and McCaughey, M. W. (1978). The development of visual information processing skills related to reading. *Journal of Experimental Child Psychology, 25*, 459-476.

Just, M. A., and Carpenter, P. A. (1987). *The psychology of reading and language comprehension.* Boston: Allyn and Bacon.

Kampwirth, T. J., and Bates, M. (1980). Modality preference and teaching method: A review of the research. *Academic Therapy, 15*, 597-605.

Kant, I. (1781/1929). *Critique of pure reason,* Translated by N. K. Smith. London: Macmillan.

Karpova, S. N. (1955). Osoznanie slovesnogo sostave rechi rebenkom doshkol'nogo vozrasta. *Voprosy Psikhologiya, 4*, 43-55. Abstracted in translation in Slobin, D. E. (1966), Abstracts of Soviet studies of child language. In F. Smith and G. A. Miller (eds.), *The genesis of language,* 363-386. Cambidge, MA: MIT Press.

Kaye, D. B., and Sternberg, R. J. (1982). *The development of lexical decomposition ability.* Unpublished manuscript. New Haven, CT: Yale University.

Kelly, M. H. (1988). Phonological biases in grammatical category shifts. *Journal of Memory and Language, 27*, 343-358.

Kintsch, W., and Keenan, J. (1973). Reading rate and retention as a function of the number of propositions in the base structure of sentences. *Cognitive Psychology, 5*, 257-274.

Kirk, C. (1979). Patterns of word segmentation in preschool children. *Child Study Journal, 9*, 37-49. Cited in Blachman, 1984, *op. cit.*

Klare, G. R. (1974-1975). Assessing readability. *Reading Research Quarterly, 10*, 62-102.

Klare, G. R. (1984). Readability. In P. D. Pearson, R. Barr, M. L. Kamil, and P. Mosenthal (eds.), *Handbook of reading research,* 681-744. New York: Longman.

Klatt, D. H. (1980). Speech perception: A model of acoustic-phonetic analysis and lexical access. In R. Cole (ed.), *Perception and production of fluent speech,* 243-288. Hillsdale, NJ: Erlbaum Associates.

Kleiman, G. M. (1975). Speech recoding in reading. *Journal of Verbal Learning and Verbal Behavior, 14*, 323-339.

Koffka, K. (1931). *The growth of the mind.* New York: Harcourt.

Koffka, K. (1935). *Principles of Gestalt psychology.* New York: Harcourt, Brace, and World.

Köhler, W. (1925). *The mentality of apes.* Translated by Ella Winter. New York: Harcourt.

Kolers, P. (1972). Experiments in reading. *Scientific American, 227*, 84-

Kolers, P. (1976). Buswell's discoveries. In R. A. Monty and J. W. Senders (eds.), *Eye movements and psychological processes,* 373-395. Hillsdale, NJ: Erlbaum Associates.

Kucer, S. B. (1987). The cognitive base of reading and writing. In J. R. Squire (ed.), *The dynamics of language learning: Research in Reading and English*, 27-51. Urbana, IL: ERIC Clearinghouse on Reading and Communication Skills and National Conference on Research in English.

Kucera, H., and Francis, W. N. (1967). *Computational analysis of present-day American English.* Providence, RI: Brown University Press.

Lapp, D., and Flood, J. (1983). *Teaching reading to every child.* New York: Macmillan Publishing Company.

Larkin, J. H., McDermott, J., Simon, D. P., and Simon, H. A. (1980). Models of competence in solving physics problems. *Cognitive Science, 4,* 317-345.

Larrick, N. (1987). Illiteracy starts too soon. *Phi Delta Kappan, 69,* 184-189.

Laubach, F. C., Kirk, E. M., and Laubach, R. S. (1969). *The new streamlined English series.* Syracuse, NY: New Readers Press.

Lefton, L. A., and Spragins, A. B. (1974). Orthographic structure and reading experience affect the transfer from iconic to short-term memory. *Journal of Experimental Psychology, 103,* 775-781.

Lefton, L. A., and Spragins, A. B., and Byrnes, J. (1973). English orthography: Relation to reading experience. *Bulletin of the Psychonomic Society, 1973, 2,* 281-282.

Leinhardt, G., Zigmond, N., and Cooley, W. W. (1981). Reading instruction and its effects. *American Educational Research Journal, 18,* 343-361.

Lenneberg, E. H. (1967). *Biological foundations of language.* New York: Wiley.

Lerner, J. W. (1988). Theories for intervention in reading. In C. N. Hedley and J. S. Hicks (eds.), *Reading and the special learner*, 7-20. Norwood, NJ: Ablex Publishing Corporation.

Levy, B. A. (1977). Reading: Speech and meaning processes. *Journal of Verbal Learning and Verbal Behavior, 16,* 623-628.

Levy, B. A. (1978). Speech processes during reading. In A. M. Lesgold, S. W. Pellegrino, S. W. Fokkema, and R. Glaser (eds.), *Cognitive psychology and instruction.* New York: Plenum Press.

Levy, B. A. (1981). Interactive processing during reading. In A. M. Lesgold and C. A. Perfetti (eds.), *Interactive processes in reading*, 1-36. Hillsdale, NJ: Erlbaum Associates.

Lewkowicz, N. A. (1980). Phonemic awareness training: What to teach and how to teach it. *Journal of Educational Psychology, 72,* 686-700.

Liberman, A. M. (1970). The grammars of speech and language. *Cognitive Psychology, 1,* 301-323.

Liberman, A. M., Cooper, F., Shankweiler, D., and Studdert-Kennedy, M. (1967). Perception of the speech code. *Psychological Review, 74,* 431-461.

Liberman, I. Y. (1973). Segmentation of the spoken word and reading acquisition. *Bulletin of the Orton Society, 23,* 65-77.

Liberman, I. Y. (1987). Language and literacy: The obligation of the schools of education. In W. Ellis (ed.), *Intimacy with language: A forgotten basic in teacher education.* Baltimore: Orton Dyslexia Society.

Liberman, I. Y., and Shankweiler, D. (1979). Speech, the alphabet, and teaching to read. In L. B. Resnick and P. A. Weaver (eds.), *Theory and practice of early reading, vol. 2,* 109-132. Hillsdale, NJ: Erlbaum Associates.

Liberman, I. Y., Rubin, H., Duques, S., and Carlisle, J. (1985). Linguistic abilities and spelling proficiency in kindergartners and adult poor spellers. In D. B. Gray and J. F. Kavanagh (eds.), *Biobehavioral measures of dyslexia,* 163-176. Parkton, MD: New York Press.

Liberman, I. Y., Shankweiler, D., Blachman, B., Camp, L., and Werfelman, M. (1980). Steps toward literacy: A linguistic approach. In P. Levinson and C. Sloan (eds.), *Auditory processing and language: Clinical and research perspectives.* New York: Grune and Stratton.

Liberman, I. Y., Shankweiler, D., Fischer, F. W., and Carter, B. (1974). Reading and the awareness of linguistic segments. *Journal of Experimental Child Psychology, 18,* 201-212.

Liberman, I. Y., Shankweiler, D., Liberman, A. M., Fowler, C., and Fischer, F. W. (1977). Phonetic segmentation and recoding in the beginning reader. In A. S. Reber and D. L. Scarborough (eds.), *Toward a psychology of reading,* 207-225. Hillsdale, NJ: Erlbaum Associates.

Liberman, I. Y., Shankweiler, D., Orlando, C., Harris, K. S., and Berti, F. B. (1971). Letter confusions and reversals of sequence in the beginning reader: Implications for Orton's theory of developmental dyslexia. *Cortex, 7,* 127-142.

Lindamood, C. H., and Lindamood, P. C. (1971). *Lindamood auditory conceptualization test.* Boston: Teaching Resources Corporation.

Lindamood, C. H., and Lindamood, P. C. (1975). *Auditory discrimination in depth.* Boston: Teaching Resources Corporation.

Lomax, R. G., and McGee, L. M. (1987). Young children's concepts about print and reading: Toward a model of word reading acquisition. *Reading Research Quarterly, 22,* 237-256.

Lord, F. M. (1969). Statistical adjustments when comparing preexisting groups. *Psychological Bulletin, 72,* 336-337.

Lundberg, I., Frost, J., and Petersen, O-P. (1988). Effects of an extensive program for stimulating phonological awareness in preschool children. *Reading Research Quarterly, 23,* 264-284.

Lundberg, I., Olofsson, A., and Wall, S. (1980). Reading and spelling skills in the first school years predicted from phonemic awareness skills in kindergarten. *Scandinavian Journal of Psychology, 21,* 159-173.

Lunzer, R., Dolan, T., and Wilkinson, J. (1976). The effectiveness of measures of operativity, language and short-term memory in the prediction of reading and mathematical understanding. *British Journal of Educational Psychology, 46,* 295-305.

MacGinitie, W. (1976). Difficulty with logical operations. *Reading Teacher, 29,* 371-375.

MacKay, D. G. (1972). The structure of words and syllables: Evidence from errors in speech. *Cognitive Psychology, 3,* 210-227.

Mackworth, N. H., and Bruner, J. S. (1970). How adults and children search and recognize pictures. *Human Development, 13,* 149-177.

Mackworth, N. H., and Morandi, A. J. (1967). The gaze selects informative details within pictures. *Perception and Psychophysics, 2,* 547-552.

Maclean, M., Bryant, P., and Bradley, L. (1987). Rhymes, nursery rhymes, and reading in early childhood. *Merrill-Palmer Quarterly, 33,* 255-281.

Manelis, L., and Tharp, D. (1977). The processing of affixed words. *Memory and Cognition, 5,* 690-695.

Mann, V. A. (1984). Longitudinal prediction and prevention of early reading difficulty. *Annals of Dyslexia, 34,* 115-136.

Mann, V. A. (1986). Phonological awareness: The role of reading experience. *Cognition, 24,* 65-92.

Mann, V. A., and Liberman, I. Y. (1984). Phonological awareness and verbal short-term memory. *Journal of Learning Disabilities, 17,* 592-598.

Mann, V. A., Tobin, P., and Wilson, R. (1987). Measuring phonological awareness through the invented spellings of kindergartners. *Merrill-Palmer Quarterly, 33,* 365-391.

Marcel, A. (1980). Phonological awareness and phonological representation: Investigation of a specific spelling problem. In U. Frith (ed.), *Cognitive processes in spelling,* 373-403. New York: Academic Press.

Marcus, S. M. (1981). ERIS-context sensitive coding in speech perception. *Journal of Phonetics, 9,* 197-220.

Marsh, G., and Desberg, P. (1978). Mnemonics for phonics. *Contemporary Educational Psychology, 3,* 57-61.

Marsh, G., Friedman, M., Welch, V., and Desberg, P. (1980). The development of strategies in spelling. In U. Frith (ed.), *Cognitive processes in spelling,* 339-353. New York: Academic Press.

Marslen-Wilson, W. D. (1987). Functional parallelism in spoken word recognition. *Cognition, 25,* 71-102.

Marslen-Wilson, W. D., and Welsh, A. (1978). Processing interactions and lexical access during word recognition in continuous speech. *Cognitive Psychology, 10,* 29-63.

Martin, S. E. (1972). Nonalphabetic writing systems: Some observations. In J. F. Kavanagh and I. G. Mattingly (eds.), *Language by ear and by eye: The relationships between speech and reading,* 81-102. Cambridge, MA: MIT Press.

Mason, J. M. (1980). When do children begin to read: An exploration of our year old children's letter and word reading competencies. *Reading Research Quarterly, 15,* 203-227.

Mason, M. (1975). Reading ability and letter search time: Effects of orthographic structures defined by single letter positional frequency. *Journal of Experimental Psychology: General, 104,* 146-166.

Masonheimer, P. E. (1982). *Alphabetic identification by Spanish speaking three to five year olds.* Unpublished Manuscript. Santa Barbara: University of California.

Masonheimer, P. E., Drum, P. A., and Ehri, L. C. (1984). Does environmental print identification lead children into word reading? *Journal of Reading Behavior, 16,* 257-271.

Massaro, D. W., and Taylor, G. A. (1980). Reading ability and the utilization of orthographic structure in reading. *Journal of Educational Psychology, 72,* 730-742.

Massaro, D. W., Venezky, R. I., and Taylor, G. A. (1979). Orthographic regularity, positional frequency and visual processing of letter strings. *Journal of Experimental Psychology: General, 108,* 107-124.

Mathews, M. M. (1966). *Teaching to read: Historically considered.* Chicago: University of Chicago Press.

Mayzner, M. S., and Tresselt, M. E. (1965). Tables of single-letter and digram frequency counts for various word-length and letter position combinations. *Psychonomic Monograph Supplements, 1,* 13-32.

McCaughey, M. W., Juola, J. F., Schadler, , M., and Ward, N. J. (1980). Whole-word units are used before orthographic knowledge in perceptual development. *Journal of Experimental Child Psychology, 30,* 411-421.

McClelland, J. L. (1976). Preliminary letter identification in perception of words and nonwords. *Journal of Experimental Psychology: Human Perception and Performance, 2,* 80-91.

McClelland, J. L., and Elman, J. L. (1986). The TRACE model of speech perception. *Cognitive Psychology, 18,* 1-86.

McClelland, J. L., and Johnston, J. D. (1977). The role of familiar units in perception of words and nonwords. *Perception and Psychophysics, 22,* 249-261.

McClelland, J. L., and O'Regan, J. K. (1981). Expectations increase the benefit derived from parafoveal visual information in reading words aloud. *Journal of Experimental Psychology: Human Perception and Performance, 7,* 634-644.

McClelland, J. L., and Rumelhart, D. E. (1981). An interactive activation model of context effects in letter perception: Part 1. An account of basic findings. *Psychological Review, 88,* 373-407.

McClelland, J. L., and Rumelhart, D. E. (1986). A distributed model of human learning and memory. In J. L. McClelland and D. E. Rumelhart (eds.), *Parallel distributed processing, vol. 2: Psychological and biological models,* 170-215. Cambridge, MA: MIT Press.

McClelland, J. L., and Rumelhart, D. E. (eds.). (1986). *Parallel distributed processing, vol. 2: Psychological and biological models.* Cambridge, MA: MIT Press.

McClelland, J. L., Rumelhart, D. E., and Hinton, G. E. (1986). The appeal of parallel distributed processing. In D. E. Rumelhart and J. L. McClelland (eds.), *Parallel distributed processing, vol. 1: Foundations,* 3-44. Cambridge, MA: MIT Press.

McConkie, G. W. (1979). On the role and control of eye movements in reading. In P. A. Kolers, M. E. Wrolstad, and H. Bouma (eds.), *Processing visible language, vol. 1.* New York: Plenum Press.

McConkie, G. W., and Zola, D. (1981). Language constraints and the functional stimulus in reading. In A. M. Lesgold and C. A. Perfetti (eds.), *Interactive processes in reading,* 155-175. Hillsdale, NJ: Erlbaum Associates.

McConkie, G. W., Kerr, P.W., Reddix, M. D., and Zola, D. (1987). *Eye movement control during reading: I. The location of initial eye fixations on words.* Technical Report No. 406. Champaign, IL: Center for the Study of Reading, University of Illinois.

McConkie, G. W., Zola, D., Blanchard, H. E., and Wolverton, G. S. (1982). *Perceiving words during reading: Lack of facilitation from prior peripheral exposure.* Technical Report No. 243. Champaign, IL: Center for the Study of Reading, University of Illinois.

McCormick, C. E., and Mason, J. M. (1986). Intervention procedures for increasing preschool children's interest in and knowledge about reading. In W. H. Teale and E. Sulzby (eds.), *Emergent literacy: Writing and reading,* 90-115. Norwood, NJ: Ablex Publishing Corporation.

McCormick, S. (1977). Should you read aloud to your children? *Language Arts, 54,* 139-143.

McGill-Franzen, A. (1988). *Curriculum coherence: A qualitative dimension of at-risk second graders experiences with reading instruction in special education, Chapter 1, and regular classrooms.* Unpublished manuscript. Albany, NY: State University of New York at Albany.

McKeown, M. G., Beck, I. L. Omanson, R. C., and Perfetti, C. A. (1983). The effects of long-term vocabulary instruction on reading comprehension: A replication. *Journal of Reading Behavior, 15,* 3-18.

McKeown, M. G., Beck, I. L. Omanson, R. C., and Pople, M. T. (1985). Some effects of the nature and frequency of vocabulary instruction on the knowledge and use of words. *Reading Research Quarterly, 20,* 522-535.

McMahon, W. E. (1968). *A, B, C, dictation skills program.* Cambridge, MA: Educators Publishing Service.

McNeil, J. D., and Stone, J. (1965). Note on teaching children to hear separate sounds in spoken words, *Journal of Educational Psychology, 56,* 13-15.

Meltzer, N. S., and Herse, R. (1969). The boundaries of written words as seen by first graders. *Journal of Reading Behavior, 1,* 3-14.

Meuhl, S., and DiNello, M. C. (1976). Early first-grade skills related to subsequent reading performance: A·seven-year follow-up study. *Journal of Reading Behavior, 8,* 67-81.

Mewhort, D. J. K. (1974). Accuracy and order of report in tachistoscopic identification. *Canadian Journal of Psychology, 28,* 383-398.

Mewhort, D. J. K., and Beal, A. L. (1977). Mechanisms of word identification. *Journal of Experimental Psychology: Human Perception and Performance, 3,* 629-640.

Mewhort, D. J. K., and Campbell, A. J. (1981). Toward a model of skilled reading: An analysis of performance in tachistoscoptic tasks. G. E. MacKinnon and T. G. Waller (eds.), *Reading research: Advances in theory and practice, vol. 3,* 39-118. New York: Academic Press.

Meyer, L. A. (1983). Increased student achievement in reading: One district's strategies. *Research in Rural Education, 1,* 47-51.

Meyer, L. A., Greer, E. A., and Crummey, L. (1987). An analysis of decoding, comprehension, and story text comprehensibility in four first-grade reading programs. *Journal of Reading Behavior, 19,* 69-98.

Mickish, B. (1974). Children's perceptions of written word boundaries. *Journal of Reading Behavior, 6,* 19-22.

Mikulecky, L. (1986). Effective literacy training programs for adults in business and municipal employment. In J. Orasanu (ed.), *Reading comprehension: From research to practice,* 319-334. Hillsdale, NJ: Erlbaum Associates.

Miller, G. A. (1988). The challenge of universal literacy. *Science, 241,* 1293-1299.

Miller, G. A., and Friedman, E. A. (1957). The reconstruction of mutilated English texts. *Information and Control, 1,* 38-55.

Miller, G. A., and Gildea, P. M. (1987). How children learn words. *Scientific American, 257* (3), 94-99.

Miller, G. A., Newman, E. B., and Friedman, E. A. (1958). Length-frequency statistics for written English. *Information and Control, 1,* 370-389.

Miller, J. L. (1981). Effects of speaking rate on segmental distinctions. In P. D. Eimas and J. L. Miller (eds.), *Perspectives on the study of speech,* 39-74. Hillsdale, NJ: Erlbaum Associates.

Miller, N. E., and Dollard, J. (1941). *Social learning and imitation.* New Haven: Yale University Press.

Miller, P., and Limber, J. (1985). *The acquisition of consonant clusters: A paradigm problem.* Paper presented at the Boston University Child Language Conference.

Monroe, M. (1932). *Children who cannot read.* Chicago: University of Chicago Press.

Montessori, M. (1966). *The secret of childhood.* New York: Ballantine Books.

Morais, J., Bertelson, P., Cary, L., and Alegria, J. (1986). Literacy training and speech segmentation. *Cognition, 24,* 45-64.

Morais, J., Cary, L., Alegria, J., and Bertelson, P. (1979). Does awareness of speech as a sequence of phones arise spontaneously? *Cognition, 7,* 323-331.

Morais, J., Cluytens, M., Alegria, J., and Content, A. (1984). Segmentation abilities of dyslexics and normal readers. *Perceptual and Motor Skills, 58,* 221-222.

Morphett, M. V., and Washburne, C. (1931). When should children begin to read? *Elementary School Journal, 31,* 495-503.

Morris, D. (1981). Concept of word: A developmental phenomenon in the beginning reading and writing processes. *Language Arts, 58,* 659-668.

Morris, D., and Perney, J. (1984). Developmental spelling as a predictor of first-grade reading achievement. *Elementary School Journal, 84,* 440-457.

Murphy, H. A. (1957). The spontaneous speaking vocabulary of children in primary grades. *Journal of Education, 140,* 1-105.

Nagy, W. E., and Anderson, R. C. (1984). How many words are there in printed school English? *Reading Research Quarterly, 19,* 304-330.

Nagy, W. E., Anderson, R. C., and Herman, P. A. (1987). Learning word meanings from context during normal reading. *American Educational Research Journal, 24,* 237-270.

Nagy, W. E., Herman, P. A., and Anderson, R. C. (1985). Learning words from context. *Reading Research Quarterly, 20,* 233-253.

Nagy. W. E., and Herman, P. A. (1987). Breadth and depth of vocabulary knowledge: Implications for acquisition and instruction. In M. McKeown and M. Curtis (eds.), *The nature of vocabulary acquisition,* 19-35. Hillsdale, NJ: Erlbaum Associates.

Nash-Webber, B. (1975). The role of semantics in automatic speech understanding. In D. G. Bobrow and A. Collins (eds.), *Representation and understanding,* 351-382. New York: Academic Press.

National Assessment of Educational Progress. (1981a). "Reading, thinking and writing." In *The 1979-80 National assessment of reading and literature.* Denver: National Assessment of Educational Progress.

National Assessment of Educational Progress (1981b). *Three national assessments of reading: Changes in performance, 1970-1980.* Report 11-R-01. Denver: Education Commission of the States.

National Assessment of Educational Progress (1985). *The reading report card, progress toward excellence in our schools: Trends in reading over four national assessments, 1971-1984.* Report No. 15-R-01. Princeton, NJ: Educational Testing Service.

National Commission on Excellence in Education (1983). *A nation at risk: The imperative for educational reform.* Washington, DC: U. S. Department of Education.

Neely, J. H. (1977). Semantic priming and retrieval from lexical memory. Roles of inhibitionless spreading activation and limited-capacity attention. *Journal of Experimental Psychology: General, 106,* 226-254.

Neisser, U. (1967). *Cognitive psychology.* New York: Appleton Century Crofts.

Nurss, J. R. (1979). Assessment of readiness. In T. G. Waller and G. E. MacKinnon (eds.), *Reading research: Advances in theory and practice, vol. 1.* New York: Academic Press.

Odom, R. D., McIntyre, C. W., and Neale, G. S. (1971). The influence of cognitive style on perceptual learning. *Child Development, 42,* 883-891.

Ohnmacht, D. C. (1969). *The effects of letter knowledge on achievement in reading in first grade.* Paper presented at the American Educational Research Association, Los Angeles.

Orton, S. T. (1937). *Reading, writing, and speech problems in children.* New York: W. W. Norton.

Orton Dyslexia Society (1986). Some facts about illiteracy in America. *Perspectives on dyslexia, 13*(4), 1-13.

Otterman, L. M. (1955). The value of teaching prefixes and word-roots. *Journal of Educational Research, 48,* 611-616.

Otto, W., Rudolph, M., Smith, R., and Wilson, R. (1975). *The Merrill linguistic reading program,* 2d ed. Columbus, OH: Charles E. Merrill.

Patterson, K. E., and Coltheart, V. (1987). Phonological processes in reading: A tutorial review. In M. Coltheart (ed.), *Attention and performance XII: The psychology of reading.* London: Erlbaum Associates.

Patterson, K. E., Seidenberg, M. S., and McClelland, J. L. (in press). Word recognition and dyslexia: A connectionist approach. In P. Morris (ed.), *Connectionism: The Oxford symposium.* Cambridge: Cambridge University Press.

Patterson, K., Marshall, J., and Coltheart, M. (eds.). (1985). *Surface dyslexia.* London: Erlbaum Associates.

Perfetti, C. A. (1985). *Reading ability.* New York: Oxford University Press.

Perfetti, C. A., and Lesgold, A. M. (1977). Discourse comprehension and sources of individual differences. In M. A. Just and P. A. Carpenter (eds.), *Cognitive processes in comprehension,* 141-183. Hillsdale, NJ: Erlbaum Associates.

Perfetti, C. A., and McCutcheon, D. (1982). Speech processes in reading. In N. Lass (ed.), *Speech and language: Advances in basic research and practice, vol. 7,* 237-269. New York: Academic Press.

Perfetti, C. A., and Roth, S. (1977). Some of the interactive processes in reading and their role in reading skill. In A. M. Lesgold and C. A. Perfetti (eds.), *Interactive processes in reading,* 269-297. Hillsdale, NJ: Erlbaum Associates.

Perfetti, C. A., Beck, I., Bell, L., and Hughes, C. (1987). Phonemic knowledge and learning to read are reciprocal: A longitudinal study of first grade children. *Merrill-Palmer Quarterly, 33,* 283-319.

Perfetti, C. A., Bell, L. C., and Delaney, S. M. (1988). Automatic (prelexical) phonetic activation in silent word reading: Evidence from backward masking. *Journal of Memory and Language, 27,* 1-22.

Perry, N. J. (1988). Saving the schools: How business can help. *Fortune,* November 7, 1988, 42-56.

Petrick, S., and Potter, M. C. (1979). *RSVP sentences and word lists: Representation of meaning and sound.* Paper presented at the Annual Meeting of the Psychonomic Society, Pheonix.

Pflaum, S. W., Walberg, H. J., Karegianes, M. L., and Rasher, S. P. (1980). Reading instruction: A quantitative analysis. *Educational Researcher, 9,* 12-18.

Piaget, J. (1972). Some aspects of operations. In M. Piers (ed.), *Play and development.* New York.

Pick, A. D. (1965). Improvement of visual and tactual form discrimination. *Journal of Experimental Psychology, 69,* 331-339.

Pillsbury, W. B. (1897). A study in apperception. *American Journal of Psychology, 8,* 315-393.

Pollack, I., and Pickett, J. M. (1964). Intelligibility of excerpts from fluent speech: Auditory versus structural context. *Journal of Verbal Learning and Verbal Behavior, 3,* 79-84.

Popp, H. M. (1975). Current practices in the teaching of beginning reading. In J. B. Carroll and J. S. Chall (eds.), *Toward a literate society: The report of the committee in reading of the National Academy of Education.* New York: McGraw-Hill.

Posnansky, C. J., and Rayner, K. (1977). Visual-feature and response components in a picture-word interference task with beginning and skilled readers. *Journal of Experimental Child Psychology, 24,* 440-460.

Posner, M. E., and Snyder, C. R. R. (1975). Attention and cognitive control. In R. Solso (ed.), *Information processing and cognition: The Loyola symposium,* 55-85. Hillsdale, NJ: Erlbaum Associates.

Pryzwansky, W. B. (1972). Effects of perceptual-motor training and manuscript writing on reading readiness skills in kindergarten. *Journal of Educational Psychology, 63,* 110-115.

Rayner, K. (1975). The perceptual span and peripheral cues in reading. *Cognitive Psychology, 7,* 65-81.

Rayner, K., and Pollatsek, A. (1987). Eye movements in reading: A tutorial review. In M. Coltheart (ed.), *Attention and performance XII: The psychology of reading,* 327-362. London: Erlbaum Associates.

Read, C. (1971). Preschool children's knowledge of English phonology. *Harvard Educational Review, 41,* 1-34.

Read, C. (1975). *Children's categorization of speech sounds in English.* Research Report No. 17. Urbana, IL: National Council of Teachers of English.

Read, C., Yun-Fei, Z., Hong-Yin, N., and Bao-Qing, D. (1986). The ability to manipulate speech sounds depends on knowing alphabetic writing. *Cognition, 24*(1,2), 31-44.

Reid, J. F. (1966). Learning to think about reading. *Educational Research, 9,* 56-62.

Reitsma, P. (1983). Printed word learning in beginning readers. *Journal of Experimental Child Psychology, 36,* 321-339.

Repp, B. H., and Liberman, A. M. (1984). *Phonetic categories are flexible.* Haskins Laboratories Status Report on Speech Research, SR-77/78, 31-53. New Haven, CT: Haskins Laboratories.

Resnick, D. P., and Resnick, L. B. (1977). The nature of literacy: An historical exploration. *Harvard Educational Review, 47,* 370-385.

Richek, M. (1977-1978). Readiness skills that predict initial word learning using two different methods of instruction. *Reading Research Quarterly, 13,* 200-222.

Robinson, H. M. (1972a). Perceptual training: Does it result in reading improvement? In R. C. Aukerman (ed.), *Some persistent questions on beginning reading*. Newark, DE: International Reading Association.

Robinson, H. M. (1972b). Visual and auditory modalities related to methods for beginning reading. *Reading Research Quarterly, 8,* 7-39.

Robinson, H. M., Monroe, M., and Artley, A. S. (1956). *The new basic readers curriculum foundation series*. Chicago: Scott, Foresman.

Rodenborn, L. V., and Washburn, E. (1974). Some implications of new basal readers. *Elementary English, 51,* 885-888.

Rosenshine, B., and Stevens, R. (1984). Classroom instruction in reading. In P. D. Pearson, R. Barr, M. L Kamil, and P. Mosenthal (eds.), *Handbook of reading research,* 745-799. New York: Longman.

Roser, N., and Juel, C. (1982). Effects of vocabulary instruction on reading comprehension. In J. Niles and L. Harris (eds.), *New inquiries in reading research and instruction,* 110-118. Rochester, NY: National Reading Conference.

Rosinski, R. R., and Wheeler, K. E. (1972). Children's use of orthographic structure in word discrimination. *Psychonomic Science, 26,* 97-98.

Rosner, J. (1974). Auditory analysis training with prereaders. *Reading Teacher, 27,* 379-384.

Rosner, J., and Simon, D. P. (1971). The auditory analysis test: An initial report. *Journal of Learning Disabilities, 4,* 384-392.

Roswell, F., and Natchez, G. (1971). *Reading disability*. New York: Basic Books.

Roth, S. F., and Beck, I. L. (1987). Theoretical and instructional implications of the assessment of two microcomputer word recognition programs. *Reading Research Quarterly, 22,* 197-218.

Routh, D. K., and Fox, B. (1984). "MM . . . is a little bit of May": Phonemes, reading, and spelling. In K. D. Gadow and I. Bialer (eds.), *Advances in learning and behavioral disabilities, vol. 3.* Greenwich, CT: JAI Press.

Rozin, P., and Gleitman, L. R. (1977). The structure and acquisition of reading II: The reading process and the acquisition of the alphabetic principle. In A. S. Reber and D. L. Scarborough (eds.), *Toward a psychology of reading,* 55-141. Hillsdale, NJ: Erlbaum Associates.

Rozin, P., Bressman, B., and Taft, M. (1974). Do children understand the basic relationship between speech and writing? The mow-motorcycle test. *Journal of Reading Behavior, 6,* 327-334.

Rozin, P., Poritsky, S., and Sotsky, R. (1971). American children with reading problems can easily learn to read English represented by Chinese characters. *Science, 171,* 1264-1267.

Rudnicky, A. I. (1980). *Units of perception in phoneme monitoring*. Paper presented at the Psychonomic Society Meeting, St. Louis, MO.

Rumelhart, D. E., and McClelland, J. L. (1986). On learning the past tenses of English verbs. In J. L. McClelland and D. E. Rumelhart (eds.), *Parallel distributed processing, vol. 2: Psychological and biological models,* 216-271. Cambridge, MA: MIT Press.

Rumelhart, D. E., and McClelland, J. L. (eds.) (1986). *Parallel distributed processing, vol. 1: Foundations.* Cambridge, MA: The MIT Press.

Rumelhart, D. E., Smolensky, P., McClelland, J. L., and Hinton, G. E. (1986). Schemata and sequential through processes in PDP Models. In J. L. McClelland and D. E. Rumelhart (eds.), *Parallel distributed processing, vol. 2: Psychological and biological models,* 7-57. Cambridge, MA: MIT Press.

Russell, D. H., et al. (1961). *The Ginn basic readers.* Boston: Ginn and Company.

Samuels, S. J. (1967). Attentional processes in reading: The effect of pictures in the acquisition of reading responses. *Journal of Educational Psychology, 58,* 337-342.

Samuels, S. J. (1970a). *An experimental program for teaching letter names of the alphabet.* Project No. 9-F-009. Washington, DC: U. S. Office of Education.

Samuels, S. J. (1970b). Effects of pictures on learning to read, comprehension and attitudes. *Review of Educational Research, 40,* 397-407.

Samuels, S. J. (1985). Automaticity and repeated reading. In J. Osborn, P. T. Wilson, and R. C. Anderson (eds.), *Reading education: Foundations for a literate America,* 215-230. Lexington, MA: Lexington Books.

Samuels, S. J., LaBerge, D., and Bremer, C. D. (1978). Units of word recognition: Evidence for developmental changes. *Journal of Verbal Learning and Verbal Behavior, 17,* 715-720.

Samuels, S.J., Begy, G., and Chen, C. C. (1975-1976). Comparison of word recognition speed and strategies of less skilled and more highly skilled readers. *Reading Research Quarterly, 11,* 72-86.

Sanford, A. J., and Garrod, S. C. (1981). *Understanding written language.* New York: Wiley.

Santa, C. M. (1976-1977). Spelling patterns and the development of flexible word recognition strategies. *Reading Research Quarterly, 7,* 125-144.

Savin, H. B., and Bever, T. G. (1970). The nonperceptual reality of the phoneme. *Journal of Verbal Learning and Verbal Behavior, 9,* 295-302.

Schatz, E. K., and Baldwin, R. S. (1986). Context clues are unreliable predictors of word meanings. *Reading Research Quarterly, 21,* 439-453.

Schreiber, R. (1980). On the acquisition of reading fluency. *Journal of Reading Behavior, 12,* 177-186.

Scott, Foresman and Company (1974). *The new open highways,* 2d ed. Glenview, IL: Scott, Foresman.

Searfoss, L. W., and Readence, J. E. (1985). *Helping children learn to read.* Englewood Cliffs, NJ: Prentice Hall.

Seidenberg, M. S. (1985). The time course of information activation and utilization in visual word recognition. In D. Besner, T. G. Waller, and G. E. MacKinnon, *Reading research: Advances in theory and practice, vol. 5,* 199-252. Orlando, FL: Academic Press.

Seidenberg, M. S. (1987). Sublexical structures in visual word recognition: Access units or orthographic redundancy. M. Coltheart (ed.), *Attention and performance XII: The psychology of reading*, 245-263. Hillsdale, NJ: Erlbaum Associates.

Seidenberg, M. S., and McClelland, J. L. (1989, in press). A distributed, developmental model of word recognition and naming. *Psychological Review*.

Seidenberg, M. S., and Tannenhaus, M. K. (1979). Orthographic effects on rhyme monitoring. *Journal of Experimental Psychology: Human Learning and Memory, 5*, 546-554.

Seidenberg, M. S., Bruck, M., Fornarolo, G., and Backman, J. (1986). Word recognition skills of poor and disabled readers: Do they necessarily differ? *Applied Psycholinguistics, 6*, 161-180.

Seidenberg, M. S., Tanenhaus, M. K., Leiman, J. M., and Bienkowski, M. (1982). Automatic access of the meanings of ambiguous words in context: Some limitations of knowledge-based processing. *Cognitive Psychology, 14*, 489-537.

Selfridge, O. G. (1955). Pattern recognition and modern computers. *Proceedings of the Western Joint Computer Conference.* Los Angeles.

Selkirk, E. O. (1982). The syllable. In H. Van der Hulst and N. Smith (eds.), *The structure of phonological representations (Part II).* Dordrecht, Holland: Floris.

Shankweiler, D., and Liberman, I. Y. (1972). Misreading: A search for causes. In J. F. Kavanaugh and I. G. Mattingly (eds.), *Language by eye and by ear*, 293-317. Cambridge, MA: MIT Press.

Shannon, P. (1987). Commercial reading materials, a technological ideology, and the deskilling of teachers. *Elementary School Journal, 87*, 307-329.

Share, D. L., Jorm, A. F. Maclean, R., and Matthews, R. (1984). Sources of individual differences in reading acquisition. *Journal of Educational Psychology, 76*, 1309-1324.

Simon, D. P., and Simon, H. A. (1973). Alternative uses of phonemic information in spelling. *Review of Educational Research, 43*, 115-137.

Simpson, G. B. (1981). Meaning dominance and semantic context in the processing of lexical ambiguity. *Journal of Verbal Learning and Verbal Behavior, 20*. 120-136.

Singer, H. (1974). IQ is and is not related to reading. In S. Wanat (eds.), *Intelligence and reading.* Newark, DE: International Reading Association.

Singer, H. (1981). Teaching the acquisition phase of reading development: An historical perspective. In O. J. L. Tzeng and H. Singer (eds.), *Perception of print: Reading research in experimental psychology*, 9-28. Hillsdale, NJ: Erlbaum Associates.

Singer, H., Samuels, S. J., and Spiroff, J. (1973-1974). The effect of pictures and contextual conditions on learning responses to printed words. *Reading Research Quarterly, 9*, 555-567.

Slavin, R. E. (1984). Meta-analysis in education: How has it been used? *Educational Researcher, 13*(10), 6-15.

Sloboda, J. A. (1980). Visual imagery and individual differences in spelling. In U. Frith (ed.), *Cognitive processes in spelling*, 231-250. New York: Academic Press.

Smith, F. (1971). *Understanding reading*. New York: Holt, Rinehart, and Winston.

Smith, F. (1973). *Psycholinguistics and reading*. New York: Holt, Rinehart, and Winston.

Smith, F., and Goodman, K. S. (1971). On the psycholinguistic method of teaching reading. *Elementary School Journal, 71*, 177-181.

Smith, N. B. (1974). *American reading instruction*. Newark, DE: International Reading Association.

Smith, P. T. (1980). Linguistic information in spelling. In U. Frith (ed.), *Cognitive processes in spelling*, 33-49. New York: Academic Press.

Smythe, P. C., Stennett, R. G., Hardy, M., and Wilson, H. R. (1970-1971). Developmental patterns in elemental skills: Knowledge of upper-case and lower-case letter names. *Journal of Reading Behavior, 3*(3), 24-33.

Snow, C. E. (1983). Literacy and language: Relationships during the preschool years. *Harvard Educational Review, 53*, 165-189.

Snow, C. E., and Ninio, A. (1986). The contracts of literacy: What children learn from learning to read books. In W. H. Teale and E. Sulzby (eds.), *Emergent literacy: Writing and reading*, 116-138. Norwood, NJ: Ablex Publishing Corporation.

Sorenson, N. A. (1983). *A study of the reliability of phonic generalizations in five primary-level basal reading programs*. Doctoral dissertation, Arizona State University.

Spache, G. D., and Spache, E. B. (1973). *Reading in the elementary school*, 3d ed. Boston: Allyn and Bacon.

Spalding, R. B., and Spalding, W. T. (1986). *The writing road to reading*. New York: Quill/William Morrow.

Speer, O. B., and Lamb, G. S. (1976). First grade reading ability and fluency in naming verbal symbols. *Reading Teacher, 26*, 572-576.

Spoehr, K. T. (1981). Word recognition in speech and reading: Toward a theory of language processing. In P. D. Eimas and J. L. Miller (eds.), *Perspectives on the study of speech*. Hillsdale, NJ: Erlbaum Associates.

Squire, J. R. (1987). *The dynamics of language learning: Research in Reading and English*. Urbana, IL: ERIC Clearinghouse on Reading and Communication Skills and National Conference on Research in English.

Stahl, S. A. (1988). Is there evidence to support matching reading styles and initial reading methods? A reply to Carbo. *Phi Delta Kappan, 70*, 317-322.

Stahl, S. A., and Fairbanks, M. M. (1986). The effects of vocabulary instruction: A model-based meta-analysis. *Review of Educational Research, 56*(1), 72-110.

Stahl, S. A., and Miller, P. D. (1989, in press). Natural language approaches to beginning reading: A quantitative research synthesis. *Review of Educational Research*.

Stanovich, K. E. (1980). Toward an interactive-compensatory model of individual differences in the development of reading fluency. *Reading Research Quarterly, 16*, 32-71.

Stanovich, K. E. (1981). Attentional and automatic context effects in reading. In A. M. Lesgold and C. A. Perfetti (eds.), *Interactive processes in reading*, 241-267. Hillsdale, NJ: Erlbaum Associates.

Stanovich, K. E. (1984). The interactive-compensatory model of reading: A confluence of developmental, experimental, and educational psychology. *Remedial and Special Education, 5*, 11-19.

Stanovich, K. E. (1986). Matthew effects in reading: Some consequences of individual differences in the acquisition of literacy. *Reading Research Quarterly, 21*, 360-406.

Stanovich, K. E. (1988, in press). The language code: Issues in word recognition. In S. R. Yussen and M. C. Smith (eds.), *Reading across the life span*. New York: Springer-Verlag.

Stanovich, K. E. (1989, in press). The right and wrong places to look for the cognitive locus of reading disability. *Annals of Dyslexia*.

Stanovich, K. E., Cunningham, A. E., and Cramer, B. B. (1984). Assessing phonological awareness in kindergarten children: Issues of task comparability. *Journal of Experimental Child Psychology, 38*, 175-190.

Stanovich, K., E., Cunningham, A. E., and Feeman, D. J. (1984). Intelligence, cognitive skills, and early reading progress. *Reading Research Quarterly, 19*, 278-303.

Stebbins, L. B., St. Pierre, R. G., Proper, E. C., Anderson, R. B., and Cerva, T. R. (1977). *Education as experimentation: A planned variation model (vol. IV-A)*, An evaluation of Project Follow Through. Cambridge, MA: Abt Associates.

Stedman, L. C., and Kaestle, C. F. (1987). Literacy and reading performance in the United States, from 1880 to the present. *Reading Research Quarterly, 22*, 8-46.

Stevens, A. L. (1978). Distortions in judged spatial relations. *Cognitive Psychology, 10*, 422-437.

Stevenson, H. W. (1984). Making the grade: School achievement in Japan, Taiwan, and the United States. *Annual report of the center for advanced study in the behavioral sciences*, 41-51. Stanford: Stanford University.

Stevenson, H., Parker, T., Wilkinson, A., Hegion, A., and Fish, E. (1976). Longitudinal study of individual differences in cognitive development and scholastic achievement. *Journal of Educational Psychology, 68*, 377-400.

Sticht, T. G. (1979). Applications of the audread model to reading evaluation and instruction. In L. B. Resnick and P. A. Weaver (eds.), *Theory and practice of early reading, vol. 1*, 209-226. Hillsdale, NJ: Erlbaum Associates.

Stotsky, S. (1983). Research on reading/writing relationships: A synthesis and suggested directions. *Language Arts, 60*, 627-742.

Stotsky, S. (1984). Research on reading/writing relationships: A synthesis and suggested directions. In J. Jensen (ed.), *Composition and comprehending.* Urbana, IL: ERIC Clearinghouse on Reading and Communication Skills and National Conference on Research in English.

Sulzby, E. (1983). A commentary on Ehri's critique of five studies related to letter-name knowledge and learning to read: Broadening the question. In L. M. Gentile, M. L. Kamil, and J. S. Blanchard (eds.), *Reading research revisited.* Columbus, OH: Charles E. Merrill.

Swinney, D. A. (1979). Lexical access during sentence comprehension: (Re)consideration of context effects. *Journal of Verbal Learning and Verbal Behavior, 18,* 645-659.

Taft, M. (1985). The decoding of words in lexical access: A review of the morphographic approach. In D. Besner, T. G. Waller, and G. E. MacKinnon (eds.), *Reading research: Advances in theory and practice, vol. 5.* New York: Academic Press.

Tannenhaus, M. K., Flanigan, H., and Seidenberg, M. S. (1980). Orthographic and phonological code activation in auditory and visual word recognition. *Memory and Cognition, 8,* 513-520.

Tannenhaus, M. K., Leiman, J. M., and Seidenberg, M. S. (1979). Evidence for multiple stages in the processing of ambiguous words in syntactic contexts. *Journal of Verbal Learning and Verbal Behavior, 18,* 427-440.

Taraban, R., and McClelland, J. L. (1987). Conspiracy effects in word pronunciation. *Journal of Memory and Language, 26,* 608-631.

Tarver, S., and Dawson, M. M. (1988). Modality preference and the teaching of reading. *Journal of Learning Disabilities, 11,* 17-29.

Taylor, N. E., Wade, M. R., and Yekovich, F. R. (1985). The effects of text manipulation and multiple reading strategies on the reading performance of good and poor readers. *Reading Research Quarterly, 20,* 566-574.

Teale, W. H. (1984). Reading to young children: Its significance for literacy development. In H. Goelman, A. Oberg, and F. Smith (eds.), *Awakening to literacy,* 110-121. Portsmouth, NH: Heinemann.

Teale, W. H. (1986). Home background and young children's literacy development. In W. H. Teale and E. Sulzby (eds.), *Emergent literacy,* 173-206. Norwood, NJ: Ablex Publishing Corporation.

Teale, W. H., and Sulzby, E. (eds.) (1986). *Emergent literacy: Writing and reading.* Norwood, NJ: Ablex Publishing Corporation.

Tenney, Y. J. (1980). Visual factors in spelling. In U. Frith (ed.), *Cognitive processes in spelling,* 215-229. New York: Academic Press.

Thomas, H. (1968). Children's tachistoscopic recognition of words and pseudowords varying in pronounceability and consonant vowel sequence. *Journal of Experimental Psychology, 77,* 511-513.

Thorndike, R. L. (1973). *Reading comprehension education in fifteen countries: An empirical study.* New York: Wiley.

Tinker, M. A. (1931). The influence of form of type on the perception of words. *Journal of Applied Psychology, 16,* 167-174.

Treiman, R. (1983). The structure of spoken syllables: Evidence from novel word games. *Cognition, 15,* 49-74.

Treiman, R. (1984). On the status of final consonant clusters in English syllables. *Journal of Verbal Learning and Verbal Behavior, 23,* 343-356.

Treiman, R. (1985a). Onsets and rimes as units of spoken syllables: Evidence from children. *Journal of Experimental Child Psychology, 39,* 161-181.

Treiman, R. (1985b). Phonemic analysis, spelling, and reading. In T. H. Carr (ed.), *The development of reading skills,* 5-18. San Francisco: Jossey-Bass.

Treiman, R. (1985c). Phonemic awareness and spelling: Children's judgments do not always agree with adults'. *Journal of Experimental Child Psychology, 39,* 182-201.

Treiman, R. (1985d). Spelling of stop consonants after /s/ by children and adults. *Applied Psycholinguistics, 6,* 262-282.

Treiman, R. (1986). The division between onsets and rimes in English syllables. *Journal of Memory and Language, 25,* 476-491.

Treiman, R. (1987). *Spelling in first grade children.* Paper presented at Midwestern Psychological Association, Chicago.

Treiman, R. (1988a, in press). The internal structure of the syllable. In G. Carlson and M. Tanenhaus (eds.), *Linguistic structure in language processing.* Dordrecht, Holland: D. Reidel.

Treiman, R. (1988b, in press). The role of intrasyllabic units in learning to read and spell. In P. Gough (ed.), *Learning to read.* Hillsdale, NJ: Erlbaum Associates.

Treiman, R., and Baron, J. (1981). Segmental analysis ability: Development and relation to reading ability. In G. E. MacKinnon and T. G. Waller (eds.), *Reading research: Advances in theory and practice, vol. 3,* 159-198. New York: Academic Press.

Treiman, R., Baron, J., and Luk, K. (1981). Speech recoding in silent reading: A comparison of Chinese and English. *Journal of Chinese Linguistics, 9,* 116-125.

Treiman, R., and Chafetz, J. (1987). Are there onset- and rime-like units in printed words? In M. Coltheart (ed.), *Attention and performance XII: The psychology of reading,* 281-298. Hillsdale, NJ: Erlbaum Associates.

Tunmer, W. E., and Nesdale, A. R. (1985). Phonemic segmentation skill and beginning reading. *Journal of Educational Psychology, 77,* 417-427.

Tunmer, W. E., Herriman, M. L., and Nesdale, A. R. (1988). Metalinguistic abilities and beginning reading. *Reading Research Quarterly, 23,* 134-158.

Tyler, A., and Nagy, W. E. (1987). *Use of derivational morphology during reading.* Unpublished manuscript. Champaign, IL: University of Illinois.

Tyler, L. K., and Frauenfelder, U. H. (eds.). (1987). Spoken word recognition. *Cognition (Special Issue), 25*(1,2), 1-234.

Tzeng, O. J. L., and Wang, W. S.-Y. (1983). The first two R's. *American Scientist, 71,* 238-243.

Tzeng, O. J. L., Hung, D. L., and Wang, W. S.-Y. (1977). Speech recoding in reading Chinese characters. *Journal of Experimental Psychology: Human Learning and Memory, 3,* 621-630.

Underwood, N. R., and McConkie, G. W. (1985). Perceptual span for letter distinctions during reading. *Reading Research Quarterly, 20,* 153-162.

Van Orden, G. C. (1987). A ROWS is a ROSE: Spelling. sound, and reading. *Memory and Cognition, 15,* 181-198.

Van Orden, G. C., Johnston, J. C., and Hale, B. L. (1988). Word identification in reading proceeds from spelling to sound to meaning. *Journal of Experimental Psychology: Learning, Memory, and Cognition, 14,* 371-386.

Vellutino, F. R. (1979). *Dyslexia: Theory and research.* Cambridge, MA: MIT Press.

Vellutino, F. R., and Scanlon, D. M. (1987). Phonological coding, Phonological awareness, and reading ability: Evidence from a longitudinal and experimental study. *Merrill-Palmer Quarterly, 33,* 321-363.

Venezky, R. L. (1967). English orthography: Its graphical structure and its relation to sound. *Reading Research Quarterly, 2,* 75-106.

Venezky, R. L. (1975). The curious role of letter names in reading instruction. *Visible Language, 9,* 7-23.

Venezky, R. L. (1980). From Webster to Rice to Roosevelt: The formative years for spelling instruction and spelling reform in the U.S.A. In U. Firth (ed.), *Cognitive processes in spelling,* 9-30. New York: Academic Press.

Vernon, M. D. (1971). *Reading and its difficulties.* Cambridge: Cambridge University Press.

Vygotsky, L. S. (1962). *Thought and language.* Edited and translated by E. Hanfmann and G. Vakar. Cambridge, MA: MIT Press.

Wagner, R. K., and Torgesen, J. K. (1987). The nature of phonological processing and its causal role in the acquisition of reading skills. *Psychological Bulletin, 101,* 192-212.

Wallach, L., Wallach, M. A., Dozier, M. G., and Kaplan, N. E. (1977). Poor children learning to read do not have trouble with auditory discrimination but do have trouble with phoneme recognition. *Journal of Educational Psychology, 69,* 36-39.

Wallach, M. A., and Wallach, L. (1979). Helping disadvantaged children learn to read by teaching them phoneme identification skills. In L. A. Resnick and P. A. Weaver (eds.), *Theory and practice of early reading, vol. 3,* 227-259. Hillsdale, NJ: Erlbaum Associates.

Walsh, D. J., Price, G. G., and Gillingham, M. G. (1988). The critical but transitory importance of letter naming. *Reading Research Quarterly, 23,* 108-122.

Wang, W. S.-Y. (1979). Language change: A lexical perspective. *Annual Review of Anthropology, 88,* 353-371.

Warren, R. M. (1971). Identification times for phonemic components of graded complexity and for spelling of speech. *Perception and Psychophysics, 9,* 345-349.

Waters, G. S., and Seidenberg, M. S. (1985). Spelling-sound effects in reading: Time course and decision criteria. *Memory and Cognition, 13,* 557-572.

Waters, G. S., Seidenberg, M. S., and Bruck, M. (1984). Children's and adults' use of spelling-sound information in three reading tasks. *Memory and Cognition, 12,* 293-305.

Waters, G., Caplan, D., and Hildebrandt, N. (1987). Working memory and written sentence comprehension. In M. Coltheart (ed.), *Attention and performance XII: The psychology of reading,* 531-555. Hillsdale, NJ: Erlbaum Associates.

Watson, R. I. (1971). *The great psychologists.* Philadelphia: Lippencott.

Weber, R.-M. (1970a). A linguistic analysis of first-grade reading errors. *Reading Research Quarterly, 5,* 427-451.

Weber, R. -M. (1970b). First-graders' use of grammatical context in reading. In H. Levin and J. P. Williams (eds.), *Basic studies on reading,* 147-163. New York: Basic Books.

Wells, G. (1985). Preschool literacy-related activities and success in school. In D. Olson, N. Torrance, and A. Hildyard (eds.), *Literacy, language, and learning: The nature and consequences of reading and writing,* 229-255. New York: Cambridge University Press.

West, R. F., and Stanovich, K. E. (1978). Automatic contextual facilitation in readers of three ages. *Child Development, 49,* 717-727.

Whitehurst, G. J., Falco, F., Lonigan, C. J., Fischal, J. E., DeBaryshe, B. D., Valdez-Manchaca, M. C., and Caulfield, M. (1988). Accelerating language development through picturebook reading. *Developmental Psychology, 24,* 552-559.

Whittlesea, B. W. A. (1987). Preservation of specific experiences in the representation of general knowledge. *Journal of Experimental Psychology: Learning, Memory, and Cognition, 13,* 3-17.

Whittlesea, B. W. A., and Cantwell, A. L. (1987). Enduring influence of the purpose of experiences: Encoding-retrieval interactions in word and pseudoword perception. *Memory and Cognition, 15,* 465-472.

Wigfield, A., and Asher, S. R. (1984). Social and motivational influences on reading. In P. D. Pearson, R. Barr, M. L. Kamil, and P. Mosenthal (eds.), *Handbook of research on reading,* 423-452. New York: Longman.

Wijk, A. (1966). *Rules of pronunciation for the English language.* London: Oxford University Press.

Williams, J. P. (1969). Training kindergarten children to discriminate letter-like forms. *American Education Research Journal, 6,* 501-514.

Williams, J. P. (1975). Training children to copy and to discriminate letterlike forms. *Journal of Educational Psychology, 67,* 790-795.

Williams, J. P. (1977). Building perceptual and cognitive strategies into a reading curriculum. In A. S. Reber and D. L. Scarborough (eds.),

Toward a psychology of reading, 257-288. Hillsdale, NJ: Erlbaum Associates.

Williams, J. P. (1979). The ABD's of reading: A program for the learning disabled. In L. A. Resnick and P. A. Weaver (eds.), *Theory and practice of early reading, vol. 3,* 227-259. Hillsdale, NJ: Erlbaum Associates.

Williams, J. P. (1980). Teaching decoding with a special emphasis on phoneme analysis and phoneme blending. *Journal of Educational Psychology, 72,* 1-15.

Williams, J. P. (1987). Educational treatments for dyslexia at the elementary and secondary levels. In R. F. Bowler (ed.), *Intimacy with language: A forgotten basic in teacher education,* 24-32. Baltimore: Orton Dyslexia Society.

Williams, J. P., and Ackerman, M. D. (1971). Simultaneous and successive discrimination of similar letters. *Journal of Educational Psychology, 62,* 132-137.

Williams, M. S., and Knafle, J. D. (1977). Comparative difficulty of vowel and consonant sounds for beginning readers. *Reading Improvement, 14,* 2-10.

Willows, D. M., Borwick, D., and Hayvren, M. (1981). The content of school readers. In G. E. MacKinnon and T. G. Waller (eds.), *Reading research: Advances in theory and practice, vol. 2,* 97-175. New York: Academic Press.

Wiseman, D. (1980). The beginnings of literacy. *Reading Horizons, 29,* 311 -313.

Woodworth, R. A. (1938). *Experimental psychology.* New York: Henry Holt, and Company.

Wylie, R. E., and Durrell, D. D. (1970). *Elementary English, 47,* 787-791.

Yarbus, A. L. (1967). *Eye movements and vision.* New York: Plenum Press.

Yarington, D. (1978). *The great American reading machine.* Rochelle Park, NJ: Hayden Book Company.

Yopp, H. K. (1988). The validity and reliability of phonemic awareness tests. *Reading Research Quarterly, 23,* 159-177.

Yopp, H. K., and Singer, H. (1985). Toward an interactive reading instructional model: Explanation of activation of linguistic awareness and metalinguistic ability in learning to read. In H. Singer and R. B. Ruddell (eds.), *Theoretical models and processes of reading,* 135-143. Newark, DE: International Reading Association.

Zhurova, L. E. (1963). The development of analysis of words into their sounds by preschool children. *Soviet Psychology and Psychiatry, 2,* 17-27.

Ziegler, E. (1986). Why our children aren't reading. Foreword to R. Flesch, *Why Johnny can't read,* 2d ed. New York: Harper and Row.

Zifcak, M. (1981). Phonological awareness and reading acquisition. *Contemporary Educational Psychology, 6,* 117-126.

Zinna, D. R., Liberman, I. Y., and Shankweiler, D. (1986). Children's sensitivity to factors influencing vowel reading. *Reading Research Quarterly, 21,* 465-478.

Name Index

Subject Index